FRANK D. GILROY

Volume One
Complete Full-Length Plays
1962–1999

SMITH AND KRAUS PUBLISHERS
Contemporary Playwrights / Anthologies

Lynne Alvarez: Collected Plays
Christopher Durang: 27 Short Plays
Christopher Durang Vol.II: Full-Lengths
Horton Foote: 4 New Plays
Horton Foote Vol.II: Collected Plays
Horton Foote Vol.III: Collected Plays
John Guare Vol.I: War Against the Kitchen Sink
A.R. Gurney Vol.I: Nine Early Plays
A.R. Gurney Vol.II: Collected Plays 1977–1985
A.R. Gurney Vol.III: Collected Plays 1984–1991
A.R. Gurney Vol.IV: Collected Plays 1992–1999
Beth Henley Vol.II: Collected Plays
Israel Horovitz Vol.I: Collected Works
Israel Horovitz Vol.II: New England Blue
Israel Horovitz Vol.III: P.E.C. and 6 New Plays
Israel Horovitz Vol.IV: Two Trilogies
Romulus Linney: 17 Short Plays
Romulus Linney: Adaptations for the American Stage
Jane Martin: Collected Plays
William Mastrosimone: Collected Plays
Terrence McNally Vol.I: 15 Short Plays
Terrence McNally Vol.II: Collected Plays
Marsha Norman: Collected Plays
Eric Overmyer: Collected Plays
Theresa Rebeck Vol.I: Collected Plays 1989–1998
Lanford Wilson: 21 Short Plays
Lanford Wilson Vol.I: Collected Plays 1965–1970
Lanford Wilson Vol.II: Collected Plays 1970–1983
Lanford Wilson Vol.III: The Talley Trilogy
Lanford Wilson Vol.IV: Collected Plays 1987–1997

If you require pre-publication information about upcoming Smith and Kraus books, you may receive our semi-annual catalogue, free of charge, by sending your name and address to *Smith and Kraus Catalogue,4 Lower Mill Road, North Stratford, NH 03590. Or call us at (800) 895-4331, fax (603) 922-3348. WWW.SmithKraus.com.*

FRANK D. GILROY

Volume One
Complete Full-Length Plays
1962–1999

CONTEMPORARY PLAYWRIGHTS
SERIES

SK
A Smith and Kraus Book

A Smith and Kraus Book
Published by Smith and Kraus, Inc.
177 Lyme Road, Hanover, NH 03755

First Edition: May 2000
10 9 8 7 6 5 4 3 2 1

The Library of Congress Cataloging-In-Publication Data

Gilroy, Frank Daniel, 1925–
[Plays. Selections]
Frank D. Gilroy. —1st ed.
p. cm. — (Contemporary playwrights series)
Contents: v.1. Collected full-length plays — v.2. 15 one-act plays.
ISBN 1-57525-266-X (v.1)
I. Title. II. Series.

PS3513.I6437 A6 2000
812'.54—dc21   00-038781

CONTENTS

∽

To Ruth—yet again…
and again…

INTRODUCTION

I returned to civilian life in 1946 determined to go to college and become a writer.

The former goal, born of a new estimate of myself gained in the Army where I realized I wasn't as dumb as school records suggested.

The latter, a secret ambition since I was fourteen, when I wrote a short story that my aunt, who worked in the Photo Morgue of *The World Telegram,* showed to a reporter who wrote on it, "The boy has narrative ability."

Common to both goals was the need of a typewriter.

Having won a handsome sum in an all Easter Sunday crap game on the forward deck of the *SS Rushville Victory* en route home from Europe, the black market price for typewriters, in short supply, was no obstacle.

Someone steered me to the Royal Typewriter office located in Rockefeller Center or thereabouts.

I asked for Mr. So-and-So.

A small, pale, eye-glassed man acknowledged me furtively and said to wait in the corridor.

After several minutes, the man appeared with a brand new Royal portable.

I handed him one hundred and twenty-five dollars—possibly one fifty.

He, anxious about what was a less than kosher activity, was about to return to his office. I, feeling a sense of occasion, could not let it end thus.

"I'm going to become a writer," I announced grandly.

I recall a look of supreme disinterest and he was gone.

That Royal portable on which all my plays have been written, not to mention TV, movie scripts, and novels, adorns the cover of this volume.

If you look closely at the space bar you will see the shiny depression that my right thumb has worn over fifty-four years.

And we're not through yet.

WHO'LL SAVE THE PLOWBOY?

ORIGINAL PRODUCTION

Who'll Save the Plowboy? was first presented by T. Edward Hambleton and Norris Houghton at the Phoenix Theatre, New York City, on January 9, 1962. The play was directed by Daniel Petrie with the following cast in order of appearance:

Albert Cobb	Gerald O'Loughlin
Helen Cobb	Rebecca Darke
Larry Doyle	William Smithers
Doctor	Burton Mallory
Mrs. Doyle	Dorothy Peterson
The Man	Tom Sawyer
The Boy	Patrick O'Shaughnessy

Directed by Daniel Petrie; costumes and scenery by Norris Houghton; lighting by John Robertson.

INTRODUCTION

It was the make or break play.

We (wife, Ruth, and ten-month old first child, Tony) returned from Hollywood after fifteen weeks at Paramount (my first L.A. stint) with enough money to see us to the end of the year (1957).

The theater, my dream since Dartmouth where I had two full length and some half dozen one-acts produced in junior and senior years. Thoroughly hooked, I went to Yale Drama on a fellowship from Dartmouth. Left after one year because I was twenty-six, thanks to two and a half years in the army, and it was time to test my dream in the real world.

First priority: make a living.

Worked in advertising (never got out of the mail room); subsistence gambler; rented beach cabanas. Television, the so-called Golden Age, aborning, I put theater aside and tried my hand.

No series. Everything live. No rating system. New York the hub. Pre-Writers' Guild of America, you wrote on speculation.

Nothing like the prospect of renting beach cabanas for the rest of your life to galvanize and inspire.

First break: a ten-minute one-act to Kate Smith starring Robert Sterling and Ann Jeffries for three hundred and fifty dollars less agent's commission. Quit the cabana business at once. Didn't score again for many months. Then another drought. Writing non-stop all the time. And then two half-hour sales in quick succession. This occasioning a party at which only people I owed money to were invited. A sizable group that I paid off during the festivities. The high point of which was a poem written and recited by Marty Donovan, a good friend, which began: "Success has touched Frank Gilroy. Touched him lightly it is true. And touched him in a different way than he touched me and you."

From 1951 to 1957 it was a scramble to stay afloat. I had shows on Studio One, Kraft Theatre, Omnibus, The U.S. Steel Hour—produced by the Theatre Guild, Playhouse 90 and on and on.

Sounds good but for every show you sold (spec remember) there were one or two that never rang the cash register. And prices were minimal. Kraft paid one grand per hour no matter how many you sold them. The high water mark was seventeen hundred and fifty dollars for *The Last Notch* on U.S. Steel, a western done live that was subsequently sold to MGM. Retitled *The Fastest Gun Alive,* it was "MGM's box office sleeper of the year" according to *Variety.* My share (I did the screenplay) was nine grand before agent's fee. That sale allowed Ruth and me to marry.

And so it went till the aforementioned job in 1957 at Paramount.

Theater dreams deferred for six years, it was put up or shut up time.

The trouble was I had no play in mind.

The days dwindled as did our finances.

In desperation I was working on several ideas at once. This in a room for thirty dollars a month in the original Circle In The Square building where Jose Quintero presided and I first glimpsed the two best actors of my generation—Jason Robards and George C. Scott. Note that of the five most memorable nights I've experienced as a theater-goer, Jose Quintero directed four of them.

So now it's November. No play idea despite all the effort. Ruth gleans I'm flailing desperately. Blows the whistle. I take a day off.

The phone rings. A fellow I'd been in the army with is in town for a convention. He comes to dinner. As we're eating I wonder what we'd be talking about if this fellow had saved my life during combat. What if he'd suffered a wound in doing so that was soon to kill him and his visit was to convince himself that his sacrifice had been worthwhile?

That was the genesis of *Plowboy.* Nothing to do with this fellow and me. But when you're truly hungry for a play idea the slightest possibility registers mightily.

Within three days I was writing it.

By the first of the year (1958) I'd completed it.

Incidentally, that pattern (intense search for an idea leading to desperation and then when you're near the breaking point, sometimes a glimmer of hope) has proved my consistent M.O.

Much praise for the script but no production offers. In part because everyone, including me, agreed that the ending wasn't right. As it stood it concluded on the bleakest of notes.

"Let me hear it once and I'll fix the ending in five minutes," was my airy boast over the next four years.

Dan Petrie, director, early and steadfast champion of *Plowboy*, called my bluff. He learned that the Phoenix Theatre had a three-week opening. Gave them *Plowboy*. They (T. Edward Hambleton and Norris Houghton) said yes. Danny cast it. I flew from L.A. to attend rehearsals.

We're on the stage of the Phoenix Theatre. Everyone assembled for the first reading.

Except for the ending it goes extremely well.

All eyes swivel to me.

The actress, Rebecca Darke, read so brilliantly that I know exactly what to do.

I retreat with the script to an office.

I change a "no" to a "yes" and throw away the last two pages.

In less than five minutes I'm back.

Everyone agrees I've done it, which another reading confirms.

We open to raves. Rebecca wins the Clarence Derwent Award. The play wins an Obie.

I find myself sleeping better than I ever have before.

The line has been crossed irrevocably. I *am* a playwright.

Oh yes. Opening night I encountered Vincent Donahue, a director I'd worked with in TV, who was a theater veteran.

"Enjoy tonight," he counseled. "Because you'll have lots of the other kind."

Me flop? Impossible, I thought.

Stay tuned.

SYNOPSIS

The scene is New York City. The time, the present.

ACT I

Scene I: Two days before Christmas. Evening.

Scene II: One hour later.

ACT II

The following morning.

ACT I
SCENE I

Setting: The scene is a lower-middle-class apartment in New York. The living room occupies the central area of the stage. Windows open on a courtyard four floors below. A swinging door leads off to the kitchen. French doors, covered with curtains, lead to a bedroom. At stage left is a passage to the bathroom and another bedroom, neither of which are seen. At stage right the living room leads to a foyer. A door in the foyer opens on the hallway outside. When the door is open, a part of this hallway is visible, including stairs leading from the floor above and the head of the stairs leading from the floor below. There is an upright piano in the living room. Its keyboard is covered. There is a phone on a stand in the foyer. It is about nine p.m., two days before Christmas, of the present year.

At rise, Albert Cobb, thirty-five, a large man of strong build, who has gone a bit to seed, dressed in his best clothes, bounces around the room in an attitude of happy expectation. He sips from a beer can, whistles snatches of "I've Got Sixpence," and chuckles at some private memory. Helen Cobb, thirty-five, his wife, plain in appearance, is darning socks. Through a partly open window comes a muted tangle of city noises.

ALBERT: What time is it now?

HELEN: Nine fifteen.

(Albert paces a bit more.)

ALBERT: What time is it?

HELEN: Nine sixteen.

ALBERT: Why don't he get here? *(Albert continues to pace, stops, laughs.)* Me lying in the dark bleeding to death and listening. And everything so still I could hear every word they said.

HELEN: I wish you'd cut your toenails once in a while.

ALBERT: "Who'll save the Plowboy?," says the Lieutenant...For a long time nobody said a word and you couldn't blame them: The Germans were using me as bait. "You still with us, Plowboy?" the Lieutenant shouts. Well, I could have been a hero by making out I was dead. But who'd have given me credit for it?

HELEN: When was the last time you cut your toenails?

ALBERT: "I'm still here," I said back. "But I won't be much longer." And then Larry spoke up: "Hang on, Plowboy, I'm coming for you," he yells. There was a whole lot of voices after that. I couldn't make it all out but

I knew they were trying to talk him out of it. Telling him he was committing suicide. But he did it. They threw everything at him. He was hit before he got to me. He had to carry me piggyback and I could feel the blood running down his side. I passed out before we got there, but we made it. A miracle. That's what everyone said it was: a miracle.

HELEN: These don't look like your socks.

ALBERT: Did you get more beer?

HELEN: Yes. *(Holds up a pair of socks.)* Where did these socks come from?

ALBERT: How do I know?...How much beer did you get?

HELEN: Twelve cans.

ALBERT: He was always a great one for beer...or anything with alcohol, for that matter.

HELEN: It's how many years since you saw him?

ALBERT: Fifteen...I'd like to have a nickel for every time I carried him back to the barracks drunk as a coot. I'd be a millionaire.

HELEN: And vice versa I'm sure.

ALBERT: I didn't drink in those days.

HELEN: I believe that.

ALBERT: It's the truth. Not a drop. He'll tell you.

HELEN: If he ever gets here. You sure he said tonight?

ALBERT: Yes. Chances are he got lost. It's the first time he's been to New York.

HELEN: How do you know?

ALBERT: If he'd been here before, he'd have looked me up....We were like brothers.

HELEN: So you've told me. How long is he going to be in New York?

ALBERT: Just overnight. God, but he was a crazy galoot. Always raising some sort of hell. And comical...

HELEN: If you were so close, how come he stopped writing to you? How come your letters came back "address unknown?"

ALBERT: You seem bound to plant a suspicion in my mind. Well, it won't work.

HELEN: Only persons I know who don't have forwarding addresses are people trying to run away from something.

ALBERT: Wait till you see how skinny he is alongside of me. You won't believe that he was able to lift me, much less carry me as far as he did...Of course I wasn't quite so heavy then.

HELEN: I don't like it. No word in years and then suddenly he pops up...He wants something.

ALBERT: Whatever he wants that I can give him he's entitled to.

HELEN: Whatever you can give him is very little and half mine. So don't be too generous.

ALBERT: How could I be too generous to a man who risked his life to save mine? And what makes you sure he wants something? Isn't it possible he might just want to see me for old times' sake?

HELEN: Don't be disappointed when he tries to sell you an insurance policy.

ALBERT: He's not like that.

HELEN: People change.

ALBERT: He couldn't change that much…You know something—you sound like you're mad at him.

HELEN: I don't even know him. Why should I be mad?

ALBERT: You sound like you are.

(He takes a swallow of beer as a short figure played on a trumpet sounds through the window. The figure is repeated as an exercise in various keys. At the first sound Helen is transfixed; listens.)

ALBERT: That's the first time I heard Gabriel in weeks.

HELEN: The super told me he's been touring the country with one of the big symphony orchestras.

ALBERT: Too bad.

HELEN: What's too bad?

ALBERT: I was hoping he moved.

HELEN: All the noise that comes floating through that window and you object to a little music?

ALBERT: I don't hear the other noises. I'm used to them.

HELEN: You like peace and quiet so good, why don't you move to a farm, Plowboy?

ALBERT: Let's not start that.

HELEN: Well, isn't that what they used to call you…Plowboy?

ALBERT: Helen, I'm in a good mood. I want to be that way when he gets here.

HELEN: Then don't complain about a little music.

ALBERT: If he'd play a song I wouldn't mind, but all he does is… *(Parodies the trumpet figure.)*

HELEN: To me it's a pleasure just to hear someone trying to improve himself at anything.

ALBERT: I guess there's another little dig at me in there some place, but I'm going to ignore it because I want to be in a good mood when Larry gets here.

HELEN: Keep lapping that beer and you won't even be conscious.

ALBERT: Don't worry about me…What time is it?

HELEN: Nine twenty.

ALBERT: I wonder what the devil's taking him so long. *(Goes to the window, shouts in the direction of the trumpet.)* Shut up!

HELEN: Maybe he changed his mind.

ALBERT: That's what you're wishing.

HELEN: I guess so.

ALBERT: Why?

HELEN: I can't see any good coming out of it.

ALBERT: You know who you sound like when you talk gloomy like this: your mother. Old moaning low. Old laugh in the morning and cry at night. That's just who you sound like. Well, go ahead, talk all you want. You won't get a rise out of me. Not tonight.

HELEN: Why not? Just what's so special about tonight?

ALBERT: I'll tell you: My friend…the only real friend I ever had…the only one…he's coming to see me and I'm looking forward to it…I haven't looked forward to anything else in years…But I'm looking forward to seeing my friend and you're not going to spoil it…You never met him but you hate him. I asked you why, but do you think I'm so stupid that I don't know why…Well, tonight you're going to keep your mouth shut…You're going to make him feel welcome…like this was a happy house he came to.

HELEN: And the boy? What do we say about the boy?

ALBERT: Nothing.

HELEN: He'll ask.

ALBERT: We'll say he's visiting relatives.

HELEN: No.

ALBERT: Yes…I won't ruin his evening…We'll say the boy is visiting relatives upstate.

HELEN: The day after tomorrow is Christmas. Kids usually spend Christmas with their parents.

ALBERT: All right. He'll be home for Christmas. Now let's drop it…I feel lousy. I hope you're satisfied. *(Goes to the window and shouts up toward the trumpet sounds.)* Shut up that lousy horn! *(Slams the window shut. The trumpet can't be heard.)* The simplest thing: a friend is coming to visit. Why can't he just come without everything getting mixed up?

HELEN: I'd like to know where these socks came from.

ALBERT: Sometimes I think you want me to kill you.

HELEN: They're not even your size.

ALBERT: I think sometimes you purposely try to make me do that.

HELEN: Don't you have any idea where these socks came from?

ALBERT: Well, the hell with all that tonight. I'm in a good mood and I'm going to stay that way. What time is it now?

HELEN: Nine twenty-three.

ALBERT: God damn it, where is he? *(He goes into the kitchen and reappears almost immediately with a new can of beer, which he opens.)* Wouldn't it be a laugh on you and your suspicions if it turned out he came to do me a good turn. That he had some good deal he wants me in on.

HELEN: It would also be a laugh on me if Santa Claus appeared, because I don't believe in him either.

ALBERT: The fact is you don't believe in anything.

HELEN: And you?

ALBERT: I believe in Larry. I have to believe in a man who risked his life to save me…I have to believe in something.

HELEN: I don't.

ALBERT: That's the only thing I have left.

HELEN: I have nothing left.

ALBERT: You're jealous of me.

HELEN: Green with it.

ALBERT: I still have hopes. You can't stand that.

HELEN: I have hopes. Want to know what they are?

ALBERT: No.

HELEN: Every night before I go to bed I hope I won't wake up in the morning.

ALBERT: You shouldn't say things like that. Even joking.

HELEN: Who's going to hear me?

ALBERT: Please lay off that talk in front of Larry.

HELEN: I thought you said he had a sense of humor.

ALBERT: If he makes me any sort of a decent offer I'm going to take it.

HELEN: Know what my other hope is?

ALBERT: Even if it means moving to another part of the country.

HELEN: That the landlord gives us a new stove.

ALBERT: I'm only thirty-five. Today that's nothing.

HELEN: Death or a new stove. I'll settle for either one…What if he wants to see a picture of the kid?

ALBERT: We haven't got one.

HELEN: Won't he find that strange?

ALBERT: It can't be helped.

HELEN: And who ever saw a happy house with no decorations two days before Christmas?

ALBERT: What are you getting at?

HELEN: I think we ought to tell your good friend the same lie we tell everyone else.

ALBERT: Why?

HELEN: Because the idea of pretending this is a happy house galls me.

ALBERT: Then go to the movies.

HELEN: And leave you here to be taken. Oh no.

ALBERT: Where are the decorations we had?

HELEN: Thrown out years ago.

ALBERT: I'll tell him we do all our decorating on Christmas Eve...Why don't he get here?

HELEN: He probably did. Probably got as far as the entrance, took a good sniff of this building, realized there was no pickings, and went away.

ALBERT: You weren't always so hard.

HELEN: Not if you go back far enough.

ALBERT: I remember the first time we ever went out together.

HELEN: Don't butter me up.

ALBERT: That was the first blind date I ever had.

HELEN: Blind, deaf and dumb.

ALBERT: Remember the picture we saw? Gilda with Rita Hayworth—

HELEN: Stop it...When your good friend gets here we'll begin the game. Till then we'll be ourselves.

ALBERT: You're a puzzle to me. I swear you are. I reckon—

HELEN: I reckon?...Well, hark the Plowboy.

ALBERT: Now what?

HELEN: Now what?...Now I reckon; shucks; well I'll be jiggered; well I'll be tarred and feathered. And all those other cute things one expects from a Plowboy. Here they come.

ALBERT: Just what are you suggesting?

HELEN: I'm suggesting you dab a little horse manure behind your ears and your good friend won't think you've changed one bit.

ALBERT: Knock it off.

HELEN: Now who ever heard a Plowboy use words like that.

ALBERT: You sure do know how to get a fellow riled.

HELEN: Riled: Now that's better. That just drips with country. And don't forget hornswoggled and cotton picking—

ALBERT: Cut it out.

HELEN: And down the road a piece...and taters...and—

(He slaps her across the mouth. They regard each other.)

HELEN: Pappy and mammy.

ALBERT: Are you happy now? I hope you're happy now.

HELEN: Don't forget pappy and mammy.

ALBERT: Why is it that the simplest thing can't go smoothly here?
(*A bell rings.*)

HELEN: That's the downstairs bell.

ALBERT: I was in such a good mood before. Why the devil didn't he come when he was supposed to?

HELEN: Tick the button.
(*He goes to the foyer and ticks the button.*)

HELEN: And smile. It's time to play happy house.

ALBERT: Don't mention the kid unless he does.

HELEN: Remember what I said about being too generous.

ALBERT: And you remember that this man saved my life...If he makes me a good offer don't sound too eager...(*He listens at the door.*) Don't mention the farm either.

HELEN: Why not?

ALBERT: Because I say so.

HELEN: That doesn't leave us much to talk about.

ALBERT: What's taking him so long?

HELEN: Maybe somebody pushed the wrong button.

ALBERT: Here he comes. (*Opens the door. Calls out.*) Who goes there?

LARRY: (*From offstage.*) A friend.

ALBERT: Rustle your tail, friend, and be recognized.
(*He goes out into the hall and waits at the head of the stairs. As he goes out, Helen goes to the window, opens it, stands looking up, listening to the trumpet.*)

ALBERT: One more flight and you got 'er licked, buddy...Well, listen at him wheeze and puff. Just listen...Well, for crying out loud, how the hell are you?
(*Larry Doyle appears. He is thirty-five, smaller than Albert and wiry, and has a lot of gray in his hair. He is neatly dressed and carries a large package. He is winded. They contemplate each other.*)

LARRY: What do ya say, Plowboy? (*Offers his hand.*)
(*They shake.*)

ALBERT: I say you're a sight for sore eyes. What do you say?

LARRY: Nothing till I catch my breath. Four flights. That's some climb.

ALBERT: Well, let me look at you...Well, for crying out loud you're scrawnier than ever...And look at the snow on that roof...And I do believe you're uglier. Now who would have thought that was possible.

LARRY: Plowboy, how are you?

ALBERT: Couldn't be better.

(Larry jabs him in the stomach.)

LARRY: Carrying more here than you used to.

ALBERT: Blame it on the little woman. I mean, she can cook. You married?

LARRY: No.

ALBERT: Still playing the field.

LARRY: Yeah. Sorry I'm late.

ALBERT: Forget it.

LARRY: I was hoping to get here before the kid went to sleep.

ALBERT: Say, what the devil are we doing out here in the hall. Come on in-side…Fifteen years. My God, it don't seem possible.

(He leads Larry into the apartment. Helen hears them coming and closes the window.)

ALBERT: Here he is, Helen.

(Helen and Larry shake hands.)

HELEN: How do you do.

LARRY: Pleased to meet you.

ALBERT: For years she's been hearing about you but I think she gave up hope of ever meeting you in person. *(To her.)* Right?

HELEN: That's right. Albert's talked about you a lot.

LARRY: Knowing the Plowboy you probably got a very distorted picture.

HELEN: Probably.

LARRY: I was hoping to get here before the kid went to sleep. I guess I didn't make it.

ALBERT: He's not here. He's visiting relatives upstate.

LARRY: That's too bad.

ALBERT: He'll be home for Christmas. Too bad you can't stay over.

LARRY: Yeah. *(Offers the package he carries to Helen.)* I brought this for him…trains.

ALBERT: He'll get a real bang out of that. *(To Helen, who eyes the package but makes no move to accept it.)* Take it, dear…Take it.

(She takes the package and puts it on the piano.)

LARRY: I was afraid he might already have trains.

ALBERT: No.

LARRY: How about brothers and sisters. Does he have any of those?

ALBERT: Not yet but we're working on it.

HELEN: May I ask you a question?

LARRY: Sure.

HELEN: Is it true you saved Albert's life?

ALBERT: I told you it was.

HELEN: As Larry said, you distort things. I'd like to know if you distorted that.

ALBERT: *(To Larry.)* She's very forthright. Says anything that comes into her head, no matter how embarrassing it is. It's one of the things I like about her.

HELEN: Did you save his life?

LARRY: Yes.

ALBERT: And risked his own to do it as I told you a thousand times. *(To Larry.)* Say, how is that wound you got?

LARRY: No trouble.

ALBERT: Good. Well, buddy, what the devil have you been up to all these years? Last I heard you were out to California going to college. Then all of a sudden my letters started coming back.

LARRY: While I was in college I had an offer to go into business with a fellow in Florida if I accepted right away. I took it and I guess in all the rush I forgot to leave a forwarding address. On top of that I lost yours.

ALBERT: Must have been a good proposition that guy put up to you.

LARRY: Yes.

ALBERT: What line was that in?

LARRY: Real estate.

ALBERT: Is that what you're doing now?

LARRY: Yes.

ALBERT: Real estate is supposed to be going great guns down there in Florida.

LARRY: I'm not complaining.

ALBERT: *(To Helen.)* What did I tell you? *(To Larry.)* I told her how everyone used to say you'd be a big success in civilian life.

LARRY: I didn't say I was a big success.

ALBERT: You didn't have to…

HELEN: Living in Florida, how come you don't have a tan?

LARRY: Only tourists have time for that.

HELEN: This the first time you've ever been to New York?

LARRY: Yes.

ALBERT: Where you staying?

LARRY: The Statler.

ALBERT: We could put you up here.

LARRY: Thanks, but I'm with my mother.

ALBERT: I was going to ask how she was.

LARRY: Still going strong.

ALBERT: *(To Helen.)* I never met her but I sure felt like I knew his mother.

HELEN: You mean his ma, don't you, Plowboy? *(She rises.)* I'll get the beer.

LARRY: No beer for me, thanks.

HELEN: Beer is all we have.

LARRY: I'll settle for a glass of water.

ALBERT: I can jump around the corner and get some rye.

LARRY: I'm off the stuff.

ALBERT: What?

LARRY: Uh huh. For years.

ALBERT: How about that? *(To Helen.)* This guy could drink any man in the outfit under the table. I mean he was the champion guzzler of them all.

HELEN: So you've told me.

ALBERT: What made you quit, buddy?

LARRY: Wanted to retire undefeated. Now tell me about the boy. How is he?

ALBERT: Fine.

> *(Helen exits to the kitchen.)*

LARRY: Who does he favor?

ALBERT: Hard to say. Say, you should have brought your ma along tonight.

LARRY: She was tired after the trip. Do you have any pictures of him?

ALBERT: Not just now. Helen's folks keep grabbing them. We're having some more taken right after the holidays.

LARRY: You know, I've still got the telegram you sent when he was born saying you were naming him after me. I want you to know I'm very proud of that.

ALBERT: It was the least I could do. What brings you to New York?

LARRY: Business.

ALBERT: Must be a big deal to bring you this far.

LARRY: Not really. My mother and I are on our way to Boston to spend Christmas with some aunts, so I thought I'd kill two birds. Gee, I wish I could stay over and see young Larry, but it's impossible.

ALBERT: He'll be sorry he missed you. Say, you know, it's funny you should be living in Florida. I've often thought I wouldn't mind living there myself.

LARRY: It has its advantages. How's Larry doing in school?

ALBERT: Fine. The thought of all that sunshine the year round is very appealing.

LARRY: What grade is he in?

ALBERT: Sixth. The winters here are mean and I mean mean.

LARRY: Ten years old and he's in the sixth grade?

ALBERT: What about it?

LARRY: He must be a genius.

ALBERT: They skipped him a grade.

LARRY: They must have skipped him more than one grade.

ALBERT: Buddy, can't we talk about anything but the kid. I mean you're only going to be here a little while so why don't we talk about us some.

LARRY: You're right.

ALBERT: The reason I say that is because Helen misses the kid so much when he's away even a few days that it would be better if you mentioned him as little as possible in front of her. You know how women are.

LARRY: Sure.

ALBERT: I work for the electric company. Go around reading meters. Lots of leg work but I don't mind. Good exercise. There's all kind of employee benefits and the salary is good, but still and all I wouldn't hesitate to chuck it if the right offer came along.

LARRY: Last I heard you were driving a truck.

ALBERT: No future there. Soon as I saw that I got out. I've been with the electric company ever since. Outdoors a lot of the time and practically my own boss, so there's a lot to be said for it. Also it's a good place in case of a depression. But still I'd give it up for something better.

LARRY: What about the farm?

ALBERT: What farm?

LARRY: The farm you were going to buy.

ALBERT: Did I say I was going to buy a farm?

LARRY: Did you ever stop saying it?

ALBERT: Must have been one of those daydreams.

LARRY: What? How many times did I hear how your parents brought you to the city, and how you hated it, and how someday you were going back to the country, where you belonged.

ALBERT: That's a long time ago.

LARRY: You used to have everyone in tears, describing the day you moved to the city and how you hid in the barn until they found you and dragged you into the moving van.

ALBERT: You've got a good memory.

LARRY: I can still tell you exactly what the farm your parents had looked like.

ALBERT: Is that a fact?

LARRY: That's how much you talked about it. After all you said against city living I never expected to find you here.

ALBERT: She must be making that beer…Helen.

HELEN: *(From offstage.)* Be right there.

ALBERT: Fifteen years. Does it seem like fifteen years?

(*Helen enters carrying a tray with two beers and a glass of water. She gives the water to Larry.*)

LARRY: Thank you.

(*She gives Albert one beer and takes one herself.*)

ALBERT: (*Raises his glass.*) Well, buddy, here's to old times and the genuine pleasure it is to see you again. (*Drinks deeply.*)

LARRY: That's the first time I ever saw you take a drink.

ALBERT: (*To Helen.*) Ain't that what I told you? (*To Larry.*) I was telling her before I never touched a drink in those days, but she didn't believe me.

LARRY: (*To Helen.*) It's true. (*To Albert.*) What made you start?

HELEN: I did. When he met me he was just an innocent Plowboy and I corrupted him.

ALBERT: (*Forces a laugh.*) Say, you know, I'm sitting here looking at you now and wondering how you ever got into real estate. You were that dead set against going into any kind of business. (*To Helen.*) He used to rant and rave so much that some people took him for a red.

LARRY: Like you said before: That's a long time ago.

ALBERT: Said business wasn't a fit way for a man to spend his life. That he was going to do something more worthwhile.

LARRY: Now *you're* the one with the good memory.

ALBERT: A doctor! That's what it was. (*To Helen.*) He used to get drunk as a skunk and run around waking everyone up to tell them he had decided to become a doctor. And would they please stick out their tongues and say ah.

HELEN: (*To Larry.*) Why didn't you?

LARRY: Become a doctor?

HELEN: Yes.

LARRY: I'm afraid it was just a gag.

ALBERT: Gag, hell. It's what you were studying at college. I remember your letters…what happened, buddy? Why'd you quit?

LARRY: I told you: This fellow in Florida made me an offer that was too good to turn down. On top of that I found out I wasn't as interested in medicine as I thought. That's all there is to it.

ALBERT: Well, I think you did the right thing. There's a lot more money in real estate and it's not so depressing.

LARRY: True.

ALBERT: Besides, doctors never get any time off.

LARRY: Also true. Who plays the piano?

ALBERT: Helen used to but she hasn't touched it in years. Hey, do *you* still play?

LARRY: Not in a long time.

ALBERT: *(To Helen.)* He used to be good at that ragtime stuff. *(To Larry.)* Why don't you give us a sample?

HELEN: No…it's out of tune and the keys are filthy.

ALBERT: I'll wipe them off.

LARRY: I'd rather talk.

ALBERT: You're the boss.

LARRY: Does young Larry show any interest in music?

ALBERT: Not much.

LARRY: Don't tell me he's tone deaf like you?

ALBERT: Yes. You sure you don't want a beer?

LARRY: Positive.

ALBERT: Well, I'm gonna put a head on this one. *(To Helen.)* Can I get you one, dear?

HELEN: No. I have a bit of a headache. I'm going to bed soon.

ALBERT: Be right back. *(He exits.)*

> *(Larry and Helen regard each other; she impassively, he uneasily. He attempts to draw her into conversation.)*

LARRY: One of the funniest things I can remember is your husband trying to carry a tune…

> *(He chuckles but elicits no response or change of expression from her.)*

LARRY: I bet I called a dozen A. Cobbs before I got the Plowboy. Thought sure I'd recognize his voice right away but I didn't.

HELEN: Common.

LARRY: What's that?

HELEN: The name Cobb. My maiden name—there was only one in the whole Manhattan book.

> *(Silence.)*

LARRY: Albert tells me the boy is already in the sixth grade. Sounds like you have a quiz kid on your hands…

> *(No response.)*

LARRY: I was saying to Albert that I never expected to reach you people here.

HELEN: Why?

LARRY: Because all he used to talk about was buying a farm and getting out of the city.

HELEN: We talk a lot while the day is long.

LARRY: The farm was more than talk and he hated the city. Why is he still here?

HELEN: You hated business. Why are you in real estate?

(Albert reenters the room carrying a full glass of beer.)

ALBERT: In your honor I had Helen get another dozen cans. But I don't guess they'll go to waste. *(Drinks.)* You know it's a shame you didn't call earlier. You could have come for dinner. Helen's a great cook. *(Pats his stomach.)* I reckon this bears it out.

HELEN: *(To Larry.)* I'd imagine real estate would take you outdoors a lot.

LARRY: It does.

HELEN: Then I'm surprised you don't have at least a slight tan.

ALBERT: *(To Helen.)* You back to that again? *(To Larry.)* She gets a notion in her head she's like a dog with a bone. Say, why don't we go out on the town?

HELEN: I have a headache. I'm going to bed soon.

LARRY: And I'd prefer to stay right here.

ALBERT: Party poops is what you both are. Say, it's getting warm in here.

(He goes to the window and opens it. The same trumpet sound is heard.)

ALBERT: Don't he ever get tired blowing that thing? *(To Larry.)* We got a trumpet player lives upstairs. It's enough to drive you out of your mind.

HELEN: He's a classical musician.

ALBERT: He's classical all right. *(Slams the window shut.)* I think the guy is a nance.

HELEN: Why?

ALBERT: You know why. *(To Larry.)* He's as old as us, not married, and lives with his mother. And you never saw a guy so pretty.

LARRY: Except for the pretty part he sounds like me.

ALBERT: Hell no, buddy. It's different in your case.

LARRY: Why?

ALBERT: Because I was there, Charlie. *(To Helen.)* Could I tell you stories about this man in the boo-dwar department.

HELEN: *(To Larry.)* Next time you come bring your medals.

ALBERT: *(To Larry.)* Ain't she got a sense of humor? Say, will you ever forget the night we liberated Paris? Man, I never saw such gratitude.

HELEN: Anybody got a cigar?

(Albert looks at her.)

HELEN: Well, isn't this a smoker?

ALBERT: I thought you were going to bed.

HELEN: My headache isn't bad enough yet. But it's getting there.

ALBERT: I was only trying to point up the difference between Larry's situation and that trumpet player's.

HELEN: He's on the road weeks at a time. How do you know what he does then? He might have hundreds of women. Probably does.

ALBERT: Why don't we just drop it?

HELEN: In favor of what? Oh I know: Let's talk about the farm. Larry was telling me you used to have your heart set on getting one. Now he says you can't remember ever feeling that way.

ALBERT: *(To Larry.)* That's the truth, buddy. The fact is I probably used to joke about it and you took me serious…The same as I took you serious about being a doctor.

HELEN: That makes it a draw.

ALBERT: Say, did you ever bump into any of the old bunch?

LARRY: No.

ALBERT: I did, once. Old Darrow. *(To Helen.)* You remember that bald guy we ran into at Grand Central about five years ago.

HELEN: The one who kept scratching himself?

LARRY: That sounds like Darrow.

ALBERT: *(To Helen.)* Larry and I are going to be up all hours talking about old times and a lot of people you never heard of. Probably be boring for you, so any time you want to trot off to bed you do it. I mean don't just stay up to be polite on our account.

HELEN: Isn't he considerate?

LARRY: I always found him so.

HELEN: Always gives his seat to old ladies in buses and I never saw him refuse a panhandler.

ALBERT: What's wrong with that?

HELEN: Who said anything was wrong? It's probably the answer to every-thing.

LARRY: Where's the john?

ALBERT: *(Points.)* Through there.

LARRY: Pardon me. *(Exits.)*

ALBERT: *God damn you.* God damn you…What must he be thinking?

HELEN: I'd like to know.

ALBERT: You're trying to drive him out of here. Well, you're not going to get away with it. When he comes back you're going to excuse yourself and go to bed.

HELEN: No.

ALBERT: Oh, yes you are. Believe me you are.

HELEN: He won't think you're so nice if you hit me.

ALBERT: I won't hit you but it'll be worse, so don't make me do it…You know, he don't seem the way he was: cocky and wild and full of laughs. All he had to do was walk in a room and it lit up. I can't see any of that now…Of course you sitting there casting a pall over everything don't help. But even taking that into account he's not at all the way I remember.

HELEN: Maybe you just don't remember right. Like you didn't remember right about the farm.

ALBERT: You are bound to make me explode.

HELEN: How could you forget those lovely rolling acres, that adorable antique of a house, the quaint lopsided barn, that heavenly mortgage?

ALBERT: A saint couldn't keep a good mood in this house.

(Larry reenters.)

ALBERT: Hey, you know what I was just thinking, buddy? It's a shame all the boys from the old outfit just drifted apart. I mean when you consider how close we all were and what we went through together, it don't seem right to lose track of each other that way.

LARRY: Can't be helped. People change. Their interests change. Finally they don't have anything in common except a memory that gets fainter every year.

ALBERT: That ain't true in every case. Take you and I. Hell, buddy, you saved my life. No amount of time is gonna change that. I'd do anything in the world for you and I know you'd do the same for me.

HELEN: Now you should cut wrists and drink each other's blood.

ALBERT: Isn't it time for you to go to bed, Helen?

HELEN: I'll go to bed when *I'm* ready to go.

ALBERT: All right…all right. *(To Larry.)* Say, let me tell you about that kid of ours.

LARRY: I wish you would.

ALBERT: Well now, you should see him run. Fast as a deer. And climb…Well, you'd think he was Tarzan. *(To Helen.)* Ain't he a great climber? *(To Larry.)* And say, funny. You never heard a kid his age with such a fine sense of humor. *(To Helen.)* Keeps us in stitches, doesn't he? *(To Larry.)* And imagination—well, you never saw a kid with such a one as he has. *(To Helen.)* Will you ever forget the time he made out he was an elephant?

HELEN: I think I *will* go to bed.

ALBERT: *(To Larry.)* He went around on all fours for a week and we had to buy peanuts by the bushel basket.

HELEN: I'm going to bed.

ALBERT: What's that, dear?

HELEN: My headache is worse. I'm going to bed.

ALBERT: That's too bad. I was just going to suggest to Larry that we set up the trains so they'll be ready when young Larry comes home Christmas morning. *(To Larry.)* How about it?

LARRY: All right.

ALBERT: *(To Helen.)* You sure you don't want to watch us put up the kid's trains?

(She starts toward the bedroom.)

LARRY: It was nice meeting you…I hope you feel better in the morning.

(At the door she stops and turns to Larry.)

HELEN: We don't call him Plowboy any more. Nobody does. Not for years.

(She exits into the bedroom and closes the door.)

ALBERT: *(Moving to Larry confidentially.)* I guess you're wondering what that was all about?…Fact is she's due for her period. Always gets real skittish and peculiar just before that happens. Usually she's sweet as pie…Say, I've got some pictures of the old bunch. Why don't I trot them out?

LARRY: I thought we were going to set up the trains.

ALBERT: Oh yeah.

(Larry picks up the box containing the trains.)

LARRY: I guess you'll want to run them around the tree.

ALBERT: Yes.

LARRY: Where will the tree be?

ALBERT: We're getting one tomorrow.

LARRY: Where will it be?

ALBERT: *(Points.)* There.

(Larry goes to the designated place; opens the box.)

LARRY: You tell young Larry any time he wants more track or any accessories he just has to go down to the store. The name's on the box. *(Holds up a car.)* I think he'll get a real kick out of this cattle car; the cows actually move into a pen…*(He puts down that car; begins to extract others.)* You should see some of the gadgets they have.

ALBERT: Say, buddy, I shouldn't let you go to all that trouble now.

LARRY: It's no trouble.

ALBERT: No, buddy, I mean it. You leave those things be. I'll put them up tomorrow.

LARRY: I don't mind. I love trains. Besides, it's a tricky job.

ALBERT: And you don't think the old Plowboy is smart enough to figure it out on his own?

LARRY: I didn't say that.

ALBERT: I was just joking. But anyway you leave it all be and relax your-self…I insist.

LARRY: Okay.

ALBERT: We've got a lot of talking to catch up on. For instance, that Veron-ica. You and her were halfway down the aisle near as I could figure. What happened, buddy?

LARRY: Just one of those things.

ALBERT: I remember when she came down to Camp Blanding. You were al-most going to get married right then and there. And then all those let-ters you wrote one another while we were overseas. What went wrong?

LARRY: I told you: Just one of those things.

ALBERT: I figured if two people were ever going to stick, it was you and her. You fooled this country boy.

LARRY: You fooled easy in those days.

ALBERT: I guess so.

LARRY: How about now?

ALBERT: I've learned a few things.

LARRY: Such as?

ALBERT: Well, buddy, I don't keep my money in the mattress any more.

LARRY: Will you ever forget that?

ALBERT: I'm still sure it was Duffy who robbed me. No one else in the whole outfit chewed snuff and those were snuff stains on my pillow.

LARRY: You were ready to kill him.

ALBERT: I would have too, if you didn't talk me out of it.

(They both laugh. Then they look at each other a moment. Then both speak at once.)

LARRY: I'm surprised…

ALBERT: I never…

(They laugh.)

LARRY: Go on.

ALBERT: I was gonna say I never knew anyone with a better gift of gab than you had in those days. I was telling Helen before you got here that none of these jokers on the television make me laugh the way you used to.

LARRY: As I recall, you laughed at everything.

ALBERT: Say, I did, didn't I?

LARRY: And it didn't matter how many times a thing was repeated.

ALBERT: That's a fact. Like whenever someone would ask you where some-body was. You'd say, "He's lying down over in the corner, drunker than hell, but better than he was." I always got a bang out of that.

LARRY: Doesn't seem funny now, does it?

ALBERT: It was the way you used to come out with it. *(Silence.)* What were you surprised about?

LARRY: What?

ALBERT: You started to say you were surprised before. About what?

LARRY: About you being content to live in the city.

ALBERT: Who said I was content?

LARRY: Well then, what are you doing here?

ALBERT: Damn, but it's warm in here. *(Opens the window.)* Well what do you know: Our trumpet player stopped…Either we get too much heat like tonight or they don't send up nearly enough. I guess that's one nice thing about Florida, huh? Yes sir, I could take to those sunny beaches with no strain at all.

LARRY: If you don't like the city, why stay?

ALBERT: Who said I don't like the city?

LARRY: You said you weren't content here.

ALBERT: That ain't necessarily the city's fault.

LARRY: Whose fault is it?

ALBERT: Buddy, I expected to have some laughs tonight. I figured by this time we'd both be drunk as skunks. Come on, loosen up. Have a beer.

LARRY: No.

ALBERT: You know something? You have a funny look in your eye. You haven't gone religious, have you?

LARRY: No.

ALBERT: Well, praise the Lord. *(Drinks.)*

LARRY: You've got a job, a family, a home. You're in good health. Why aren't you content? What's wrong?

ALBERT: Who said anything was wrong?

LARRY: *You* did.

ALBERT: Say, why *don't* we set up those trains. I'm bound to botch it up if I do it myself…Say, they're real cute, aren't they?

LARRY: What about the farm?

ALBERT: Hey, how about this caboose?

LARRY: Plowboy?

ALBERT: And that pullman—you can actually see the people.

LARRY: *Plowboy!*

ALBERT: What?

LARRY: Why didn't you go back to the farm?

ALBERT: *(Pauses.)* I did.…Bought a place in Pennsylvania…House…barn…

chickens…cows. The works…Took every cent I could beg or borrow…
All down the drain inside of two years.

LARRY: What went wrong?

ALBERT: Me…We got there at night. The people I bought it from turned
over the keys and left. We went to bed but I couldn't sleep. I thought it
was the excitement of having my dream come true, but as the night went
on I realized there was nothing good in my feeling…Four-thirty the
alarm went off. Helen made breakfast. I couldn't eat a thing…I stepped
out of the house. The sky was beginning to get light. I stood in the doorway. I could see fields of corn and lettuce and beans and tomatoes…I
could hear pigs and chickens and cows and horses. And everything that
I could hear belonged to me…And right then, right at that instant, it hit
me what was wrong…I didn't know anything about farming.

LARRY: What do you mean?

ALBERT: I mean all that I could see and hear was my responsibility to care for
and I didn't know the first God damn thing to do.

LARRY: But you lived on a farm till you were twelve.

ALBERT: Yes, but I didn't remember anything. And no wonder when I really
thought about it. My father did everything. My mother wouldn't let me
help. She hated the farm. She was determined I was not to follow in his
footsteps. So all I used to do was loll around playing. And standing there
that morning I remembered all that for the first time…Buddy, I was par-
alyzed…The sky was getting brighter so I could see all my responsibili-
ties clearer. And the animals kept making more and more noise to be
cared for. You never heard such a racket. And I just stood there watching and listening till Helen came and shook the truth out of me…After
she got through cursing me she sent me to town to get a hired man. Even
with the hired man I didn't manage. I didn't have any talent for it. More
important, I didn't have any love for it. To be honest, I hated it. I was
my mother's boy in spades.

LARRY: Why didn't you tell me this before?

ALBERT: I was ashamed. I'd sold you a phony bill of goods. Hell, it was you
that named me Plowboy. What must you be thinking now?

LARRY: I'm thinking that maybe it was my fault. Maybe I was the one who
sold *you* the bill of goods.

ALBERT: Don't talk nonsense. I looked like a plowboy, talked like a plowboy,
and thought I was one long before I ever met you.

LARRY: But did you think of getting a farm before you met me?

ALBERT: Yes.

LARRY: That would explain why your wife looked at me the way she did. She feels I'm responsible for the farm.

ALBERT: I tell you it was my idea.

LARRY: Back to your roots. The virtues and joy of a rustic existence! I remember the lectures I used to give. My God, *was* I responsible?

ALBERT: No. Now drop it.

LARRY: You want to know something?…I'm relieved…I got the feeling from your wife that I was being indicted for the worst crime on earth. I'm relieved to know that this is all she accuses me of.

ALBERT: She don't accuse you of anything.

LARRY: Then why is she so angry?

ALBERT: She's not angry. I told you before she's due for the curse. It affects some women that way. Now damn it to hell you need a beer and I'm going to see you have one if I have to pour it down your throat.

(He would put his beer glass to Larry's lips but Larry shoves his hand away angrily.)

LARRY: I didn't come here to drink beer!

ALBERT: What did you come for?

(Silence.)

ALBERT: Let's get busy with these trains. *(He starts assembling the tracks.)* I guess it don't matter which tracks connect with which.

LARRY: I came to see if you were happy.

ALBERT: Now what's *this* wire for?

LARRY: *Are* you happy?

ALBERT: Is that all you came here for; just to ask me that?

LARRY: Yes.

ALBERT: Well, now I'm the one who's relieved. Helen figured that you were really after something. That you wanted something like money or something. You've been acting so strange that I was beginning to think maybe she was right. Of course, I'd give you anything if you asked me for it. But the fact is I don't have hardly anything *to* give so I'm relieved to know that that's all you want. Now come on and help me with the trains. I can't figure this wire sticking out of this one track here.

LARRY: You haven't answered the question…*Are* you happy?

(Silence.)

ALBERT: No.

LARRY: Not at all?

(Albert shakes his head no.)

ALBERT: You know the only things that make me get up in the morning?…

Booze and the chance of running into a piece while I'm on my route. It doesn't happen very often, the piece I mean, but now and then you come across a live one. It happened yesterday. I was reading meters in Brooklyn in this dame's apartment and out of a clear blue sky she begins to ask me what I think of husbands who play around. It seems her husband was that sort and she had just learned about it. Well, I said to her, in my opinion she should fight fire with fire. It turned out to be a most pleasant morning. Now—

LARRY: I get the picture.

ALBERT: Let me finish, buddy. There's a great punch line…You see, when I got dressed I put her husband's socks on by mistake. Helen was darning them when you came in. How's that for a close one?

LARRY: Charming.

ALBERT: You don't approve?

LARRY: What's there to approve?

ALBERT: Well, I thought a big ass man like you would surely approve… What's the matter, buddy, you look a little ill. I'm sorry if I disgusted you but you insisted on sticking your nose in and asking questions so I want to be sure and give you the answers in full. Like for instance about that job driving a truck.

LARRY: I think you better go to bed.

ALBERT: I told you I gave it up because there was no future in it. What I meant was there was no future in it for me. You see, there's always some kind of hassle going when you drive a truck and I couldn't take it. After two weeks I was shaking like a leaf. One day in the middle of a traffic jam on Thirty-fourth Street I got out of my truck, walked away and left it there. It was in all the papers, buddy. How'd you miss it?

(Larry rises.)

ALBERT: What do you want? Do you want something?

LARRY: I'm leaving.

ALBERT: *(Blocks his way.)* No you ain't. You came here to find out if I was happy and you're not going out of here without a complete answer. You try to go and I'll knock you down. *God damn it, somebody has to listen to me!*

LARRY: All right…go on.

ALBERT: That's my buddy. But, buddy, where were you ten years ago? I needed you then. I needed to talk to somebody and you were the only one and I couldn't find you. I tried everything. Well, you're here now.

Maybe it's not too late. Helen says it's too late but maybe she's wrong. She's like her mother. Gloomy...gloomy. Gloomy. Gloomy. You know what I call her mother?...Old moaning low. Old everything happens for the worst...You know the only thing they look forward to?...Dying... That's right: Dying...One time Helen and I had a terrible fight. I started to choke her. Had my hands around her neck and meant to kill her. You know what stopped me?...She never struggled. I was doing just what she wanted...She never forgave me for stopping.

LARRY: I can't hear any more. I'm sorry but I can't. *(He starts to put on his overcoat.)*

ALBERT: You've got to! You owe it to me.

(Larry regards him incredulously.)

ALBERT: That's right, you owe it to me. If it wasn't for you I wouldn't be here, so you owe it to me! *(In desperation he seizes the lapels of Larry's coat.)*

LARRY: You son of a bitch! *(Hurls him to the floor.)* You lousy son of a bitch!

ALBERT: Take me to Florida. Give me a job. Talk to me. Help me, buddy. Save the Plowboy again.

(Larry exits and slams the door, which rouses Albert, who runs after him out into the hallway.)

ALBERT: You haven't heard the worst part. If you heard that you'd understand. You would, buddy. *(Calls down the stairwell.)* Don't go, buddy. Don't go.

(There is a crashing noise from downstairs.)

ALBERT: Buddy!...Buddy! *(Albert runs down the stairs.)*

(Helen, attracted by the commotion, comes into the living room. Now Albert appears carrying Larry, who is unconscious. He brings him into the apartment.)

ALBERT: *(To Helen.)* He collapsed. He started downstairs and just crumpled up...Call the doctor.

(She goes to the phone and dials while he lays Larry on the couch; clucks at him.)

ALBERT: Buddy...buddy, wake up...buddy...buddy...

(Curtain.)

SCENE II

It is about an hour later. At rise, Helen and Albert sit on opposite sides of the room. An overcoat is draped over a chair. There is a hat beside it. Albert keeps darting nervous glances toward the off-stage bedroom.

ALBERT: What's his name again?

HELEN: Sheldon.

ALBERT: I don't see why Dr. Block couldn't come.

HELEN: I told you: Block doesn't feel well himself.

ALBERT: He's certainly taking his time…I'd feel better if it was Block in there… *(Rises, paces aimlessly, stops at the coat, examines the lapel.)* Expensive taste. I can see what he's gonna charge. *(Eyes the offstage bedroom again.)* He's been in there half an hour. How much longer is he gonna take?…Did you hear Larry then?

HELEN: No.

ALBERT: I figure it was just the excitement of coming to New York and all…I hope he snaps out of it before his mother gets here.

HELEN: What did you tell her?

ALBERT: That he wasn't feeling well and I thought it would be better if he spent the night here.

HELEN: Was she excited?

ALBERT: No, but she insisted on coming up. I'm sorry as hell now I called…What the devil is taking that doctor so long…This started out to be a wonderful night. How did it end up like this? *(Picks up the doctor's hat and looks inside it.)* This is no ten-dollar hat either. Don't pay this guy cash. That's how these jokers beat their income tax. Make him send a bill.

(The bedroom door opens and the Doctor comes out, closing the door behind him.)

DOCTOR: He appears to be suffering from complete exhaustion.

ALBERT: *(To Helen.)* What did I tell you?

DOCTOR: I gave him a sedative that should allow him to sleep well into the morning. Of course I can only make a superficial diagnosis under these conditions.

ALBERT: Oh, it's exhaustion all right. I could see how tired he was the minute he got here. Usually he's very lively, so I knew something was wrong right away.

DOCTOR: Yes. Well, you bring him to my office tomorrow. Here's my card. The hours are twelve to two. *(Starts to put on his hat and coat.)*

ALBERT: How much do I owe you?

DOCTOR: I'll send you a bill. Good night.

ALBERT: Good night.

HELEN: Good night, Doctor.

(He exits.)

ALBERT: What did I tell you? Didn't I say it was just exhaustion? I'm sorry as hell now that I called his mother.

HELEN: How do you suppose he got so exhausted?

ALBERT: Probably been on a bender. Probably never gave up booze at all. You wait and see: a good night's sleep and you won't even recognize him. He'll be his old self...Probably won't remember anything that happened tonight.

HELEN: You hope.

(He turns to her.)

HELEN: Sounded like a nice little row you were having. What was it about?

ALBERT: Nothing.

HELEN: Did you find out what he wanted?

ALBERT: He doesn't want anything.

HELEN: Did he offer you a job?

ALBERT: We didn't talk about that.

HELEN: You didn't get very far putting up the trains, did you?

(The doorbell rings.)

ALBERT: That's the upstairs bell. Probably his mother.

HELEN: Well, let her in.

ALBERT: We mustn't excite her. She's an old lady.

HELEN: Open the door.

(He goes to the door.)

ALBERT: Come in, Mrs. Doyle. Come in.

(Mrs. Doyle, a woman in her late sixties, enters. Albert closes the door.)

ALBERT: That's some climb coming up those stairs. Here, give me your coat. *(Helps her off with her coat.)* Larry's sleeping like a lamb. Doctor just left. Said it was a plain and simple case of exhaustion. I'm sorry I put you to all this trouble for nothing.

MRS. DOYLE: How much did the doctor charge?

ALBERT: He's going to send a bill.

MRS. DOYLE: *(Takes a bill from her purse and offers it to him.)* This should be enough. Here.

ALBERT: That isn't necessary.

MRS. DOYLE: I insist.

ALBERT: *(Sees how adamant she is and takes the bill.)* All right, but it isn't necessary. I'd be only too glad—

MRS. DOYLE: I'm sure you would...Where is he?

ALBERT: In the bedroom. *(Ushers her into the living room.)* This is my wife Helen.

HELEN: Hello.

MRS. DOYLE: How do you do.

(The two women regard each other.)

ALBERT: It's a shame we all had to meet under these circumstances...Say, how would you like a nice cup of tea?

MRS. DOYLE: Thank you, not just now.

ALBERT: Well, you sing out if you change your mind. I know from Larry what a great one you are for your tea.

(She sits. Albert indicates the off-stage bedroom.)

ALBERT: He's in that room there, if you want to take a look at him.

MRS. DOYLE: Not just now, thank you. *(Unaware of how uneasy she is making them, she looks about, from where she is seated, blatantly inspecting the apartment.)*

ALBERT: The doctor says he'll sleep well into the morning...

(She continues looking about.)

ALBERT: We don't put our Christmas decorations up till Christmas Eve...

(As her eye falls on the trains.)

ALBERT: It was swell of Larry to bring those trains...Young Larry will be here Christmas morning. He's upstate visiting some relatives...I guess Larry got a real kick out of me naming the kid after him.

MRS. DOYLE: He did.

ALBERT: I figured it was the least I could do for him.

(She continues looking around.)

HELEN: If you're looking for the bathroom, it's through there. *(To Albert.)* Mrs. Doyle seems to be looking for something. I thought maybe it was the bathroom.

MRS. DOYLE: No, but thank you anyway.

ALBERT: *(To Helen.)* Mrs. Doyle used to send us packages of things she'd canned herself. Greatest stuff I ever tasted. *(To Mrs. Doyle.)* Do you still can?

MRS. DOYLE: No.

ALBERT: We're having a very mild winter but I guess it still seems pretty bad to you.

MRS. DOYLE: Why?

ALBERT: Well, I mean in contrast to Florida.

MRS. DOYLE: I come from Chicago.

ALBERT: I thought you lived in Florida with Larry.

MRS. DOYLE: I'll see him now. *(She rises.)*

(Albert rises with her.)

MRS. DOYLE: I can manage alone. *(She goes off into the bedroom.)*

ALBERT: What gave me the idea she lived with Larry?

HELEN: He did. He said he was like the trumpet player because he lived with his mother.

ALBERT: We must have misunderstood him.

HELEN: Listen to me.

ALBERT: What?

HELEN: Get her out of here. I don't care what excuse you use but get rid of her as fast as you can.

ALBERT: Why?

HELEN: She gives me the creeps.

ALBERT: She's upset about Larry.

HELEN: So upset she sat here and looked over the whole room before she went in to see him. What the devil was she looking for?... And we didn't misunderstand him. He *did* say he lived with her.

ALBERT: Don't be ridiculous. Why would he lie about a thing like that?

HELEN: I don't know. I just want her out of my house. I want them both out.

ALBERT: Larry can't be moved.

HELEN: Well, get rid of *her*. I—

(Mrs. Doyle reappears.)

HELEN: How is he?

MRS. DOYLE: Asleep.

ALBERT: He gave us quite a scare.

MRS. DOYLE: Did he?

HELEN: We'd offer to put you up for the night but we don't have the room.

MRS. DOYLE: Thank you, I'll return to the hotel.

ALBERT: You must be pretty tired.

MRS. DOYLE: Yes.

HELEN: In that case we mustn't keep you any longer. *(To Albert.)* Get Mrs. Doyle's coat.

ALBERT: I think she should have a cup of tea before she goes.

HELEN: We're out of tea.

ALBERT: Are you sure?

HELEN: Yes.

ALBERT: *(To Mrs. Doyle.)* I'm sorry.

HELEN: Get the coat.

ALBERT: All right. *(He gets Mrs. Doyle's coat and holds it for her.)*
(She dons it absently.)

MRS. DOYLE: What else did Larry tell you?

ALBERT: About what?

MRS. DOYLE: About himself.

ALBERT: Just that he lived in Florida and was doing very nicely in the real estate business.

MRS. DOYLE: It's not true.

ALBERT: What's not true?

MRS. DOYLE: None of it…Not about Florida or the real estate or any of it…All lies.

HELEN: *(To Albert.)* Go down and get Mrs. Doyle a cab. When you have one, tick the button for her to come.

ALBERT: All right. *(Turns and starts toward the door.)*

MRS. DOYLE: Don't you want to know why he lied?

ALBERT: *(Stops.)* No…No, I don't think I do.

HELEN: Then go for the cab.

ALBERT: Yes. *(He continues toward the door.)*

MRS. DOYLE: He's dying.
(Albert falters as though he might stop.)

HELEN: Go for the cab!
(He continues toward the door.)

MRS. DOYLE: It's your fault.
(This stops him. He turns to her.)

HELEN: You fool. *(She turns away from both of them.)*

MRS. DOYLE: Dying and it's your fault.

ALBERT: My fault?

MRS. DOYLE: The wound…the wound he got when he saved you.

ALBERT: He recovered from that.

MRS. DOYLE: So he thought. And so it seemed for several years. Then it began to bother him. He's been in one hospital or another ever since. Now they say in a matter of months he'll be dead and he knows it…He didn't want you to find out. He didn't want you to blame yourself.

HELEN: Then why did he come here?

MRS. DOYLE: He never said, but I think it was to convince himself that he had not sacrificed his life for nothing.

ALBERT: Oh, my God.

MRS. DOYLE: If you are happy, then he accomplished something.

ALBERT: My God.

MRS. DOYLE: He must not know that I've told you any of this.

HELEN: Why *have* you told us?

MRS. DOYLE: Because my intuition tells me this is by no means a happy home. If my son hasn't discovered that, I beg you— prevent his doing so. *(Looks toward Albert.)* Did you know *he* was married? A good match, and on his way to being a fine doctor. Number one in his class. All the best in front of him when that old sore began to act up. When he realized there would be nothing but hospitals for the rest of his life he made an end of the marriage. Did it in fine style, as usual, so she wouldn't blame herself...I always live a block from the hospital...Too graceful— that was his trouble. Anyone could lean against him and as hard as they wanted. And never a peep out of him.

ALBERT: You must hate me.

MRS. DOYLE: Yes...I'll go now. I can get my own cab. *(Starts for the door, then halts.)* No child lives in this house.

HELEN: No.

MRS. DOYLE: Does he know that?

HELEN: No.

MRS. DOYLE: Good. *(She exits.)*

(Helen and Albert stand silently for a time.)

ALBERT: I'll take tomorrow off...You get prettied up soon as you get out of bed...We'll be all smiles. All lovey-dovey...First thing in the morning I'll get Christmas decorations and a Christmas tree and presents...I'll smooth everything over...Time I get through he'll think this is the happiest place he ever saw...I'll get a big tree. Not one of them midgets...I'll tell him the kid insisted on a big tree...

(As he talks the Curtain slowly descends.)

END OF ACT I

ACT II

Time: The following morning. At rise: Helen stands by the open window listening to the trumpet. She appears nervous. The trains which Larry brought have been set up. The doorbell rings—three times long, two times short. Helen closes the window, and opens the door to admit Albert, who carries a Christmas tree, a stand and several boxes of lights and ornaments.

HELEN: What took you so long?

ALBERT: I had to go all the way to Broadway to get a tree. Five bucks for this. Can you beat it?…He still sleeping?

HELEN: Yes. I thought you'd never get back.

ALBERT: I was only gone a half-hour.

HELEN: I was afraid he'd wake up while you were out.

ALBERT: What if he did?

HELEN: I don't want to be alone with him.

ALBERT: Why not?

HELEN: I'm afraid I'll say the wrong thing, that I won't act right.

ALBERT: You don't give yourself enough credit. *(Holds the tree up.)* Here, give me a hand.

(She moves to assist him.)

ALBERT: This is supposed to be the latest thing in stands. You hold the tree like that and I'll screw these things into it.

HELEN: *(As they put up the tree.)* How much did you tell him last night?

ALBERT: Don't worry about that…Will you hold the tree straight.

HELEN: You were arguing.

ALBERT: I can smooth that over. Stop jiggling the tree…And about us—I mean you and me. Well, if we seemed in a bad mood last night, it was because we had a little spat before he got here.

HELEN: About what?

ALBERT: You wanted a new coat and I said no. It was one of those little spats that got out of hand. To spite you I started drinking too much. When I drink too much I get very depressed. I exaggerate my troubles…I'm not getting anywhere with this thing.

HELEN: Let me do it.

ALBERT: No! You're always complaining how clumsy I am. Well, what the devil do you expect when you never give me a chance to finish anything…Will you please hold the damn thing straight…I told him about the farm…the whole story.

HELEN: How you going to smooth *that* over?

ALBERT: I'm not going to try. Everyone has to have some disappointments…Remember: His mother wasn't here. I never called her. I wanted to but I couldn't remember the name of the hotel.

HELEN: He'll wonder what the doctor said.

ALBERT: We'll tell him: exhaustion. *(Catches his finger in the stand.)* Ow!… Damn it to hell, I caught my finger.

HELEN: Here.

(He now supports the tree, while she sets up the stand.)

ALBERT: *(Sucking the injured finger.)* Gave myself a nice cut.

HELEN: Are you sure you've told me everything you said last night, so we don't contradict each other.

ALBERT: Uh huh…This thing's really bleeding.

HELEN: Don't move the tree.

ALBERT: You know something: You look very nice this morning…I like the way your hair is.

(No reply.)

ALBERT: I said I like the way your hair is.

HELEN: Save it. *(She secures the tree and rises.)* There.

(He seizes her arm.)

ALBERT: I hope to God you're going to cooperate. I hope you ain't going to spoil this thing.

HELEN: I'll do my best. *(She frees herself and begins to decorate the tree.)*

ALBERT: If you say the wrong thing it won't be any accident and I'll know it. *(Listens.)* He's moving around…he's getting up. Now don't be nervous…Come here.

HELEN: What do you want?

ALBERT: Come here!

(She comes to him apprehensively.)

HELEN: What do you want?

ALBERT: Put your arms around me.

HELEN: I will not.

(He grabs her and forces her to him so they are in something of an embrace when Larry, wearing pajamas and a robe, both much too big for him, appears.)

LARRY: Good morning.

(Albert and Helen separate with something that could pass for embarrassment.)

ALBERT: Good morning, and excuse us.

LARRY: I should have knocked. *(To Helen.)* Good morning.

HELEN: Good morning.

ALBERT: How you feel, buddy?

LARRY: Fine. I don't know what happened to me last night.

ALBERT: Doctor said it was just a plain and simple case of exhaustion.

LARRY: That figures. I've been going at quite a pace.

ALBERT: Well, maybe I'm speaking out of turn, but I've got to tell you for your own good that you can't keep chasing around like you did when we were youngsters. No sir. The time comes when you have to single out one filly, grab her…*(He grabs Helen around the waist and swings her in a circle.)*

HELEN: Stop it!

ALBERT: Eh-yah! *(Deposits her.)* And settle down. That's what you've got to do, buddy: Settle down.

LARRY: Maybe you're right.

ALBERT: I know I am.

LARRY: What time is it?

HELEN: Ten thirty.

LARRY: *(To Albert.)* What time do you go to work?

ALBERT: I'm not going today. Phoned in sick.

LARRY: You didn't have to do that on my account.

ALBERT: Don't talk nonsense. Say, hadn't you better call your mother and let her know where you are?

LARRY: Yes.

ALBERT: I was going to do it but I couldn't remember which hotel you said it was.

LARRY: The Statler. Where's the phone?

ALBERT: In the foyer there.

LARRY: I better do that right now.

(He goes into the foyer and phones. We can't hear the call.)

HELEN: I'll go along with all this. I'll—

ALBERT: I hope his mother doesn't give it away.

HELEN: Listen to me.

ALBERT: What?

HELEN: I'll go along with all this. I'll smile and laugh and do everything I can to make him think we get along fine, but don't put your hands on me.

ALBERT: I was just—

HELEN: You were just taking advantage of the situation.

ALBERT: I was not. I was only trying to be convincing.

HELEN: A lot of couples get along fine and they don't paw each other in public.

ALBERT: A lot of couples, maybe. Not us. When *we* got along best we were at each other every minute. In public or not.

HELEN: Don't be disgusting.

(Larry completes his call; returns to them.)

ALBERT: You get her?

LARRY: Yes.

ALBERT: *(Hanging ornaments on the tree.)* Everything all right?

LARRY: Everything's fine.

ALBERT: She wasn't too worried, I hope.

LARRY: No. She's used to my irregular hours.

ALBERT: That's good.

HELEN: *(To Larry.)* Will you have some breakfast?

ALBERT: Of course he will.

LARRY: *(To Helen.)* Well, I would like some coffee, thank you.

ALBERT: Just coffee? What the devil kind of a breakfast do you call that? We've got eggs, bacon, cereal, anything you want. Just name it.

LARRY: All I want is coffee.

ALBERT: Well, I certainly—

HELEN: Larry's old enough to know what he wants for breakfast.

LARRY: Thank you.

HELEN: Cream and sugar?

LARRY: Just cream.

(She exits to the kitchen.)

ALBERT: Is that all you have every morning? Coffee?

LARRY: Usually. Why?

ALBERT: Well then, it's no damn wonder you...

LARRY: It's no wonder I what?

ALBERT: Well, that you look so scrawny and go around collapsing from exhaustion. Man, breakfast is the most important meal of the day. It's like the foundation of a house.

LARRY: I'll make a note of it.

(Albert looks at him a moment and laughs.)

LARRY: What's funny?

ALBERT: You should see yourself in my pajamas. You look like one of them floppy clowns.

LARRY: I do feel kind of lonely in here.

ALBERT: Hey, do you remember that crazy boy from Baltimore who took his pajamas into combat?

LARRY: Novak?

ALBERT: Yeah. Swore he was gonna wear them every night as some kind of protest against the war.

LARRY: And then loused up the whole idea by getting killed the first day we saw action.

ALBERT: Say, that's right, he *was* killed, wasn't he?

LARRY: Uh huh.

ALBERT: Well, now isn't that a cheerful thing to be discussing first thing in the morning. I wonder what the devil made me bring up a thing like that.

LARRY: We were talking about pajamas.

ALBERT: That's right. That's what it was.

LARRY: I see you bought a tree.

ALBERT: Yeah. Kind of skimpy-looking but it was the best they had left. Young Larry's gonna be mad. He likes a big one.

(Larry opens one of the boxes Albert brought in.)

LARRY: New lights?

ALBERT: Our old ones were shot, and it don't pay to take chances when there's a kid around. You're always reading something about kids getting burned at this time of year.

LARRY: *(Regarding the decorations on the tree.)* I always thought you put the lights on first.

ALBERT: You're right....How do you like that?...Say, listen, while Helen's out of the room I want to tell you that I hope you didn't get me wrong about what I said before about settling down. I mean I hope I didn't sound like I was trying to give you the idea that marriage is nothing but paradise. I didn't, did I?

LARRY: No.

ALBERT: That's good. Married guys are always sounding off like that to bachelors. You know, "Come on in, the water's fine." And it don't matter a damn if the water is ten below zero. You and I are too close for crap like that. I mean I'll level with you about marriage. The plain fact is that it ain't all beer and skittles, by a long shot. No sir. But still, over the long pull, it's the only way to really live.

LARRY: This off the record or can I quote you?

ALBERT: I'm serious, buddy. Now of course appearances are deceiving. Take Helen and me: Most people meet us they think we never exchanged a cross word in our lives. Of course that would be hard for you to believe. From what you heard last night you probably got the notion we battle all the time. Well, the actual truth is somewhere between those two points. That is to say that while we're not always lovey-dovey, still we're nothing like the impression we must have given you last night.

LARRY: You don't have to explain about last night.

ALBERT: I do. I certainly do. I won't have you leaving here with any wrong ideas about us. Now what happened last night was that Helen and me had a row before you got here. One of those little stupid things that got blown up way out of reason. She wants a certain coat. I thought it was too expensive. I said no. She said something back about the money I spend on beer. And bingo, we're off. It ends up with me drinking too much to spite her. Then you called and said you were coming. Well, by that time I was already tight. You know how some guys get depressed when they get tight?

LARRY: Yeah.

ALBERT: Well, that's how it hits me. I always feel way down and sorry for myself. Any little problems I have take on the size of mountains. I don't remember everything I said to you but I know a lot of it was pretty wild and I apologize.

LARRY: Forget it.

ALBERT: The fact is Helen and I are as happy as any couple we know…We'll be married twelve years in April.

LARRY: Maybe the thing for you to do is to give up booze.

ALBERT: You know something—I think you're right. Seems I always end up the morning after apologizing for a lot of bull I said the night before.

LARRY: About the farm. Was that bull?

ALBERT: No. No, that was true. But still it wasn't the tragedy like I made out. It was just one of those disappointments that happens to everyone. I got over it. It never even crosses my mind except when I'm drinking.

(Helen enters with coffee and toast, which she sets before Larry.)

HELEN: There's some toast and jelly there in case you change your mind.

LARRY: Thank you.

ALBERT: *(To Larry, indicating Helen.)* If you lived around here she'd have you fattened up in no time.

LARRY: I'll bet.

ALBERT: *(To Helen, indicating Larry.)* Would you ever believe that such a runt as that was able to lug me on his back for fifty yards?

(The phone rings.)

ALBERT: I'll get it. *(Goes to the phone.)*

(Larry and Helen regard each other. She is now the uneasy one.)

HELEN: The coffee's very hot.

(Larry tries the coffee and puts it down.)

LARRY: Thanks for the warning.

HELEN: Burn yourself?

LARRY: Not quite.

(Pause.)

HELEN: We like our coffee hot…I hope it isn't too strong. We like it that way.

LARRY: The stronger the better.

HELEN: That's how we feel. Anything we can't stand is a weak cup of coffee…Without snow it doesn't seem like Christmas, does it?

LARRY: No.

HELEN: I hope you found the bed comfortable.

LARRY: I did. *(Tries the coffee again.)* Still too hot. I think I'll get dressed while it's cooling. Will you pardon me?

HELEN: Certainly.

(He goes into the bedroom. Albert hangs up.)

HELEN: Who was that?

ALBERT: Gavigan.

HELEN: What did he want?

ALBERT: I have to go to the office.

HELEN: I thought you told him you were sick.

ALBERT: The supervisor came around and a couple of my sheets aren't in order. It'll only take an hour.

HELEN: Don't go.

ALBERT: I have to. What's he doing?

HELEN: Getting dressed…Wait till he has his coffee, then take him with you.

ALBERT: No.

HELEN: Why not?

ALBERT: I told him the story I made up to cover last night, but I don't think he believed me.

HELEN: Is he apt to believe you any better if he hangs around here?

ALBERT: I won't let him go away thinking about us the way he does now.

HELEN: If he stays he might end up thinking a lot worse.

ALBERT: You just keep him here till I get back. I'll fix everything.

HELEN: How? What can you do?

ALBERT: Just keep him here. I'll think of something. I have to. I can't let him go like this. *(Goes to the bedroom door.)* Hey, buddy?

LARRY: *(From offstage.)* Yeah?

ALBERT: I got to run down to my office for a few minutes. I'll see you when I get back.

LARRY: *(From offstage.)* I was going to shove off pretty soon.

HELEN: *(To Albert.)* Let him go. Please.

ALBERT: *(Ignores her.)* You can stay a little longer.

(*Larry comes out buttoning his shirt.*)

LARRY: I promised my mother I'd take her to Radio City.

ALBERT: You'll have time. I'll just be a few minutes. Okay?…Okay?

LARRY: Okay.

ALBERT: That a boy. *(Puts on his coat.)* Be back in three shakes. Bye, hon.

(*Kisses Helen, who can't help averting her head.*)

ALBERT: Married twelve years and still blushes. How about that?

HELEN: Albert, really.

ALBERT: See ya. *(Exits.)*

LARRY: Same old Plowboy.

HELEN: Yes.

LARRY: I forgot they don't call him that any more. *(He takes some of his coffee.)*

HELEN: Is there enough cream in it?

LARRY: Yes…When did they stop calling him Plowboy?

HELEN: Years ago.

(*He drinks the coffee.*)

HELEN: It's probably cold now. I'll warm it up.

LARRY: It's perfectly all right the way it is…Why did they stop?

HELEN: Pardon me?

LARRY: Why did everyone stop calling him Plowboy?

HELEN: They just did…If you'll excuse me I think I'll clean up my kitchen.

LARRY: You really can't stand me, can you?

HELEN: Why do you say that?

LARRY: You won't even sit and talk awhile.

HELEN: If you want me to sit and talk I'll be glad to.

LARRY: Look, I know why you don't like me and I don't blame you. In a way I guess I was responsible.

HELEN: For what?

LARRY: The farm. Albert told me about it last night.

HELEN: Oh.

LARRY: I did name him Plowboy. And I did fill his head with a lot of talk about quitting the city and going back to the country where he belonged. So I guess I am partly responsible for what he did, and you have every right to blame me for it.

HELEN: I don't blame *you* for that.

LARRY: Then what is it?

HELEN: What is what?

LARRY: Why are you so nervous? Why do you look at me the way you do?

HELEN: What way?

LARRY: Like I was your worst enemy.

HELEN: What are you talking about?

LARRY: I'm talking about the hate in your eyes when you look at me.

HELEN: I never met you before last night. What reason could I have to feel one way or another about you?

LARRY: It's in your eyes right now!

HELEN: I think I better clean up the kitchen. *(Turns from him and starts toward the kitchen.)*

LARRY: *(Blocking her way.)* If it's the money, tell me how much the farm set you back and I'll make it good!
(She looks at him as though he'd struck her, then about to cry, runs to the kitchen.)

LARRY: *(Calls.)* Excuse the last remark. It was uncalled for…As a matter of fact forget everything I said…*(Drinks the coffee.)* The coffee is excellent…A man should never open his mouth in the morning until he's had his coffee…*(Goes to the kitchen door and listens.)* Please don't cry… There's nothing to cry about…*Will you please stop crying…(Unable to stand the sound of her crying he goes to the piano, opens it, and, reading a piece of music already on the holder, begins to play loudly in an effort to drown her out.)* Let me know when you're through.
(Helen appears immediately in the kitchen doorway.)

HELEN: Don't do that…don't play.

LARRY: *(Goes on playing.)* Am I that bad?

HELEN: Please stop.

LARRY: *(As he plays.)* I'll make a deal. You stop crying and I'll stop playing.

HELEN: You must stop.

LARRY: Well, how about it? Is it a deal?

HELEN: I said stop!
(She goes to the piano and pulls the sheet music from the stand. He stops and now aware for the first time of her intensity regards her curiously.)

HELEN: I'm sorry…I don't like anyone to touch my piano…I asked you to stop…I can't stand for anyone to touch my piano.

LARRY: Why?

HELEN: I just can't. I realize how childish that sounds, but I can't.
(Someone rattles the doorknob. Helen seems not to hear the sound.)

LARRY: There's someone at the door.

HELEN: I've always been like that about my possessions.

(The rattling of the door handle is repeated.)

LARRY: Someone's at your door.

HELEN: It's the kids. They're always doing that. If you don't pay any attention they go away.

(Now there is a gentle tapping at the door.)

LARRY: I'll get rid of them. *(He starts for the door.)*

HELEN: No. I'll go…I know them.

(She moves toward the door. Then pauses. The knock is repeated.)

HELEN: It's probably the kids.

(Again the knock sounds. She goes to the door with great reluctance, would open it only partially but the man who was knocking enters boldly.)

THE MAN: Why was it locked?

(Helen just looks at him.)

THE MAN: What's wrong?

(Now he follows her gaze and turns to face Larry.)

THE MAN: Who are you?

LARRY: Friend of the family.

THE MAN: *(To Helen.)* What's going on here?

LARRY: You took the words right out of my mouth.

HELEN: *(To the man, indicating Larry.)* He's a friend of Albert's.

THE MAN: *(To Larry.)* So am I, I live upstairs. *(To Helen.)* Mother wanted to know if she could borrow a cup of sugar.

LARRY: Where's the cup?

HELEN: *(To the man.)* We can spare him the performance.

LARRY: Thank you.

THE MAN: I think I better go. *(To Larry.)* If you tell him, you might be responsible for a murder. He's capable of that.

LARRY: You the trumpet player?

THE MAN: Yes.

LARRY: You've got nothing to worry about: He thinks you're queer.

THE MAN: He ought to consult his wife. *(To Helen.)* I'll call later. *(He exits.)*

(Larry closes the door.)

LARRY: Hubby goes to work and *you* play the piano to sound the all-clear. Clever.

HELEN: What are you going to do?

LARRY: I may never play again.

HELEN: Do you think I care if you tell him?

LARRY: No.

HELEN: That's right. Not a bit and that's why you won't tell him. No one ever tries to hurt you when you don't care and I don't care about anything.

LARRY: Including your son?

(No reply.)

LARRY: Well, don't you care about your son?

HELEN: *Yes!*...That make you happy.

LARRY: Suppose the kid found out you were playing around?

HELEN: He won't.

LARRY: Suppose he did? How would he feel?

HELEN: Are you going to preach?...If you're going to preach I'm going to walk out of this house and stay out till you're gone.

LARRY: If you and the Plowboy are so miserable together, split up. It would be easier on the kid.

HELEN: One more word and I'm walking out.

LARRY: I'm through. *(Begins to knot his tie.)*

HELEN: I'm sorry you had to see all this.

LARRY: So am I.

HELEN: Can I get you more coffee?

LARRY: No thanks. *(Puts on his jacket.)*

HELEN: You leaving?

LARRY: Yes.

HELEN: He'll wonder why you didn't wait.

LARRY: Tell him my mother called. That she wasn't feeling well.

HELEN: He'll only be a few minutes.

LARRY: I couldn't face him right now...Tell him I'll stop by tomorrow.

HELEN: Tomorrow?

LARRY: Yes. Sometime in the morning.

HELEN: I thought you and your mother were leaving town this afternoon.

LARRY: I changed my mind. We'll leave tomorrow instead.

HELEN: Why?

LARRY: I want to see the boy.

HELEN: Why?

LARRY: Because I want to.

HELEN: But that's impossible. We don't know when he'll be home.

LARRY: You said he'd be home tomorrow.

HELEN: I mean we don't know what time. These relatives will be driving him down and we never know when they'll arrive. They have an old car and it's a long ride.

LARRY: I'll wait.

HELEN: It's possible they won't come till tomorrow night.

LARRY: I'll wait.

HELEN: Just to see the boy?

LARRY: Yes.

HELEN: You make it seem like the most important thing in the world.

LARRY: *(Putting on his overcoat.)* Tomorrow when the boy arrives, call me at the hotel. I'll come right up.

HELEN: Suppose he doesn't arrive tomorrow.

LARRY: I'll stay over...I'm not leaving New York until I see him. *(Takes out a pad and pencil.)* So there won't be any excuse for not calling, I'll leave the name of the hotel and my room number. *(Writes.)* As far as me saying anything to the Plowboy about what happened this morning, you can rest easy. *(Finishes writing, offers her the paper.)* Here.
(Helen makes no move to accept the paper.)

HELEN: It's impossible to spare you if you won't spare yourself.

LARRY: What does that mean?

HELEN: That I beg you...I beg you to leave this house without another word and never come back. Never come back. Never call...I beg you.

LARRY: Not until I see the boy.

HELEN: *There is no boy!...There is no boy!*

LARRY: He's dead?

HELEN: That's what we tell people...what we should have told you in the beginning...In my heart I know it's what I should tell you now, but I'm sick of lies...Just once I'd like to tell the truth about it.

LARRY: Go on...go on.

HELEN: They have a complicated name for it...a long medical word...What it means is...What it means is I gave birth to a monster...Yes...Not boy. Not girl. Not anything human...not anything.

LARRY: He sent me a telegram when the baby was born. Said everything was fine and he was naming it after me.

HELEN: The hospital gave him the wrong report on the phone. When he got there they told him. They didn't tell me for a week...I've never seen it. They put it some place. Some institution. We pay. I don't know where it is...It took something in him and something in me. Something bad in the both of us to produce this thing. They say it couldn't happen again in fifty years...You made it possible...Again and again he'd tell that story. How he lay in the dark bleeding to death and heard the Lieutenant say, "Who'll save the Plowboy?" And then silence until you said, "I'll go." And each time I heard it my hate for you grew…Why didn't you keep your mouth shut?

LARRY: He was my friend.

HELEN: He wasn't worth your pinky. He's a stupid, pitiful fool.

LARRY: Why did you marry him?

HELEN: It was the only offer I ever got. And he was the Plowboy then: strong, honest, kind. And there would be the farm. I'd never been to the country. He made it sound like paradise. Everyone said, "You'll never do any better and you could do lots worse." So I married him. And very soon I knew that I'd been swindled…He was not strong. He was not honest…He was not kind…

LARRY: Why don't you leave? Go away?

HELEN: I did…One day I got on a bus…was walking by the Greyhound terminal and just got on a bus…Rode all across the country…passed all sorts of wonderful places…saw all sorts of beautiful sights…But you know what?…It wasn't real to me…none of it…The only thing in the world that's real to me is here…this place…*(To Larry directly.)* Why did you do it? Why did you risk your life to save him?

LARRY: I never thought why. I just did it.

HELEN: I think about it all the time. I think what a fool you were. And how wrong. The best thing you could have done was let him die that night. He'd never admit it, but he feels that way himself.

LARRY: No.

HELEN: Yes. A plowboy who hates the country. He's lost in this world. He should have died that night. None of the others would try to save him. They all saw that it was impossible…But you…you must do the impossible. And we all pay the penalty.

LARRY: We *all* pay?

HELEN: I meant he and I.

LARRY: You said we all. You included me. How do I pay?…*What do you know?*

HELEN: Your mother was here.

LARRY: She told you?

(Helen nods.)

LARRY: Everything?

HELEN: Yes.

LARRY: She told the both of you?

HELEN: Yes.

LARRY: So that's why he was knocking himself out to be so cheerful...You should have heard the stories he told me...And that explains the tree.

HELEN: I begged you to leave...I begged you.

LARRY: It's my own fault...Never should have come in the first place...Had this wild idea...Was going to prove I hadn't wasted my life...Was going to find a nice family and console myself that I was responsible for its existence...Pretty wild, huh?

HELEN: What will you do now?

LARRY: Who knows. I may have to turn to God or whatever you call it...There's nothing else left...When I was young I was always vowing to get to the bottom of things. The deepest level. I wanted to press my nose against it. I've done it now...Looked at properly, maybe the whole thing has been a tremendous success.

HELEN: I hope so.

LARRY: Thanks...You know we have accomplished one thing.

HELEN: What's that?

LARRY: You don't hate me any more.

(She takes his head in her hands, and gently kisses him; first on one cheek and then the other and then the forehead. For a moment they regard each other.)

LARRY: I think it's time for you to clean up your kitchen...time for me to go.

HELEN: Stay. Stay here. Let us care for you. We owe you that.

LARRY: Wouldn't work. I begrudge the Plowboy every breath he draws. When we got down to the wire I'd tell him so...So long.

(He turns abruptly and goes toward the door as the door bell rings—three times long, two times short. Larry halts.)

HELEN: It's Albert.

LARRY: Let him in.

HELEN: He couldn't have gone to the office and be back so soon.

(The ring is repeated.)

LARRY: Let him in.

HELEN: What are you going to say to him?

LARRY: I don't know.

(She goes to the door and admits Albert and a boy of eleven. The boy carries a gift-wrapped package.)

ALBERT: *(Indicating the boy.)* Hi. Well say, will you look who I ran into as I stepped out of the house! *(To the boy.)* Well, aren't you going to say hello to your mother?

(The boy hugs Helen, who recoils from his touch.)

ALBERT: That a boy. We stopped around the corner to get a present for Uncle Larry.

HELEN: You were supposed to go to the office.

ALBERT: I wanted to be here when the two Larrys met. *(To the boy.)* Take your coat off.

HELEN: They'll fire you. They're just looking for a reason.

ALBERT: I don't give a damn. *(Goes to Larry.)* Hey, buddy, I got a surprise for you. He wasn't due back till tomorrow, but the folks wanted to do some shopping so they drove him down this morning. They were just dropping him off when I stepped out of the house.

LARRY: *For Christ's sake, Plowboy!*

ALBERT: What's the matter?...Oh, you mean about risking my job? Hell, buddy, don't give it a thought. Plenty of jobs around for an able man and I was pretty fed up with that one. *(Introducing the boy to Larry.)* Larry junior meet Larry senior.

(Larry and the boy look at each other.)

ALBERT: *(To the boy.)* Well, aren't you going to say something?

THE BOY: Pleased to meet you.

ALBERT: How about the present?

(The boy extends the present to Larry.)

THE BOY: We bought this for you.

(Larry doesn't move to accept it.)

ALBERT: Go on, buddy. It ain't no time bomb. Take it.

(Larry finally takes the package. Albert prompts the boy.)

THE BOY: I always wanted to meet you...I heard a lot about you.

ALBERT: *(To Larry, indicating the boy.)* What do you think of him? Most people say he takes after Helen. I can't see it myself. But at least he don't resemble me and that's something to be thankful for. Huh?

THE BOY: *(Goes to the trains.)* These the trains?

ALBERT: That's right. *(To Larry.)* I told him about the trains. *(To the boy.)* You like them?

(The boy nods yes. His attention is focused on the trains.)

ALBERT: Well, what do you say to Uncle Larry?

THE BOY: *(Without turning from the trains.)* Thanks.

ALBERT: *(To Larry.)* He's a little bit bashful.

THE BOY: Make them run.

ALBERT: Sure. *(Snaps on the switch and the trains begin to run. He turns to Larry.)* I told you he'd go for those trains. *(Notices now that Larry is wearing his overcoat.)* Hey, what have you got your coat on for?

LARRY: I was just about to leave.

ALBERT: Without saying good-by to me?

LARRY: My mother called. They canceled our flight so we're taking an earlier one on another line.

ALBERT: *(Stopping the trains.)* Well, then I'm certainly glad I came home and you had a chance to meet young Larry.

(To Helen, who has kept her back to him since the boy's entrance.)

ALBERT: Hey, honey, Larry's going.

HELEN: I know.

ALBERT: Well come on, say good-bye.

HELEN: We said our good-byes before you got here.

THE BOY: How do you make it go backwards?

ALBERT: Never mind that now. Uncle Larry is leaving.

THE BOY: You said it could go backwards.

ALBERT: It does. After Uncle Larry goes I'll show you. Now say good-bye.

THE BOY: Bye.

ALBERT: *(Grabbing the boy.)* What kind of a good-by is that? Now you leave those trains alone and—

HELEN: *(Whirling.)* Stop!

ALBERT: But it's not right. He should have some manners.

LARRY: If he did, I wouldn't believe he was your son.

(The two men regard each other a moment, then Larry smiles and Albert laughs.)

ALBERT: You son of a gun you. *(To Helen.)* That's the way he used to be all the time.

LARRY: If I'm going to make that plane I better get started. *(To Helen.)* Good-bye again and good luck.

ALBERT: You've got our new address now, so there's no excuse for not writing.

(Larry goes to the boy, who is intent on the trains, and pats his head. the boy looks up, smiles.)

LARRY: Good-bye, Larry.

THE BOY: Merry Christmas.

LARRY: Same to you.

ALBERT: I wouldn't be surprised if we came down to Florida on a vacation or something before too long.

LARRY: That'll be nice. *(Offers his hand to Albert.)* So long, Plowboy.

ALBERT: So long, buddy. It's been great seeing you.

LARRY: Same here.

ALBERT: Take care of yourself.

LARRY: You too. *(To Helen and the boy.)* Bye. *(He goes out.)*

(Albert follows him out into the hall and calls after him down the stairwell.)

ALBERT: Hey, buddy, I got a question for you.

LARRY: *(From offstage.)* What's that?

ALBERT: Where's Santa Claus?

LARRY: *(From offstage.)* He's lying down over in the corner drunker than hell, but better than he was.

ALBERT: *(Laughs loudly.)* Hey, buddy, wait till I get my coat, I'll ride downtown with you…

(No answer.)

ALBERT: Buddy?…Buddy?

(No answer. Albert turns now and reenters the apartment.)

ALBERT: He's gone.

THE BOY: There's no tunnel.

ALBERT: *(To Helen.)* I think he believed it.

THE BOY: There's no station, either.

ALBERT: *(To the boy.)* Go home.

THE BOY: Where's the box they came in?

ALBERT: Go home.

THE BOY: You said I could have the trains.

ALBERT: *Get out of here!*

(He approaches the boy, who, frightened, moves toward the door.)

THE BOY: *(To Helen.)* He promised me the trains.

HELEN: Come back tomorrow.

ALBERT: He doesn't deserve them. He didn't say the things I told him to.

HELEN: *(To the boy.)* Come back tomorrow.

THE BOY: What time?

HELEN: Any time.

THE BOY: All right.

HELEN: What's your name?

THE BOY: Joey…Joey Pike.

HELEN: *(Takes a pencil and writes on the cover of the box the trains came in.)* "Property of Joey Pike." There. *(She shows it to him.)* Now you come back tomorrow.

THE BOY: All right. *(He starts out, then turns to her.)* Merry Christmas. *(He exits.)*

ALBERT: I think Larry believed it…The kid didn't say the things I told him to but I think he believed it anyway…Maybe it was better that the kid didn't make such a fuss over him. It seemed more natural…I was getting on the bus when I spotted this kid. From the side he looked a little like me. Like in those pictures on the farm when I was a kid. That's what gave me the idea...It's gonna cost me my job but if he believes it, it's worth it...Did you see the way he patted the kid on the head?...I think he believed it...Don't you think he believed it?

HELEN: Yes.

ALBERT: I'm out of a job. I've got to make plans. I can't afford to get excited.

(The trumpet, extremely muted, is heard.)

ALBERT: Well, it was worth it...He believed me...I owed him that.

(His eye is caught by the trains. He bends to them, turns a switch. The trains go backward.)

ALBERT: I told him they went backwards.

(Curtain.)

THE END

THE SUBJECT WAS ROSES

ORIGINAL PRODUCTION

The Subject Was Roses was first presented by Edgar Lansbury at the Royale Theatre, New York City, on May 25, 1964, with the following cast, in order of appearance:

John Cleary . . . . Jack Albertson
Nettie Cleary . . . . Irene Dailey
Timmy Cleary . . . . Martin Sheen

Directed by Ulu Grosbard; scenery design by Edgar Lansbury; light by Jules Fisher; costumes by Donald Foote; production stage manager, Paul Leaf.

INTRODUCTION

I wrote *The Subject Was Roses* during the epic Writers' Guild Strike in 1960. A six-month strike that began with jokes about writers borrowing to pay for swimming pools and ended as a bitter labor dispute (I can still name the scabs), including fisticuffs and enmities that never healed.

"Epic" because it led to pension, welfare, residuals, and other valued things that today's membership is inclined to take as birthrights.

Off the soapbox and to *Roses:*

It's essentially my parents and me. Insights gained later imposed on events that took place twenty years earlier.

I wrote it in a rented office on Via de la Paz in the Pacific Palisades. Except for depleted savings and the strike looking like it would go on forever, it was the happiest time of my life in L.A.

Palmer Thompson, a fellow writer, had an office close by.

Coffee at the drugstore each morning. Palmer (now dead many years) and I talked craft. Then to our work. Then a quick bite and to the Mecca Pool Room on Fifth Street in Santa Monica.

Palmer, whose father owned a pool room in Brooklyn, was too good for me at straight pool, so we, both neophytes, began to play three-cushion billiards.

Neither of us made a billiard the first time we played. By the time the strike ended, we were scoring fifteen. Another measure of the strike's duration.

"Do you know how embarrassing it is when someone calls you to give them the number of the Mecca Pool Room?" my wife asked.

By the time *Plowboy* was produced, I had *Roses* in the drawer.

When *Plowboy* succeeded, I figured getting *Roses* produced would be easy. Wrong.

It took several years. Outright rejections and numerous options that came to naught until, fed up, I decided to raise the money myself.

Good old Palmer Thompson volunteered the first grand of the fifty (yes fifty) needed to open on Broadway.

The fellows I played cards with every Wednesday (the Hi-Be-Low-Be gang) did the same.

Edgar Lansbury, a scene designer at CBS, said, "If I raise the rest of the money, can I do the set and be the producer?"

And so began the most magical (miraculous?) saga of my life. Not just mine, but I daresay the lives of everyone involved: Paul Leaf, Joe Beruh, Max Eisen, Edgar Lansbury, Irene Dailey, Jack Albertson, Martin Sheen, and Ulu Grosbard who wove the spell.

We ran for two years in four theaters, three theatres the first year during which only the actors were paid. We were about to close at theater number two when Merv Griffin, unaware of our imminent demise and seeking a home for his talk show, asked how much we wanted to vacate.

We got him up to forty thousand. Used it to move to the Helen Hayes where we hung on till the spring when we won the Drama Critics Award, the Tony, and the Pulitzer.

Let the good times roll:

Road companies. A movie. Both play and movie directed by Ulu Grosbard. Two Oscar nominations for Pat Neal and Jack Albertson. Jack won.

We were living back East (to stay) by then. A quintet: Dan and John, twins, having joined the family.

Roses is my signature play, for which I'm grateful. But my dream is some day to be introduced as the author of something other. So far no cigar, but it ain't over.

The Pulitzer guarantees the first line of my obituary.

I wouldn't give it back. But it screwed me up for several years as you'll see.

SYNOPSIS OF SCENES

ACT I

A middle-class apartment. May 1946.

Scene I: Saturday morning

Scene II: Saturday afternoon

Scene III: Two A.M. Monday morning

ACT II

The same place.

Scene I: Sunday morning

Scene II: Sunday evening

Scene III: Two A.M. Monday morning

Scene IV: Nine A.M. Monday morning

ACT I
SCENE I

Setting: The kitchen and living room of a middle-class apartment in the West Bronx. A doorway links the two rooms; an invisible wall divides them. The living room is furnished with the heavy upholstered pieces (replete with antimacassars) considered fashionable in the late twenties and early thirties. There is evidence of a party given the night before: a beer keg, a stack of camp chairs, a sagging banner that is hand lettered—"Welcome Home, Timmy." Time: A Saturday morning in May of 1946.

At rise: A man stands alone in the kitchen, lost in contemplation of an army jacket hanging from the door. The man, John Cleary, is fifty. The army jacket bears an infantry division patch, corporal chevrons, service ribbons (including the ETO with two battle stars, and a presidential unit citation), four "Hershey Bars" marking two years of overseas duty, and the "Ruptured Duck" signifying recent discharge. John Cleary's expression as he regards the jacket is one of almost reverent curiosity. He touches the jacket, feels the material, traces the outline of the chevrons inquiringly. Now, on an impulse, he takes the jacket from the hanger, dons it furtively, is enjoying what is obviously a secret moment when he hears a key turn in the front door. Quickly returning the jacket to the hanger, he takes a seat at the kitchen table and appears engrossed in a newspaper as the door opens and his wife, Nettie, forty-five, enters with a bundle of groceries.

NETTIE: It's a lovely day…Timmy still asleep?

JOHN: Haven't heard him…Better give me mine.

NETTIE: I thought we'd all have breakfast together.

JOHN: I have to go downtown.

NETTIE: Today?

JOHN: Ruskin wants to see me.

(She regards him a moment, then begins to set the food before him.)

JOHN: I'm going to stop at St. Francis on the way…to offer a prayer of thanks.

NETTIE: Toast?

JOHN: Yes…All those casualties and he never got a scratch. We're very lucky.

NETTIE: What do you want on it?

JOHN: Marmalade…The Freeman boy dead. The Mullin boy crippled for life…Makes you wonder…Think he enjoyed the party?

NETTIE: He seemed to.

JOHN: First time I ever saw him take a drink.

NETTIE: He drank too much.

JOHN: You don't get out of the army every day.

NETTIE: He was sick during the night.

JOHN: Probably the excitement.

NETTIE: It was the whiskey. You should have stopped him.

JOHN: For three years he's gotten along fine without anyone telling him what to do.

NETTIE: I had to hold his head.

JOHN: No one held his head in the army.

NETTIE: That's what *he* said.

JOHN: But that didn't stop *you*.

NETTIE: He s not in the army any more.

JOHN: It was a boy that walked out of this house three years ago. It's a man that's come back in.

NETTIE: You sound like a recruiting poster.

JOHN: *You* sound ready to repeat the old mistakes.

NETTIE: Mistakes?

JOHN: Pardon me.

NETTIE: You said mistakes.

JOHN: Slip of the tongue.

NETTIE: I'd like to know what mistakes you're referring to.

JOHN: The coffee's excellent.

NETTIE: I d really like to know.

JOHN: He was eighteen when he went away. Until that time, he showed no special skill at anything, but you treated him like he was a protégé.

NETTIE: I think you mean prodigy.

JOHN: What I really mean is baby.

NETTIE: For a baby he certainly did well in the army.

JOHN: I didn't say he *was* a baby. I said you treated him like one.

NETTIE: You were surprised he did well. You didn't think he'd last a week.

JOHN: Bless us and save us, said Mrs. O'Davis.

NETTIE: Do you know why you were surprised?

JOHN: Joy, joy, said Mrs. Malloy.

NETTIE: Because you never understood him.

JOHN: Mercy, mercy, said old Mrs. Percy.

NETTIE: I never doubted that he'd do as well as anyone else.

JOHN: Where he's concerned you never doubted, period. If he came in here right now and said he could fly, you'd help him out the window.

NETTIE: If you're saying I have confidence in him, you're right. And why not? Who knows him better?

JOHN: Is there more coffee?

NETTIE: He's exceptional.

JOHN: Here we go again.

NETTIE: Yes—exceptional!

JOHN: In what way?

NETTIE: I refuse to discuss it.

JOHN: A person who's going to be famous usually drops a *few* clues by the time they're twenty-one.

NETTIE: I didn't say famous—I said exceptional.

JOHN: What's the difference?

NETTIE: You wouldn't understand.

JOHN: Here's something you better understand—you can't treat him as though he'd never been away. He's not a kid.

NETTIE: If you had stopped him from drinking too much that would have been treating him like a kid?

JOHN: This is where I came in.

NETTIE: He was trying to keep up with you and you knew it.

JOHN: You sound like you're jealous.

NETTIE: The two of you so busy drinking you hardly paid attention to anyone else.

JOHN: You *are* jealous!

NETTIE: Don't be absurd.

JOHN: He and I got along better yesterday than we ever did before and you're jealous.

(She turns away.)

JOHN: Well, well, well. *(He finishes the last of his coffee. Rises to leave.)*

NETTIE: Can't Ruskin wait till Monday?

JOHN: No. And don't pretend you're disappointed. What a charming little breakfast you and he will have together.

NETTIE: You're welcome to stay.

JOHN: My ears are burning already.

NETTIE: I've never said a word against you and you know it.

JOHN: Don't forget my excursion to Montreal.

NETTIE: It was always your own actions that turned him against you.

JOHN: And the convention—don't leave that out. *(He starts from the room.)*

NETTIE: The curtains.

(He regards her.)

NETTIE: The curtains for Timmy's room. They're coming today.

JOHN: I don't know anything about curtains.

NETTIE: Yes, you do.

JOHN: I do not.

NETTIE: They'll be ten dollars.

JOHN: What's the matter with the old ones?

(Timmy Cleary, twenty-one, wearing army sun-tans, open at the neck, emerges from his room, starts toward the kitchen, is arrested by their voices. He stops, listens.)

NETTIE: They're worn out.

JOHN: They look all right to me.

NETTIE: They aren't all right.

JOHN: Ten dollars for curtains.

NETTIE: Timmy will want to bring friends home.

JOHN: The old squeeze play.

(Timmy puts his hands over his ears.)

NETTIE: Are you going to give me the money?

(John extracts a bill from his wallet, slaps it on the table.)

JOHN: Here!

NETTIE: I need five dollars for the house.

JOHN: I gave you fifteen yesterday.

NETTIE: That went for the party.

JOHN: That party cost close to a hundred dollars.

NETTIE: It was worth it.

JOHN: Did I say it wasn't? *(He takes another bill from his wallet and puts it down.)* There.

(Timmy goes back, slams the door of his room to alert them, then approaches the kitchen. Nettie and John compose themselves cheerfully as Timmy, equally cheerful, enters.)

TIMMY: Good morning.

JOHN: Champ.

NETTIE: Morning, son.

(Timmy shakes hands with his father; kisses his mother on the cheek.)

JOHN: We thought you were going to sleep all day.

TIMMY: I smelled the coffee.

JOHN: Mother said you were sick during the night.

TIMMY: I'm fine now.

JOHN: I was a little rocky myself.

TIMMY: I wonder why.

(They both laugh.)

NETTIE: *(To John.)* What time is your appointment?

JOHN: Eleven-fifteen.

NETTIE: It's twenty-five of.

JOHN: *(To Timmy.)* Mr. Ruskin wants to see me.

TIMMY: That's too bad.

JOHN: Why?

TIMMY: Thought we might take in the Giant game.

NETTIE: *(To John.)* Why don't you?

JOHN: You know I can't. *(To Timmy.)* This thing with Ruskin means a sure sale.

TIMMY: I understand.

JOHN: We'll go tomorrow.

NETTIE: My mother expects us for dinner tomorrow.

(John looks at Nettie as though he might say something, thinks better of it, turns to Timmy.)

JOHN: How about *next* Saturday?

TIMMY: All right.

JOHN: We'll get box seats—the works.

TIMMY: Sounds fine.

JOHN: Swell.

NETTIE: What time will you be home?

JOHN: I'll call you.

NETTIE: I'll be at my mother's.

JOHN: *(Appraising Timmy.)* I understand none of your old clothes fit.

TIMMY: That's right.

JOHN: Meet me downtown on Monday and we'll get you some new ones.

TIMMY: Okay.

(John feints a jab. Timmy covers up. They spar good-naturedly until Timmy drops his hands.)

JOHN: I still think I can take you.

TIMMY: I wouldn't be surprised.

JOHN: See you later.

TIMMY: Right.

(John moves toward the door, stops before the army jacket, indicates one of the ribbons.)

JOHN: What did you say this one was for?

TIMMY: It's a combat infantry badge.

JOHN: How about that?

TIMMY: It's not as important as it sounds.

JOHN: We'll have to sit down and have a real talk. I want to hear all about it.

TIMMY: All right.

JOHN: It's great to have you home.

TIMMY: It's great to be home.

JOHN: The Mullin boy crippled. The Freeman boy dead. We're very lucky.

TIMMY: I know.

JOHN: I'm stopping off at St. Francis this morning to offer a prayer of thanks…
   See you later.

TIMMY: Right.

   (John exits from the apartment. Timmy looks after him.)

NETTIE: How did you sleep?

TIMMY: Fine…How's he feeling?

NETTIE: All right.

TIMMY: He looks a lot older.

NETTIE: It's been two years…It must have seemed strange.

   (He glances at her.)

NETTIE: Sleeping in your own bed.

TIMMY: *(Turning away again.)* Yes…How's his business?

NETTIE: Who knows?

TIMMY: The coffee market's off.

NETTIE: I hope you're hungry.

TIMMY: I can't get over the change in him.

NETTIE: Guess what we're having for breakfast.

TIMMY: It's not just the way he looks.

NETTIE: *Guess what we're having for breakfast.*

   (He turns to her.)

NETTIE: Guess what we're having.

TIMMY: What?

NETTIE: Guess.

TIMMY: I don't know.

NETTIE: Yes, you do.

TIMMY: No.

NETTIE: Sure you do.

TIMMY: What is it?

NETTIE: You're fooling.

TIMMY: What is it?

NETTIE: What's your favorite?

TIMMY: Bacon and eggs?

NETTIE: Now I know you're fooling.

TIMMY: No.

NETTIE: I forgot what a tease you were.

TIMMY: I'm not teasing.

NETTIE: Waffles. We're having waffles.

TIMMY: Fine.

NETTIE: You used to be crazy about waffles.

TIMMY: I still am.

NETTIE: I've got the waffle batter ready.

TIMMY: Swell.

NETTIE: Your first morning home, you're entitled to whatever you want.

TIMMY: I want waffles.

NETTIE: I used the last egg in the batter.

TIMMY: *I want waffles.*

NETTIE: Really?

TIMMY: Cross my heart.

NETTIE: All right.

   (While she prepares things, he goes to a window, gazes out.)

TIMMY: I see a new butcher.

NETTIE: Quite a few new stores.

TIMMY: Pop said the Bremens moved.

NETTIE: And the Costellos…Remember old Zimmer the tailor?

TIMMY: Sure?

NETTIE: A few weeks ago a woman brought him a coat she wanted altered.
   Zimmer started to fix it, then very politely excused himself, went up to
   the roof and jumped. No one knows why.

TIMMY: Who was the woman?

NETTIE: Mrs. Levin.

TIMMY: That explains it.

NETTIE: That's not funny.

TIMMY: Sorry.

NETTIE: What a thing to say.

TIMMY: I said I'm sorry.

NETTIE: I'm surprised at you.

TIMMY: Bless us and save us.

NETTIE: *What?*

TIMMY: Bless us and save us. As in "Bless us and save us, said Mrs. O'Davis;
   Joy, joy, said Mrs. Malloy…"
   (She regards him incredulously.)

TIMMY: What's the matter?

NETTIE: I never expected to hear that nonsense from you!

TIMMY: It beats swearing.

NETTIE: You used to cover your ears when your father said it.

TIMMY: *(With mock solemnity.)* I'll never say it again.

NETTIE: *Don't talk to me like that!*...I'm sorry. I don't know what's wrong with me this morning. I don't think I slept well...Too much excitement— the party and all.

(She resumes the preparation of breakfast: pours batter on the waffle iron while he, still not recovered from her outburst, studies her.)

NETTIE: Will you have bacon with it?

TIMMY: Just the waffles will be fine.

NETTIE: Did you like the party?

TIMMY: Yes.

NETTIE: I wish the house had looked better.

TIMMY: What's wrong with it?

NETTIE: It needs painting. The sofa's on its last legs. And the rugs...Well, now that you're here I'll get it all fixed up.

TIMMY: It looks fine to me.

NETTIE: I still can't believe you're here.

TIMMY: I find it a little hard to believe myself.

NETTIE: You *are* here?

TIMMY: Want to pinch me?...Go ahead.

(She hesitates. He holds out his hand.)

TIMMY: Go on.

(She takes his hand.)

TIMMY: Believe it now?

(She continues to hold his hand. He becomes uneasy.)

TIMMY: Hey.

(Oblivious to his resistance, she still clings to his hand.)

TIMMY: What are you doing?

(She persists. His agitation mounts.)

TIMMY: Cut it out...Cut it out! *(He jerks free of her; immediately tries to make light of it.)* One pinch to a customer...House rule.

(She regards him mutely.)

TIMMY: The waffles must be ready; the light on the iron went out.

(She just looks at him.)

TIMMY: Isn't that what it means when that little light goes out?

(She looks at him a moment more, then goes to the waffle iron, lifts the cover,

*starts to remove the waffles, stops, moves to a chair, sits, folds her hands in
her lap and begins to cry.)*

TIMMY: What's the matter?…What's wrong?…What is it?…*What is it?*

NETTIE: *(Continuing to cry.)* They stuck.

TIMMY: What?

NETTIE: Why did they have to stick today?

TIMMY: The waffles?

NETTIE: I can't remember the last time they stuck.

TIMMY: What's that to cry about?

NETTIE: I've looked forward to this morning for three years and nothing's right.

TIMMY: Why do you say that?

NETTIE: Not one thing.

TIMMY: What isn't right?

NETTIE: Not one single thing.

TIMMY: Will you please stop?

NETTIE: The things you've been saying—your attitude.

TIMMY: What things? What attitude?

NETTIE: You haven't even asked about Willis.

TIMMY: …How is he?

NETTIE: Every time I look at you, you avoid me.

TIMMY: *(Turning away.)* That's ridiculous.

NETTIE: You're doing it now.

TIMMY: I am not!

NETTIE: How could you forget waffles were your favorite?

TIMMY: I just forgot?

NETTIE: Then you must have forgotten a lot of things.

TIMMY: I'll tell you one thing I didn't forget.

    (She looks at him.)

TIMMY: The dance.

    (No reaction from her.)

TIMMY: The one we were going to have the first morning I was home.

NETTIE: What made you think of that?

TIMMY: It's been on my mind all along.

NETTIE: I'll bet.

TIMMY: I was about to turn the radio on when you started crying.

NETTIE: I'll bet.

TIMMY: If you're through, I'll do it now. Are you through?

NETTIE: I haven't danced in so long I've probably forgotten how.

(He goes to the living room, snaps on the radio, dials to a band playing a slow fox trot, returns to the kitchen.)

TIMMY: Shall we have a go at it?

NETTIE: I can't remember the last time I danced.

TIMMY: Come on.

NETTIE: You really want to?

TIMMY: Yes.

NETTIE: *(Rising.)* You asked for it.

TIMMY: That-a-girl. *(He puts his arms about her.)* Here we go.

(They move smoothly, gracefully.)

TIMMY: Forgot how to dance—who you kidding?

NETTIE: I guess it's one of those things you never forget.

TIMMY: Remember this?

(He goes into a maneuver that she follows perfectly.)

TIMMY: You've been taking lessons.

NETTIE: Of course.

(They dance from the kitchen into the living room.)

TIMMY: Come here off-ten?

NETTIE: Foist time.

TIMMY: Me likewise…By yuhself?

NETTIE: Widda goil friend.

(The song ends.)

ANNOUNCER'S VOICE: That's all the time we have on Dance Parade this morning. I hope—

(Timmy goes to the radio, dials, picks up a polka band going full blast.)

TIMMY: What do you say?

NETTIE: The spirit's willing.

TIMMY: Let's go!

(They take off.)

TIMMY: Not bad…not bad.

NETTIE: What will the neighbors think?

TIMMY: The worst.

(The rhythm begins to accelerate.)

TIMMY: We're coming into the home stretch. Hang on.

(They move faster and faster.)

NETTIE: I'm getting dizzy.

(As they whirl about the room they begin to laugh.)

TIMMY: Hang on.

NETTIE: I can't do any more.

(The laughter grows.)

TIMMY: Hang on!

NETTIE: I can't!

(The laughter becomes hysterical.)

TIMMY: Hang on! Hang on!

NETTIE: I can't! I...

(They trip, collapse to the floor.)

TIMMY: You all right?

NETTIE: I think so.

(Both breathe laboredly. The laughter subsides. He snaps the radio off, then sits on the floor facing her.)

TIMMY: I'm dead...absolutely dead.

NETTIE: So am I.

TIMMY: I can't remember the last time I laughed like that.

NETTIE: I can...We were driving to the lake and stopped at that dinky carnival.

TIMMY: The time I got you to go on that ride.

NETTIE: Your father thought we'd lost our minds. He kept begging the man to stop the engine.

TIMMY: Which made us laugh all the harder.

NETTIE: Know something?

TIMMY: What?

NETTIE: I really believe you're here now.

TIMMY: So do I.

NETTIE: What are you going to do today?

TIMMY: I don't know.

NETTIE: Why don't you come to Mama's with me?

TIMMY: We're going there for dinner tomorrow.

NETTIE: Willis would love to see you.

TIMMY: I'll see him tomorrow.

NETTIE: When we told him you were coming home he began to sing. It's the first time he's done that in months.

TIMMY: All right, I'll go.

NETTIE: We won't stay long.

TIMMY: All right.

(The door opens and John enters, sees them on the floor.)

JOHN: Well, hello.

(Timmy rises.)

JOHN: Don't get up on my account.

TIMMY: We were dancing and fell down.

NETTIE: *(To John.)* What did you forget?

JOHN: Nothing.

NETTIE: *(Rising.)* Why did you come back?

JOHN: I changed my mind. *(To Timmy.)* If you still want to go to the ball game, it's a date.

NETTIE: What about Ruskin?

JOHN: The hell with him. *(To Timmy.)* Still want to go?

TIMMY: Yes.

NETTIE: What about Willis?

JOHN: What *about* Willis?

NETTIE: Timmy was going to see him this afternoon.

TIMMY: I'll see him tomorrow.

NETTIE: I told him you'd be over today.

TIMMY: Before you even asked me?

NETTIE: I thought sure you'd want to.

TIMMY: You had no right to do that.

NETTIE: What will I tell him?

TIMMY: Tell him I'll be there tomorrow.

NETTIE: He'll be disappointed.

TIMMY: That's not my fault.

JOHN: The game starts at twelve.

TIMMY: Just have to get my tie.

NETTIE: You haven't eaten.

TIMMY: We'll grab something on the way. *(He exits.)*

JOHN: I came out of St. Francis and started for the subway. Was halfway there when I thought of Mr. Freeman: What wouldn't *he* give to be able to spend a day with his son?…It made me turn around and come back. *(She just looks at him.)*

JOHN: You're mad.

(No reply.)

JOHN: You told me to take him to the game.

NETTIE: And you always do what I tell you.

JOHN: Bless us and save us.

(Timmy, knotting his tie, reappears, puts on his jacket, snaps to attention.)

TIMMY: Corporal Cleary reporting for duty.

JOHN: Kiss your mother good-bye.

TIMMY: That's not a duty.

(He kisses Nettie on the cheek. She receives the kiss impassively.)

TIMMY: So long, Mom.

JOHN: We won't be late.

> *(He and Timmy exit. She stands as she is. Curtain.)*

SCENE II

> *Time: Late afternoon—the same day. At rise: John and Timmy enter the apartment. Timmy carries a bouquet of red roses. John has just concluded a joke and they are both laughing.*

JOHN: I haven't told that one in years.

TIMMY: I was considered a very funny fellow. Thanks to you.

JOHN: Hello?…Anybody home?

> *(No answer.)*

JOHN: Still at her mother's.

TIMMY: *(Indicating the roses.)* I better put these in water.

> *(They move into the kitchen.)*

JOHN: Stand another beer?

TIMMY: Sure.

> *(While Timmy puts the roses in a vase, John gets two cans of beer from the refrigerator.)*

JOHN: *(Opening the beers.)* How did you remember all those jokes of mine?

TIMMY: Just came to me.

JOHN: I don't remember most of them myself…*(Hands Timmy a beer.)* Here you go.

TIMMY: Thanks.

JOHN: What'll we drink to?

TIMMY: The Chicago Cubs.

JOHN: Think it'll help them?

TIMMY: Can it hurt?

JOHN: *(Raising the can.)* To the Cubs.

TIMMY: To the Cubs.

> *(They both drink.)*

JOHN: Sixteen to three.

TIMMY: I'm still glad we went.

JOHN: So am I. *(Drinks.)* That was a beautiful catch Ott made.

TIMMY: Yes.

JOHN: For a moment I thought he lost it in the sun.

> *(Timmy says nothing. John drinks.)*

JOHN: So they really went for the old man's jokes?

TIMMY: Especially the ones about Uncle Mike.

JOHN: Such as?

TIMMY: The Pennsylvania Hotel gag.

JOHN: Columbus told that one to the Indians.

TIMMY: Uncle Mike was a famous man in our outfit.

JOHN: Joking aside, he was quite a guy. Stood six three. Weighed close to two fifty.

TIMMY: I remember his picture.

JOHN: He was in the Spanish American War.

TIMMY: I know.

JOHN: Got hit by a bullet once that knocked him out. When he came to, he was lying in a field full of wounded men. The ones that were sure goners were marked with yellow tags so no one would waste time on them. The others had blue tags. Mike found a yellow tag around his wrist. The fellow next to him who was unconscious had a blue one. Quick as a wink Mike switched the tags and…How about that? I'm telling you war stories. Go on—you do the talking.

TIMMY: About what?

JOHN: You must have seen some pretty bad things.

TIMMY: Not as much as a lot of others.

JOHN: Maybe you'd rather not talk about it.

TIMMY: I don't mind.

JOHN: I'd like to hear what you have to say.

TIMMY: I don't know how to begin.

JOHN: Anything that comes to mind.

TIMMY: Want to hear the bravest thing I ever did?

JOHN: Yes.

TIMMY: The first night we were in combat I slept with my boots off.

JOHN: Go on.

TIMMY: That's it.

JOHN: You slept with your boots off?

TIMMY: Doesn't sound like much, does it?

JOHN: Not offhand.

TIMMY: The fellows who eventually cracked up were all guys who couldn't sleep. If I hadn't decided to take my boots off I'd have ended up being one of them.

JOHN: I see.

TIMMY: Want to know the smartest thing I did?

JOHN: Sure.

TIMMY: I never volunteered. One day the lieutenant bawled me out for it. I said, "Sir, if there's anything you want me to do, you tell me and I'll do it. But if you wait for me to volunteer you'll wait forever."

JOHN: What did he say to that?

TIMMY: Nothing printable. The fact is I wasn't a very good soldier, Pop.

JOHN: You did everything they asked you.

TIMMY: The good ones do more. You'd have been a good one.

JOHN: What makes you say that?

TIMMY: I can tell.

JOHN: Well, thanks.

TIMMY: You're welcome.

JOHN: It's one of the big regrets of my life that I was never in the service.

TIMMY: I know.

JOHN: The day World War One was declared I went to the recruiting office. When they learned I was the sole support of the family, they turned me down.

TIMMY: I know.

JOHN: A lot of people made cracks. Especially guys like Clayton and Harper who waited to be drafted and then wangled safe jobs at Governor's Island and the Navy Yard...I fixed their wagons one night—sent the army flying one way and the navy the other. That was the last about slacking I heard from them...Still it bothers me—missing out on the whole thing...I keep wondering what difference it might have made in my life...And then I wonder how I'd have made out...I wouldn't have settled for a desk job. I'd have gotten to the front.

TIMMY: I'm sure of that.

JOHN: But once there, how would I have done?

TIMMY: Fine.

JOHN: How do you know?

TIMMY: You're a born fighter.

JOHN: They say a lot of fellows who were terrors as civilians turned to jelly when they heard those bullets.

TIMMY: Not you.

JOHN: It doesn't seem so. But you can't be sure...That's always bothered me. *(Drinks the last of his beer.)* How about another?

TIMMY: Fine.

JOHN: Maybe we shouldn't.

TIMMY: Why?

JOHN: Your mother blames me for your getting sick last night; says I encouraged you to drink too much.

TIMMY: It wasn't what I drank. It was the excitement.

JOHN: That's what I told her.

TIMMY: *I'll* open two more.

JOHN: All right.

(*While Timmy gets the beers, John regards the roses.*)

JOHN: Her father used to send her roses every birthday…A dozen red ones…Never missed…Even at the end.

TIMMY: Tell her they were your idea.

JOHN: What?

TIMMY: Tell her the roses were your idea.

JOHN: Why?

TIMMY: She'll get a kick out of it…All right?

JOHN: If you like.

TIMMY: (*Handing him a beer.*) Here you go.

JOHN: Thanks.

TIMMY: You call it this time.

JOHN: (*Raising his beer.*) To the two nicest fellows in the house.

TIMMY: I'll buy that.

(*They drink. Timmy regards the can.*)

TIMMY: Funny how you acquire a taste for things.

JOHN: Yes.

TIMMY: When I was a kid I couldn't even stand the smell of beer.

JOHN: Believe it or not I was the same.

TIMMY: We seem to have gotten over it.

JOHN: Yes…Can I say something to you?

TIMMY: Sure.

JOHN: You won't take it the wrong way?

TIMMY: No.

JOHN: I owe you an apology.

TIMMY: For what?

JOHN: You were always sick; always home from school with one thing or another. I never thought you'd last in the army.

TIMMY: Neither did I.

JOHN: Really?

TIMMY: Really.

JOHN: When Dr. Goldman heard they took you he said it was ridiculous. When they put you in the infantry he said it was inhuman.

TIMMY: And when I survived?

JOHN: He said it was a miracle.

(They both laugh.)

JOHN: I don't think it was a miracle. I think we just underestimated you... Especially me...That's what I wanted to apologize for.

TIMMY: Remember that corny thing you used to recite—about how a boy thinks his father is the greatest guy in the world until he's fifteen. Then the doubts start. By the time he's eighteen he's convinced his father is the worst guy in the world. At twenty-five the doubts start again. At thirty it occurs to him that the old man wasn't so bad after all. At forty—

JOHN: What about it?

TIMMY: There's some truth to it.

JOHN: I think you've had too much to drink.

TIMMY: I'm not saying you're a saint.

JOHN: That's a relief.

TIMMY: But taking into account where you started from, and the obstacles you had to overcome, what you've done is something to be proud of.

JOHN: Well, thank you.

TIMMY: How many guys that you grew up with even turned out legitimate?

JOHN: Not many.

TIMMY: And most of *them* are still scraping along where they started.

JOHN: That's true.

TIMMY: How many years of school did you have?

JOHN: I had to quit after the fourth grade.

TIMMY: I've met college graduates who don't know nearly as much as you about the things that really count.

JOHN: Must have been Yale men.

TIMMY: I'm serious.

JOHN: Speaking of college...If you get into one of those big ones and it's more than the G.I. Bill pays for, I'll help you out.

TIMMY: Thanks.

JOHN: That's just between you and me.

TIMMY: Why?

JOHN: I don't want people getting wrong notions.

TIMMY: About what?

JOHN: That I'm loaded.

TIMMY: *Are* you loaded?

JOHN: Don't be ridiculous.

TIMMY: That doesn't answer my question.

JOHN: The question's ridiculous.

TIMMY: That's still no answer.

JOHN: No, I'm not loaded.

TIMMY: How much do you have?

JOHN: What?

TIMMY: How much money do you have?

JOHN: Is this your idea of a joke?

TIMMY: No.

JOHN: Then why are you doing it?

TIMMY: I don't want to take money from you if you can't afford it.

JOHN: I can afford it.

TIMMY: Some of the places I applied at are pretty expensive.

JOHN: I can afford it!

TIMMY: Then you must be loaded.

JOHN: *I am not loaded!*

TIMMY: We have a summer place, a car. Now you tell me you can afford any
school in the country. You must be fairly loaded.

JOHN: *If I hear that word once more, I'm marching right out the door!*
(Timmy is unable to suppress his laughter any longer.)

TIMMY: You haven't changed a bit.
(John regards him uncertainly.)

TIMMY: You look as though I'd asked you to betray your country.
(John, against his will, smiles.)

JOHN: You son of a gun.

TIMMY: I really had you going.

JOHN: Some joke.

TIMMY: Oh, say, Pop.

JOHN: What?

TIMMY: How much *do* you have?

JOHN: *Enough's enough!*
(Timmy laughs anew.)

JOHN: I think we better change the subject.

TIMMY: How did you meet Mother?
(John regards him.)

TIMMY: You said change the subject.

JOHN: You know all about that.

TIMMY: Just that you picked her up on the subway.

JOHN: It wasn't like that at all.

TIMMY: Then I don't know all about it.

JOHN: "Picked her up" makes it sound cheap.

TIMMY: Sorry.

JOHN: The first time I spoke to her was on the subway but there's more to it.

TIMMY: Tell me.

JOHN: Why?

TIMMY: I might become a writer and want to do a story about it someday.

JOHN: A writer?

TIMMY: Maybe.

JOHN: Well, that's the first I heard about that.

TIMMY: Me, too. Must be the beer...What year was it you met her?

JOHN: Nineteen twenty-one...A writer?

TIMMY: A writer...Where were you working then?

JOHN: At Emerson's...

TIMMY: And?

JOHN: One morning I saw her walk by. That afternoon she passed again. Same the next day. Turned out she worked around the corner. I...You sure you want to hear this?

TIMMY: Uh-huh.

JOHN: One evening I happened to be leaving at the same time she did. Turned out we took the same subway. She got off at Seventy-second Street...To make a long story short, I got a seat next to her one day and we started talking.

TIMMY: That's it?

JOHN: Yes.

TIMMY: Sounds like an ordinary pickup to me.

JOHN: *Well, it wasn't...*I left some things out.

TIMMY: Such as?

JOHN: I don't remember...It was twenty-five years ago.

TIMMY: The way I heard it, you followed her for a month before you finally got the nerve to speak.

JOHN: I thought you didn't know the story.

TIMMY: To convince her your intentions were honorable, you asked if you might call at her home. True or false?...Well?

JOHN: True. (*Chuckles.*) You wouldn't believe how nervous I was. And she didn't make it any easier...Pretended the whole thing was a complete surprise. Bernhardt couldn't have done it nicer...Or looked nicer...All in blue...Blue dress, blue hat, blue shoes...Everything blue...Light blue... And dignified...One look at her, you knew she was a lady...My family called her The Lady. To their minds it was an insult. *(Regards Timmy.)* How did we get on this?

TIMMY: You were—

(He is interrupted by the opening of the outside door. Nettie enters.)

JOHN: Join the party.

(She enters the kitchen.)

TIMMY: We're having a little hair of the dog.

NETTIE: How was the game?

JOHN: One-sided.

TIMMY: Pop was just telling me how you and he met.

(Nettie turns to John questioningly.)

JOHN: He asked me.

TIMMY: *(To his mother, indicating his father.)* His version is a little different from yours.

NETTIE: What do you mean?

TIMMY: He says *you* chased *him.*

NETTIE: That'll be the day.

TIMMY: Says you did everything but stand on your head to attract his attention.

(Nettie is not sure now whether he's kidding or not.)

TIMMY: That's what he said.

(Nettie looks uncertainly from Timmy to John. They break up simultaneously.)

NETTIE: You two.

JOHN: How about a beer?

NETTIE: No thanks.

JOHN: Come on—

TIMMY: Be a sport.

NETTIE: All right.

JOHN: That-a-girl.

NETTIE: Just a glass. *(To Timmy, while John gets the beer.)* What did he tell you?

TIMMY: He said you were dressed in blue and nobody ever looked nicer.

NETTIE: I'll bet.

TIMMY: *(To John.)* Didn't you say that?

JOHN: I'm a stranger here.

NETTIE: Did he tell you how he used his friend Eddie Barnes?

JOHN: Bless us and save us.

NETTIE: Every night they'd get on the subway, stand right in front of me, and have a loud conversation about how well they were doing in business.

JOHN: It wasn't every night.

NETTIE: Poor Eddie had to go an hour out of his way.

TIMMY: That's what I call a friend.

JOHN: The best I ever had. *(Extends a glass of beer to Nettie.)* Here you go.
   (She stares past him.)

JOHN: Here's your beer.
   (She continues looking off. He follows her gaze to the roses.)

NETTIE: Where did they come from?

TIMMY: Pop got them…for you.

NETTIE: *(To John.)* You did?

JOHN: Yes.
   (She goes to the roses.)

NETTIE: They're beautiful…Thank you.

JOHN: You're welcome.

NETTIE: What made you do it?

JOHN: We happened to pass a place and I know you like them.

NETTIE: I haven't had red roses since Papa died. *(To Timmy.)* He used to send
   me a dozen on my birthday. Never missed.

TIMMY: I remember.

NETTIE: *(To John.)* Thank you.

JOHN: You're welcome.

NETTIE: I'm going to cry. *(She does.)*

JOHN: You don't bring flowers—they cry. You do—they cry.

NETTIE: I'm sorry.

TIMMY: What's to be sorry?

NETTIE: He was the kindest, gentlest man that ever lived.

TIMMY: I know.

NETTIE: I'm all right now.

JOHN: *(Handing her the glass of beer.)* Here's what you need.

NETTIE: Maybe so.

TIMMY: *(Raising his beer.)* To happy days.

JOHN AND NETTIE: To happy days.
   (They all drink.)

NETTIE: *(Regarding the roses.)* They're just beautiful.

JOHN: *(Anxious to change the subject.)* Talking of Eddie Barnes before, God
   rest his soul, reminds me of the time old Emerson put up a second-hand
   car for the man who sold the most coffee over a three-month period. I
   won it, but couldn't drive. Eddie said he'd teach me. We didn't get two
   blocks from the office when he ran broadside into an ice truck.

NETTIE: How about that ride to Connecticut? He practically killed us all.

JOHN: What was the name of the place we stayed at?

NETTIE: The Rainbow Grove.

JOHN: That's right. Big fat red-haired dame ran it.

NETTIE: Mrs. Hanlon.

JOHN: *(Mimicking Mrs. Hanlon à la Mae West.)* "My friends all call me Daisy."
   (He and Nettie laugh.)

JOHN: I dubbed her the Will Rogers of Connecticut—she never met a man
   she didn't like.
   (They all laugh.)

NETTIE: Remember the night you, Eddie, and a couple of others picked her
   up, bed and all, and left her sleeping in the middle of the baseball field.

JOHN: In the morning when we went out to play, she was still there.

TIMMY: What did you do?

JOHN: We ruled that any ball hitting her on the fly was a ground rule double.
   (They all laugh.)

JOHN: We had a lot of fun at that place.

NETTIE: Yes.

JOHN: I wonder if it's still there.

NETTIE: I wonder.

JOHN: Let's take a ride someday and see.

NETTIE: All right. *(She starts to rise.)*

JOHN: Where you going?

NETTIE: Have to start supper.

JOHN: Forget it—we're eating out!

NETTIE: I bought a steak.

JOHN: It'll keep. *(To Timmy.)* Where would you like to go, Champ?

NETTIE: Maybe he has a date.

JOHN: Bring her along.

TIMMY: I don't have a date.

NETTIE: I thought you'd be seeing that Davis girl?

TIMMY: That's finished.

NETTIE: She was a nice girl.

JOHN: She was a dunce.

NETTIE: John!

TIMMY: Pop's right.

NETTIE: You men are terrible.

TIMMY: You're too kind.

JOHN: Well, where are we going?

TIMMY: You two settle it while I see a man about a dog. *(He exits.)*

JOHN: How about the Concourse Plaza?

NETTIE: All right.

JOHN: I had a nice day today.

NETTIE: I'm glad.

JOHN: He's quite a boy.

NETTIE: That's what I've been telling you for years.

JOHN: We talked about things. Really talked. The way Eddie and I used to... The hell with the Concourse Plaza! Let's go downtown! Let's go to the New Yorker!

NETTIE: You *are* in a good mood.

JOHN: Because I want to go downtown?

NETTIE: That and the roses.

JOHN: Are you going to talk about those roses all night?

NETTIE: I just wanted to thank you for them.

JOHN: You already have.

NETTIE: You sound as though you're sorry you got them.

JOHN: Don't be ridiculous.

NETTIE: Then what are you angry about?

JOHN: I'm just tired of hearing about them. A guy gets some roses—big deal.

NETTIE: You're embarrassed.

JOHN: I am not.

NETTIE: You did something nice and you're embarrassed.

JOHN: You don't know what you're talking about.

NETTIE: Don't worry, I won't tell anyone.

JOHN: *Nettie, please.*

NETTIE: All right, but I want to let you know how much I appreciate it.

JOHN: Good. I'm glad.

NETTIE: I do...I really do. *(On an impulse she touches his shoulder. The contact is mutually startling. Flustered, she turns away.)* We haven't been to the New Yorker in years...I wonder if they still have the ice show?...Do you suppose we'll have any trouble getting in on a Saturday night? *(Timmy enters.)*

TIMMY: What did you decide?

JOHN: We're going to the Hotel New Yorker.

TIMMY: Well, digga digga doo.

JOHN: After that we're going to the Diamond Horseshoe. And then the Sawdust Trail.

TIMMY: Sounds like our night to howl.

JOHN: That's what it is. *(He howls.)*

TIMMY: You call that a howl? *(He howls louder.)*
(*Now John howls. Now Timmy. Now John. Now Timmy. Each howl is louder than the last. Curtain.)*

SCENE III

Time: Two A.M. Sunday morning. At rise: The apartment is in darkness. From the hallway outside the apartment, we hear Timmy and John in loud but dubious harmony.

TIMMY AND JOHN: *(Offstage.)* Farewell, Piccadilly…Hello, Leicester Square… It's a long, long way to Tipperary…But my heart's right there."
NETTIE: *(Offstage.)* You'll wake the Feldmans.
JOHN: *(Offstage.)* Nothing could wake the Feldmans.
(*Timmy and John laugh.)*
NETTIE: *(Offstage.)* Open the door.
JOHN: *(Offstage.)* Can't find my keys.
TIMMY: *(Offstage—giggling.)* I can't find the door.
NETTIE: *(Offstage.)* Honestly.
JOHN: *(Offstage.)* Where would you be if you were my keys?
NETTIE: *(Offstage.)* Here—I'll do it.
JOHN: *(Offstage.)* Did you ever see such pretty hair?
NETTIE: *(Offstage.)* Stop.
TIMMY: *(Offstage.)* Beautiful hair.
NETTIE: *(Offstage.)* Will you please let me open this door?
(*A key turns. The door opens. Nettie followed by John and Timmy, enters. She turns on the lights.)*
JOHN: Home to wife and mother.
NETTIE: *(To John.)* Someday we'll break our necks because you refuse to leave a light.
TIMMY: *(Sings.)* By the light…
(*John joins in.)*
TIMMY AND JOHN: Of the silvery moon—"
NETTIE: That's just enough.
JOHN: Whatever you say, Antoinette.
NETTIE: I say to bed.
JOHN: Shank of the evening.

(He grabs her around the waist and manages a squeeze before she breaks away. Ignoring the look of censure she directs at him, he turns to Timmy.)

JOHN: No sir, you can't beat a law degree. Spring board for anything.

TIMMY: So they say.

NETTIE: *(To John.)* Anyone can be a lawyer. How many people become writers?

JOHN: That's my point.

NETTIE: You should be proud to have a son who wants to try something different.

JOHN: Did I say I wasn't proud of him?

TIMMY: Abra ka dabra ka deedra slatter-in.

(They regard him.)

TIMMY: The fellow in the red jacket who leads the horses to the post at Jamaica always says that when they reach the starting gate. Abra ka dabra ka deedra slatter-in. And here are your horses for the fifth race…Long as you can say it, you're not drunk…*Abra ka dabra ka deedra slatter-in.*

JOHN: Abra ka dabra…

TIMMY: Ka deedra slatter-in.

NETTIE: Honestly.

JOHN: Ka zebra—

TIMMY: Not zebra. Deedra…Ka deedra slatter-in…Abra ka dabra ka deedra slatter-in.

JOHN: Abra…ka dabra…ka deedra…slatter-in.

TIMMY: Faster.

JOHN: Abra, ka dabra, ka deedra, slatter-in.

TIMMY: Faster.

JOHN: Abra ka dabra ka deedra slatter-in.

NETTIE: Have you both lost your minds?

JOHN: Nothing wrong with us that a little nightcap wouldn't cure. *(He enters the kitchen.)*

NETTIE: *(Following him.)* I'll nightcap you.

TIMMY: I can't bear to hear married people fight.

JOHN: *(To Nettie.)* We ought to go dancing more.

NETTIE: Now I know you're drunk.

TIMMY: *(Calling from the living room.)* Who was it that used to call us The Four Mortons?

JOHN: *(Calling back.)* Harold Bowen.

TIMMY: *(Staring at the audience.)* I wish we were.

JOHN: *(To Nettie.)* Remember the first dance I took you to?

NETTIE: Of course.

JOHN: I'll bet you don't.

NETTIE: Of course I do.

TIMMY: *(Lost in contemplation of the audience.)* I have this magical feeling about vaudeville.

JOHN: *(To Nettie.)* Where was it, then?

NETTIE: The Crystal Terrace.

JOHN: And what was the first song?

NETTIE: It's too late for quiz games.

TIMMY: It doesn't matter how cheap and tinny the show is…Soon as the house lights go down and the band starts up, I could cry.

JOHN: *(To Nettie.)* The first song we ever danced to was "Pretty Baby." A blond guy crooned it.

NETTIE: Through a gold megaphone.

JOHN: You *do* remember.

NETTIE: Of course.

(John moves to touch Nettie. To elude him, she reenters the living room. He follows.)

TIMMY: *(To the audience—à la Smith and Dale.)* "I've got snew in my blood"…"What's snew?"…"Nothing. What's snew with you?"

NETTIE: *(To John—indicating Timmy.)* What's he doing?

JOHN: Playing the Palace.

TIMMY: *(To the audience.)* "Take off the coat, my boy…Take…off…the…coat…Tay-ake…o-f-f-f-f…the coat-t-t-t-t."

JOHN AND TIMMY: The coat is off.

NETTIE: *(To Timmy.)* Will you please go to bed?

TIMMY: *(To the audience.)* In closing I would like to do a dance made famous by the inimitable Pat Rooney. *(Nods to John.)* Maestro, if you please.

(John begins to hum "The Daughter of Rosie O'Grady" as both he and Timmy dance in the manner of Pat Rooney.)

NETTIE: John! Timmy!

(They stop dancing.)

NETTIE: Mama expects us at twelve.

TIMMY: *(To the audience.)* We're running a bit long, folks: No dance tonight. My mother thanks you. My father thanks you. My sister thanks you. And the Feldmans thank you. *(He goes into Jimmy Durante's closing song.)* "Good night…Good night…Good night—"

NETTIE: *Good night.*

TIMMY: *(Kisses Nettie.)* Good night, Mrs. Cleary—whoever you are.

NETTIE: Good night, dear.

TIMMY: *(To John—indicating the audience.)* Tough house, but I warmed them up for you.

JOHN: Thanks.

TIMMY: Don't look now, but your leg's broken.

JOHN: The show must go on.

TIMMY: *(To Nettie—indicating John.)* Plucky lad. *(Extends his hand to John.)* Honor to share the bill with you.

JOHN: *(Shaking with him.)* Likewise.

TIMMY: Sleep well, chaps.

JOHN: Night, Champ.

NETTIE: Sure you don't want an Alka Seltzer?

TIMMY: Abra ka dabra ka deedra slatter-in…see you in the morning.

JOHN: With the help of God.

TIMMY: *(Moving toward his room.)* Abra ka dabra ka deedra slatter-in… Abra ka dabra ka deedra slatter-in… And here are your horses for… *(He enters his room, closes the door.)*

NETTIE: Home two days and both nights to bed like that.

JOHN: He's entitled. You should hear some of the things he's been through. They overran one of those concentration camps—

NETTIE: I don't want to hear about it now.

JOHN: You're right. It's no way to end a happy evening.

NETTIE: I think we have some aspirin in the kitchen.

(She moves into the kitchen. He follows, watches her take a bottle of aspirin from a cabinet.)

JOHN: You didn't say anything before about a headache.

NETTIE: I don't have a headache.

JOHN: Then what—

NETTIE: I read that if you put an aspirin in cut flowers they keep longer. *(She drops an aspirin in the vase, regards the roses.)* I wonder what made you get them?

JOHN: I don't know.

NETTIE: There must have been some reason.

JOHN: I just thought it would be nice to do.

(She turns to him.)

NETTIE: It was.

(They regard each other a moment.)

JOHN: I like your dress.

NETTIE: You've seen it before.

JOHN: It looks different…Everything about you looks different.

NETTIE: What Mass are you going to?

JOHN: Ten o'clock.

NETTIE: *(Picking up the vase of roses and starting toward the living room.)* I better set the alarm.

JOHN: Nettie?

> *(She turns to him.)*

JOHN: I had a good time tonight.

NETTIE: So did I. *(Nettie enters the living room and places the roses on a table.)*

JOHN: *(Following her into the living room.)* Did you really? Or were you putting it on for his sake?

NETTIE: I really did.

JOHN: So did I.

NETTIE: I'll set the alarm for nine-fifteen. *(She starts away again.)*

JOHN: Now that he's back we'll have lots of good times.

> *(She stops.)*

NETTIE: What's wrong between you and I has nothing to do with him.

JOHN: I didn't say it did.

NETTIE: We have to solve our own problems.

JOHN: *(Coming up behind her.)* Of course.

NETTIE: They can't be solved in one night.

JOHN: *(Touching her.)* I know.

NETTIE: One nice evening doesn't make everything different.

JOHN: Did I say it did? *(His lips brush the nape of her neck.)*

NETTIE: I guess you don't understand.

JOHN: I forgot how nice you smelled.

NETTIE: You'll spoil everything.

JOHN: I want things right between us.

NETTIE: You think this is going to make them right?

JOHN: *(His hand moving to her breasts.)* We have to start some place.

NETTIE: *(Breaking away.)* Start?

JOHN: Bless us and save us.

NETTIE: *That's not my idea of a start.*

JOHN: Nettie, I want you…I want you like I never wanted anything in my life.

NETTIE: *(Covering her ears.)* Stop.

JOHN: *Please?*

NETTIE: You're drunk.

JOHN: *Do you think I could ask again if I wasn't?*

NETTIE: I'm not one of your hotel lobby whores.

JOHN: If you were I wouldn't have to ask.

NETTIE: A couple of drinks, a couple of jokes, and let's jump in bed.

JOHN: Maybe that's my mistake.

NETTIE: How do you suppose Ruskin managed without you today?

JOHN: Maybe you don't want to be asked! *(He seizes her.)*

NETTIE: Let me alone.

JOHN: *(As they struggle.) You've had the drinks! You've had the jokes!*

NETTIE: *Stop!*

(She breaks free of him; regards him for a moment, then picks up the vase of roses and hurls them against the floor. The impact is shattering. They both freeze. For a moment there is silence. Now Timmy's door opens.)

TIMMY: *(Entering.)* What happened?

NETTIE: The roses...I knocked them over.

TIMMY: Sounded like a bomb.

NETTIE: I'm sorry I woke you.

(Timmy bends to pick up a piece of the vase.)

NETTIE: Don't...I'll clean up. You go back to bed.

(He hesitates.)

NETTIE: Please.

TIMMY: All right...Good night.

NETTIE: Good night.

TIMMY: Good night, Pop.

(John, his back to Timmy, remains silent. Timmy hesitates a moment, then goes off to his room and closes his door.)

NETTIE: *(To John.)* You moved me this afternoon...When you brought the roses, I felt something stir I thought was dead forever. *(Regards the roses on the floor.)* And now this...I don't understand.

JOHN: *(Without turning.)* I had nothing to do with the roses...They were his idea.

(She bends and starts to pick up the roses. Curtain.)

END OF ACT I

ACT II
SCENE I

Time: Nine-fifteen A.M. Sunday morning. At rise: John and Nettie are at the breakfast table.

JOHN: Coffee's weak.

NETTIE: Add water.

JOHN: I said *weak*…Waste of time bringing good coffee into this house…
(*He looks for a reaction. She offers none.*)

JOHN: I'm thinking about renting the lake house this summer…
(*Still no reaction from her.*)

JOHN: Business is off…
(*Still no reaction.*)

JOHN: Well, what do you say?

NETTIE: About what?

JOHN: Renting the lake house.

NETTIE: Timmy will be disappointed.

JOHN: How about you?

NETTIE: I'm in favor of it.

JOHN: Of course you are.

NETTIE: I wonder why.
(*Timmy enters.*)

TIMMY: Morning.

NETTIE: Good morning.
(*Timmy kisses her.*)

TIMMY: (*To John.*) Morning.

JOHN: Nice of you to join us.

TIMMY: My pleasure.

JOHN: This isn't a hotel. We have our meals at certain times. (*Timmy now senses his father's irritation.*)

TIMMY: You should have woke me.

NETTIE: (*To Timmy.*) It's all right.

JOHN: Of course it is.

NETTIE: (*To Timmy, who regards his father puzzledly.*) Sit down.
(*Timmy sits.*)

NETTIE: What do you want?

TIMMY: Coffee.

NETTIE: Just coffee?

TIMMY: Stomach's a bit shaky.

NETTIE: You should have taken that Alka Seltzer.

TIMMY: I'll be all right.

JOHN: Two days—two hangovers. Is that what they taught you in the army?

TIMMY: *(To John.)* Cream, please?

(John passes the cream.)

TIMMY: Thank you.

JOHN: I'm thinking of renting the lake house.

TIMMY: How come?

JOHN: I can use the money.

TIMMY: Oh...

JOHN: That all you're going to say?

TIMMY: What do you expect me to say?

JOHN: I thought that house meant something to you.

TIMMY: It does. But if you need the money—

JOHN: A bunch of strangers sleeping in our beds, using our things—doesn't bother you at all?

TIMMY: If it has to be it has to be.

JOHN: Of course! I forgot! What's a little summer cottage, after the earth-shattering things you've been through?

TIMMY: *(To Nettie—holding up the cream pitcher.)* Do you have more cream?

NETTIE: *(Taking the pitcher.)* Yes.

JOHN: What do you want more cream for?

TIMMY: Coffee's strong.

JOHN: It's weak.

TIMMY: It's too strong for me.

(Nettie returns the refilled pitcher to him.)

TIMMY: Thanks. *(He adds cream to his coffee.)*

JOHN: A few months in the army and they're experts on everything. Even coffee.

TIMMY: Who said that?

JOHN: By the time I was your age I was in the coffee business nine years... Nine years...When I was seventeen they sent me to Brazil for three months.

TIMMY: I know.

JOHN: I'd never even been out of New York before but I went down there on my own and did my job.

TIMMY: For Emerson, wasn't it?

JOHN: No uniform. No buddies. No Uncle Sam to lean on. Just myself…All alone in that strange place.

TIMMY: That's the time you grew the mustache to look older.

JOHN: Who's telling the story?

TIMMY: Sorry.

JOHN: Thirty-five years in the business and he's going to tell me about coffee.

TIMMY: I wasn't telling you anything about anything. I just said that for me, the coffee was too strong.

JOHN: It isn't strong!

TIMMY: *(To Nettie.)* What time's dinner?

NETTIE: Mama expects us at twelve.

JOHN: I suppose you'll wear your uniform.

TIMMY: It's the only thing I have that fits.

JOHN: Are you sure? I mean maybe you haven't grown as much as you think.

(Timmy, studiously trying to avoid a fight, turns to Nettie.)

TIMMY: Ravioli?

NETTIE: And meat balls.

JOHN: G.I. Bill, home loans, discharge bonus, unemployment insurance— you boys did pretty well for yourselves.

NETTIE: They did pretty well for us, too.

JOHN: *(Sings.)* "Oh, say can you see."

TIMMY: What's your point, Pop?

JOHN: The war's over.

TIMMY: I'll buy that.

JOHN: The world doesn't owe anyone a living—including veterans.

TIMMY: I'll buy that too.

JOHN: Let the Jews support you.

TIMMY: Come again?

JOHN: Wasn't for them we wouldn't have gotten in it in the first place.

TIMMY: I thought you broke that record.

JOHN: Lousy kikes.

NETTIE: John!

TIMMY: *(To Nettie.)* I changed my mind—I'll have some toast.

JOHN: *(To Timmy.)* Don't tell me you've lost your great love for the Jews?

NETTIE: *Stop it!*

TIMMY: *(To Nettie.)* It's all right.

JOHN: How nice of you to let me talk in my own house. And me not even a veteran.

TIMMY: Would you mind telling me what you're mad about?

JOHN: Who's mad?

NETTIE: *(To Timmy.)* Anything on the toast?

TIMMY: Honey, if you've got it.

JOHN: A man states a few facts and right away he's mad.

NETTIE: *(At the cupboard.)* How about strawberry jam?

TIMMY: No.

JOHN: If I get a halfway decent offer I might sell the lake house.

NETTIE: Peach?

TIMMY: All right.

JOHN: Hurry up with your breakfast.

TIMMY: What for?

JOHN: Mass starts in twenty minutes and you're not even dressed.

TIMMY: Mass?

JOHN: Mass.

TIMMY: I haven't been to Mass in over two years. You know that.

JOHN: Lots of bad habits you boys picked up that you'll have to get over.

TIMMY: Not going to Mass isn't a habit I picked up. It's a decision I came to after a lot of thought.

JOHN: What way is that for a Catholic to talk?

TIMMY: I haven't considered myself a Catholic for quite a while.

JOHN: Must be something wrong with my ears.

NETTIE: *(To John.)* You knew this was coming. Why pretend it's such a shock?

JOHN: Now there's a familiar alliance. *(To Timmy.)* So you've outgrown the Faith?

TIMMY: It doesn't answer my needs.

JOHN: Outgrown your old clothes and outgrown the Faith.

TIMMY: Pop, will you listen to me—

JOHN: Billions of people have believed in it since the beginning of time but it's not good enough for you.

TIMMY: It's not a question of good enough.

JOHN: What do you say when people ask what religion you are?

TIMMY: Nothing.

JOHN: You say you're nothing?

TIMMY: Yes.

JOHN: The Clearys have been Catholics since…since the beginning of time. And now you, a Cleary, are going to tell people that you're nothing?

TIMMY: Yes.

JOHN: *You're an atheist!*

NETTIE: John!

JOHN: When you come to the blank after religion on those college applications, put down atheist. Make a big hit in those Ivy League places, from what I hear.

TIMMY: I'm not an atheist.

JOHN: Then what are you?

TIMMY: I don't know…But I'd like a chance to find out.

JOHN: You don't know what you believe in?

TIMMY: Do you?

JOHN: Yes.

TIMMY: Tell me…Well, go on!

JOHN: I believe in the Father, the Son and the Holy Ghost…I believe that God created man in his own image…I—

TIMMY: Pop, look…if your faith works for you, I'm glad. I'm very glad. I wish it worked for me…But it doesn't.

JOHN: Do you believe in God—yes or no?

TIMMY: I don't believe in Heaven, or Hell, or Purgatory, or—

JOHN: *Yes or no?*

TIMMY: I believe there's something bigger than myself. What you call it or what it is I don't know.

JOHN: Well, this is a fine how-do-you-do.

NETTIE: *(To John.)* Yesterday you said he was a man. A man has a right to decide such things for himself.

JOHN: "Good morning, Father Riley." "Good morning, Mr. Cleary. I understand your boy's out of service." "Yes, Father." "Where is he this fine Sunday morning, Mr. Cleary?" "Home, Father." "Is he sick, Mr. Cleary?" "No, Father" "Then why isn't he here in church, Mr. Cleary?" "He's become an atheist, Father."

TIMMY: I'm not an atheist!

JOHN: Whatever you are, I won't have it! I'm the boss of this house. If you want to go on living here you'll do as I say. And I say you're going to church with me this morning.

NETTIE: *(To John.)* Do you know what you're doing?

JOHN: *(To Nettie.)* Keep out! *(To Timmy.)* Well?

NETTIE: *(To Timmy.)* Don't pay any attention to him.

TIMMY: *(To Nettie.)* It's all right. *(To John.)* I'll go to church with you. *(Rises.)* Be out in a minute. *(He starts from the room.)*

JOHN: Forget it!

TIMMY: What?

JOHN: I said forget it. The Lord doesn't want anybody in His house who has to be dragged there. *(To Nettie as he puts on his jacket.)* Score another one for your side.

TIMMY: It has nothing to do with her.

JOHN: *(To Timmy.)* Wait till you're down on all fours someday—you'll be glad to see a priest then. *(He starts out.)*

NETTIE: We'll meet you at Mama's.

JOHN: I won't be there.

NETTIE: She expects us.

JOHN: We all have our disappointments.

TIMMY: I said I'd go with you.

(John exits, slamming the door.)

NETTIE: Now what was that all about?

TIMMY: *(Furious with himself.)* I should have gone with him.

NETTIE: I'll never understand that man.

TIMMY: Why didn't I just go? Why did I have to make an issue?

NETTIE: It wasn't your fault.

TIMMY: It never is.

NETTIE: When he's in one of those moods there's nothing anyone can do.

TIMMY: The alliance, he called us.

NETTIE: Everyone's entitled to their own beliefs.

TIMMY: That's what we must seem like to him—an alliance. Always two against one. Always us against him...Why?

NETTIE: If you're through eating, I'll clear the table.

TIMMY: Didn't you hear me?

NETTIE: Evidently your father's not the only one who got up on the wrong side of the bed this morning.

TIMMY: *I'm not talking about this morning.*

NETTIE: There's no need to shout.

TIMMY: You, and him, and me, and what's been going on here for twenty years...It's got to stop.

NETTIE: What's got to stop?

TIMMY: *We've* got to stop ganging up on him.

NETTIE: Is that what we've been doing?

TIMMY: You said you've never understood him.

NETTIE: And never will.

TIMMY: Have you ever really tried?...

NETTIE: Go on.

TIMMY: Have you ever tried to see things from his point of view?

NETTIE: What things?

TIMMY: The lake house, for instance.

NETTIE: The lake house?

TIMMY: It's the pride and joy of his life and you're always knocking it.

NETTIE: Do you know why?

TIMMY: Because he bought it without consulting you.

NETTIE: Drove me out to this Godforsaken lake. Pointed to a bungalow with no heat or hot water and said, "That's where we'll be spending our summers from now on."

TIMMY: An hour's ride from New York City isn't exactly Godforsaken.

NETTIE: It wasn't an hour's ride twenty years ago.

TIMMY: The point is, would he have gotten it any other way? If he had come to you and said he wanted to buy a cottage on a lake in New Jersey, would you have said yes?

NETTIE: I might have.

TIMMY: No. Not if it had been a palace with fifty servants.

NETTIE: I don't like the country.

TIMMY: We'd have spent every summer right here.

NETTIE: My idea of a vacation is to travel—see something new.

TIMMY: You had a chance to see Brazil.

NETTIE: That was different.

TIMMY: The fellow who took that job is a millionaire today.

NETTIE: And still living in Brazil.

TIMMY: Which is not to be compared with the Bronx.

NETTIE: So it's my fault we're not millionaires.

TIMMY: Who knows—your mother might have loved Brazil!

(This causes her to turn from him.)

TIMMY: You violently objected to moving from Yorkville to the Bronx…Why?

NETTIE: *(Clearing the table in an effort to avoid him.)* I hate the Bronx.

TIMMY: *(Pursuing her.)* But you insisted that your mother move up here.

NETTIE: They tore down her building. She had to move somewhere.

TIMMY: Except for summers at the lake, have you ever gone two days without seeing her?

NETTIE: Only because of Willis.

(He starts from the room.)

NETTIE: Where are you going?

TIMMY: To get dressed. Then I'm going to church and apologize to him for acting like a fool.

NETTIE: You'll be at Mama's for dinner?

TIMMY: Only if he'll come with me.

NETTIE: You disappointed Willis yesterday. You can't do it again.

TIMMY: Oh yes I can!

NETTIE: How cruel.

TIMMY: Not as cruel as your dragging me over there every day when I was little. And when I was bigger, and couldn't go every day, concentrating on
Sunday. "Is it too much to give your crippled cousin one day a week?"
And when I didn't go there on Sunday, I felt so guilty that I couldn't
enjoy myself anyway…I hate Sunday, and I don't think I'll ever get over
it. But I'm going to try.

NETTIE: How fortunate for the cripples in this world that everyone isn't as
selfish as you.

TIMMY: Why do you keep calling him a cripple? That's not the worst thing
wrong with Willis. It's his mind. He's like a four-year-old.

NETTIE: Can a four-year-old read a book?

TIMMY: *(Pressing his attack relentlessly.)* Yes, he reads. After you drilling him
every day for twenty years. But does he have any idea what he's reading
about?…If you and the rest of them over there want to throw your lives
away on him, you go ahead and do it! But don't try and sacrifice me to
the cause!

*(Nettie, stunned by Timmy's assault, exits from the kitchen, disappears into
the bedroom. Immediately regretful at having vented his feelings so strongly,
Timmy moves into the living room; is pondering the best way to apologize,
when Nettie, carrying a pocketbook, appears, takes a coat from the hall
closet, puts it on.)*

TIMMY: Where are you going?

(No answer.)

TIMMY: Your mother doesn't expect us till twelve.

(No answer.)

TIMMY: Give me a minute to dress and I'll go with you.

(No answer.)

TIMMY: Now look—

*(As Nettie reaches for her pocketbook, Timmy also reaches for it in an effort
to prevent her departure. He wrests it from her. As he does so, his face registers surprise.)*

TIMMY: This is like lead. *(He opens the bag, regards the contents, looks at her
puzzledly.)* You've got all your coins in here…You're taking your
coins…What for?

(She extends her hand for the bag. He surrenders it. She moves toward the door.)

TIMMY: *Will you please say something?*

NETTIE: Thank you for the roses. *(She exits.)*

(Curtain.)

SCENE II

Time: Ten P.M. Sunday. At rise: Timmy, highball glass in hand, whiskey bottle on the coffee table before him, sits on the sofa in the living room. It is plain that he has been drinking for some time. John, cold sober, moves about the room nervously.

TIMMY: I remember sitting here like this the night she went to have John.

JOHN: Why would she just walk out and not tell anyone where she was going?

TIMMY: I was six.

JOHN: Without any reason.

TIMMY: Dr. Goldman came at midnight and took her to the hospital.

JOHN: It doesn't make sense.

TIMMY: After they left, I started to cry. You did too.

JOHN: It's not like her.

TIMMY: I asked you if you loved her. You nodded. I asked you to say it. You hesitated. I got hysterical. To quiet me you finally said, "I love her."

JOHN: Maybe she's at Sophie's.

TIMMY: No.

(John regards him questioningly.)

TIMMY: I called Sophie.

JOHN: *(Looking at a pocket watch.)* It's after ten.

TIMMY: I called everybody.

JOHN: She's been gone twelve hours.

TIMMY: They all said they'd call back if they heard from her.

JOHN: If she's not here by eleven o'clock I'm calling the police.

TIMMY: I wonder what difference it would have made if John lived.

JOHN: I wonder what department you call.

TIMMY: I remember you and I going to visit her at the hospital on a Sunday afternoon. I had to wait downstairs. First time I ever heard the word incubator...In-cubator.

JOHN: I guess you call Missing Persons.

TIMMY: As we left the hospital and started down the Concourse, we ran into an exotic Spanish-looking woman whom you'd met on one of your trips to Brazil. She was a dancer. Very beautiful. You and she spoke awhile and then you and I went to a movie. Fred Astaire and Ginger Rogers in *Flying Down to Rio.*

JOHN: What are you talking about?

TIMMY: I always thought that was a coincidence—meeting a South American woman and then seeing a picture about Rio…Was it a coincidence?

JOHN: What?

TIMMY: *(Sings.)* "Hey Rio, Rio by the sea-o. Got to get to Rio and I've got to make time."

JOHN: You're drunk.

TIMMY: Abra ka dabra ka deedra slatter-in.

JOHN: Fine time you picked for it.

TIMMY: A bunch of chorus girls stood on the wings of a silver plane singing that song—"Hey Rio. Flying down to Rio—"

JOHN: You're the last one who saw her. The police will want to question you.

TIMMY: She left the house at ten A.M., your Honor. Didn't say boo but I assumed she was going to her mother's. Brown coat. Brown hat. When I got to her mother's, she wasn't there. They hadn't seen her—hadn't heard from her. I had two helpings of ravioli and meat balls. Came back here to wait. When she didn't call by three o'clock I started to worry—

JOHN: And drink.

TIMMY: *When she didn't call by three o'clock I started to worry…*I tried to get in touch with my father. Called all the bars I could think of—"Is Mr. Cleary there?"…"If he comes in would you please tell him to call his house?"… It was like old times.

JOHN: I told you—I had dinner and went to a movie.

TIMMY: "Is Mr. Cleary there?"—Shows how long I've been away. You never say, "*Is* Mr. Cleary there?" You say, "Let me speak to Mr. Cleary." As though you knew he was there.

JOHN: I was at a movie.

TIMMY: Did it have a happy ending?

JOHN: *Gilda,* with Rita Hayworth and Glenn Ford.

TIMMY: I didn't ask you what it was.

JOHN: At the Loew's Paradise.

TIMMY: *I didn't ask you what it was!*

JOHN: What's the matter with you?

TIMMY: *(About to pour another drink.)* Join me?

JOHN: No, and I think you've had enough.

TIMMY: First time I ever saw you refuse a drink.

JOHN: I want you to stop.

TIMMY: But you're powerless to stop me. It's a lousy position to be in, *I* know.

JOHN: That's your last one. *(He starts to remove the bottle.)*

TIMMY: Take it and I leave!

(John hesitates, puts the bottle down.)

JOHN: Joy, joy, said Mrs. Malloy.

TIMMY: Louder louder, said Mrs....What rhymes with louder?

JOHN: You were sick Friday night. Sick last night.

(The phone rings. By the time Timmy gets to his feet. John is picking up the receiver.)

JOHN: *(On the phone.)* Hello?...Oh...

(The abrupt disinterest in his voice causes Timmy to sit down.)

JOHN: Nothing...I said we haven't heard anything...I know how long she's been gone...Of course I'm concerned...*I don't care how I sound—I'm concerned*...If she's not here by eleven, that's what I'm going to do... That's a comforting bit of information. *(He hangs up, returns to the living room.)* Her mother again. Wanted to let me know how many muggings there's been lately.

TIMMY: I've got it! Earl Browder.

JOHN: What?

TIMMY: Louder, louder, said Mrs. Earl Browder.

JOHN: I'm glad you can take the whole thing so calmly.

TIMMY: To quote a famous authority: "I don't care how I sound—I'm concerned."

JOHN: *(Regards his watch.)* Ten after ten.

TIMMY: Trouble with you is you haven't had enough experience in these matters.

JOHN: Where the devil can she be?

TIMMY: I'm an old hand.

JOHN: Never done anything like this before in her life.

TIMMY: All those nights I lay in bed waiting for your key to turn in the door. Part of me praying you'd come home safe, part of me dreading the sound of that key because I knew there'd be a fight.

JOHN: I'll give her a few minutes more.

TIMMY: All those mornings I woke up sick. Had to miss school. The boy's delicate, everyone said, has a weak constitution.

JOHN: I'll give her till half-past.

TIMMY: From the day I left this house I was never sick. Not once. Took me a long time to see the connection.

JOHN: Where can she go? She has no money.

TIMMY: Wrong.

JOHN: What?

TIMMY: Nothing.

JOHN: You said wrong.

TIMMY: *(Sings.)* "Hey Rio. Rio by the—"

JOHN: I want to know what you meant.

TIMMY: She took her coins.

(John goes into the bedroom.)

TIMMY: *(Quietly.)* "Hey Rio. Rio by the sea-o."

(John reappears.)

JOHN: Why didn't you mention it before?

TIMMY: Slipped my mind.

JOHN: Over fifty dollars in dimes and quarters, and she took them all.

TIMMY: Person could go quite a ways with fifty dollars.

JOHN: You saw her take them?

TIMMY: Yes.

JOHN: Didn't it strike you as peculiar?

TIMMY: Everything strikes me as peculiar.

JOHN: There's something you're not telling me.

TIMMY: We all have our little secrets.

JOHN: There is something!

TIMMY: Take you and your money for instance.

JOHN: I want to know what it is.

TIMMY: For all I know, we're millionaires.

JOHN: I want to know why she walked out.

TIMMY: Just between us chickens, how much do you have?

(Timmy reaches for the bottle to pour another drink, but John snatches it out of his reach.)

JOHN: Answer me.

TIMMY: If you don't put that bottle down, I'm leaving.

JOHN: I want an answer!

TIMMY: *(Rising.)* See you around the pool hall.

JOHN: *(Shoving him down hard on the sofa.)* I want an answer!

TIMMY: Hell of a way to treat a veteran.

JOHN: I've taken all the crap from you I'm going to.

TIMMY: You want an answer. I want a drink. It's a deal.

(He reaches for the bottle but John keeps it from him.)

JOHN: First the answer.

TIMMY: I forget the question.

JOHN: Why did your mother leave this house?…Well?

TIMMY: We had an argument.

JOHN: About what?

TIMMY: I don't remember.

JOHN: Probably something to do with your drinking.

TIMMY: Yes, that's what it was. She said I drank too much.

JOHN: She's right.

TIMMY: Yes.

JOHN: I never thought I'd see the day when you and she would argue.

TIMMY: Neither did I.

JOHN: She didn't say where she was going? Just took the coins and left?

TIMMY: That's right.

JOHN: Beats me. *(He starts toward the kitchen.)*

TIMMY: Where you going?

JOHN: To get something to eat.

TIMMY: *Eat?*

JOHN: I didn't have any supper.

TIMMY: A minute ago you were so worried you couldn't even sit down.

JOHN: I'm just going to have a sandwich.

TIMMY: Have a banquet!

JOHN: What are you getting mad at *me* for? You're the one who argued with her.

TIMMY: Which absolves you completely! She might jump off a bridge but *your* conscience is clear!

JOHN: A person doesn't take a bunch of change along if they're planning to do something like that.

TIMMY: *She thanked me for the roses!*
(John just looks at him.)

TIMMY: Don't you have any consideration for other people's feelings?

JOHN: Consideration?

TIMMY: Don't you know how much it pleased her to think they were from you?

JOHN: *You* talk about consideration?

TIMMY: How could you do it?

JOHN: Do you have any idea how I looked forward to this morning? To Mass, and dropping in at Rafferty's afterwards with you in your uniform?

TIMMY: Always the injured party.

JOHN: You'll be the injured party in about two minutes.

TIMMY: I already am.

JOHN: Real rough you had it. Good food. Good clothes. Always a roof over your head.

TIMMY: Heigh-ho, everybody, it's count-your-blessings time.

JOHN: I'll tell you what rough is—being so hungry you begged. Being thrown out in the street with your few sticks of furniture for all the neighbors to enjoy. Never sleeping in a bed with less than two other people. Always hiding from collectors. Having to leave school at the age of ten because your father was crippled for life and it was your job to support the house...You had it rough, all right.

TIMMY: The subject was roses.

JOHN: Where I couldn't have gone with your advantages...What I couldn't have been.

TIMMY: I still want to know why you told her about the roses.

JOHN: We were having words and it slipped out.

TIMMY: Words about what?...Well?

JOHN: Stop pushing or I'll tell you.

TIMMY: Go on! Go on!

JOHN: *The humping I'm getting is not worth the humping I'm getting.*

TIMMY: *(Rising.)* You pig.

JOHN: I'm warning you!

TIMMY: *You pig.*

(John's right hand shoots out, catches Timmy hard across the side of his face. Nettie enters.)

TIMMY: Bon soir.

(Nettie regards them with an air of detached curiosity.)

TIMMY: Had one too many... Lost my ka deedra slatter-in.

(Nettie removes her hat and coat.)

JOHN: Where have you been?

(Nettie lays her hat, coat and pocketbook on a chair in the foyer.)

JOHN: I was about to call the police.

(Nettie gives no indication that she even hears him.)

JOHN: I want to know where you've been.

(Nettie moves through the living room, stops in front of Timmy, who has just poured himself another drink.)

JOHN: Are you going to tell me where you've been?

NETTIE: You wouldn't believe me.

JOHN: Of course I'd believe you.

NETTIE: *(To Timmy.)* You don't look well.

TIMMY: Appearances are deceiving—I feel terrible.

JOHN: Why wouldn't I believe you?

NETTIE: You just wouldn't.

JOHN: Tell me and see.

NETTIE: I went to the movies.

JOHN: Go on.

NETTIE: That's it.

JOHN: You just went to the movies?

NETTIE: That's right.

JOHN: You've been gone over twelve hours.

NETTIE: I stayed for several shows.

JOHN: Are you trying to tell me you were at a movie for twelve hours?

NETTIE: I knew you wouldn't believe me.

TIMMY: I believe you.

NETTIE: Thank you.

TIMMY: What did you see?

NETTIE: That means you *don't* believe me.

TIMMY: No, I guess not.

JOHN: I demand to know where you were.

NETTIE: I went to the Hotel Astor, picked up a man, had a few drinks, a few jokes, went to his room and—

JOHN: Stop it!

NETTIE: I was just getting to the best part.

JOHN: You're making a fool of yourself.

NETTIE: Is there anything I could say that you *would* believe?

TIMMY: Say you took a bus downtown, walked around, visited a museum, had dinner, went to Radio City, and came home.

NETTIE: I took a bus downtown, walked around, visited a museum, had dinner...

TIMMY: Went to Radio City and came home.

NETTIE: Went to Radio City and came home.

TIMMY: I'll buy that. *(To John.)* If you had any sense you'd buy it, too.

JOHN: I don't have any sense. I'm just a poor, ignorant slob whose wife's been missing twelve hours—and I want to know where she was.

TIMMY: What difference does it make?

JOHN: Stay out of this!

TIMMY: How?

JOHN: *(To Nettie.)* What are you going to tell your mother?

NETTIE: Nothing.

JOHN: The poor woman's almost out of her mind.

TIMMY: There's a joke there some place.

JOHN: At least call her and say you're home.

NETTIE: She'll want an explanation. When I tell her, she won't believe me any more than you did.

JOHN: I'll believe you when you tell the truth.

TIMMY: What is truth?

(John shoots him a furious glance.)

TIMMY: Sorry.

NETTIE: I'll tell you this…In all my life, the past twelve hours are the only real freedom I've ever known.

TIMMY: Did you enjoy it?

NETTIE: Every moment.

TIMMY: Why did you come back?

NETTIE: I'm a coward.

JOHN: *Will somebody tell me what's going on?*

TIMMY: *(To the audience.)* You heard the question. *(He peers out into the theatre, points.)* Up there in the balcony. The bearded gentleman with the…*(He stops abruptly, rubs his stomach, regards the audience wanly.)* Sorry, folks, but I'm about to be ill.

(He hastens offstage. Nettie follows him. John takes advantage of her absence to examine her pocketbook, is going through it when she returns.)

NETTIE: He wouldn't let me hold his head, ordered me out of the bathroom, locked the door.

JOHN: What happened to your coins?

NETTIE: I spent them.

JOHN: How?

NETTIE: I took a bus downtown, walked around, visited a museum—

(John interrupts her by slamming the pocketbook to the table.)

JOHN: Wasn't for his drinking, none of this would have happened.

NETTIE: Why do you say that?

JOHN: If he didn't drink, you and he wouldn't have argued.

(She regards him uncomprehendingly.)

JOHN: Isn't that why you left? Because you had an argument about his drinking?

NETTIE: We had an argument, but it wasn't about drinking.

JOHN: What was it about?

NETTIE: You, mostly.

JOHN: Go on.

NETTIE: He thinks I don't give you enough credit…Feels you're quite a guy…Said we had to stop ganging up on you.

(John turns away. Curtain.)

SCENE III

Time: Two A.M. Monday. At rise: The apartment is in darkness. Now a crack of light appears beneath the door to Timmy's room. The door opens. Timmy, in pajamas, emerges, goes to the living room, turns on a lamp, which reveals Nettie, in nightgown and robe, sitting on the sofa.

NETTIE: I couldn't sleep.

TIMMY: Neither could I. Came out to get a magazine.

NETTIE: You feel all right?

TIMMY: Yes. *(He looks through a pile of magazines, selects one.)*

NETTIE: What time is it?

TIMMY: Almost two…Are *you* all right?

NETTIE: Yes.

TIMMY: Well, I guess I'll turn in.

(She offers no comment.)

TIMMY: Good night.

(Again, no response. He starts away.)

NETTIE: Isn't there something you want to tell me?

TIMMY: As a matter of fact there is…but it'll keep till morning.

NETTIE: You've decided to leave.

TIMMY: Yes.

NETTIE: When?

TIMMY: It's not a sudden decision.

NETTIE: When are you leaving?

TIMMY: In the morning.

(He looks for a comment from her, but she remains silent.)

TIMMY: This fellow I went to high school with has a flat on Twenty-second Street. His roommate just got married and he's looking for a replacement. I figured…*(He becomes aware that she isn't listening.)* Hey…

(Still no reaction.)

TIMMY: Hey.

(She regards him absently.)

TIMMY: Give you a penny for them.

NETTIE: An apple core.

TIMMY: What?

NETTIE: An apple core…I was due to start working for a law firm. Passed all the interviews and had been notified to report for work the following Monday…On Sunday, my sister and I were walking in the park when a blond boy who had a crush on me but was too bashful to speak, demonstrated his affection by throwing an apple core which struck me here. *(She indicates the area beneath her left eye.)* When I woke up Monday morning, I had the most beautiful black eye you ever saw. Too embarrassed to start a new job looking like that, I called in sick. They called back to say the position had been filled by someone else...The next job I found was the one that brought your father and I together...I often think of that apple core and wonder what my life would be like if it had never been thrown.

TIMMY: Everyone wonders about things like that.

NETTIE: I was going in early to type up some dictation I'd taken the night before...Front Street was deserted...As I walked, I had the sensation of being watched...I glanced up at the office I was passing and saw this young man, your father, staring down...He regarded me intensely, almost angrily, for a moment, then suddenly realized I was looking back at him and turned away...In that moment, I knew that that young man and I were not suited to each other...And at the same time I knew we would become involved...that it was inevitable.

TIMMY: Why? You had others to choose from.

NETTIE: Oh yes...All gentle, considerate men. All very much like my father...One of them was the baker from Paterson, New Jersey, that we always joke about.

TIMMY: The fellow who brought a hatbox full of pastries whenever he called on you.

NETTIE: Yes...What a sweet man...How he begged me to marry.

TIMMY: What was it that drew you to Pop?

NETTIE: I think it was his energy...a certain wildness. He was not like my father at all...I was attracted...and I was afraid. I've always been a little afraid of him...And then he was clearly a young man who was going places. Twenty-four when I met him and making well over a hundred a week. Great money in those days and his prospects were unlimited... Money was never plentiful in our house. We weren't poor like his people, you understand. Never without rent, or food, or tickets to the opera, or nice clothes. But still we weren't well-to-do...My father brought home stories from the hotel about the various bigwigs who came in and what they wore and how they talked and acted. And we went to the opera. And we had friends who were cultured. Musical Sunday afternoons. Those were Papa's happiest moments...Yes, I liked good things. Things that the baker from Paterson and the others could never give me…But your father surely would. The way he was going he would be a millionaire…That was his dream, you know—to be a millionaire by the time he was forty…Nineteen twenty-nine took care of that. He was never quite the same afterwards…But when I met him he was cock of the walk. Good-looking, witty young Irishman. Everyone liked him and those who didn't at least feared him because he was a fierce fellow. Everyone wanted to go into business with him. Everyone wanted to be social with him…He was immediately at home on a ship, a train…in any bar. Strangers thought he was magnificent. And he was…as long as the situation was impersonal…At his best in an impersonal situation…But that doesn't include the home, the family…The baker from Paterson was all tongue-tied outside, but in the home he would have been beautiful…Go to bed now.

(He kisses her on the forehead.)

TIMMY: Want the light off?

NETTIE: Please.

(He moves to the lamp, is about to turn it off, hesitates.)

TIMMY: When I left this house three years ago, I blamed *him* for everything that was wrong here…When I came home, I blamed you…Now I suspect that no one's to blame…Not even me. *(He turns the light off.)* Good night.

NETTIE: Good night.

(Timmy exits into his room, closes the door. For a moment there is silence. Then.)

NETTIE: "Who loves you, Nettie?"…"You do, Papa"…"Why, Nettie?"…"Because I'm a nice girl, Papa."

(Curtain.)

SCENE IV

Time: Nine A.M. Monday. At rise: John and Nettie are in the kitchen.

JOHN: One word from you…That's all it would take.

NETTIE: I'm not so sure.

JOHN: Try.

NETTIE: No.

JOHN: Do you want him to go?

NETTIE: No.

JOHN: Then say something before it's too late.

NETTIE: What do you want for breakfast?

JOHN: Who cares about breakfast?

NETTIE: Timmy's having scrambled eggs.

JOHN: *Am I the only one who's upset by what's going on here?*

NETTIE: No.

JOHN: Then how can you just stand there?

NETTIE: Would you feel better if I wept?

JOHN: You'll weep when he's gone.

NETTIE: But not now.

JOHN: All I want you to do is tell him how you feel.

NETTIE: He knows that.

JOHN: You won't speak to him.

NETTIE: I can't.

JOHN: You're the one who'll miss him most…With me it's different. I've got my business.

NETTIE: I envy you.

JOHN: Just ask him to wait a couple of days and think it over.

NETTIE: After a couple of days, we'd be used to having him around. It would be that much harder to see him leave.

JOHN: He might change his mind. Might not want to leave.

NETTIE: He has to leave sometime.

JOHN: But not now. Not like this.

NETTIE: Twenty-second Street isn't the end of the world.

JOHN: If he leaves this house today I don't want to see him ever again!

NETTIE: If you say that to him, make it clear that you're speaking for yourself.

JOHN: Who's this fellow he's moving in with?

NETTIE: A boy he knew at high school.

JOHN: Everything he wants right here—food, clothing, a room of his own. And he has to move into a dirty cold-water flat.

NETTIE: I think I understand his feeling.

JOHN: Home two days and gone again. The neighbors will have a field day.

NETTIE: I'm going in to call him now.

JOHN: I want to see him alone.

NETTIE: If you're wise you won't start a row.

JOHN: *I want to see him alone.*

NETTIE: All right. *(She goes inside, knocks at Timmy's door.)*

TIMMY'S VOICE: Come in.

(She enters the room, closes the door after her.)

JOHN: *(Addresses Timmy's place at the table.)* I understand you've decided to
leave us…*(Not satisfied with this opening, he tries another.)* What's this
nonsense about your leaving?…*(And another.)* Your mother tells me
you're moving out. I would like to know why. *(The first part of this opening pleases him, the last part doesn't. He tries variations on it.)* I demand to
know why…Would you be so good as to tell me why?…Why, God-
damn it?

*(He is puzzling over these various approaches when Timmy enters the
kitchen.)*

TIMMY: Good morning.

JOHN: Morning.

TIMMY: Mother said you wanted to see me.

JOHN: Sleep well?

TIMMY: Yes.

JOHN: Good…

TIMMY: You wanted to see me?

JOHN: Mother says you're leaving.

TIMMY: Yes.

JOHN: Rather sudden, isn't it?

TIMMY: Not really.

JOHN: Mind telling me why?

TIMMY: I just think its best.

JOHN: For who?

TIMMY: Everyone.

JOHN: Crap!

(Timmy starts from the room.)

JOHN: Wait.

(The note of entreaty in his voice causes Timmy to halt.)

JOHN: I didn't mean that…The fact is I don't blame you for wanting to leave.
I had no business hitting you.

TIMMY: That's not why I'm going.

JOHN: If there was any way I could undo last night, I would.

TIMMY: It's not a question of last night.

JOHN: If I had to do it over again I'd cut my arm off.

TIMMY: Pop, listen—

JOHN: I don't know what gets into me sometimes.

TIMMY: Pop!

(John looks at him.)

TIMMY: I'm not leaving because of anything that happened last night...I always intended to leave.

JOHN: You never mentioned it.

TIMMY: I planned to stay a couple of weeks and then go.

JOHN: A couple of days isn't a couple of weeks.

TIMMY: It's not like I'm going to China.

JOHN: Why two days instead of two weeks?

TIMMY: Because I know that if I stay two weeks I'll never leave.

JOHN: If it's what I said yesterday, about me being the boss and you'd have to do what I said—forget it.

TIMMY: It's not that.

JOHN: I was just letting off steam.

TIMMY: *It's not that.*

JOHN: As far as I'm concerned you're a man—you can come and go as you please, do as you please. That goes for religion, drinking, anything.

TIMMY: How can I make you understand?

JOHN: Even girls. I know how it is to be your age. Give me a little advance notice and I'll see that you have the house to yourself whenever you want.

TIMMY: Pop, for Chrissake.

JOHN: *(Flares momentarily.)* What kind of language is that? *(Then hastily.)* I'm sorry. I didn't mean that. Talk any way you want.

TIMMY: I don't know what to say to you.

JOHN: What I said yesterday about the Jews, I was just trying to get a rise out of you.

TIMMY: I know.

JOHN: The time those bums from St. Matthew's jumped the I-cash-clothes man. I was the one who saved him.

TIMMY: I know.

JOHN: Whole crowd of people watching but I was the only one who did anything.

TIMMY: Do you think I could forget that?

JOHN: Stay another week. Just a week.

TIMMY: I can't.

JOHN: Stay till Wednesday.

TIMMY: No.

JOHN: Do you have any idea how your mother looked forward to your coming home?

TIMMY: Yes.

JOHN: Then how can you do it?

TIMMY: We're just going around in circles.

JOHN: What happens to the lake house?

TIMMY: What do you mean?

JOHN: Without you, what's the good of it?

TIMMY: I'll be spending time there.

JOHN: I thought we'd have a real summer together like before the war.

TIMMY: You're making this a lot tougher than it has to be.

JOHN: Did you expect me to say nothing? Like her?…

TIMMY: Are you through?

JOHN: *(Trying a new tack.)* I know what the trouble is. You know what the trouble is? You're like me…Stubborn…All the Clearys are stubborn… Would rather die than admit a mistake…Is that a fact? Yes or no?

TIMMY: I don't know.

JOHN: *(Points to himself.)* Well, here's one donkey who's seen the light. I've been wrong in my dealings with you and I admit it.

TIMMY: Pop—

JOHN: Not just wrong last night, but all along. Well, those days are gone forever, and I'll prove it…You know how much money I have?

TIMMY: I don't want to know.

JOHN: Fourteen thousand three hundred and fifty-seven dollars.

TIMMY: Pop!

JOHN: Plus a bit more in stocks…Now *you* admit that you made a mistake— admit you don't really want to leave and we'll forget the whole thing.

TIMMY: I *don't* want to leave.

JOHN: See—

TIMMY: But I'm leaving.

JOHN: *(Turning away.) Then go and good riddance!*

TIMMY: Listen to me.

JOHN: The sooner the better.

TIMMY: *Listen to me! (Pauses—then goes on quietly, intensely.)* There was a dream I used to have about you and I…It was always the same…I'd be told that you were dead and I'd run crying into the street…Someone would stop me and ask why I was crying and I'd say, "My father's dead and he never said he loved me."

JOHN: *(Trying unsuccessfully to shut out Timmy's words.)* I only tried to make you stay for her sake.

TIMMY: I had that dream again last night…Was thinking about it this morning when something occurred to me that I'd never thought of before.

JOHN: She's the one who'll miss you.

TIMMY: It's true you've never said you love me. But it's also true that I've never said those words to you.

JOHN: I don't know what you're talking about.

TIMMY: I say them now—

JOHN: *I don't know what you're talking about.*

TIMMY: I love you, Pop.

(John's eyes squeeze shut, his entire body stiffens, as he fights to repress what he feels.)

TIMMY: I love you.

(For another moment, John continues his losing battle, then, overwhelmed, turns, extends his arms. Timmy goes to him. Both in tears, they embrace. Nettie emerges from Timmy's room, closes the door with emphasis to alert them to her approach. Timmy and John separate hastily.)

JOHN: What I said about the money—that's strictly between us.

TIMMY: I understand.

(Nettie enters the kitchen. If she is aware of anything unusual in their appearance or manner, she doesn't show it.)

NETTIE: Ready for breakfast?

(They nod.)

NETTIE: Sit down.

(They sit. She pours the coffee.)

NETTIE: *(To Timmy.)* Your bag is packed and ready to go.

TIMMY: I've changed my mind.

NETTIE: What?

TIMMY: I've changed my mind. I'm going to stay a few more days.

JOHN: I'm afraid that's out of the question.

(Timmy and Nettie regard him incredulously.)

JOHN: When you said you were going, I called the painters. They're coming in to do your room tomorrow…You know how hard it is to get the painters. If we don't take them now, it'll be months before they're free again.

TIMMY: Then I guess I better leave as scheduled.

JOHN: I think so. *(To Nettie.)* Don't you?

NETTIE: …Yes.

(John tastes the coffee—scowls.)

JOHN: I don't know why I bother to bring good coffee into this house. If it isn't too weak, it's too strong. If it isn't too strong, it's too hot. If it isn't…

(Curtain.)

THE END

THAT SUMMER—THAT FALL

ORIGINAL PRODUCTION

That Summer—That Fall was first presented by Edgar Lansbury at the Helen Hayes Theatre in New York City, on March 16, 1967, with the following cast in order of appearance:

Angelina Capuano	Irene Papas
Steve Flynn	Jon Voight
Zia Filomena	Elena Karam
Josephine Marino	Tyne Daly
Victor Capuano	Richard Castellano

Directed by Ulu Grosbard; settings and lighting by Jo Mielziner; costumes by Theoni V. Aldredge; music composed and conducted by David Amram.

INTRODUCTION

Asked at the time what effect the Pulitzer had on my life, I would have answered sincerely, "None at all."

In retrospect, I realize I was kidding myself.

Ideas for new plays came and went. Discarded not because they weren't valid but because they didn't seem big enough for a Pulitzer winner.

Two years, going into three, passed. Pressure growing. What would our fair-haired boy (two successes in a row) do next?

How and when I fastened on the Hippolytus-Phaedra myth I don't recall.

That's the one about Hippolytus, a handsome youth, spurning love of Phaedra, his stepmother. She turns his father (Theseus) against him with false accusations. Theseus has his son killed. Phaedra commits suicide.

Big enough for Euripides, it was big enough for me.

I made it present day.

If anyone involved had misgivings, they weren't voiced. That's how it is after success. You, and those around you, begin to think you're infallible.

What a cast: Irene Papas in the Phaedra role. John Voight as the winsome lad. Richard Castellano as his father. Tyne Daly.

Ulu Grosbard directing. Set by the dean of designers: Jo Mielziner. Costumes by Theoni Aldredge.

A far cry from the threadbare circumstances that attended *Roses*.

We opened in Chicago.

First intimation something amiss via the late Sam Freedman, press agent who never pulled his punches. After a run-through he told us bluntly we were in trouble.

Second bad augury: We opened in a blizzard.

The Chicago critics split: two pro—two con. But we knew something was wrong.

The actors uniformly excellent, all fingers pointed to the script.

I wrote and rewrote to no avail.

The terrible truth leaked in: Plays are ultimately decided at the moment of conception. *That Summer* had been forced into being. No amount of rewriting would correct innate deficiencies.

I could make it better but I couldn't make it good.

A momentary hope when Claudia Cassidy, the legendary Chicago theater critic of awesome clout, came out of retirement a week after we opened and wrote:

"*That Summer—That Fall* is told in taut, laconic, contemporary terms with a caustic austerity in the humor and violence...Despite the fluid, impressionist, almost pointillist technique, the play is classic in design. Yet none of it is remote in myth, but rather warmly, vividly, compassionately alive...It expands in imagination...the play casts a spell."

Can you blame me for quoting? Business jumped.

Maybe we were too close to the play to appraise it accurately.

I recalled Mischa Elman, the late violinist, saying, "We are not always the best judges of our own performance."

On to New York.

We did one preview in which everything worked. The actors so brilliant that any script flaws went unnoticed.

Ah if the critics had only been there.

Unfortunately they came the next night when the play played as usual and we were deservedly judged wanting. Closed in two weeks.

What did I learn besides the fact that the genuine article can't be willed?

When actors have to be incandescent to make a play work, beware. Valid plays, like corks, surface regardless of circumstances.

Don't open in Chicago in February.

Bronx boys (at least this one) shouldn't mess with the Greeks.

SYNOPSIS

ACT I

ACT II

ACT I
SCENE I

The setting is part of a playground in lower Manhattan, including a hand-ball court and two benches. The time is mid-morning, a warm day in August. As the house lights dim, we hear the rhythmic bounce of a ball. As the curtain rises we see a young man in his early twenties, dressed in a T-shirt, playing handball. Well built, handsome in a winning boyish way, he hits the ball in desultory fashion—as though he were preoccupied, killing time. Seated on one of the benches bordering the court, reading a book, is Angelina Capuano. She is thirty-six, an attractive woman whose severely arranged hair and matronly dress make her appear prim and older than she is. Head bowed, absorbed in her book, she seems oblivious to the young man's presence. He interrupts a volley to look at his wrist watch, then crosses to a second bench over which are draped a jacket and a knapsack. He dons the jacket, shoulders the knapsack, goes offstage. As the sound of his steps recede, Angelina lifts her head, rises, and looks after him. As she looks, her right hand moves slowly to her mouth—as though to stifle an utterance. Lights down.

SCENE II

The setting is now the Capuanos' apartment, in an Italian neighborhood in lower Manhattan. The stage is divided between the living room and Victor and Angelina's bedroom. A hallway (visible when required) links these rooms and offers the door to Zia's room. Upstage in the living room is an opening that gives access to the rest of the apartment and the entrance door, which is offstage. The furnishings, expensive, in good repair, contrast with the building, which is old and worn. Religious pictures and relics are in evidence. The time is afternoon, the same day. As the lights come up, Angelina sits in a rocker in the living room; she rocks in a way that denotes agitation. The source of her discomfort seems to be an open window and the sounds (children's voices predominate) emanating from it. Across the room, knitting, apparently oblivious to Angelina's mounting irritation, is her aunt Zia Filomena, in her late fifties. A chorus of shouts prompts Angelina to go to the window; she slams it shut. Zia regards her.

ANGELINA: I wish they never built that playground.
ZIA: There was a breeze.

ANGELINA: I have a headache.

(*Zia resumes her knitting. Angelina rocks a bit more; then she stops.*)

ANGELINA: Maybe we'll go away for a couple of weeks—to the shore.

ZIA: He won't take the time.

ANGELINA: You and I.

ZIA: I don't like the shore.

ANGELINA: The mountains then.

ZIA: We'll see.

ANGELINA: That means no.

ZIA: Go yourself.

ANGELINA: Sure.

ZIA: What do you care what a bunch of old ladies say?

ANGELINA: (*In Italian, sharply.*) Smettila!

(*Zia glances at her, then returns to her knitting.*)

ANGELINA: I'm sorry.

ZIA: It's all right.

ANGELINA: I didn't sleep well.

ZIA: It's the heat.

(*The doorbell rings.*)

ZIA: Stay.

(*She rises; goes off; returns with Josie [Josephine Marino], a pretty, vivacious girl of eighteen.*)

JOSIE: (*To Angelina.*) How about a wash and set?

ANGELINA: I don't know.

JOSIE: You could use it.

ANGELINA: Thanks.

ZIA: You were complaining about your hair.

ANGELINA: (*To Josie.*)… All right.

(*Josie's attention is drawn to the entrance of Victor Capuano, a large, barrel-chested man, in his mid-fifties. Well groomed, manicured nails, custom-made suit, he exudes an air of prosperity, self-satisfaction, and authority. At the moment he is exceedingly disturbed and trying unsuccessfully not to show it.*)

JOSIE: Hi, Victor.

VICTOR: Josie.

ANGELINA: What brings you home?

VICTOR: (*To Josie.*) Would you excuse us?

JOSIE: Sure. (*To Angelina.*) I'll get my things. (*She exits.*)

ANGELINA: (*To Victor.*) What is it?

(Victor, his agitation mounting, listens for the sound of the front door closing after Josie; he mops his forehead.)

ANGELINA: What's wrong?

VICTOR: Nothing.

(Zia blesses herself.)

VICTOR: There's nothing wrong.

ANGELINA: Say it...Go on.

VICTOR: ...Before we were married I told you about a woman I went with...Irish.

ZIA: God help us.

VICTOR: Don't start.

ANGELINA: You heard from her...? Well?

VICTOR: From the child—a boy...He came to the restaurant.

ZIA: *(Sarcastically.)* Nothing's wrong.

VICTOR: "My name is Steve Flynn. I think I'm your son." Just like that.

ZIA: What's he want?

VICTOR: Nice-looking. From California. Goes to college.

ZIA: What does he want?

VICTOR: Nothing.

ANGELINA: Why's he here?

VICTOR: I'm the father!

ZIA: Tell the world.

ANGELINA: How come he waited so long?

VICTOR: Lilly never told him about me. He was going through some things she left—found papers.

ANGELINA: Left?

VICTOR: She's dead.

ANGELINA: ...Where is he?

VICTOR: Downstairs.

ANGELINA: Tell him to come up.

VICTOR: It's his first trip East.

ANGELINA: Bring him up.

VICTOR: He doesn't know anybody in New York.

ANGELINA: ...You invited him to stay here.

VICTOR: What could I do?

ZIA: Leave it to you.

ANGELINA: How long?

VICTOR: The end of the summer—three weeks.

ANGELINA: ... All right.

VICTOR: What could I do?

ANGELINA: I said all right.

VICTOR: *(To Zia.)* What could I do? *(He goes to a window fronting the street and calls down.)* Steve…Two B. *(To Angelina and Zia.)* He hitchhiked across the country—got everything he owns in one of those canvas bags like soldiers carry.

ANGELINA: A knapsack?

VICTOR: Yeah.

(Angelina turns away.)

VICTOR: Very polite—kept calling me "sir." I—

ANGELINA: *(Maintaining her back to him.)* —Victor.

VICTOR: Yeah?

ANGELINA: I've changed my mind: Say there's no room—give him money for a hotel.

VICTOR: Why?

ZIA: …The neighbors.

VICTOR: What do I care about the neighbors?

(There is a knock at the door. Victor goes off.)

ZIA: *(To Angelina.)* You should have said no in the beginning.

(Angelina exits into the kitchen. Victor returns with Steve—the young man we saw in the playground.)

VICTOR: *(To Steve, indicating Zia.)* My wife's aunt. *(To Zia.)* This is Steve.

STEVE: Pleased to meet you.

(Zia nods.)

VICTOR: Aunt, in Italian, is zia. That's what we call her.

ZIA: *(To Steve.)* Do you travel one road or two?

STEVE: Pardon me?

ZIA: Do you travel one road or two?

(Steve, puzzled, turns to Victor for explanation.)

VICTOR: She was born with a caul, tells fortunes—like the gypsies. Treat her nice or she'll stick pins in your doll.

ZIA: Don't ridicule when you don't understand!

VICTOR: Give him a break—he just got here. *(Calling.)* Angy…Angy.

(Angelina appears.)

VICTOR: I'd like you to meet Steve.

STEVE: How do you do?

(She just looks at him.)

VICTOR: I figured he'd use the back room.

ANGELINA: Yes.

STEVE: *(To Angelina.)* You're sure I'm not putting you out?

VICTOR: Positive. Zia'll show you the way.

(Steve follows Zia off.)

VICTOR: *(To Angelina.)* I don't like it any more than you do, but he's here—let's make the best of it.

ANGELINA: What do we do with him for three weeks?

VICTOR: Show him the sights.

ANGELINA: I thought you were so busy.

VICTOR: *You* can take him.

ANGELINA: No!

(Zia and Steve, minus his knapsack, return.)

STEVE: It's a nice room.

VICTOR: Kind of small.

STEVE: You should see some of the places I've been staying.

VICTOR: Sit.

(Steve sits.)

VICTOR: *(To Angelina.)* He hitchhiked across the country.

(This elicits no response from her. He returns his attention to Steve.)

VICTOR: How long did it take?

STEVE: Two weeks.

VICTOR: I always wanted to do that—cross the country. But not hitchhiking. *(He forces a laugh. Steve smiles politely. The women's expressions are unchanged.)*

VICTOR: Maybe you'd like to take a rest or something.

STEVE: No.

VICTOR: Sure?

STEVE: Positive.

VICTOR: Hungry?

STEVE: No.

VICTOR: Coffee maybe?

STEVE: No, thanks.

(Silence ensues until Victor can't bear it.)

VICTOR: A lot of people wonder why we still live here. For one thing, it's near the restaurant—besides, I own the building… *(No response. Victor turns to Angelina and ZIA: he indicates Steve.)*

VICTOR: Nice-looking, huh? *(To Steve.)* Like they say, it don't come from the sticks and stones. *(Victor starts to laugh—stops when he sees that no one else finds it funny; he mops his forehead.)* Some weather you picked—hottest summer in years. But then you're used to it…California.

STEVE: Yes.

(Silence.)

VICTOR: *(Rising.)* I'm going to get a glass of water. Anyone else?

STEVE: No, thanks.

(Victor exits into the kitchen. Steve glances at Zia, who regards him uninterruptedly. Uncomfortable, he looks away; he tries to make conversation.)

STEVE: *(To Angelina.)* It's very nice of you.

(She looks at him uncomprehendingly.)

STEVE: To put me up.

(She offers no reaction, and turns away. He tries again.)

STEVE: Were you in the playground this morning?

ANGELINA: What?

STEVE: I was waiting for the restaurant to open. I went to the playground. I think I saw you sitting on a bench by the handball court.

ZIA: You were there?

ANGELINA: Did I say I wasn't? You've got a good memory.

(Victor enters with a glass of water.)

VICTOR: There's all kinds of things to do in New York: shows, sports, museums, concerts—anything.

STEVE: I'd like to try all of them.

(Silence.)

VICTOR: *(Rising. He speaks to Steve.)* Well, you'll have to excuse me.

ANGELINA: Why?

VICTOR: *(To Steve.)* We're shorthanded at the restaurant.

STEVE: Can you use a busboy?

ANGELINA: You know how?

STEVE: Yes.

ANGELINA: *(To Victor.)* There you go.

VICTOR: He's here for a vacation.

STEVE: I'd enjoy it.

VICTOR: It's hard work.

STEVE: I'm used to that.

ANGELINA: *(To Victor.)* What can you lose?

VICTOR: I'm a tough boss.

STEVE: I'll take my chances.

ANGELINA: Well?

VICTOR: …Okay.

ZIA: What do we tell people?

(They turn to her, uncomprehending.)

ZIA: When they ask who he is.

VICTOR: To mind their own business!

STEVE: Why not tell them the truth?

(They regard him apprehensively.)

STEVE: That I'm the son of an old friend.

(It takes a moment, until he smiles, to realize he's offering them a graceful way out.)

VICTOR: *(Laughing, but still taken aback by the audacity of the joke.)* That's it—the son of an old friend. *(To Steve.)* Come on.

STEVE: *(To Angelina.)* Thanks.

(He follows Victor out.)

ZIA: You should have said no—right away.

ANGELINA: It's only three weeks.

(Josie, with her hair-setting equipment, enters, looking back to the door.)

JOSIE: Who was that?

ZIA: With Victor?

JOSIE: Uh-huh.

ZIA: The son of an old friend.

JOSIE: Wow!

ZIA: He's staying with us.

JOSIE: Hurray for our side.

ZIA: Till the end of the month—three weeks.

JOSIE: I'll have to work fast.

ANGELINA: I've changed my mind.

JOSIE: This may not be such a bad summer after all.

ANGELINA: I've changed my mind…

(Josie regards her.)

ANGELINA: My hair's all right.

JOSIE: I was going to do it different.

ANGELINA: No.

JOSIE: Just a set.

ANGELINA: Nothing! *(Angelina turns away.)*

(Josie is perplexed. Zia ushers Josie off. Angelina remains as she is. Lights down.)

SCENE III

Time: Three A.M. the next morning. As the lights come up, there is a single light on in the living room. The stage is deserted. We hear the outside door open; Victor and Steve enter.

VICTOR: Tired?

STEVE: I won't have any trouble sleeping.

VICTOR: I warned you.

STEVE: True.

VICTOR: *(Pouring himself a glass of wine.)* Want something to drink or eat?

STEVE: No.

VICTOR: No bad habits, huh?

> *(Steve smiles.)*

VICTOR: You're a good worker.

STEVE: Thanks.

VICTOR: I think I'll promote you.

> *(Steve regards him questioningly.)*

VICTOR: You'll relieve me a few hours a day—show people to their tables, and like that.

STEVE: I don't have a suit.

VICTOR: My tailor'll fix you up.

> *(He looks for a reaction. Steve offers none.)*

VICTOR: You don't like that?

STEVE: No.

VICTOR: You don't want to be obligated to me.

STEVE: To anyone.

VICTOR: Good for you...How about if I take the suit out of your pay?

STEVE: Pay?

VICTOR: Don't thank me until you see how much...Well?

STEVE: The way you worked me tonight, it better be pretty substantial.

VICTOR: If you're not satisfied you can always quit.

STEVE: Fair enough.

VICTOR: And if I'm not satisfied I'll fire you.

STEVE: You've got a deal.

VICTOR: *(Finishes his drink, then rises.)*...Well, I guess I'll turn in. Good night.

STEVE: Good night.

VICTOR: You change your mind about something to eat—help yourself.

STEVE: Thanks.

(Victor starts from the room; he stops and turns.)

VICTOR: Your mother and me went together over a year. Had a lot of good times, but it didn't take. We said all the good-byes—then she found out she was expecting. I was willing to do the right thing, but she disappeared. I tried to find her. Hired detectives. *(He extracts a packet of papers from his pocket.)* It's all here. *(He drops the packet on a coffee table.)* Good night.

STEVE: Good night.

(Victor exits. Steve removes the rubber band holding the packet; he starts to read the contents. Victor enters the bedroom, turns on a light, starts to undress. Angelina sits up in bed; she regards him.)

ANGELINA: Well?

VICTOR: Good worker…been working since he was twelve.

ANGELINA: …That's all?

VICTOR: His mother's mother was Swedish…The blonde hair. *(Victor massages the back of his neck.)*

ANGELINA: Stiff neck?

VICTOR: Yes.

ANGELINA: Come here.

(He looks at her.)

ANGELINA: Come here!

(Victor moves to the bed.)

ANGELINA: Sit down.

(He sits facing her.)

ANGELINA: Turn around.

VICTOR: What for?

ANGELINA: Turn!

(He turns away. She kneels, starts to rub his neck, kneads it slowly and deliberately with both hands.)

ANGELINA: How am I doing?

VICTOR: Fine.

ANGELINA: Relax.

VICTOR: I am relaxed. *(He allows her to continue a few moments more, then stands up.)* That's much better—thanks

ANGELINA: That's all—thanks?

VICTOR: What do you mean?

ANGELINA: One good turn deserves another.

VICTOR: Uh-uh.

ANGELINA: Why?

VICTOR: You know why.

ANGELINA: I'm fine now.

VICTOR: The doctor said eight weeks.

ANGELINA: Your concern doesn't touch me.

VICTOR: What's that supposed to mean?

ANGELINA: You want me to say it?

VICTOR: Say what?

ANGELINA: I think that since there's no chance for a child, you've lost interest.

VICTOR: That's ridiculous.

ANGELINA: Prove it.

VICTOR: Not tonight.

ANGELINA: Please...! It's very important to me.

VICTOR: I can't.

ANGELINA: *Won't.*

VICTOR: *Can't.*

ANGELINA: Can't?

VICTOR: It'll pass—just don't force me.

(She goes back to bed, turning away from him.)

VICTOR: Good night.

(She doesn't reply. In the living room, Steve continues to read. Lights down.)

SCENE IV

Time: Afternoon, one week later. When the lights come up, Angelina is at the window overlooking the playground; she stares out raptly. The doorbell rings, and rings again before she hears it. She goes to the door and returns, accompanied by Josie.

JOSIE: Steve here?

ANGELINA: No.

JOSIE: Where'd he go?

ANGELINA: I have no idea.

JOSIE: Expect him for supper?

ANGELINA: Yes.

(Josie wanders to the window overlooking the playground.)

JOSIE: There he is!

(Angelina regards her blankly.)

JOSIE: Steve—he's in the playground.

ANGELINA: Oh.

JOSIE: He's playing ball—has his shirt off…What a body…

ANGELINA: Josie!

JOSIE: Well, he *has.* You must have noticed.

ANGELINA: I've never seen him with his shirt off.

JOSIE: Here's your chance.

ANGELINA: I don't like that kind of talk!

JOSIE: I'm sorry…I don't know what's the matter with me…Yes, I do…Angy.
(Angelina regards her.)

JOSIE: I'm in love.

ANGELINA: What?

JOSIE: I love him.

ANGELINA: Steve?

JOSIE: Yes.

ANGELINA: You hardly know him.

JOSIE: Everything you're going to say, I told myself.

ANGELINA: A week ago he didn't exist.

JOSIE: I'm sick about him.

ANGELINA: Does he know?

JOSIE: No. Help me.

ANGELINA: Two weeks from tomorrow, he'll be gone.

JOSIE: Invite me to dinner.

ANGELINA: There's twenty fellows on the block ready to die for you. Why him?

JOSIE: After dinner, make up a reason to go out—leave us alone.

ANGELINA: Would you like me to hypnotize him?

JOSIE: Please, Angy.

ANGELINA: Put a little something in his soup?

JOSIE: Don't…

ANGELINA: You ought to be ashamed of yourself.

JOSIE: We all can't be like you!

ANGELINA: …What does *that* mean…? *What does that mean?*

JOSIE: Some people have feelings they can't control.
(Angelina turns away.)

JOSIE: I'm sorry…I didn't mean anything wrong…Angy…
(She hesitates, sees that Angelina will not respond, and then exits. We hear the door close. Angelina goes to the window overlooking the playground. She looks for an instant, and then draws the shade. Lights down.)

SCENE V

Time: It is now the next morning, eleven A.M. As the lights come up, Victor stands before a mirror, knotting his tie.

VICTOR: *(To Angelina, who is offstage in the kitchen.)* He gave me a great idea for fixing up the bar.
(He waits for a response from her. There is none.)

VICTOR: It'll look better and make more room.
(Again he waits in vain for a response.)

VICTOR: Tell him I said he should take the day off.
(Angelina, wearing a robe, appears.)

ANGELINA: How come?

VICTOR: He deserves it.

ANGELINA: Don't get too used to him.
(Victor regards her.)

ANGELINA: He leaves in two weeks.
(Victor returns his attention to the mirror and his tie.)

VICTOR: He's very popular with the customers—the help, too.

ANGELINA: What do you want for supper?

VICTOR: I'll bring lobsters. See you later. *(He exits.)*
(We see Zia, hat and coat on, emerge from her room and enter the living room.)

ZIA: Want anything from Colluci's?

ANGELINA: Colluci's?

ZIA: I'm going to Theresa's.

ANGELINA: Now?

ZIA: No—yesterday…Well?

ANGELINA: Why today?

ZIA: They expect me.

ANGELINA: It's so warm.

ZIA: Do you want anything—yes or no?

ANGELINA: Stay. We'll have lunch out…go to the movies.

ZIA: They're expecting me.

ANGELINA: Then go!

ZIA: What's the matter?

ANGELINA: Nothing.

ZIA: You want to have lunch and go to the movies—go. What do you need *me* for?

ANGELINA: You're right! *(She hugs Zia.)*

ZIA: What's *with* you?

(Steve enters.)

STEVE: Good morning.

ZIA: Good morning.

ANGELINA: Zia, wait—I've changed my mind, I'll go with you.

ZIA: I'm late now.

ANGELINA: I'll only be a minute.

ZIA: *(Starting to go.)* I'll be home six o'clock. *Ciao. (She exits.)*

ANGELINA: Zia…!

STEVE: Good morning.

ANGELINA: There's coffee on the stove, juice in the refrigerator, and rolls on the table.

STEVE: Thanks.

ANGELINA: I'd fix it, but I'm on my way out.

STEVE: I'll manage. Where's Victor?

ANGELINA: He left. He said you should take the day off.

STEVE: How come?

ANGELINA: He said you earned it.

STEVE: He's right.

ANGELINA: I've got to go. *(She exits from the living room and reappears in the bedroom.)*

STEVE: Where?

ANGELINA: What?

STEVE: Where are you going?

ANGELINA: …To the movies. *(She removes her robe, is wearing a slip; she starts to dress.)*

STEVE: I've got a better idea: Let's go to the beach.

ANGELINA: …No.

STEVE: Why not?

ANGELINA: …I don't like the beach.

STEVE: How do you feel about Central Park?

ANGELINA: No.

STEVE: Then *you* pick a place.

ANGELINA: …I'm going to the movies.

STEVE: We can't talk in a movie.

(Angelina, dressed, ready to leave, reappears in the living room.)

ANGELINA: Talk?

STEVE: I've been here a week—we've never talked.

ANGELINA: There's coffee on the stove—

STEVE: —Juice in the refrigerator, and rolls on the table.

ANGELINA: It's a picture I've been wanting to see.

STEVE: I understand.

(Angelina starts to exit as Victor enters.)

VICTOR: I forgot the papers for Rosen.

(She goes to the bedroom to get the papers.)

VICTOR: *(To Steve.)* Good morning.

STEVE: Good morning. I understand you're giving me the day off.

VICTOR: With pay.

STEVE: Its a deal.

VICTOR: The Yankees are home.

STEVE: I'm going to the beach.

VICTOR: Every man to his own taste.

STEVE: You don't like the beach either.

(Victor regards him questioningly. Steve indicates Angelina, who returns with the papers.)

STEVE: I invited your wife to go. She prefers a movie.

VICTOR: *(To Angelina.)* How come? *(To Steve.)* She's crazy about the beach— always pestering me to go.

ANGELINA: *(To Steve.)* I thought you were just asking to be polite. I didn't want to impose.

STEVE: The offer's still open.

VICTOR: Go—it'll be good for you.

ANGELINA: I have shopping.

VICTOR: It'll keep.

STEVE: They say it'll hit ninety today.

VICTOR: *Go.* You'll hurt his feelings.

ANGELINA: …All right.

VICTOR: Thatta girl. *(To Steve.)* Gotta run. *(Kisses Angelina.)* Have a good time. *(He exits.)*

(We hear the door close.)

ANGELINA: While you're having breakfast, I'll get my things.

STEVE: Right.

ANGELINA: There's coffee on the stove—

STEVE: —And juice in the refrigerator.

(For a moment they regard each other, then give way simultaneously to laughter. Abruptly Angelina stops laughing and reverts to her previous mood and manner.)

ANGELINA: The earlier we get started, the better.

STEVE: Right.

(*She goes off. He looks after her. Lights down.*)

SCENE VI

Time: Five P.M., the same day. As the lights come up, we hear Steve and Angelina, returned from their day at the beach, entering the apartment.

ANGELINA: (*Offstage.*) The days.

STEVE: (*Offstage.*) *Lunedi…Martedi…Mercoledi…Giovedi…Venerdi… Sabato… Dominica.*

ANGELINA: (*Correcting him.*) Domen*ica.*

STEVE: Domenica.

ANGELINA: The greeting?

STEVE: *Bon giorno, Signore.*

ANGELINA: To a girl?

STEVE: *Bon giorno, Signorina.*

ANGELINA: To a pretty girl?

STEVE: (*With comic leer.*) *Bon giorno, Signorina.*
(*They laugh.*)

ANGELINA: You learn fast.

STEVE: I owe it all to my teacher. (*He flops into a chair and reacts as though in pain when his back makes contact.*)

ANGELINA: You really got a burn.

STEVE: Is there a doctor in the house?

ANGELINA: I'll see what we have.
(*She goes off. In her absence, Steve gingerly removes his shirt.*)

STEVE: I'm glad you changed your mind.

ANGELINA: (*Offstage.*) What?

STEVE: I'm glad you came to the beach.

ANGELINA: (*Offstage.*) Why?

STEVE: Because I had a good time. How about you?
(*Angelina, bearing a tube of ointment, reappears. The sight of Steve bare chested, facing away, stops her. She regards him for a moment.*)

ANGELINA: (*Offering the tube.*) Try this.

STEVE: (*Accepting the tube.*) Thanks.
(*As he opens the tube and begins to apply the contents, she averts her gaze.*)

ANGELINA: I'd like to live by it—the ocean.

STEVE: Why don't you?

ANGELINA: Try and get Victor to leave this neighborhood.

STEVE: *(Studying her as he applies the ointment.)* Why do you dress like that?

ANGELINA: *(Turning to him involuntarily.)* What?

STEVE: You look ten years younger in a bathing suit.

ANGELINA: You always say what you think?

STEVE: Why not…? I meant it as a compliment.

ANGELINA: Thanks.

STEVE: You're angry.

ANGELINA: Yes.

STEVE: Why?

ANGELINA: I don't know.

STEVE: How old *are* you?

ANGELINA: Thirty-six.

STEVE: And Victor?

ANGELINA: Why all the questions?

STEVE: I'm nosey. *(He resumes the application of the ointment.)*

ANGELINA: It happens every day.

    (Steve regards her.)

ANGELINA: Girls marrying older men.

STEVE: How did you meet?

ANGELINA: Zia raised me after my parents died. Victor went to her—said he was interested.

STEVE: How old were you then?

ANGELINA: Seventeen. I used to pass the restaurant—knew him to say hello. He was friendly, but I had no idea what he had in mind till Zia told me. You know what I did when she told me?

STEVE: What?

ANGELINA: I laughed so hard I had a pain.

    (Steve smiles.)

ANGELINA: It's true…When I got through laughing, Zia warned me not to be hasty—told me what a good man he was, how well off he was, begged me to go out with him just once…Why not…? We took a ride—Zia, he, and I—brand-new Buick convertible, lunch at a fancy restaurant, anything I admired—a dog, an ashtray, a bushel of tomatoes—he wanted to buy it for me…It was painful. You know what I mean?

STEVE: I think so.

ANGELINA: As far as *I* was concerned, that was the end. Not Zia. She kept at me to give him another chance. To quiet her, I said all right. He was better the second time—not so nervous, so anxious to please…I began to see him occasionally. In my mind, it was casual—but one step leads to another…The next thing you know, you see yourself in a mirror trying on a wedding gown…how can that be you?…How did it happen? *(Suddenly aware that she's been talking too much and too intimately, she stops, trying to shift the focus to Steve.)* And you? What's your story?

STEVE: Just what you know.

ANGELINA: No secrets?

STEVE: No.

ANGELINA: No girls?

STEVE: No.

ANGELINA: I'll bet.

STEVE: Never had time. *(He goes through futile contortions trying to apply the ointment to an area that proves unreachable.)*

ANGELINA: What are you doing?

STEVE: There's a spot I can't reach. Can you give me a hand?

(He offers the tube to her. She accepts it, goes behind him, and starts to apply the ointment.)

ANGELINA: *(As she rubs his back.)* Zia was right about him—Victor. You couldn't ask for a more wonderful man, a better husband…There isn't a woman on the block who wouldn't change places with me. *(Abruptly she stops applying the ointment, puts the tube down, moves away.)*

ANGELINA: What time is it?

STEVE: *(Glancing at his watch.)* Five-fifteen. How do you say that in Italian?

ANGELINA: School is over.

STEVE: …I see. *(Puzzled by her behavior, he turns away and dons his shirt.)*

ANGELINA: What I meant is that I have things to do.

(He offers no reaction.)

ANGELINA: I did enjoy myself today.

(He turns to her.)

ANGELINA: If I told you how much, you'd laugh. *(She goes off.)*

(Lights down.)

SCENE VII

Time: Midnight, several days later. The lights come up on Zia, alone, playing cards. She hears the door open.

ZIA: Angy?

ANGELINA: *(Offstage.)* Yes.
 (Angelina and Victor appear. He is drunk—she is angry.)

ZIA: *(To Angelina.)* How was the party?
 (Angelina doesn't reply.)

ZIA: Well?

VICTOR: *(To Zia.)* I'm in the doghouse.

ZIA: *(To Angelina.)* What happened?

VICTOR: I made a speech.

ZIA: What?

VICTOR: A speech...*a speech!*

ZIA: *(To Angelina.)* What's he talking about?

ANGELINA: He stood on a chair; said he had an important announcement—told them that Steve is his son.

ZIA: *O Signore!*

ANGELINA: I prayed the floor would swallow me.

ZIA: What did they do?

VICTOR: Nothing!

ZIA: Where is he—Steve?

ANGELINA: He ran—like the place was on fire.

VICTOR: Anybody says anything...*anything*...they have to answer to me!

ZIA: I'm not going out tomorrow.

VICTOR: You'll go!

ZIA: *(To Angelina.)* He's drunk—maybe they didn't pay any attention.

ANGELINA: *(Studying Victor.)* He's not *that* drunk.

ZIA: Then why...?

ANGELINA: That's a good question.

VICTOR: One more word, I'm gonna open the window and shout it to the block!

ANGELINA: *(To Zia.)* Come on.
 (They go off. Victor, not so drunk as he seemed previously, goes to the street window; he peers anxiously; paces; is about to look out the window again when he hears something. He waits. Steve appears. They regard each other uncertainly.)

VICTOR: I was worried.

STEVE: I took a walk.

VICTOR: You left so sudden…I didn't mean to embarrass you.

STEVE: That wasn't it.

VICTOR: I should have asked you first.

STEVE: There's no need to apologize.

VICTOR: I don't use my head.

STEVE: I'm glad you did it…

(Victor regards him.)

STEVE: Really.

(Victor extends his hand. Steve takes it. Victor, delighted and embarrassed, laughs—pumps Steve's hand. Steve, similarly affected, also laughs. The mood spirals: They shake with mounting vigor—their laughter swells. Lights down.)

SCENE VIII

Time: Several nights later. As the lights come up, Zia and Angelina are sitting together in the living room. Angelina glances repeatedly at Victor and Steve, who, oblivious of Zia and her, are playing chess.

ZIA: My father, your grandfather, was a terrible spend thrift. Every payday he'd go on a tear—have all his money spent before he went to bed…

VICTOR: Check!

ZIA: …Well, this payday he did just like usual—went celebrating and buying drinks for everyone, from one bar to another. By midnight he was broke. He went home, went to bed—but he couldn't fall asleep. Kept turning and tossing. Something was bothering him, but he didn't know what…

VICTOR: Did you say "resign?"

ZIA: …Finally he couldn't stand it any more; got up, started to get dressed, was putting on his pants when he felt something in one of his pockets…

STEVE: Check to *you!*

ZIA: …He reached in—found a penny; opened the window, tossed the penny out into the street, went back to bed, and slept like a baby.

STEVE: Announcing mate in four.

ANGELINA: So you think I have a penny in my pocket?

ZIA: What?

ANGELINA: Maybe you're right.

ZIA: What's the penny got to do with you?

ANGELINA: *You* tell *me.*

ZIA: What are you talking about?

ANGELINA: Well, doesn't everything you say have a point, a moral?

(*The doorbell rings. Zia goes to the door.*)

VICTOR: I resign.

STEVE: I accept.

VICTOR: You're pretty good.

STEVE: You're not bad yourself. Another?

VICTOR: All right.

(*Zia returns with Josie, who is trying unsuccessfully to hide her nervousness.*)

JOSIE: Hi.

VICTOR: Hey—Josie.

STEVE: Hello.

JOSIE: Am I interrupting?

VICTOR: Anybody else, I'd say yes—but the prettiest girl on the block—

JOSIE: —You.

VICTOR: (*To Steve.*) She's blushing.

ANGELINA: (*To Josie.*) What is it?

JOSIE: What?

ANGELINA: Don't you want something?

JOSIE: No.

ANGELINA: It's a social visit?

JOSIE: Yes—well, that is…

(*All attention focuses on her.*)

VICTOR: What is it, Josie?

JOSIE: There's going to be a dance at the Waldorf Astoria, Thursday night. It's for charity. All the big celebrities are going to be there. The tickets cost a hundred dollars apiece.

ZIA: We'll take fifty.

JOSIE: I'm not selling them…

ANGELINA: What then?

JOSIE: My boss bought two tickets, but he can't go…he gave them to *me.*

VICTOR: What time should I pick you up?

JOSIE: What?

VICTOR: Isn't that why you came—to invite me?

ANGELINA: She came to invite Steve. (*To Josie.*) Didn't you?

JOSIE: …Yes. (*To Steve.*) Would you like to go?

VICTOR: A hundred bucks a ticket—the Waldorf! Of course he would.

JOSIE: There'll be a lot of celebrities.

VICTOR: Formal?

JOSIE: Yes.

VICTOR: *(To Steve.)* Max'll fix you up.

ANGELINA: He hasn't said he wants to go.

VICTOR: Of course he wants to go. *(To Steve.)* Right?

(*Steve doesn't answer immediately.*)

JOSIE: Don't feel obligated. I mean, it was just a thought. Actually, there's someone else I should have asked. I just thought you might get a kick out of it.

STEVE: I don't know how to dance.

JOSIE: That doesn't matter.

(*Steve regards her uncertainly.*)

JOSIE: Really.

VICTOR: It'll be mostly entertainment.

STEVE: *(To Josie.)* You're sure?

JOSIE: Positive…Will you go?

STEVE: Yes.

JOSIE: Thursday—eight o'clock.

STEVE: Right.

VICTOR: And don't worry about the dancing—Josie'll teach you.

STEVE: In a week?

VICTOR: What week? The dances today—a monkey could learn in five minutes. *(To Josie.)* Show him.

JOSIE: Now?

VICTOR: Why not? *(He turns on the radio.)*

JOSIE: *(To Steve.)* You want to?

STEVE: I don't think we have any choice.

(*Victor finds a rock-and-roll number.*)

VICTOR: You're on!

JOSIE: *(To Steve.)* It's simple—just do what I do. *(She demonstrates one of the current dances with great vigor.)*

STEVE: It's hopeless. *(He starts away from her.)*

JOSIE: *(Pulling him back.)* No, it isn't. It's easy. It's just this. *(She guides him, manipulating his hips. Victor laughs.)*

STEVE: *(To Victor.)* You think it's so easy, you try it.

(*Josie goes to Victor with the intention of getting him to dance.*)

JOSIE: Come on.

VICTOR: *(Waving her away.)* I'll get my own partner.

(Josie returns to Steve and resumes teaching him. Victor beckons Angelina to dance with him. She refuses. He goes to Zia.)

VICTOR: Come on.

ZIA: No.

VICTOR: Come on!

(He gives Zia no choice; he pulls her to her feet and compels her to dance.)

ZIA: You crazy thing!

VICTOR: *(To Josie and Steve.)* We challenge you.

STEVE: We accept.

JOSIE: *(To Victor and Zia as she breaks into a new step.)* Try this.

(Victor and Zia try to emulate the kids. A happy mood spirals until Angelina, unable to bear what is happening, snaps the radio off. They all regard her curiously.)

ANGELINA: *(Trying to make light of what she's done.)* Have you lost your minds?…It's late.

(They continue to regard her.)

ANGELINA: I hate that music! *(She hastens to the bedroom.)*

ZIA: *(To the others.)* Stay.

(She follows Angelina off.)

JOSIE: I think I better go.

VICTOR: You were doing fine—don't stop.

(Josie regards Steve uncertainly.)

STEVE: I could use another lesson.

(Victor turns the radio on and locates a fox trot, slow and dreamy.)

VICTOR: Try that.

(As Josie starts to teach Steve this step, Victor turns from them and directs his attention toward the bedroom, where Zia is confronting Angelina.)

ZIA: *Che cosa è? Che succede?*

ANGELINA: I have a headache.

ZIA: I don't mean tonight.

ANGELINA: I don't know what you're talking about.

ZIA: Victor don't see—but I see: You haven't been yourself for weeks.

ANGELINA: Do me a favor—leave me alone!

ZIA: Will you go to the doctor?

ANGELINA: For what?

ZIA: For me.

ANGELINA: …All right.

ZIA: Tomorrow.

ANGELINA: All right.

ZIA: You'll take a warm bath now—go to bed.

(In the living room Josie emits a burst of laughter as she and Steve dance. Angelina breaks down; she lays her head in Zia's lap and weeps. Zia cradles her.)

ZIA: What's the matter…? What is it…?

(Josie laughs again. Curtain.)

END OF ACT I

ACT II
SCENE I

Time: Eight P.M., the night of the dance. As the curtain rises, Zia sits in an attitude of imminent departure. Angelina, preoccupied, fans herself. Victor moves about impatiently.

VICTOR: What's taking them so long?

ZIA: She's a girl.

VICTOR: He promised they'd stop in.

ZIA: *(To Angelina.)* Remember how long you used to take?

VICTOR: Maybe he forgot—maybe they went.

ANGELINA: Suppose they did. What's the tragedy?

ZIA: *(To Victor.)* What time is it?

VICTOR: *(Checking his watch.)* Five after eight.

ZIA: I can't wait any more.

VICTOR: I'm going to see what's what. *(He goes off.)*
   (Zia rises.)

ZIA: *(To Angelina.)* It's all right if I go?

ANGELINA: What do I care?

ZIA: You won't come?

ANGELINA: No.

ZIA: Saint Jude's been good to you.

ANGELINA: Please!

ZIA: I won't say another word.

ANGELINA: Thank you.
   (Zia puts on her hat—turns to Angelina.)

ZIA: I'm going.

ANGELINA: All right!

ZIA: …It might be just what you need.

ANGELINA: All I need is for the summer to be over.

ZIA: …Those pills are in your nightstand.

ANGELINA: I know!

ZIA: A good night's sleep wouldn't do you any harm. I won't be late. *(Zia exits.)*
   (A moment later, Victor returns.)

VICTOR: She had to have a hem fixed—they'll be right down. *(He resumes his fitful movement about the room; he goes to the window fronting the street and gazes down.)* I was figuring the other day that if I had supported him all these years, it would have cost twenty-five thousand dollars. *(Turns to Angelina.)* At least twenty five.

ANGELINA: So what?

VICTOR: It's something to keep in mind.

ANGELINA: Why?

(The bell rings. He goes off and reappears a few moments later. He poses in the living-room entrance.)

VICTOR: Announcing the arrival of the prince and the princess.

(He steps aside. Steve and Josie, in formal attire, their youth and beauty breathtaking to behold, enter.)

VICTOR: *(To Angelina.)* Are *they* something? *(To Steve and Josie.)* In my whole life, I've never seen a prettier looking…*(Overwhelmed, he is unable to continue.)*

STEVE: Hey.

VICTOR: Sorry.

JOSIE: *(Revolving to show the gown to Angelina.)* You really like it?

ANGELINA: Yes.

JOSIE: Where's Zia?

ANGELINA: Novena.

VICTOR: I wish I had a camera.

JOSIE: *(To Steve.)* We better get started.

STEVE: Yes.

VICTOR: How you going?

STEVE: Cab.

VICTOR: I got a better idea. Come here.

(He moves to the window overlooking the street. Steve and Josie follow him. He is pointing.)

VICTOR: See there—that white car—the convertible?

STEVE: Yes.

VICTOR: Here. *(He holds out a set of car keys to Steve.)* The registration's in the glove compartment.

JOSIE: Whose is it?

VICTOR: Steve's.

STEVE: *What?*

VICTOR: If you don't like the color or the model, you can have it changed.

STEVE: *(To Angelina.)* What's he talking about?

ANGELINA: Offhand, I'd say he's giving you a car.

(Steve regards Victor incredulously.)

VICTOR: Go.

STEVE: Why?

VICTOR: Don't ask dumb questions.

STEVE: But—

VICTOR: —The dance already started.

STEVE: My head's spinning.

VICTOR: I'll be your first passenger. You can drop me at the restaurant.

STEVE: At least let me say thank you.

VICTOR: You're welcome—let's go.

STEVE: *(To Angelina.)* And thank *you*.

ANGELINA: I had nothing to do with it.

VICTOR: *(To Steve.)* Come on.

> *(Josie dashes over to Angelina—kisses her warmly.)*

JOSIE: This is the happiest night of my life.

VICTOR: Let's go!

STEVE: *(To Angelina.)* Good night.

JOSIE: *(To Angelina.)* Good night.

VICTOR: Don't wait up.

> *(They exit. Angelina remains as she is for a moment, goes to the window and looks down. She then turns back into the room, goes to a sideboard bearing a wine decanter and glasses, and pours a glass of wine. She is drinking the wine when her attention is arrested by her reflection in the mirror above the sideboard. She regards herself; she lets her hair down. She then moves closer to the mirror and becomes lost in contemplation of herself. Lights down.)*

SCENE II

> *Time: Three hours later. As the lights come up, Angelina, in her slip, reclines on the sofa. The apartment is in darkness until Zia enters, turns on a light, discovers Angelina. She then notes the half-filled wine decanter and empty glass on the table beside her.*

ZIA: Angy…Angy, what do you call this?

ANGELINA: *(Regarding Zia with drunken amusement.)* How's Saint Jude?

ZIA: *What?*

ANGELINA: Poor Zia.

ZIA: Get up.

ANGELINA: *(Sings loudly.)* "*Vidi na croce su questu canone…Muriva senza suono di campane…*"

ZIA: Go to bed—we'll talk in the morning.

ANGELINA: Nothing serious he said—just nerves.

ZIA: *(Trying to help her up.)* Come.

ANGELINA: What killed her? Nothing serious—just nerves. *(She laughs.)*

ZIA: *(Attempting unsuccessfully to get her to her feet.)* I can't do it alone.

ANGELINA: *(Pushing her away—savagely.)* You've done enough! *(Angelina gets up on her own. She takes her wine glass and wanders about.)*

ZIA: Are you trying to frighten me?

ANGELINA: Poor Zia…Tell me something, poor Zia: Did I advertise? Did I go looking for him?

ZIA: For who?

ANGELINA: A punishment? For what?

ZIA: I don't understand.

ANGELINA: Did I ever look at another man?

ZIA: What are you talking about?

ANGELINA: *Did I ever look at another man?*

   (Zia regards her—says nothing.)

ANGELINA: *(Screams.) Answer me!*

ZIA: *(Hastily closing the window.)* You want the police?

   (Angelina laughs at her.)

ANGELINA: Not once…not once.

   (Zia, sensing real trouble, moves to Angelina.)

ZIA: *(Probing.)* What?

ANGELINA: *(Moving away from her and to the window.)* "Vidi na croce su questu canone…"

ZIA: *Who?*

ANGELINA: *(Looking out the window.)* It hurt my eyes to look at him the first time—like he was the sun. *(Turns to Zia.)* And he is. *(She laughs.)*

ZIA: *(Explosively.) Who?*

ANGELINA: It took everything I had not to follow him, and then Victor brought him here.

   (Laughing, Angelina goes into the bedroom—sits on the bed. Zia, horrified by what she's learned, takes a moment to collect herself, then follows.)

ZIA: Listen to me.

ANGELINA: A punishment? For what?

ZIA: Listen!

   (She gains Angelina's attention.)

ZIA: *Has he touched you?*

ANGELINA: No.

ZIA: Does he know how you feel?

ANGELINA: No.

ZIA: Then it will be all right.

ANGELINA: What did she die of? Nothing serious. Just nerves.

ZIA: He's leaving in a week!

ANGELINA: A week?

ZIA: The thirtieth—a week from yesterday.

ANGELINA: *(Softly, almost to herself.)* "Vidi na croce su questu canone…"

ZIA: Less than a week.

ANGELINA: "…Muriva senza suono di campane…"
    (Lights down.)

SCENE III

Time: The next morning. The lights come up on Angelina, asleep in the bedroom. Zia, alone in the living room, is packing the tuxedo Steve wore. Victor, a cup of coffee in his hand, enters.

VICTOR: I'll drop it off. He didn't get in till three.

ZIA: You waited up?

VICTOR: Yes…Angy's still asleep.

ZIA: She was very tired.

VICTOR: I have some news.

ZIA: What?

VICTOR: I want her to hear first…I'm going to wake her.

ZIA: No!

VICTOR: I've got to go.

ZIA: …I'll get her. *(She goes off.)*
    (Victor sits down. He picks up a newspaper, drinks his coffee, and reads. Zia enters the bedroom; she raises the shades. The light rouses Angelina.)

ANGELINA: Hey!

ZIA: It's after ten.

ANGELINA: Go away.

ZIA: Victor wants to talk to you.

ANGELINA: …What is it?

ZIA: I don't know.

ANGELINA: You put me to bed?

ZIA: Yes.

ANGELINA: I drank too much.

ZIA: No kidding.

ANGELINA: I think I carried on.

ZIA: Yes.

ANGELINA: Talked a lot.

ZIA: Yes.

ANGELINA: About what?

ZIA: Who could tell?

ANGELINA: It didn't make sense?

ZIA: Not to me.

ANGELINA: Not a word?

ZIA: Not a word.

ANGELINA: I never did that before—got drunk!

ZIA: Victor's waiting.

(*Angelina gets out of bed. Zia is helping her on with her robe. Angelina hesitates.*)

ZIA: The other arm.

ANGELINA: You don't know what he wants?

ZIA: No.

ANGELINA: Does he know I was drunk?

ZIA: No.

ANGELINA: Maybe I talked in my sleep—said something that upset him.

ZIA: Once you got in bed, you were dead to the world.

ANGELINA: Does he look upset?

ZIA: No…Come.

(*Angelina follows Zia into the living room.*)

VICTOR: Good morning.

ANGELINA: Morning.

VICTOR: Sorry to wake you.

ANGELINA: That's all right…Zia said you have something to tell me.

VICTOR: Yes…

ANGELINA: What is it?

VICTOR: I waited up for Steve…We talked…

ANGELINA: And?

VICTOR: He's staying.

ANGELINA: What?

VICTOR: He's not going back.

ZIA: (*To Victor.*) What are you talking about?

VICTOR: (*To Zia.*) Steve's going to live here—in New York.

(He looks to Angelina for a reaction. She offers none.)

VICTOR: Well?

(She just looks at him.)

VICTOR: What do you say?

(She continues to look at him.)

VICTOR: You don't like it.

(No reaction.)

VICTOR: Why not?

(No reaction.)

VICTOR: Once he gets the hang of the restaurant, you and I can take vacations—travel.

(Still no reaction.)

VICTOR: What have you got against him?

(Still no reaction.)

VICTOR: He's the only son I'll ever have!

ANGELINA: If you love him, send him away.

VICTOR: Why?

(She starts from the room.)

VICTOR: He's staying!

ANGELINA: *(She stops and turns to him.)* I saw the look on your face when you came to the hospital: You wanted to be rid of me so someone else could give you children.

VICTOR: No.

ANGELINA: You wished me dead.

(Victor is unable to respond.)

ANGELINA: The tickets for the dance: you got them—not her boss. *(She exits to the bedroom.)*

VICTOR: *(To Zia.)* What's the matter with her?

ZIA: The house is on fire—where are you?

(She hands Victor the tuxedo. He regards her a moment, then exits from the house. Zia goes to the bedroom. Angelina, who has been contemplating a vial of pills, pockets them guiltily as Zia enters.)

ANGELINA: Get out.

ZIA: What are you doing?

ANGELINA: Get out!

ZIA: What have you got there?

ANGELINA: Nothing.

ZIA: *(Reaching for Angelina's pocket.)* What have you got there?

ANGELINA: *Lasciamme!*

ZIA: *Che cos'è?*

ANGELINA: You really want to know? *(Taking the vial from her pocket, she thrusts it at Zia.)*

ZIA: *(Taking the vial—regarding it.)* These are…What for…? *(Now the monstrous implication hits her. She regards Angelina.)* You fool!… You fool!

ANGELINA: If you knew.

ZIA: How it hurt your eyes to look at him in the playground?
(Angelina regards her incredulously.)

ZIA: Yes!

ANGELINA: Everything?

ZIA: What "everything?" You got a crush.

ANGELINA: Don't.

ZIA: Nothing happened—you told me yourself.

ANGELINA: Stop!

ZIA: Something *did* happen.

ANGELINA: No!

ZIA: *(Indicating the pills.)* Then why?

ANGELINA: After, it will be too late.

ZIA: He'll be out of the house tonight—I guarantee!

ANGELINA: I wouldn't have the will.

ZIA: You'll never seen him again!

ANGELINA: I think that would kill me too.

ZIA: *(Commandingly.)* Look at me!
(Angelina regards her. Zia indicates the vial.)

ZIA: This is a worse sin than the other.

ANGELINA: And it's better to bend than to break.

ZIA: Yes.

ANGELINA: No!

ZIA: So all lovers have to die.

ANGELINA: *(Shocked.)* You say that? *You*, who helped to crucify Mrs. Alvarez?

ZIA: You want to blame someone—blame *me!*

ANGELINA: Now what?

ZIA: *I* made you marry Victor. Put it on *my* head.

ANGELINA: Of course.

ZIA: And what would happen to *him*—Victor?

ANGELINA: *(Savagely.)* You would take care of him—just like you always dreamed!
(Zia slaps her hard across the face. For a moment, equally shocked and regretful, they regard each other.)

ANGELINA: I'm so sorry.

ZIA: Give me time.

ANGELINA: For what?

ZIA: I'll think of something…Have I ever failed you…? Give me time…All right?

ANGELINA: …All right.

ZIA: Lie down now—rest—trust me. *(She starts from the room, bearing the vial of pills.)*

ANGELINA: Leave them.

(Zia hesitates.)

ANGELINA: Trust me.

(Zia puts the vial on a nightstand, then exits. Angelina returns to bed. Zia enters the living room. The desperate feelings she suppressed in Angelina's presence are apparent now as she searches for a solution. Steve enters the living room.)

STEVE: Zia—the tuxedo, did Victor take it?

(She nods almost imperceptibly. Steve regards her more closely—senses something wrong.)

STEVE: You all right?

(She offers no reaction.)

STEVE: What is it? What's the matter?

ZIA: Angelina…

STEVE: What's wrong…? Well?

ZIA: She won't say.

STEVE: You mean sick?

ZIA: No.

STEVE: Then what?

ZIA: I don't know.

STEVE: Anything I can do?

(This question spawns a thought in Zia's mind. She rises and faces Steve.)

ZIA: Yes…

STEVE: Name it…Well?

ZIA: Talk to her—find out what's the matter.

STEVE: Me?

ZIA: She likes you, trusts you.

(Steve regards her skeptically.)

ZIA: She told me so…Will you do it?

STEVE: Talk to her?

ZIA: Yes.

STEVE: About what?

ZIA: You noticed she hasn't been herself: Is there anything wrong?…can you help?…*(To Steve directly.)* All right?

STEVE: I don't know.

ZIA: You don't care about her.

STEVE: Of course I do.

ZIA: She's in her room.

STEVE: You mean, now?

ZIA: Yes…Please.

STEVE: You're really worried.

   (Zia nods.)

STEVE: Just talk to her and…

   (Zia nods.)

STEVE: She might resent it.

   (Zia's look tells that any further protest is futile.)

STEVE: Her room?

ZIA: Yes.

   (He exhales resignedly, braces himself, and starts from the room.)

ZIA: One thing.

   (He turns to her.)

ZIA: Your word you won't say anything about this to anyone.

STEVE: Wild horses couldn't drag it out of me.

ZIA: It's not a joke!

STEVE: Sorry.

   (She turns away. He regards her an instant, then goes off. Zia sits. There is a knock at the bedroom door. Silence. Another knock. Angelina stirs.)

ANGELINA: What?

STEVE: *(Outside her bedroom door.)* It's me—Steve.

   (Angelina, instantly alert, sits up.)

STEVE: Angelina?…Angelina?

ANGELINA: …What do you want?

STEVE: *(Still outside.)* I'd like to talk to you.

   (No response.)

STEVE: Angelina?

ANGELINA: …It's open.

STEVE: *(Still outside.)* What?

ANGELINA: The door's open.

   (He enters the shadowed room tentatively.)

STEVE: Good morning.

(She studies him.)

STEVE: I woke you.

(She continues to regard him.)

STEVE: It can wait till later.

ANGELINA: Close it.

(He closes the door and turns to her; he hesitates.)

ANGELINA: You're embarrassed.

STEVE: Yes.

ANGELINA: I'm glad.

STEVE: Why?

ANGELINA: Excuse the way I look.

STEVE: You look fine. How do you feel?

ANGELINA: Like in a dream—like nothing's real.

STEVE: What's wrong?

ANGELINA: Maybe it is.

(He regards her uncomprehendingly.)

ANGELINA: A dream—maybe it is, huh?

STEVE: Maybe.

ANGELINA: …You wanted to talk to me.

STEVE: Yes…

ANGELINA: Go on.

STEVE: You haven't been yourself lately. I thought maybe there was something wrong, something you might like to tell me…Well?

ANGELINA: If I asked you to leave and never come back—would you do it?

STEVE: What?

ANGELINA: If I asked you to leave this house, right now, and never come back—would you do it?

STEVE: Why?

ANGELINA: *Would you do it?*

STEVE: If I thought you really wanted me to…Do you?…Well?

(She begins to cry. He goes to her, sits on the bed, takes her hand.)

STEVE: What is it?…What is it?

ANGELINA: You came here—I didn't go to you. *(She looks to him for confirmation.)* You came to *me.*

STEVE: That's right.

(She kisses his hand.)

STEVE: Angy—what is it…? Tell me…I want to help.

(She kisses him on the mouth. A moment of deep contact, then Steve recoils;

he would pull away, but she holds him fast. With a violent jerk he breaks her grip, rises, and then backs away.)

ANGELINA: What's the matter?

(He just looks at her.)

ANGELINA: What is it?

(Expression unchanged, he continues to regard her.)

ANGELINA: You never kissed a girl before?

(Still no response.)

ANGELINA: What? *(She gets out of bed; she studies him. The truth begins to occur to her.)* Why did you come here?…For what?

STEVE: Zia said something was wrong.

ANGELINA: Zia—of course…That's very funny…Don't you see?…Look at the face on him…! Say it!

STEVE: What is there to say?

ANGELINA: I love you.

STEVE: Get off it.

ANGELINA: What do I do now?

STEVE: Go back to the playground—get yourself another boy.

ANGELINA: *(Turns from him as though struck.)*…Yes…Of course.

STEVE: *(Realizing how deeply he's hurt her, he is regretful.)* I'm sorry.

ANGELINA: Get out.

(He just stands there.)

ANGELINA: *(She screams.)* Get out!

(He exits and enters the living room; he now confronts Zia.)

STEVE: You bitch…You dirty old bitch…You knew what would happen—didn't you…? *Didn't you?*

ZIA: Yes…and so did *you.*

(He regards her an instant; then he exits from the apartment. In the bedroom, Angelina sits on the edge of the bed.)

ANGELINA: *(Coldly, bitterly.)* "I've been here a week—we haven't talked"… "You look ten years younger in a bathing suit"…"Rub my back." *(She removes the crucifix from about her neck; she removes her wedding ring; she places both of them on the pillow and then freezes. Lights down.)*

SCENE IV

Time: Late that night. When the lights come up the apartment is in darkness, except for the light coming in from the street. Victor, barely discernible, preferably unnoticed, sits alone in the living room. The sound of the front door opening is heard. Steve enters the living room, turns on a lamp; he is startled to discover Victor who, expression glazed, regards him as though he were an apparition.

STEVE: *(Tapping his heart.)* Hey—what are you trying to do to me...?
(Victor, expression unchanged, continues to regard him.)

STEVE: What's up—what are you sitting in the dark for...?
(No response.)

STEVE: You all right...?
(No response.)

STEVE: Matter of fact, I'm glad you're up. I was going to speak to you in the morning—I'll do it now...
(Still no response. Steve, increasingly uneasy, moves about to avoid Victor's gaze.)

STEVE: I don't know exactly how to put it, but I've been doing a lot of thinking, and I've come to a decision: I'm going to leave, go back out West—at least till I finish school... *(Forces himself to face Victor.)* You understand, I like it here—can't remember a better time, or when people were nicer to me—especially you...
(Still no reaction from Victor. Steve turns away.)

STEVE: I figure I should look around a bit, learn more, before I settle down...I know this is a lot to spring on you all of a sudden, and I apologize for not saying anything sooner...
(No response. Steve regards him.)

STEVE: Well, what do you say?...
(No response, no reaction.)

STEVE: What's wrong with you?...Something the matter...? *What is it...?*
(He still gets no response. Steve, fighting to retain control of himself, turns away.)

STEVE: Look—I don't know what's bothering you, but I— *(Steve's movement has brought him to the rear of a chair over which Victor's suit jacket is draped. Something he sees arrests his attention. He stops, stares, looks from the jacket to Victor, and back again. He then slowly reaches for the jacket and lifts it to expose a mourning band on the left sleeve; he regards it.)*

What's this for?...Why?...For who? *(As though it were suddenly hot to the touch, Steve drops the jacket; he turns to Victor, exercising great control.)* Where's Angelina?

(Victor remains unchanged.)

STEVE: I want to speak to her.

(No reaction.)

STEVE: Wake her up.

(No reaction.)

STEVE: If you don't—I will!

(Still no reaction. Steve rushes to the bedroom. He turns on the light. The bed is stripped. A crucifix on the wall above the bed is draped in black. An unmistakably funereal air pervades the room. He snaps the light off—returns to the living room.)

STEVE: How?...An accident...? What?...Say something!

(Victor takes a letter from his pocket; he proffers it. Steve hesitates a moment, moves to Victor, takes the letter. He reads it and regards Victor incredulously.)

STEVE: It's not so—not any of it.

VICTOR: She lied?

STEVE: Yes.

VICTOR: Why?

STEVE: I don't know.

VICTOR: Maybe she was disturbed—unbalanced?

STEVE: I don't know.

VICTOR: Hated the son she could never give me?

STEVE: I don't know.

VICTOR: Took her life to spite you?

STEVE: I could have had lots of girls. Why *her?*

VICTOR: A bastard's revenge.

STEVE: For what? You loved me, acknowledged me.

VICTOR: How long did you plan it?

STEVE: Don't!

VICTOR: How long did you watch the house?

STEVE: Stop!

VICTOR: You're shouting. Why? You can't outshout what's written there.

(Steve, searching desperately for a way to rebut the charge, goes to Zia's closed door.)

STEVE: Zia?

(No answer. He knocks.)

STEVE: Zia!

(No answer. He tries the handle, but finds the door locked; he beats on it.)

STEVE: *Zia—Zia, please?*

(Still no answer. Victor rises; he faces Steve as he re-enters the living room.)

VICTOR: Get out!

(Steve weeps.)

VICTOR: Tears...? What for?...You shouldn't have any trouble finding another house where you can sneak into the husband's heart—the·wife's bed.

STEVE: Stop! For your *own* sake!

VICTOR: My sake?

STEVE: I beg you.

VICTOR: *Before* you took her—*that* was the time for "my sake."

STEVE: If you really believe that, why don't you kill me?...Go on!

VICTOR: It wants more than that.

(Steve regards Victor with vaulting horror; he dashes out. Victor remains as he is. Zia emerges from her room.)

ZIA: He's gone?

VICTOR: Yes.

ZIA: ...Can I get you something?

VICTOR: I showed him the letter. He swore it wasn't so.

ZIA: What did you expect?

VICTOR: Was I too quick?

ZIA: He's guilty!

VICTOR: Then why do I have this feeling, this doubt?

ZIA: You're tired.

VICTOR: He said—

ZIA: *(In an outburst.) —Who cares what he said?*
(This outburst draws Victor's attention. He regards Zia. His scrutiny unsettles her. She becomes increasingly agitated.)

ZIA: Said what...? Whatever he said, there's nothing to it...Want some tea? I'll make you some...In his condition he'd accuse anyone. Why not? What has he got to lose?...What's the matter? Why're you looking like that...? I'll bet he even brought me into it—huh?...Sure...All right, what did he say about me?

VICTOR: Nothing—not a word.

ZIA: Then why are you looking like that?

VICTOR: You're so nervous.

ZIA: The blackest day of my life—who wouldn't be?

VICTOR: Trembling.

ZIA: I'm going back to bed.

VICTOR: Why didn't you come out when he called?

ZIA: I was asleep.

VICTOR: How did you know he was here?

ZIA: We'll talk in the morning.

VICTOR: Why didn't you come out when he called?

ZIA: I didn't want to see him.

VICTOR: Miss a chance to accuse, to punish? *You?*

> *(She would escape to her room—he blocks the way.)*

VICTOR: Tell me.

ZIA: Let me go.

VICTOR: Tell me!

ZIA: I feel faint.

VICTOR: Tell me!

ZIA: She loved him!

> *(Victor regards her incredulously.)*

ZIA: Yes.

> *(Victor turns away.)*

ZIA: She was dying for him, and he had no idea. Could I just let her die? Do nothing...? I made up a reason—sent him to her...When he realized what it was all about, he walked out.

VICTOR: Nothing happened?

ZIA: Nothing—everything: What's it matter now?

> *(They are interrupted by the sound of Josie, who bursts into the apartment crying hysterically.)*

JOSIE: *Victor! Victor!*

VICTOR: What is it?

> *(She grabs him, pulls him toward the door.)*

JOSIE: Come with me...? Please come with me!

> *(Victor grips her, immobilizes her.)*

VICTOR: What's the matter?

JOSIE: *(Numbly.)* He got in the car—raced off. I saw him turn the corner. I heard a crash...so loud.

VICTOR: He's hurt?

JOSIE: He's dying.

> *(Victor dashes out.)*

JOSIE: Nothing will ever be so wonderful again...Nothing.

> *(Lights down.)*

SCENE V

Setting: The playground, the same as in Scene I, Act I. Time: The immediate continuation of the last scene. As the lights come up, the playground is in darkness, except for light from a street lamp. Steve lies in the circle of light. Victor kneels behind him.

VICTOR: *(To the audience as though they were a crowd of onlookers.)* Keep off!...*Keep off!*

STEVE: Father?

VICTOR: Yes?

STEVE: I can't see.

VICTOR: The light's gone out.

STEVE: Father?

VICTOR: Yes?

STEVE: My legs are numb.

VICTOR: The summer's over—there's a chill in the air.

STEVE: Father?

VICTOR: Yes?

STEVE: Hold me. Raise me up.

VICTOR: To heaven, if I could.

(Curtain.)

THE END

THE ONLY GAME IN TOWN

ORIGINAL PRODUCTION

The Only Game in Town opened at the Broadhurst Theatre, New York City on May 20, 1968. The play was produced by Edgar Lansbury and directed by Barry Nelson. Scenery designed by George Jenkins. The cast was as follows:

Fran Walker . . . . Tammy Grimes

Joe Grady . . . . Barry Nelson

Thomas Lockwood . . . . Leo Genn

INTRODUCTION

The failure of *That Summer—That Fall* broke the Pulitzer spell.

From Greek mythology I turned to earthly matters and a subject I knew well—gambling.

The result: *The Only Game in Town.*

The title derived from a hoary joke about one gambler telling another that the card game he's about to play in is crooked. "I know," says the guy, "but it's the only game in town."

Stung by my first failure, eager to prove it a momentary glitch, I worked demonically. Completed the play within six months of *That Summer* closing.

It was the custom in pre-computer days to send your play to Studio Duplicating, where unemployed actors and the like retyped your manuscript, ran off as many copies as ordered, and bound them in colorful bindings of your choosing.

I'd heard rumors that Hollywood movie studios paid some of the typists at Studio Duplicating to tip them off if anything with possible movie interest caught their eye.

The rumors proved true.

Witness that I'd yet to show the play to anyone, when H. N. Swanson (my Hollywood agent) called and said he'd had an inquiry from one of the studios about a new play of mine he wasn't privy to.

Thus began a whirlwind period that saw *The Only Game* purchased by Twentieth Century Fox as a vehicle for Elizabeth Taylor and Frank Sinatra to be directed by George Stevens.

All this before plans for the play production were finalized.

Edgar Lansbury produced the play with most of the old team.

With Ulu Grosbard committed elsewhere, I went back to Dan Petrie (*Plowboy*), who had turned down *Roses.*

We could have had just about any actors we wanted for the play.

Hubris reared its head: With stars set for the movie, we (largely me) opted to do the play with relative unknowns, which would make the play the star.

Baltimore, where we opened, set the critical tone that rarely varied. The play heralded as a million-dollar pre-production deal—a gross exaggeration. Sinatra, Taylor, and Stevens noted. And then our modest offering was savaged. Those who felt I'd aimed too high with the Greeks indicted me for aiming too low via Vegas.

Thus it was in Baltimore, New Haven, and Boston.

Twentieth Century Fox leaning heavily, we dismissed the actors and director. As painful an event as I can recall.

Recast with names, we came to New York.

Burdened by weeks of negative reports, there was no way we could win. We closed in two weeks.

The movie (about an over-the-hill dancer and a second-rate piano player who's a hooked gambler—same as the play) should have been a small, intimate picture made for a dollar ninety-eight.

Shot in Paris (yes Paris) because Taylor wouldn't be parted from Burton who was doing a film there, it cost an astronomical sum. Vegas built on a Paris sound stage. Crap tables flown in. Sinatra bowed out. Warren Beatty stepped in.

The movie failed resoundingly.

As a life experience (I was in Paris for three months pre-production) I profited enormously. Freddie Kohlmar, the producer, and George Stevens were an education and a delight to be around. George kept having me look through his view finder. When I asked why, he said "You're going to be a director one day." This two years before I directed my first film.

Some seven years later, *Only Game,* the play, was done in Paris.

Marta Andras (my late foreign agent and dear friend) invited me to the opening. The wounds from previous experience not yet healed, I passed.

"We have a huge hit," Marta wired next morning.

Invited to the hundredth performance I, still gun shy, declined.

Finally at the two hundred or two hundred and fifty mark I went over.

In Paris they put the playwright's photo on the program cover. All eyes on me as the curtain rose. I, certain it wouldn't work that night, experienced a chill.

All went well.

It ran for two years in Paris and on the road. Other successful productions, foreign and domestic, followed.

I see now that plays of mine which had the hardest time getting produced ultimately worked best because by the time they were produced I knew
them fully.

Bad cess to the typist at Studio Duplicating responsible for *Only Game*
being snatched from the cradle before it was weaned.

SYNOPSIS

The entire action of the play takes place in Fran Walker's second-floor garden apartment just off the Strip in Las Vegas, Nevada.

ACT I

Is composed of seven scenes. The first six scenes take place two years ago
within a period of thirty-six hours. The final scene occurs three months
later.

ACT II

Consists of two scenes that happen tonight.

ACT I
SCENE I

Setting: A second-floor garden apartment just off the Strip in Las Vegas. A bedroom and living room (stage right and left) divided by a partial wall and connecting door, share the stage. The upstage wall, common to both rooms, contains two picture windows (one in the bedroom—one in the living room) that offer a view of the Strip: The neon glow of hotel and casino signs by night—the hotels and surrounding desert and mountains by day. The bedroom: downstage in the right wall is a door opening on a bathroom. Upstage, in that same wall, is a closet door. Between these doors, its head against the wall, is a king-size bed. The living room: in the upstage wall (stage left of the window) is the entrance door. When it's open we have another view of the Strip. Upstage in the left wall is a closet door. Downstage, in the same wall, is the entrance to a kitchenette. The area between the closet and the kitchenette is marked by table and chairs as the dining area. The furnishings should indicate that a girl lives here alone. The clutter and accumulation should tell us that she has dwelled here for some time, and suffers no compulsion to neatness or order. The apartment itself, except for its view of the Strip, should be indistinguishable from the unimaginatively designed and cheaply constructed warrens that populate the nation everywhere. A vaguely claustrophobic air would not be amiss.

Time: Spring two years before the present, three A.M. At rise: The apartment, deserted, is lit by a lamp or two, and the drawn curtains hide all signs of Vegas. The bed is unmade. A clothes-drying rack, draped with a girdle, bra, and slips, stands in the bedroom. The living-room closet door is open, revealing a jumble of odds and ends. Three hangers, suspended from the door that connects the bedroom and living room, bear a negligee, a dress, and a coat, all modish and colorful. A portable sewing machine rests on the dining table. Leotards are draped over one of the chairs at the dining table. A newspaper (The Las Vegas Sun) *is scattered about the sofa. A bag of laundry rests on the sofa. A vase of dead flowers is prominent. The total effect should indicate more than carelessness, should hint at some loss of hope. Among the other more conspicuous items in the living room are: an air conditioner and liquor stand. In the bedroom we note a large blowup of Humphrey Bogart that lines the inside of an open closet door, a shelf above the bed lined with fancy mugs and vases, a telephone beside the bed, and a photograph of a man, mid-fifties, authoritative, vital (Thomas J. Lockwood), which stand on the vanity. The telephone rings…again…again…we hear some one approach at a run. A key turns, the door opens, Fran Walker bursts in, snaps on a central light switch, races toward the bedroom, leaving the outside door open.*

FRAN: *(On the phone.)* Hello?…Hello?…
(Too late. She returns the receiver to its cradle, stands dejectedly. Joe Grady, mid-thirties, wearing a tuxedo, enters the apartment, glances about the living room in a way that tells us he's never been here before, moves to a bookcase, is inspecting the contents, accidentally drops a book. The sound of the book hitting the floor rouses Fran. She enters the living room still absorbed in her disappointment.)
JOE: You didn't make it, huh?
FRAN: No.
(He moves to her, cups her face consolingly.)
JOE: Don't take it so hard.
FRAN: I hate things like that—missing calls.
JOE: As mother used to say: "If it's important they'll call back."
(He would ease into a kiss, but she, anticipating him, turns away, surveys the room.)
FRAN: Excuse the way things look—I wasn't expecting company.
JOE: Neither was I.
FRAN: *(Making a lame effort to tidy up.)* It's not much but it's home.
JOE: Compared to my place it's the Taj Mahal.
FRAN: Where's "your place"?
JOE: Downtown. Allow me.
(Helps her off with coat, turns her head, kisses her lightly—introductorily. Fran accepts the kiss impassively, moves to the liquor closet, inventories her supply. Joe puzzled by her reaction, uncertain how to proceed, studies her.)
FRAN: I don't have bourbon.
JOE: Anything.
FRAN: Scotch?
JOE: Fine.
FRAN: I'm out of soda.
JOE: On the rocks is fine.
FRAN: *(Making drinks.)* Make yourself comfortable.
JOE: I always do.
FRAN: I'm a lousy bartender.
JOE: A minor flaw.

FRAN: Thanks. *(Hands him his drink.)*

JOE: Thanks.

FRAN: I haven't been downtown in—

JOE: —Cheers.

FRAN: Cheers.

> *(They drink.)*

JOE: You were saying?

FRAN: I haven't been downtown in almost a year.

JOE: You haven't missed anything.

FRAN: It depresses me—downtown.

JOE: What's different about the Strip?

FRAN: The people look better. I mean they don't look like they're gambling their last cent.

JOE: You think gambling should be restricted to the well-to-do?

FRAN: I hate to see people risking what they can't afford.

JOE: If you're *not* risking what you can't afford, you're not really gambling.

FRAN: I've seen some terrible scenes.

JOE: Tell me about them.

> *(There is a bitter edge in his voice that causes her to regard him. He tries to make light of it: smiles.)*

JOE: How did we get on this?

FRAN: I said I hadn't been downtown in a long time.

JOE: Which helps to explain why we never met before.

FRAN: It was only by accident I happened to be with that bunch tonight. I've been trying to give up smoking—went three weeks, but tonight I couldn't stand it any more. I was buying cigarettes when I ran into them.

JOE: I'm glad you don't have much will power.

> *(She doesn't understand.)*

JOE: If you did we wouldn't have met.

FRAN: How long have you been playing there?

JOE: Seven months.

FRAN: I like the way you play.

JOE: I figured that.

> *(She regards him questioningly.)*

JOE: When you didn't leave with the others.

FRAN: *(Unsettled by his unswerving, vaguely suggestive attention, she goes to the window, partially opens the drape.)* Used to be I could see the mountains—now every time you look there's another hotel.

JOE: How long you been here—in Vegas?

FRAN: Too long.

JOE: How long is that?

FRAN: Five years. Can you imagine if they ever voted gambling out—what a ghost town this would make?

JOE: You missed your cue.

(She regards him.)

JOE: You're supposed to ask how long I've been here.

FRAN: Why?

JOE: It lends continuity to the conversation.

FRAN: I don't *care* how long you've been here.

JOE: Good for you.

(She regards him.)

JOE: Not being particularly honest myself, I admire it in other people.

FRAN: That sounds like a warning.

JOE: Let the buyer beware.

FRAN: *(She appraises him a moment. Then.)* In that case maybe I should ask you to leave.

JOE: I'd rather have a refill. *(Drains drink.)* Please?

(She replenishes their drinks.)

JOE: Three years going on four.

(She regards him.)

JOE: That's how long I've been here.

FRAN: Funny we never bumped into each other before this.

JOE: Better late than never—to coin a phrase.

(She hands him his drink.)

JOE: Pros-it.

FRAN: Cheers.

(They drink.)

FRAN: Do you like Vegas?

JOE: Loathe, despise, and detest it.

FRAN: Why do you stay?

JOE: Financial reasons. Roughly translated: I used to gamble a little—got in a bit of a hole from which I have only recently extricated myself. How about you?

(She doesn't grasp the question.)

JOE: You like it here?

FRAN: No.

JOE: Why do *you* stay?

FRAN: Inertia.

JOE: That's one of my favorite words—"inertia." It conjures an image of soft satin pillows—a whole mountain of them and me sitting on top... Where *were* we?

FRAN: I'm not sure.

JOE: I think it's your move. *(He waits, making it plain that he expects her to speak next.)*

FRAN: *(Unsettled, she says the first thing that comes to mind.)* I don't get around as much as I used to.

(He regards her uncomprehendingly.)

FRAN: That's probably why we never met.

JOE: Probably.

FRAN: The first couple of years it was like one long party. Now I just do the shows and come back here. Tonight was the first time I've been out in a month.

JOE: What do you do with yourself?

FRAN: Read a bit, mostly it's TV—old movies. I'm an addict. Do you like Bogart?

JOE: *(À la Bogart)* "If you want anything just whistle."

FRAN: That's Lauren Bacall's line.

JOE: Who do you think I was I doing?

FRAN: I'm crazy about him—Bogart. I think if he was alive I'd do everything I could to meet him.

JOE: I used to be married to a woman who was flipped over George Brent.

FRAN: You're divorced?

JOE: Twice.

FRAN: What I like about Bogart is that he's so ugly. I've never liked pretty men.

JOE: I guess that rules me out.

(She laughs.)

JOE: Hold that pose while I get a camera.

FRAN: What?

JOE: That's the first time I've seen you really smile.

FRAN: I won't let it happen again.

JOE: And jokes to boot. Things are looking up.

FRAN: *(Sharply.)* Don't tease me...I can't stand being teased.

JOE: I'm sorry.

FRAN: ...You sang a song from a Bogart movie.

JOE: *(Sings.)* "You must remember this, a kiss is still a kiss."

FRAN: It gives me goose pimples.

JOE: The song or my singing?

FRAN: The song.

JOE: Ouch.

FRAN: I *do* like the way you play.

JOE: Hit him again, he's still moving.

FRAN: I'm sorry.

JOE: I guess that pays me back for teasing.

FRAN: I wasn't trying to pay you back.

JOE: I know: You're just so full of honesty you can't help yourself.

FRAN: Are you the sort who has to be lied to?

JOE: Come on back to my place—I'll buy you a drink and kick your head in.

FRAN: Do *you* think you're a *good* singer?

JOE: That's not the point!

(*The ridiculousness of the exchange hits them simultaneously. They regard each other.*)

JOE: Ain't we touchy?

FRAN: I had a rotten day. What's your excuse?

JOE: I come from a broken home.

FRAN: Do you always have to joke?

JOE: Only when I'm nervous.

FRAN: What are you nervous about?

JOE: I don't know how to get you from here to the bedroom.

FRAN: That's the lousiest approach I ever heard.

JOE: Thanks for the drink...Just for the record, why did you drape yourself all over the piano—ask me back here?

FRAN: You appealed to me.

JOE: The feeling was more than mutual.

(*He waits for her to speak. She doesn't.*)

JOE: Well?

FRAN: Well what?

JOE: Do I stay or do I go?

FRAN: I couldn't care less.

JOE: That's a lie.

FRAN: Walk out that door and see if I try to stop you.

JOE: You wouldn't stop me, but that doesn't mean you don't care.

FRAN: What are you—a psychiatrist?

JOE: I don't have to be a psychiatrist to know that you're as hard up and as lonely as I am.

FRAN: I don't like that kind of talk.

JOE: I thought you were all for honesty.

FRAN: Get out of here! *(She turns her back on him.)*

JOE: *(He hesitates a moment; goes to her.)* Look, I don't wrestle—I don't coax. I can't. If you want to go to bed—we go. If you don't—we don't…Well?

FRAN: Carry me.

JOE: What?

FRAN: Carry me into the bedroom. I like to be carried…Please?
(Lights down.)

SCENE II

Time: An hour later. At rise: They are in bed—barely discernible. Joe hums a song (unknown to us) in a way that mirrors complete relaxation and contentment.

JOE: Cigarette?

FRAN: Please.
(He strikes a match; lights two cigarettes; hands her one.)

FRAN: Thanks.

JOE: *(He hums a bit more of the song. Then.)* If they ever drop the bomb, I hope this is how it finds me.

FRAN: That's a cheerful thought.

JOE: I'm a cheerful fellow.

FRAN: Warning number three?

JOE: Five—you missed a couple. *(Hums a bit more.)* Where did you say you danced?

FRAN: The Tropicana.

JOE: Line or specialty?

FRAN: Line.
(He hums.)

FRAN: What's that you keep humming?

JOE: A little thing I wrote…Like it?

FRAN: It sounds familiar.

JOE: Who asked you?

FRAN: Why can't you wrestle or coax?

JOE: What?

FRAN: You said before that you couldn't wrestle or coax.

JOE: That's right.

FRAN: Why?

JOE: It's very Freudian and complicated.

FRAN: Try me.

JOE: I grew up in a house with paper thin walls.

FRAN: So?

JOE: So my childhood memories are filled with sounds of father making vigorous advances and mother protesting plaintively.

FRAN: So what?

JOE: So if I have to wrestle or coax, the girl becomes my mother and the whole thing's ruined.

FRAN: That must put you at a great disadvantage.

JOE: True, but occasionally I meet someone who has the courage to participate without lies or pretense, and then it's very nice...I just paid you a compliment.

FRAN: Thanks—I guess...Do you still gamble?

JOE: Haven't touched the stuff in months. Have satisfied all my creditors. Have started a bank account which, when it reaches five thousand dollars, will be my instantaneous passport out of this cesspool.

FRAN: I hope you make it.

JOE: Thanks.

FRAN: This is a treat—smoking in bed.

JOE: Why?

FRAN: I never do it when I'm alone. All those terrible stories you read about people falling asleep.

JOE: When was the *last* time you smoked in bed?

FRAN: That's sneaky.

JOE: Strike the question.

FRAN: You have a nice body.

JOE: That's what everyone says.

FRAN: What are you nervous about?

JOE: Who's nervous?

FRAN: You said you only make jokes when you're nervous.

JOE: I think we better take it from the top: How do you feel?

FRAN: Fine. How about you?

JOE: Not as good as I did a minute ago.

FRAN: How come?

JOE: I don't know.

FRAN: ...Three months.

JOE: What?

FRAN: It's been three months since I smoked in bed.

JOE: Regular or king-sized?

FRAN: That's not funny.

JOE: I know.

FRAN: I'm not sure I like you.

JOE: I knew we had something in common.

FRAN: Stop it!

JOE: What are you doing?…Crying?…What are you crying for?…I'm sorry…
      I said I'm sorry…Hey…All right—I apologize. I'm not sure what for—
      but I do.

FRAN: *(Tearfully.)* Thanks a lot.

JOE: *I can't stand crying.*

FRAN: Then leave.

JOE: I'll do worse than that: *(He sings.)* "It must have been moonglow."

FRAN: All right—you win.

JOE: No more tears?

FRAN: Providing there are no more jokes.

JOE: It's a deal. *(He takes her cigarette; extinguishes it along with his own.)*

FRAN: What are you *doing?*

JOE: Smoking is bad for you.

FRAN: What are you doing?

JOE: You make a deal, you have to seal it.

FRAN: There must be a better way.

JOE: Name one…Well?
      (Silence. Lights down.)

SCENE III

*Time: Noon the next day. At rise: Fran, in a housecoat, humming Joe's song,
enters the living room from the kitchen; removes the sewing machine from
the dining table; sets two places for breakfast. The bedroom door is closed.
Joe emerges from the bathroom into the bedroom. He has his trousers, socks
and shoes on—is bare from the waist up. He has just shaved; is toweling his
face. As he does this, he moves about studying various items (souvenirs, photographs, books) that decorate the room. The picture of Thomas J. Lockwood
claims his attention. As he dons his shirt he studies it; picks it up for closer
examination; puts it down; finishes buttoning his shirt; enters the living room.*

FRAN: Good morning.

JOE: Morning.

FRAN: I didn't know you were up.

JOE: Up, shaved, and showered.

FRAN: What can I make you?

JOE: Juice and coffee is fine.

FRAN: I have eggs, bacon—you name it.

JOE: Juice and coffee.

FRAN: All right.

JOE: I'm not much for breakfast.

FRAN: Neither am I. *(She disappears into the kitchen.)*

JOE: Looks like a nice day.

FRAN'S VOICE: *(Offstage.)* Yes…Pineapple or orange?

JOE: Pineapple…You could use a new blade in that razor.

FRAN: *(Returning with juice and coffee.)* I'll put it on my list.

JOE: *(He joins her at the table. Taking his juice glass.)* Cheers.

FRAN: Cheers.

(As they sip their juice, they appraise each other.)

JOE: Here we are again.

FRAN: Yes.

JOE: You *don't* remember me.

FRAN: Of course I do.

JOE: I'm serious.

FRAN: So am I.

JOE: Where was it?

FRAN: Where was what?

JOE: I knew it.

FRAN: What are you talking about?

JOE: You don't remember.

FRAN: Remember what?

JOE: Three summers ago—a party at Al Russo's.

FRAN: Who's Al Russo?

JOE: We got high, you and I—hey that rhymes; left the party; ended up at my place.

FRAN: What?

JOE: Don't feel bad—I once knew a girl who couldn't even remember the first guy she went to bed with.

FRAN: *I never met you before last night.*

JOE: Are you sure?

FRAN: Positive!

JOE: Congratulations.

(She just looks at him.)

JOE: There aren't many girls in this town who remember every guy they went to bed with.

(She continues to look at him.)

JOE: Something wrong?

FRAN: What kind of a person *are* you?

JOE: The kind who likes to be remembered.

FRAN: I think you better finish your coffee and get out of here.

JOE: Why?

FRAN: Because I have long antennae for bad news.

JOE: I mean why finish my coffee. *(Rising.)* I had a hat when I came in.

FRAN: All right. *(She collects his tie and jacket; hands them to him.)* Here.

JOE: Thanks. You're wise. *(He waits, but this fails to elicit a response.)* "Why?" she said, unable to stifle her curiosity. "Because I'd only break your heart," he said cavalierly. "Don't flatter yourself," she said bitingly.

FRAN: I've made nuts before, but *you* take the cake.

JOE: "Made?"

FRAN: I meant "met."

JOE: You *said* "made."

FRAN: You're too much.

JOE: Does that mean I can finish my coffee?

FRAN: Suit yourself.

JOE: *(Picks up his cup—drinks.)* How many years have we been married?

FRAN: It feels like forever.

JOE: If it wasn't for the kids, I'd leave.

FRAN: Me too.

JOE: What do you say we abandon the little monsters—tell them we're going to a movie and skip?

FRAN: I couldn't do that.

JOE: I could.

FRAN: I believe it.

JOE: Nelson Algren says you should never go to bed with anyone who has more problems than *you* do.

FRAN: Who's he?

JOE: You don't know who Nelson Algren is and you call yourself an intellectual?

FRAN: It's a free country.

JOE: Smile when you say that.

FRAN: Do you *ever* touch the ground?

JOE: I have my moments.

FRAN: Call me the next time you feel one coming on. (*She holds up his jacket as an invitation to leave.*)

JOE: This is it?

FRAN: This is it.

JOE: (*Donning the jacket.*) That guy in the photograph in the bedroom—is he something special?

FRAN: Why do you ask?

JOE: I'm the jealous type...Well?

FRAN: Yes, he's something special.

JOE: It would be in bad taste to ask anything else about him.

FRAN: Yes.

JOE: Where is he?

FRAN: In San Francisco with his wife.

JOE: Serves you right for getting mixed up with a guy who has beady eyes.

FRAN: I've always been a sucker for beady eyes.

JOE: (*Extending his hand.*) It's been real.

FRAN: (*Shaking his hand.*) Likewise.

JOE: As my friend Jose Cristobal would say, "Una buena aventura sin mala consequencia." "A good adventure without bad consequence."

FRAN: Olé.

JOE: I'm having a little trouble leaving—can't find an exit line.

FRAN: I've noticed.

JOE: How about something simple like "I enjoyed last night"?

FRAN: Try it.

JOE: I enjoyed last night.

FRAN: So did I.

JOE: Maybe we can do it again sometime.

FRAN: Maybe.

JOE: Why don't you drop in at the club tonight?

FRAN: I don't think so.

JOE: It's better than old movies.

FRAN: Don't flatter yourself.

JOE: I won't sing.

FRAN: You're getting to me.

JOE: My interest is purely physical, you understand?

FRAN: Perfectly.

JOE: In short—no ulterior motives.

FRAN: I'm relieved.

JOE: You'll stop in tonight?

FRAN: We'll see.

JOE: I'll keep a candle in the window.

FRAN: You do that.

JOE: Ta-ta. *(He exits.)*
(Lights down.)

SCENE IV

Time: Two A.M, the following morning. At rise: the apartment in darkness. A key turns. The door opens. Fran enters, turns on a light. She is fuming; hurls her pocketbook across the room.

FRAN: *(Mimicking angrily.)* "I'll keep a candle in the window." *(She kicks off her shoes; pours a drink.)* "Ta-ta."
(She downs the drink; is pouring another when there is a knock at the door.)

FRAN: Who is it?

JOE'S VOICE: *(Offstage. A la a house detective.)* Have you got a man in there?

FRAN: What do you want?

JOE'S VOICE: *(Offstage.)* Can I come in?

FRAN: No.

JOE'S VOICE: *(Offstage.)* I'd like to apologize.

FRAN: For what?

JOE'S VOICE: *(Offstage.)* Standing you up.

FRAN: I don't know what you're talking about.

JOE'S VOICE: *(Offstage.)* Didn't you come to the club tonight?

FRAN: No.

JOE'S VOICE: *(Offstage.)* Then what are you mad about?

FRAN: Who's mad?

JOE'S VOICE: *(Offstage.)* I have to talk to you.

FRAN: Go ahead.

JOE'S VOICE: *(Offstage.)* It's confidential.

FRAN: Send me a letter.

JOE'S VOICE: *(Offstage. Roughly, à la Bogart if possible.)* All right sister—open this door or else. *(Falsetto.)* Or else what? *(Bogart.)* Or else I'll huff and I'll puff and I'll blow your house in.

FRAN: Go away.

JOE'S VOICE: *(Offstage. Loudly, à la Ezio Pinza.)* "Oh say can you see by the dawn's early light…"

FRAN: You'll wake the house!

JOE'S VOICE: *(Offstage.)* "What so proudly we hailed…."

(She opens the door.)

JOE: *(He enters.)* I also do Al Jolson, Ed Sullivan, and a very good Herbie Steinkraut. Unfortunately Herbie never made it…Hello there.

FRAN: Say what you have to say and go.

JOE: I wanted to explain why I wasn't at the club tonight.

FRAN: Neither was I—so no explanation is necessary.

JOE: I stopped at the club. They said you'd just left.

FRAN: So what?

JOE: So I apologize.

FRAN: Your apology is accepted—good night.

JOE: Don't you want to know *why* I wasn't there?

FRAN: No.

JOE: Even though it was *your* fault?

FRAN: My fault?

JOE: What time did I leave here yesterday?

FRAN: Noon.

JOE: Noon—a cloudless sunny day. Temperature eighty-seven degrees. I knew it was eighty-seven degrees because I passed the Sahara Hotel just as the sign said "Temperature eighty-seven." With me so far?

FRAN: Cloudless sunny day—temperature eighty-seven.

JOE: Eighty-eight—the sign just changed.

FRAN: There better be a good punchline.

JOE: *(Clapping his hands loudly.)* Bang!

(She eyes him curiously.)

JOE: Just as I was looking at the sign, one of my tires blew out.

FRAN: Which one? I love details.

JOE: Left rear. Did I mention that I was in a good mood yesterday?

FRAN: No.

JOE: Well I was—a *very* good mood. Thanks to you.

FRAN: I'm touched.

JOE: To demonstrate: Ordinarily a flat tire ruins my day. Not yesterday. I went right on singing—pulled into a gas station. Did I mention I was singing?

FRAN: No.

JOE: "I love you as I never loved before—"

FRAN: —I've got the picture.

JOE: Where am I?

FRAN: The gas station.

JOE: The attendant says he's busy—says it will take an hour to change the tire. Do I get steamed up—blow my top? I do not. I can't. I'm in too good a mood.

FRAN: Thanks to *me*.

JOE: Thanks to *you*. What to do for an hour? The Sahara is just up the street. I have a bartender friend on the day shift. I'll drop in—say hello.

FRAN: This is fascinating.

JOE: *(Moving to the liquor stand.)* He isn't there—my bartender friend. I have a drink anyway. *(He spots a new bottle of bourbon; picks it up.)* Bourbon— for me?

FRAN: Don't flatter yourself.

JOE: As I was saying—I have a drink anyway. *(He pours a drink.)* I have another drink. *(He pours a bit more.)* I don't want a third drink so I stroll about the casino. I stop to observe at one of the crap tables. The table is cold—ice cold. Five shooters in a row go down without a pass. And then up steps Harold C. Carver. I know it's Harold C. Carver because he has a tag that says "Harold C. Carver—Ridgeway Products Ink." I also know, with sudden and absolute certainty, that Harold is going to have a very hot hand.

FRAN: You didn't—

JOE: Don't anticipate. I have eighty dollars. I bet ten that Harold passes. He throws a twelve. I bet ten more. He repeats. Ten more. He craps again. To make a long story short, Harold craps out eight times in a row. My eighty is gone. I need money to pay the gas station guy. I walk to the bank. I intend to draw two hundred dollars—am writing that figure on the withdrawal slip when something comes over me: I watch my hand write "two thousand"—which happens to be my total worth.

FRAN: I don't want to hear any more.

JOE: I returned to the Sahara—

FRAN: Lost everything, and would like me to lend you five bucks so you can get your car.

JOE: I returned to the Sahara; won six thousand dollars—which gives me a total of eight thousand; am leaving this crummy town tomorrow, and would like to celebrate my last night here with you.

FRAN: Eight thousand?

JOE: *(Displaying a roll of bills.)* Eight thousand. And I owe it all to you.

FRAN: Why?

JOE: How could I lose when I was in such a good mood?

(*She starts to cry.*)

JOE: What's the matter?

FRAN: I'm sorry.

JOE: Can't bear to see me go—huh?

FRAN: I'm so happy for you.

JOE: You always cry when you're happy?

FRAN: Always.

JOE: How long does it go on?

FRAN: I'm through.

JOE: Feel up to doing the town?

FRAN: Yes.

JOE: Lots of people I should say good-bye to—we'll kill two birds.

FRAN: Lead on.

JOE: Give me a kiss.

FRAN: Why should I?

JOE: Because I'm a winner—and winners are irresistible.

(*She kisses him.*)

JOE: Not a very big kiss.

FRAN: Not a very big winner. (*He would embrace her. She fends him off.*) We're doing the town—remember?

JOE: I'd rather do you.

FRAN: The town first.

JOE: It's a deal....*Hold the phone!* (*He freezes.*)

FRAN: What's the matter?

JOE: One night, when I was sixteen. I was on my way to a dance at a summer resort. I was walking. When I got about a half mile away, I could hear the orchestra. The sound of the music, the anticipation of the dance, the quality of the night—everything combined to make a moment that was so perfect, I wept. Right now is a moment just like that. I'm letting it sink in so that I'll remember it forever. (*He shuts his eyes for a beat, then opens them.*) It's a take. Let's go! We'll start at the end of the Strip and work our way back.

FRAN: Whatever you say.

JOE: The first drink will be a toast to Harold C. Carver and Ridgeway Products Ink.

(*They exit. Their laughter echoes back. Lights down.*)

SCENE V

Time: Seven A.M., five hours after the previous scene. At rise: neon competes with early morning light in the window. Fran, dressed as she was, sits in an attitude of deep and troubled preoccupation, watching TV. There is a knock at the door, weak and uncertain. The knock is repeated. Fran, reluctantly, almost against her will, goes to the door; opens it. Joe, a little drunk, a little disheveled, and totally spent, stands framed in the doorway.

JOE: Top of the morning. "Won't you come in?" "Don't mind if I do." *(He enters; closes the door; regards her.)* Okay, say it.

FRAN: What is there to say?

JOE: For openers you could call me a fool, a jackass, a moron, an idiot.

FRAN: Would that make you feel better?

JOE: A little.

FRAN: All right: You're a fool, a moron, a weakling, a baby.

JOE: Stick to the script.

FRAN: I thought you wanted to be punished.

JOE: I think I'm in the wrong apartment.

FRAN: So do I.

JOE: So much for small talk—can you lend me twenty bucks?

FRAN: *(Shocked.)* You lost it *all?*

JOE: Every farthing—every sou.

FRAN: You still had five thousand when I left.

JOE: Want to search me?

FRAN: How *could* you?

JOE: It was easy.

FRAN: *I've had enough jokes!*

JOE: Give me the twenty and I'll never darken your door again.

FRAN: *(Placing herself between him and the door, mimicking cruelly.)* "I used to gamble a little. Haven't touched the stuff in months."

JOE: Do I get the twenty—yes or no?

FRAN: "As soon as I have five thousand I'm going to flee this cesspool."

JOE: I didn't come here for a lecture!

FRAN: Do I detect anger?

JOE: *Get out of my way or…*

FRAN: Or what?

JOE: *(Caving in.)* Or you're going to see a grown man cry.

FRAN: I'd prefer that to jokes.

JOE: *(Close to tears, he turns away.)* I had eight thousand dollars. Had it in my hand. Am I crazy—or what? *(Slams the fist of one hand against the palm of the other.)* God damn me! *God damn me!*

FRAN: I can't tell you how sorry I am.

JOE: Eight grand…*Eight thousand dollars.*

FRAN: How about a drink?

JOE: Got any hemlock?

FRAN: I'll see. *(She prepares drinks.)*

JOE: Did you know that Las Vegas has the highest suicide rate, per capita, in the country?

FRAN: I don't like that kind of talk—even kidding.

JOE: Who's kidding?

FRAN: Now look.

JOE: Relax. I don't have the guts. If I did, I wouldn't be here.

FRAN: Maybe you better stick to jokes. *(She hands him his drink.)*

JOE: All I needed was *five* thousand—and I had *eight.*

FRAN: Shut up and drink your whiskey.

JOE: *(Raising his glass.)* To Harold C. Carver—may he rot in hell. *(He drinks.)* All I needed was *five*—and I had *eight.*

FRAN: Why do you need *anything?* Why can't you just leave?

JOE: You have to be in New York six months to get your eight-o-two card. Until you get it, you can only work one nighters.

FRAN: You need five thousand dollars to live six months?

JOE: I'm a big tipper.

FRAN: That's two hundred dollars a week.

JOE: *I'm not in the mood for an economics lesson.*

FRAN: Sorry.

JOE: Speaking of economics—do I get the twenty?

FRAN: No.

JOE: Why not?

FRAN: You'd go to the nearest casino and blow it.

JOE: You've got it all figured out.

FRAN: Well, wouldn't you?

JOE: *(Drains his drink.)* Thanks for the use of the hall. *(Starts out.)*

FRAN: Hey…You're welcome to spend the night.

JOE: Is that an indecent proposal—or pity?

FRAN: Pity.

JOE: In that case—I accept. The fact is I'm not up to the other.

FRAN: How would you like a warm bath?

JOE: I wouldn't.

FRAN: It'll relax you.

JOE: I don't want to relax.

FRAN: I'll scrub your back.

JOE: I don't want my back scrubbed.

FRAN: Get undressed. I'll run the water. *(She exits into the bathroom.)*
(We hear the sound of running water.)

JOE: Five grand—and I had eight…Five, and I had eight. *(He breaks down; cups his head in his hands.)*

FRAN: *(Returning.)* The bath will be ready in a— *(She sees him; stops; goes to him; puts her arms about him.)* You'll be all right.

JOE: How could I do it?…How?

FRAN: Tomorrow it will hurt less. The next day, a little less. The next day, still less…You'll see…Come now—take your bath.
(Lights down.)

SCENE VI

Time: Three P.M. the same day. At rise: Joe, alone in the bedroom, is getting dressed.

JOE: "If you can make one heap of all your winnings, and risk it on one turn of pitch-and-toss…and lose, and start again at your beginnings, and never breathe a word about your loss."
(Fran, in a housecoat, emerges from the bathroom.)

FRAN: Is that what you're going to do—start again at your beginnings?

JOE: What else?

FRAN: How long will it take to save five thousand dollars?

JOE: Six months if I give up food and drink, and don't forget the lyrics to "Sweet Adeline." You know how many choruses of "Sweet Adeline" there are in five thousand dollars?

FRAN: Twelve hundred and thirty-four.

JOE: "If *you* can keep your head when all about you are losing theirs and blaming it on you." That's how it begins—it's a poem by Kipling. It enumerates all the virile virtues and ends: "If you can fill the unforgiving minute with sixty seconds worth of distance run. Yours is the earth and everything that's in it. And—which is more —you'll be a Man, my son!"*

FRAN: What do you do for an encore?

JOE: A framed copy of that poem decorated the wall above my bed in Hackensack, New Jersey. Did I mention that I was born and raised in Hackensack, New Jersey?

FRAN: No.

JOE: Well, I was.

FRAN: Braggart.

JOE: I think it was my father's idea—the framed poem. I think he looked upon it as an antidote to mother's permissive coddling. Did I mention that I was an only child whose mother permissively coddled?

FRAN: No.

JOE: Well, I was. I think my old man lived in mortal fear that I'd turn out queer. Hey, that rhymes. When they caught *me* and Morton Conway examining each other's equipment, he was convinced. That's when Kipling appeared above my bed.

FRAN: Is your father still alive?

JOE: No.

FRAN: Too bad.

JOE: Why?

FRAN: I'd have sent him an affidavit that you're straight.

JOE: I did better than that: When I was seventeen I knocked up the best cheerleader Hackensack High ever had. My father made indignant noises, but I always suspected I had pleased him enormously.

FRAN: Was she your first wife—the cheerleader?

JOE: Yes.

FRAN: How long?

JOE: Three months.

FRAN: What happened to the child?

JOE: Miscarriage.

FRAN: What time is it?

JOE: Ten after three.

FRAN: ...*I* used to be a cheerleader.

JOE: I knew it.

_____

*Lines from "If" by Rudyard Kipling are taken from *Rewards and Fairies,* by Rudyard Kipling. © 1910 by Rudyard Kipling. Reprinted by permission of Mrs. George Bambridge, Doubleday & Company, Inc. and The Macmillan Company of Canada.

FRAN: How?

JOE: The way you handle a baton.

FRAN: Don't flatter yourself.

JOE: *You* ever been married?

FRAN: No.

JOE: You prefer freedom and a career.

FRAN: On the contrary, it's my fondest wish to get married and raise a family.

JOE: I think my mother's calling me.

FRAN: Relax—I'm already spoken for.

JOE: Beady eyes?

FRAN: Beady eyes.

JOE: How long's it been going on?

FRAN: You'll laugh if I tell the truth.

JOE: Try me.

FRAN: Ten years.

JOE: You must have been nine when it started.

FRAN: Thanks, but I'm twenty-eight.

JOE: You could have fooled *me.*

FRAN: Why should I?

JOE: *(Sings.)* "A wild sort of devil, but dead on the level."

FRAN: You're pretty wild your *own* self.

JOE: But not dead on the level.

FRAN: Warning number two hundred and three.

JOE: How did you meet him?

FRAN: On a train. The seat next to me was vacant. I heard someone say, "All right if I sit here, kid?" I said, "Help yourself, Mister."

JOE: That was *him?*

FRAN: That was *him,* and that was *it.*

JOE: When did you begin to suspect he was a white slaver?

FRAN: He's a businessman.

JOE: You're too modest: He's a tycoon, a leading member of the financial community.

FRAN: How did *you* know?

JOE: Elementary, dear Watson: You studiously refrain from saying his name.

FRAN: What's *that* prove?

JOE: He's someone prominent, someone wealthy, someone I might go to San Francisco and blackmail if I were so inclined.

FRAN: I *never thought any such thing.*

JOE: Sure you did—and why not? You hang around this town a few years, you learn to trust no one or you're dead…Well?

FRAN: You're too much.

JOE: You concede the thought crossed your mind?

FRAN: I concede. Nothing personal, you understand?

JOE: Perfectly.

FRAN: His name's Lockwood—Thomas J. Lockwood.

JOE: Thanks.

FRAN: You're welcome.

JOE: Ten years?

FRAN: Ten years.

JOE: Ever hear of the statute of limitations?

FRAN: I'm afraid it doesn't apply.

JOE: You've got it that bad?

FRAN: Yes.

JOE: What are you doing about it?

FRAN: I gave him an ultimatum: "Never darken my door again—unless it's for keeps."

JOE: What happened?

FRAN: I haven't seen him in three months.

JOE: The last time you smoked in bed?

FRAN: Check.

JOE: What's your next move?

FRAN: I wait.

JOE: How long?

FRAN: Till he comes.

JOE: You're sure he will?

FRAN: If I wasn't I'd—

JOE: You'd what?

FRAN: I don't know.

JOE: *(Sings.)* "Poor Butterfly—'neath the blossoms waiting."

FRAN: He has a family, social position, a big business. He can't just pull out. It takes time.

JOE: That sounds like a direct quote.

FRAN: *It's true.*

JOE: *I'm* convinced—how about *you?*

FRAN: Don't.

JOE: Sorry…A thought occurs.

FRAN: What is it?

JOE: How do *I* fit into this picture of eternal love and devotion?

FRAN: I had an overpowering urge to smoke in bed.

JOE: Glad to have been of service.

FRAN: Sorry to put it so bluntly, but I don't want to mislead you.

JOE: Nothing to be sorry about. The fact is I'm relieved.

FRAN: I thought you would be.

JOE: To tell you the truth, I was afraid you were falling for me.

FRAN: Not a chance.

JOE: That's what they all say, and then *pow*—they're head over heels.

FRAN: I'll try to be the exception.

JOE: If I start getting to you, let me know and I'll turn it off.

FRAN: It?

JOE: The charm—the old je ne sais quoi. I've been keeping it in check but it's bound to leak out sooner or later.

FRAN: I'll protect myself at all times.

JOE: Do that. I'd hate to see you end up like all the others.

FRAN: I'm willing to take my chances.

JOE: Where does that leave us?

FRAN: If you want to move in with me, you can.

JOE: This is so sudden.

FRAN: If you're going to get cute—forget it.

JOE: Sorry.

FRAN: …Well?

JOE: No strings—no obligations?

FRAN: No strings—no obligations.

JOE: Both of us free to pull out at any time and no questions asked?

FRAN: Both of us free to pull out at any time and no questions asked.

JOE: Fifty-fifty on all household expenses?

FRAN: Fifty-fifty on all household expenses.

JOE: What's the rent?

FRAN: One-forty a month.

JOE: You just got yourself a roommate.

FRAN: Welcome.

JOE: Thanks.

FRAN: What time do you go to work?

JOE: See that?

FRAN: What?

JOE: Married less than a minute and already you're nagging.

FRAN: This has nothing to do with marriage!

JOE: I like your attitude…Nine o'clock. That's when I start playing.

FRAN: I usually eat at six.

JOE: Fine.

FRAN: Any preferences or dislikes?

JOE: I eat anything but curry.

FRAN: I don't like curry either. *(She commences a series of exercises appropriate to a dancer's needs.)*

JOE: How long you been dancing?

FRAN: Professionally since I was seventeen.

JOE: Are you good?

FRAN: No.

JOE: But you like it.

FRAN: No.

JOE: Why do you keep on?

FRAN: I like to eat.

JOE: I thought your boy friend was loaded.

(She stops exercising, regards him angrily.)

JOE: Methinks I goofed.

FRAN: I pay my own way—and always have.

JOE: I should have known.

FRAN: Look in that closet—no furs. Look in those drawers—no jewelry.

JOE: More fool you.

FRAN: *Fool?*

JOE: *Fool.*

FRAN: If *you* were *me*, you would have taken them?

JOE: No—*and you know why?*

FRAN: Why?

JOE: *I'm* a fool too.

FRAN: Ha-ha. *(Resumes her exercises.)*

JOE: How much longer?

FRAN: Just a bit…You know it wouldn't hurt *you* to exercise—tighten those stomach muscles.

JOE: "Where are you from originally?" he said—changing the subject.

FRAN: Pittsfield, Massachusetts.

JOE: What does your father do?

FRAN: I wish I knew.

JOE: What's *that* mean?

FRAN: He vanished when I was ten—has never been heard from again.

JOE: That rhymes. How do you mean "vanished"?

FRAN: One day we were the happiest family on the block—the next day he was gone. We never found out *where*—we never found out *why.*

JOE: That must have been a jolt.

FRAN: It eventually killed my mother.

JOE: What effect did it have on *you?*

FRAN: I decided to become a famous dancer. *So* famous that my father wouldn't be able to resist getting in touch with me.

JOE: You loved him.

FRAN: Oh, yes. You know something?

JOE: What?

FRAN: I think he came to my room the night he left. I think I woke up and found him sitting on my bed. He was crying. I asked him why. He didn't say anything—just leaned down; kissed me; and patted my head till I went back to sleep...How did we get on *this?*

JOE: You said I had flabby stomach muscles.

FRAN: You do.

JOE: Nonsense. *(Tenses his abdomen.)* Feel.
(She hesitates.)

JOE: Go on.
(She digs him, none too gently, in the solar plexus. He winces; clutching his middle—exaggeratedly.)

JOE: "If you can force your heart and nerve—"

FRAN: Juice and coffee?

JOE: Please.
(She exits from the bedroom, is passing through the living room when he calls.)

JOE: *Hey.*

FRAN: *(Stopping.)* What?

JOE: Why do you want me to live here?

FRAN: So I can smoke in bed whenever I like.

JOE: Besides that.

FRAN: Seriously?

JOE: Seriously.

FRAN: I've given him ultimatums before but never had the guts to stick to them: got too lonely—always ended up begging him to come back.

JOE: With *me* for immoral support, you hope to *make* it this time.

FRAN: Something like that.

JOE: I'll do my best: Any time I think you're weakening, I'll sing a few choruses of "A Bird in a Gilded Cage."

FRAN: And any time *you* seem headed for a crap table, I'll do "Sweet Adeline."

JOE: United we conquer—divided we fall.

FRAN: In union there is strength.

JOE: *(Sings.)* "She's only a bird in a gilded cage…"

FRAN: *(Sings.)* "Sweet Adeline, my Adeline…"

JOE: "A beautiful sight to see…"

FRAN: "At night, dear heart, for you I pine…"

JOE: "You may think she's happy and free from care…"

FRAN: "In all my dreams, your fair face beams…"

(Lights down.)

SCENE VII

Time: Two A.M., three months later. At rise: The only light on is the one in the bathroom. The rest of the apartment is in shadows. We pick up the figure of a man seated on the easy chair in the living room. It is the man in the photograph, Thomas J. Lockwood. His attitude is one of deep and somber reflection. One should sense that he has been sitting thus for some time. After several beats (as many as the traffic will bear) he is roused by the sound of laughter (Joe and Fran) approaching the outside door. Their laughter must not be hysterical, hilarious or feigned, but rather of the low key and genuine sort indicative of two people in intimate, practiced, and comfortable relationship.

FRAN: *(Offstage.)* You know something? You ought to keep a diary, write down everything that happens there every night.

JOE: *(Offstage.)* Why?

FRAN: *(Offstage.)* You might have a best-seller.

JOE: *(Offstage.)* Who'd believe it?

(She laughs. A key turns in the door. As they enter both carry bags of groceries.)

JOE: We can use Chuck's boat on Sunday—you want to?

FRAN: Yes.

JOE: I'm beat.

FRAN: So am I, and we start rehearsing the new show tomorrow. I think—

(She turns on the central light switch. They discover Lockwood. Guilt, fear, and anger flood the room. The moment lengthens ominously.)

LOCKWOOD: Good evening.

FRAN: *(Numb, deeply shaken.)* You always phone…Why didn't you phone?
  (Lockwood maintains his silence, allows her confusion to work in his behalf.)
FRAN: *(Almost hysterical.)* Why didn't you phone?
LOCKWOOD: I thought I'd surprise you.
JOE: *(As gracefully as possible.)* Aren't you going to introduce me?
FRAN: *(Distraught.)* What?
JOE: Introduce me.
FRAN: Yes—of course: Thomas Lockwood—Joe Grady.
JOE: How do you do?
  (Lockwood doesn't reply, regards him disdainfully; looks away.)
JOE: Can you speak a little louder?
LOCKWOOD: I can—
FRAN: *(To avoid the fight that is imminent, she appeals to Joe.)* Thanks for
  bringing me home.
  (Joe turns from Lockwood to her.)
FRAN: Thanks for bringing me home.
JOE: *(He rejects her appeal for an instant, then gives in.)* My pleasure…Well, I
  guess I better shove off.
FRAN: Yes.
JOE: I think I'll pay Chuck a visit.
  (She just looks at him.)
JOE: *(He turns to Lockwood.)* Nice meeting you.
  (Lockwood doesn't reply.)
JOE: *(To Fran.)* Take care of yourself.
FRAN: I will.
JOE: *(To Fran.)* Ta-ta. *(With obvious reluctance and misgivings, he departs.)*
  (Fran and Lockwood regard each other.)
FRAN: I've been living with him.
  (He offers no reaction.)
FRAN: I've been living with him.
LOCKWOOD: Did I ask?
FRAN: I was so lonely.
LOCKWOOD: You don't owe me any explanations.
FRAN: If he hadn't come along, I don't know what I would have done.
LOCKWOOD: *I don't want any explanations.*
FRAN: It wasn't anything serious.
  (He just looks at her.)
FRAN: *It wasn't—I swear.*
LOCKWOOD: Prove it.

FRAN: How?

LOCKWOOD: I'm on my way to Europe for a month. Pack your bags and come with me.

FRAN: The same old deal?

LOCKWOOD: The same old deal.

FRAN: No.

LOCKWOOD: Then it *is* serious.

FRAN: You know it isn't.

LOCKWOOD: Good-bye.

> *(He would leave. She blocks his way.)*

FRAN: You don't give a damn about him! You're just using it to make me do what you want!

LOCKWOOD: *Good-bye. (He brushes by her, moves toward the door.)*

FRAN: *(Frightened, confused.)* All right…All right.

LOCKWOOD: You'll come with me?

FRAN: *(Joylessly.)* Don't I always?

LOCKWOOD: *(Her surrender alters his mood abruptly. Confident, elated, he moves to her.)* There's my girl. We'll have a grand time in Europe.

FRAN: Whoopee.

LOCKWOOD: We can stay longer than a month if you like.

FRAN: *(Unconsoled.)* Let's not talk any more, let's just go.

LOCKWOOD: Such a sad face. Charming holiday this is going to be.

FRAN: I'm sorry—it's the best I can do right now.

LOCKWOOD: It's not good enough. Before we leave here I want to see you smile.

FRAN: Stop.

LOCKWOOD: Now, how do we accomplish that?

FRAN: *Stop it.*

LOCKWOOD: I have it. *(He extracts a gift box such as a wrist watch might come in from his pocket, proffers it.)*

FRAN: *(Suspiciously.)* What's that?

LOCKWOOD: Take it and see.

FRAN: *(Moving to him, still suspicious.)* What is it? *(Mistrustful, she takes the box from him, opens it, removes a document; regards it. It takes a moment for her to focus on the page. When she does so, her face registers shock. She glances at Lockwood incredulously.)*

LOCKWOOD: That's right.

FRAN: *(She returns to the document; scans it feverishly; finds what she's looking for. Reading from the document.)* "…is hereby given and granted a final and absolute divorce from Defendant Thomas J. Lockwood."…Oh, my God. Oh, my God. *(Overwhelmed.)* You did it—you really did it.

LOCKWOOD: Didn't I say I would.

FRAN: *(Beside herself.)* How come? I mean why now? I don't know what I mean. So what happens now?

LOCKWOOD: You pack your bag and come with me: London, Paris, Stockholm—any place you like for as long as you like.

FRAN: A honeymoon?

LOCKWOOD: A honeymoon.

FRAN: Don't they usually come after weddings?

LOCKWOOD: I know a beautiful little church in Paris.

FRAN: I'm sure it's the most beautiful church in the world, but if it's all the same to you I'd like to be married here.

LOCKWOOD: You still don't trust me.

FRAN: *You* I trust—*airplanes* I'm not so sure about. If we crash, I want to go down as Mrs. Thomas Lockwood.

LOCKWOOD: That's a cheerful thought.

FRAN: Indulge me—okay?

LOCKWOOD: Okay. Now start packing.

FRAN: What's the rush?

LOCKWOOD: I have us booked on a seven A.M. flight to New York.

FRAN: It'll take me hours.

LOCKWOOD: One suitcase—essentials only.

FRAN: I have things at the cleaner's—and what about my job?

LOCKWOOD: One suitcase—essentials only. That's an order.

FRAN: Leave everything—just like that?

LOCKWOOD: Everything—just like that. Now get packing.

FRAN: Aye, aye, sir.

LOCKWOOD: On the double.

FRAN: Yes, *sir.* My head's spinning. *(She takes a suitcase from the living room closet.)*

LOCKWOOD: Before I forget—come here.
(She moves to him. He takes a ring box from his pocket, opens it, extracts a diamond ring. The diamond is huge.)

FRAN: Holy hat!

LOCKWOOD: May I? *(He takes the ring, slips it on her finger.)*

FRAN: Don't tell me how many carats or I'll be scared to wear it.

LOCKWOOD: All right.

FRAN: How many?

LOCKWOOD: Ten.

FRAN: One for each year?

LOCKWOOD: *Get packing.*

FRAN: Essentials only.

LOCKWOOD: Essentials only.

FRAN: *(Regarding the ring.)* It's beautiful.

LOCKWOOD: I'm glad you like it.

FRAN: Thanks.

LOCKWOOD: You're more than welcome. Get going!

FRAN: *(She enters the bedroom; lays the open suitcase on the bed; contemplates her diamond; buffs it on her sleeve; starts to pack.)* How do you define "essential"?

LOCKWOOD: Anything you can't duplicate in New York.

FRAN: *(As she packs.)* This isn't really happening, is it?

LOCKWOOD: No.

FRAN: It's a dream.

LOCKWOOD: That's right.

FRAN: I don't know what I'm doing...Hey.

LOCKWOOD: What?

FRAN: How did you know I didn't change my mind— that I'd still marry you?

LOCKWOOD: I didn't.

FRAN: You must have been pretty confident—getting the divorce and all.

LOCKWOOD: Let's say I had a reasonable expectation.

FRAN: What you mean is you felt you had a "lock."

LOCKWOOD: You said it—I didn't.

FRAN: I should have played harder to get.

LOCKWOOD: That isn't your style.

FRAN: I wish it was.

LOCKWOOD: What does he do for a living—your friend?

FRAN: He's a musician—a piano player.

LOCKWOOD: A good one?

FRAN: Average...Say something every once in a while so I know you're there.

LOCKWOOD: I'm here.

FRAN: I'm *not* dreaming.

LOCKWOOD: Want me to pinch you?

FRAN: Later...What about the rest of my clothes and things?

LOCKWOOD: I'll have somebody pick them up...Where does he play?

FRAN: Joe?

LOCKWOOD: Yes.

FRAN: Downtown…Is a travel iron "essential"?

LOCKWOOD: No…How did you get mixed up with someone like that?

FRAN: What do you mean "someone like that?"

LOCKWOOD: A loser.

FRAN: What makes you think he's a loser?

LOCKWOOD: Isn't he?…Well, isn't he?

FRAN: *(It's never occurred to her before.)* Yes, I guess he is.

LOCKWOOD: How did you get mixed up with him?

FRAN: I guess I was sick and tired of winners.

LOCKWOOD: I'll take that as a compliment…How are you doing?

FRAN: Almost finished…Hey.

LOCKWOOD: What?

FRAN: This furniture belongs to *me*—and it's worth something.

LOCKWOOD: Leave it for what's-his-name.

FRAN: He wouldn't take it.

LOCKWOOD: Why not?

FRAN: His pride wouldn't allow it.

LOCKWOOD: No talent and lots of pride.

FRAN: I didn't say "*no* talent"—I said "average."

LOCKWOOD: Pardon me.

FRAN: So what about it—the furniture?

LOCKWOOD: I'll have someone dispose of it.

FRAN: *(She locks the suitcase.)* Ready when you are.

LOCKWOOD: That was fast.

FRAN: I've had ten years' practice. How about that chapel by the New Frontier?

LOCKWOOD: Fine.

FRAN: *(She takes a last, sweeping look of the room.)* So long, drapes I made myself. So long sofa. So long chairs. *(To Lockwood.)* Let's go.

LOCKWOOD: Aren't you forgetting something?

FRAN: What?

LOCKWOOD: What's-his-name. Shouldn't you let him know what happened?

FRAN: Of course. What's the matter with me!

LOCKWOOD: I suggest you leave him a note.

FRAN: That's very considerate of you—she said suspiciously.

LOCKWOOD: "In defeat: defiance. In victory: magnamity."

FRAN: I'll just be a minute. *(She starts for the bedroom.)*

LOCKWOOD: What are you doing?

FRAN: I'm going to phone—it's easier.

(She blows him a kiss; closes the door, sits on the bed; picks up the phone; dials. We hear one ring, then someone picks up the receiver at the other end.)

CHUCK'S VOICE: *(Offstage.)* Hello.

FRAN: Chuck?

CHUCK'S VOICE: *(Offstage.)* Speaking.

FRAN: It's Fran. Is Joe there?

chuck's voice: *(Offstage.)* I'll get him.

(While she waits for Joe to come to the phone, Fran holds her left hand up, surveys her diamond ring from various angles.)

JOE'S VOICE: *(Offstage.)* Duffy's Tavern—Archie the manager speaking.

(The sound of his voice has a tremendous impact on her. Startled by her reaction, she just holds the receiver, regards it.)

JOE'S VOICE: Anybody there?…Hello America…*Hey.*

FRAN: *(With great effort.)* Joe?

JOE'S VOICE: *(Offstage.)* Hi.

FRAN: *(Fighting to gain control of herself.)* Is that you?

JOE'S VOICE: *(Offstage.)* As far as I know.

FRAN: *(Her confusion growing.)* What?

JOE'S VOICE: *(Offstage.)* I said…forget it. So what's the good word?

FRAN: Joe?

JOE'S VOICE: *(Offstage.)* Yes?

FRAN: *(Piteously.)* *Oh,* Joe.

JOE'S VOICE: *(Offstage.)* What is it?

(Unable to speak, she rests the receiver on her lap.)

JOE'S VOICE: What's the matter?…What's going on?… Are you still there?… Hey…Hey—

(She hangs up; sits a moment more in dazed reaction; rises like a somnambulist; enters the living room.)

LOCKWOOD: Mission accomplished?

(She offers no reaction.)

LOCKWOOD: What's the matter?

(No reaction.)

LOCKWOOD: Something wrong?

(No reaction.)

LOCKWOOD: What is it?…He took it badly—said something that upset you…*What is it?*

FRAN: I can't do it.

LOCKWOOD: Can't call him?

FRAN: Can't marry you.

LOCKWOOD: What?

FRAN: I can't marry you.

LOCKWOOD: What are you talking about?

FRAN: His voice on the phone…I couldn't say good-bye.

LOCKWOOD: *What?*

FRAN: Why did you make me do it? Why didn't we just leave?

LOCKWOOD: That's insane.

FRAN: You're telling me.

LOCKWOOD: Two minutes ago you were ready to walk out that door—

FRAN: Never mind *that*—What do I do *now?*

LOCKWOOD: Very simple: You're coming with me just as we planned.

FRAN: I can't.

LOCKWOOD: *(Picking up her suitcase.) Just as we planned*…come on.

FRAN: Of all the lousy, rotten, stupid, damn luck.

LOCKWOOD: Come on.

FRAN: Don't you understand? I want to—but I can't.

LOCKWOOD: A month from now you won't remember his name.

FRAN: You think so?

LOCKWOOD: I'm positive. Come.

FRAN: *(She starts toward the door; stops.)* It's no use.

LOCKWOOD: Come!

FRAN: When you used to order me like that, I did whatever you said—couldn't help myself. Now it means nothing. I wish it *did.*

LOCKWOOD: Fran, look—I've divorced my wife, disrupted my life.

FRAN: That rhymes. *(Hastily.)* Sorry.

LOCKWOOD: If this whole thing's a joke, it's in very poor taste.

FRAN: If this whole thing's a joke, it's on *me.*

LOCKWOOD: A second-rate piano player—that's wonderful.

FRAN: Don't.

LOCKWOOD: Still the schoolgirl I met on that train: love conquers all.

FRAN: *Don't.*

LOCKWOOD: You stay with him and this is the most your world will ever be!

FRAN: *So do something*—help me!

LOCKWOOD: *(He moves close to her.)* Is it all right if I sit here, kid?
    (She regards him.)

LOCKWOOD: Well?

FRAN: Help yourself, Mister.
    (He embraces her. She wants to respond; tries to; can't; breaks it off.)

FRAN: It's no use…it's no good.

LOCKWOOD: *Don't say that!*...Don't say that.

FRAN: I think you better go.

LOCKWOOD: Before I give you my blessing?

FRAN: You hate me.

LOCKWOOD: I'm trying not to.

FRAN: Go ahead—I guess I deserve it.

LOCKWOOD: *He must be exceptional in bed! (He is immediately embarrassed by what he's just said.)*

FRAN: What a way for us to end.

LOCKWOOD: End? What makes you think it's ending? *(He cups her face as though she were an errant child.)* You've just picked up a bad little habit that you have to get over. *(He kisses her gently.)*

FRAN: *(Repelled by the touch of his lips, she involuntarily averts her head.)* Don't.

LOCKWOOD: *(His grip tightens; his voice for all its coolness betrays desperation.)* A bad little habit that you have to get over—and I'm going to help you. *(He tries to compel a kiss; she resists.)*

FRAN: Stop!

(The struggle escalates. In danger of being overpowered, she screams.)

FRAN: Stop it!

(Her shout brings Lockwood to his senses. He releases her. She regards him for an instant as though she'd never seen him before, then exits into the bedroom, locking the door behind her. Lockwood takes a moment to collect himself; resumes his dignity as best he can; goes to the bedroom door, turns the handle. Finding the door locked, his dignity vanishes.)

LOCKWOOD: Open this door! *Open it!* All right, I'm sorry—I apologize. Now, open it...You dropped a bombshell on me. What was I supposed to do—pat you on the head and go?...Isn't this a bit childish? I mean, isn't it?...I won't touch you—my word of honor...I can't say what I have to say through a door. What's the matter—afraid I'll convince you you're making a mistake? It wouldn't be hard...If I walk out now, it's for keeps. No "Call me when you come to your senses." No "Remember me if you ever need a friend."...This is it then. Ten years wiped out just like that. Bermuda, Mexico, Hawaii. All those places, all those times. They never happened—they're *nothing* to you... *Well, to me they're something!*... This will hand you a laugh but I'm going to say it anyway...If I could relive any day in my life, *any* day, it would be a Sunday we spent together in New York...It was cold and rainy—we never left the room...Ring a bell?...So much for romance. Perhaps we can interest you in something a little more practical. Consider our ages. You're twenty-eight—I'm fifty-two. I drink too much, work too hard, play too hard. Ten years from now you could be one of the wealthier widows in the nation...Well, what do you say?...I guess that brings us to good-bye...Good-bye...Not even a good-bye?...You know one of the guiding principles of my life? "What I can't get—I don't want." It's a must for those who would survive and above all *I* am a survivor. "What I can't get—I don't want." Just saying it makes me feel better. I begin to see flaws in you that I have previously been blinded to. For instance—your intellect. Have you and I ever talked about anything but love? Then there's the matter of your slothfulness. Who but a sloth could live the way you've lived all these years. And your looks—*yes*, even your looks! Peek in the mirror. That's not an eighteen-year-old girl looking back at you. That's a woman whose chances are running out—a woman who can't afford many more mistakes...Having said all that, I now, for the last time, ask you, beg you, to open that door and come with me...I now depart.

(He starts away—is about to exit when he hears the bedroom door open. He turns hopefully as Fran enters the living room.)

FRAN: The ring. *(She removes the ring from her finger; proffers it.)*

LOCKWOOD: Keep it.

FRAN: I can't. *(She puts the ring in his hand.)*

LOCKWOOD: Do you remember that Sunday in New York.

FRAN: Yes.

LOCKWOOD: It *was* a great day—wasn't it?

FRAN: The greatest.

LOCKWOOD: Take care of yourself, kid.

FRAN: You too, Mister.

(Lockwood exits. Fran looks after him a moment; then, stunned by all that has happened, she sits and is trying to sort the pieces when there is a knock at the door. Instantly alert, she listens. The knock is repeated.)

FRAN: Who is it?

JOE'S VOICE: *(Offstage.)* The egg man.

(Fran thrusts her suitcase into the closet. Joe knocks again.)

FRAN: Just a minute. *(She composes herself; opens the door.)*

JOE: You sounded funny on the phone—I got worried.

FRAN: I'm all right.

JOE: *(Peering about.)* Where's himself?

FRAN: Gone.

JOE: What happened? What happened?

FRAN: *You really want to know?*

JOE: Only if you want to tell me.

(*She appraises him intently, trying to determine how much truth he can handle.*)

JOE: Well?

FRAN: (*Her decision made; turning away.*) He wanted to resume on the same old basis. I said no.

JOE: What did *he* say to *that?*

FRAN: He said he couldn't live without me. He said he was going to go home and start divorce proceedings immediately.

JOE: What did *you* say?

FRAN: I said I'd believe it when he brought me the decree—put it in my hand.

JOE: What did *he* say?

FRAN: He said he would.

JOE: Congratulations.

(*She turns to him.*)

JOE: For sticking to your guns.

FRAN: Thanks.

JOE: What did he say about *me?*

FRAN: Nothing.

JOE: It must have been obvious I was living here.

FRAN: It didn't seem to bother him.

JOE: That's an insult.

FRAN: I'm sorry.

JOE: Seriously—I'm relieved: I was afraid I might have loused things up for you.

FRAN: You can rest easy.

JOE: What happens now?

FRAN: I wait.

JOE: How long will it take him—to get the divorce?

FRAN: I don't know.

JOE: A couple of months, probably.

FRAN: Probably.

JOE: Well, I guess I better start packing.

FRAN: Packing?

JOE: Packing.

FRAN: What for?

JOE: I don't think you should press your luck.

FRAN: What do you mean?

JOE: He may not have said anything but I'm sure he didn't like the idea of me being here.

FRAN: I see.

JOE: I'd hate to be the cause of any trouble.

FRAN: If you want to go—go, but spare me the *noble* crap.

JOE: Are you saying I can stay—that we can go on the way we have been?

FRAN: I'm saying go if you want to go—*stay* if you want to *stay*.

JOE: It doesn't worry you that he might not like it?

FRAN: All right, he *doesn't* like it. He was furious about you! That's why he's getting the divorce—because you made him so jealous. *Feel better now?*

JOE: In other words by staying I'm really *helping* the cause.

FRAN: Enormously.

JOE: I'll have my money in another six or seven weeks. It would be silly to get a place of my own for six or seven weeks...Wouldn't it?

FRAN: You're a big boy—you have to make those decisions for yourself.

JOE: You're not just being polite? I mean if you didn't want me to stay, you'd say so.

FRAN: Do it or get off the pot!

JOE: Same ground rules? Both of us free to come and go—no strings?

FRAN: Yes, God damn it.

JOE: I'll stay.

FRAN: Hoo-ray. *(She breaks down; throws herself on the sofa; weeps in a mood of anger and despair.)*
(He moves to comfort her.)

JOE: Don't...You'll see—everything's going to work out fine: Before you know it, you'll be Mrs. Thomas Lockwood.
(She wails all the harder.)

JOE: How would you like a nice warm bath?

FRAN: No.

JOE: I'll scrub your back and anything else you like.

FRAN: *No.*

JOE: As a famous authority once said: "Tomorrow it will hurt less. The next day a little less. And so on—and so on—and so on."

FRAN: You're a son-of-a-bitch.

JOE: Did I ever say I wasn't? Come on, now. Get undressed—take your bath.
(Curtain.)

END OF ACT I

ACT II
SCENE I

Time: The present; evening. At rise: There is a piano in the living room. Other changes in the furnishings should indicate the passage of two years. Joe is intent on the radio account of a ballgame. Fran is at the sewing machine working on a skirt.

ANNOUNCER'S VOICE: The count on Mays is three and two...Drysdale checks the runner on first...pumps...throws...Willie tags it—a liner to left that's going, going...*It's gone!*
(Joe grimaces.)
ANNOUNCER'S VOICE: A home run for Willie Mays. His twenty-fourth of the season—and the Giants go ahead three to two.
JOE: *(Furious, he snaps the radio off.)* Damn!
FRAN: I thought you were a Giant fan.
JOE: I am.
FRAN: So why the long face?
JOE: *(Screwing his face into a smile.)* That better?
FRAN: Pardon me. *(She returns to her sewing.)*
JOE: "You've got to cut down on those intermissions."...Three customers in the whole joint and he hollers because I take five extra minutes.
FRAN: You going to start on *that* again?
JOE: Pardon *me.*
FRAN: Besides, you really can't blame him.
JOE: "But soft."
FRAN: Business is off—you said so yourself. He's nervous.
JOE: Is that any reason to jump on *me?*
FRAN: I can't imagine Tony jumping on anyone—*you* least of all.
JOE: Now I'm a liar.
FRAN: Look—assume the worst: He jumped on you. You've been playing there three years. He's a dear sweet man who loves you like a son. So he criticizes you once in three years? So he's entitled.
JOE: I should have known whose side *you'd* take.
FRAN: Fasten your seat belts, folks. *(She returns to her sewing.)*
JOE: Just because I don't come home and complain doesn't mean that job is any bed of roses.
FRAN: There's a good picture at the drive-in.
JOE: The fact is I have to put up with a *lot* of crap.

FRAN: Elizabeth Taylor and Richard Burton.

JOE: And I've had just about all I can take.

FRAN: I move we go to the movies. All in favor?

JOE: No.

FRAN: Why not?

JOE: I've got an idea for a song I want to work on.

FRAN: We so rarely get the same night off.

JOE: Maybe that's fortunate.

FRAN: Maybe it is. *(She returns to her sewing.)*

JOE: Cut down on the intermissions...The day I leave here I'm going to tell that "dear sweet" man what I really think of him. *(He looks at her for a reaction.)*
(She offers none.)

JOE: It won't be long now...till I leave.
(Still no reaction from her.)

JOE: I've got thirty-six hundred dollars.
(Still no reaction.)

JOE: What do you say to that?
(No reaction.)

JOE: *Well, what do you say?*

FRAN: No comment.

JOE: What's that mean?

FRAN: It means that since whatever I say would be misinterpreted, I choose to say nothing.

JOE: That's a new twist. *(He turns on the radio.)*

ANNOUNCER'S VOICE: McCovey scores—and the Giants lead four to two in the top half of the ninth. That—
(Joe all but pulls the knob loose as he turns the radio off. Fran, studiously ignoring him, concentrates on her sewing.)

JOE: You're dying to know why I'm so steamed up, but you won't ask.

FRAN: If you want to tell me, you will.

JOE: How philosophical you can be when you think you've got a "lock."

FRAN: What's that supposed to mean?

JOE: She said naively.

FRAN: Can I make a suggestion?

JOE: Be my guest.

FRAN: Go to bed—get a good night's sleep.

JOE: Wouldn't it *frost* you if I *did.*
(She gives up—returns to the sewing.)

JOE: The "thirty-six hundred" surprised you. You had no idea I was getting that close again.

(No reaction from her.)

JOE: What did you mean before about my misinterpreting anything you might say?

(No reaction.)

JOE: Why would I misinterpret you?

(No reaction. Determined to provoke a response, he goes to the piano—plays the first eight bars of "Moonglow.")

JOE: I wrote it this afternoon—what do you think?

(No reaction.)

JOE: Aren't you going to say it sounds familiar?

(No reaction.)

JOE: It's a good thing Irving Berlin wasn't married to *you*.

FRAN: You're not married to me either.

JOE: Thank heaven for *small* favors.

(That does it: Fran rises purposefully, goes to the bedroom.)

JOE: Where are you going?

(No reply.)

JOE: Where are you going?!

FRAN: To the movies.

(She prepares to go. He looks on with mounting concern till she is about to leave; then.)

JOE: Don't go.

(The note of genuine entreaty in his voice causes her to hesitate, regard him.)

JOE: I did a stupid thing today.

FRAN: What?

JOE: What Tony said about the intermissions, plus some other things—it got me down…

FRAN: Go on.

JOE: I felt if I stayed here another day I'd lose my mind.

FRAN: What did you do?

JOE: I took my money out of the bank. All I needed was fourteen hundred dollars more and the Giants were six to five.

FRAN: You bet all that money on the game?

JOE: I wish I *had*—I'd be leaving here tomorrow.

FRAN: I don't understand.

JOE: I went up to the counter—but I couldn't do it. The words stuck in my throat.

FRAN: You didn't bet?

JOE: Not a penny.

FRAN: Where is it—the money?

(*Joe extracts a packet of bills from his pocket; lays them on the table.*)

JOE: Thirty-six hundred and the night is young. Help me?

FRAN: (*Sings.*) "Sweet Adeline, my Adeline…"

JOE: It'll take more than that.

FRAN: What did you have in mind?

JOE: I want you to do me a favor.

FRAN: What is it?

JOE: I want you to take the money and—

FRAN: No!

JOE: I don't trust myself.

FRAN: *The answer is no.*

JOE: I want the money to be somewhere where I can't get it.

FRAN: *No!*

JOE: I want you to put it in your account—keep it till I have five thousand.

FRAN: No-no-no-no-no-no-no.

JOE: Why?

FRAN: I can't.

JOE: If you don't, I'm going to blow the whole thing again—I can feel it.

FRAN: Why me?

JOE: I don't trust anyone else.

FRAN: What about Chuck?

JOE: What are you afraid of?

FRAN: Or Tony.

JOE: *What are you afraid of?*

FRAN: I don't know.

JOE: Could it be you want me to fail again?

FRAN: Don't.

JOE: Want me to fail—but don't want to be held responsible?

FRAN: *No.*

JOE: *Prove it!*

(*She regards him.*)

JOE: If you're really on my side—help me. Take the money…Well?

FRAN: (*Resigned.*) All right.

JOE: You'll put it in your account?

FRAN: Yes.

JOE: You won't give me a cent until I have the whole five thousand?

FRAN: Once that money is in the bank, you won't see it again until the day you leave.

JOE: I really think you mean it.

FRAN: Wait and see.

JOE: *(Indicates the money.)* Take it.

(She makes no move.)

JOE: Go on.

FRAN: I can't put it in the bank until morning.

JOE: I don't want to look at it.

(She is still reluctant.)

JOE: *Go on.*

·*(She picks up the money.)*

JOE: Thirty-six hundred even.

(She starts toward the bedroom.)

JOE: Where are you going?

FRAN: To put it away.

(He regards her uncertainly.)

FRAN: You said you didn't want to look at it. *(She leaves the living room; passes through the bedroom; disappears into the bathroom.)*

JOE: I'll be out of here by Christmas…If the tips pick up, it could be Thanksgiving… Wouldn't that be something to be thankful for?…I said wouldn't that be something to be thankful for?

FRAN'S VOICE: *(Offstage.)* Yes.

JOE: What are you doing? What are you doing?

(Fran emerges from the bathroom, reenters the living room.)

JOE: I hope you put it in a safe place.

FRAN: Yes.

JOE: Lot of robberies lately.

FRAN: It's in a safe place.

JOE: Where's my receipt?

(She frowns.)

JOE: Just kidding.

(She returns to the sewing machine.)

JOE: It's a real load off my mind. Thanks.

FRAN: You're welcome.

JOE: Of course I won't really rest easy until it's in the bank.

FRAN: Neither will I.

JOE: Why?

FRAN: As you said—there have been a lot of robberies.

JOE: What time does the bank open?

FRAN: Ten o'clock.

JOE: *(Glancing at his watch.)* Thirteen to go.

FRAN: What?

JOE: Thirteen hours to go till the bank opens. That's a long time. A lot could happen...For instance, I might change my mind—ask for my money back...Would you give it to me?

FRAN: Didn't I just say I wouldn't?

JOE: You said that once it was in the bank you wouldn't. That doesn't cover the next thirteen hours.

FRAN: Your imagination is working overtime.

(He crosses to her; compels her to give him her attention; confronts her in deadly earnest.)

JOE: I've changed my mind—give me my money.

(She just looks at him.)

JOE: Give me my money.

(She continues to regard him. After a moment, he smiles.)

JOE: Now I know my money's safe.

(She still looks at him, expression unchanged.)

JOE: Don't look so upset—I was just testing you. How about a little double solitaire? *(Takes two packs of cards from shelf.)*

(She regards him uncertainly.)

JOE: You're always pestering me to play...Well? Choose your weapon.

(When she doesn't choose, he forces a deck on her.)

JOE: Come on, come on. *(He removes the sewing machine from the table.)* Ones or threes?

FRAN: I don't care.

JOE: Let's live dangerously: ones. I'll play you for the thirty-six hundred... Just kidding.

(They begin to lay out the cards.)

JOE: I feel good tonight...Feel I really have it licked...It's what I should have done from the start—let *you* hold the money.

(They finish laying out the cards.)

JOE: Ready?

FRAN: Yes.

JOE: *Go.*

(They start to play. He goes at it with feverish intensity. She proceeds methodically, regards him curiously from time to time.)

JOE: That time I had over four thousand saved...Lost the whole thing...

Wouldn't have happened if you had the money...*Couldn't* have happened...Banks shouldn't allow you to draw money when you're drunk. *(He puts a card out.)* First blood for our side. *(He follows up with three more.)* And again...And again...And again.

(The game continues. Both put cards out. He beats her to one.)

JOE: You'll have to move faster than that. *(He hits another three-card streak.)* Looks like my night.

(The game proceeds.)

JOE: If I had let you hold the money in the beginning, I'd be well established... *(Each of the following words underlines the putting out of a card.)* in...New...York...by...now! *(He regards her triumphantly.) Am I hot or am I hot?*

(She makes no comment; starts to turn a card. He stays her hand.)

JOE: Wait. *(He squeezes his eyes shut; concentrates.)* The next card you turn will be...will be...*a jack. (He opens his eyes, releases her hand.)* Go on.

(She just looks at him.)

JOE: Turn it over.

(She turns the card. His face lights jubilantly.)

JOE: What did I tell you?

FRAN: You said it would be a jack.

JOE: I said queen.

FRAN: You said jack.

JOE: I said queen.

(Realizing it would be futile to argue, she resumes the game.)

JOE: All afternoon I was calling the dice like that. Stood by this one table and could have made a fortune if I'd been betting...Fellow threw four elevens in a row. I called the turn every time. Know what the odds against that are?...Then the ball game...I knew the Giants would win.

FRAN: *(Turning her last card.)* I'm through.

JOE: *(He turns his remaining cards. Rising.)* You sort them.

(While she separates the cards, he goes to the bedroom entrance, peers in.)

JOE: I hope you know what you're talking about when you say the money is in a safe place...Anyone could walk in here.

FRAN: I think you won.

(He turns to her.)

FRAN: I think you won the game.

JOE: Was there any doubt about it?

FRAN: Want to play another?

JOE: What for? I couldn't lose if I tried.

(She shuffles the cards, begins to lay out a game of solitaire for herself. He goes to the radio, turns it on.)

ANNOUNCER'S VOICE: That wraps it up from Dodger Stadium: The Giants lose a heartbreaker on Haller's three-run homer in the bottom of the ninth. Final score, the Los Angeles Dodgers, five—The San Francisco Giants, four. Winning pitcher—

(Joe turns the radio off, regards it dumbly.)

FRAN: If you'd bet on the Giants, you'd be broke. Still think this is your lucky day?

JOE: But I didn't bet on them…Something stopped me. *(He has it! Whirls to her.)* I said I couldn't lose if I tried. That proves it!

(She resumes her game. He begins to pace excitedly.)

JOE: You know something—I'm being too rigid…What I should do is take a little of my money and see what happens…One hot hand and I can leave here tomorrow. If I lose—no harm done. *(He stops, regards her.)* Well?

(She goes on playing.)

JOE: Well?

FRAN: Well what?

JOE: I want some of my money.

FRAN: No.

JOE: Just a little.

FRAN: No.

JOE: Two hundred.

FRAN: No.

JOE: *One* hundred.

FRAN: No.

JOE: Now, look—

FRAN: *You* look: You're not getting a *hundred*—you're not getting a *cent!* *(She resumes her game.)*

JOE: No doubt about it—I made a wise choice.

(She regards him.)

JOE: I was just testing again.

FRAN: *Bull. (She returns to her game.)*

JOE: I was and I'll prove it…If I really wanted the money—would I have to ask for it?…I'd just go in there and take it…Of course I'd have to find it first— but would that be so difficult? *(He moves to the bedroom entrance, peers.)* Where would you hide it in a room this size?…Knowing you and the way your mind works, I can tell you right now where it is…It's in that cookie jar or whatever you call it, isn't it?...Of course it is. And just to prove it... *(He enters the bedroom; picks up the jar from the vanity; turns it upside down. Empty.)* You fooled me. I was sure it would be here. *(She concentrates determinedly on the cards.)*

JOE: Nothing I like better than a challenge.

(She goes on playing. He deliberately drops the jar. It shatters against the floor. She whirls to him.)

JOE: I'm terribly sorry. I know how fond you were of it. I'll try to be more careful. *(He turns, surveys the bedroom.)* Now let's see...Under the rug?...No...The bed?...No...The night stand?...Too obvious...One of those fancy mugs your grandmother gave you?...Of course—just the place...That one.

(He takes one of the mugs from the shelf; drops it to the floor. It breaks. Fran winces; covers her ears.)

JOE: Would you believe that anyone could be so clumsy?...If my curiosity wasn't so aroused, I'd give up. *(He regards the mugs.)* Now let's see— what's the next most likely one?

(Fran can take no more; rises, brushes by him; disappears into the bathroom; reappears with a tissue box from which she extracts the money.)

FRAN; *(Proffering the money.)* Here.

JOE: Well, aren't you the clever miss?

FRAN: Take it.

JOE: I don't want it.

FRAN: *Take it.*

JOE: I just wanted to know where it was.

FRAN: Take it!

JOE: You know what will happen if I do.

FRAN: *Take it! (She throws the money. It strikes his chest, falls to the floor.)*

JOE: You disappoint me. I thought you'd hold out a good deal longer. *(He retrieves the money; regards her.)* Why so sad? If past performance is any indication, I should be broke and crying on your shoulder by morning. *(He exits. Lights down.)*

SCENE II

Time: Dawn the next morning. At rise: Fran, in nightgown and robe, is asleep on the sofa. A key turns. The door opens. Joe, disheveled and spent, enters; closes the door; sees Fran; regards her a moment; pours a drink; sits in a chair opposite her; studies her thoughtfully. She stirs; opens her eyes.

JOE: *(Raising his glass to her.)* Top of the morning.
    (She stares at him, trying to focus.)
JOE: When I snap my fingers, you'll feel rested and refreshed. *(He snaps his fingers.)* How do you feel?
FRAN: How do *you* feel?
JOE: What's the opposite of rested and refreshed?
FRAN: You lost.
JOE: That's what I like about you—no beating around the bush.
FRAN: Everything?
JOE: Give you three guesses.
FRAN: I'm sorry.
JOE: Easy come—easy go.
FRAN: Want something to eat? I have those sweet rolls.
JOE: I knew you would. As I was coming up the stairs, I said to myself, "I'll bet she has those sweet rolls."
FRAN: I'll run the water—you'll take a warm bath first.
JOE: Like I always do?
FRAN: Yes.
JOE: And you'll scrub my back like you always do?
FRAN: Yes.
JOE: Then I'll go to bed, and you'll cradle me.
FRAN: Yes.
    (He chuckles.)
FRAN: You'll be all right.
    (He continues to chuckle.)
FRAN: Think of the other times.
    (The chuckles become a laugh.)
FRAN: Will you please stop that?
    (His laughter grows.)
FRAN: Stop it!
JOE: *(Soberly.)* Sorry.
FRAN: I'll run the water. *(She starts from the room.)*

JOE: "Come unto me, all ye who labor and are burdened, and I shall refresh thee."

(*Sensing that this is a dig at her, she turns to him. He smiles disarmingly.*)

JOE: You never saw anything like it. I went to the Sands first—was out five hundred bucks in ten minutes. From the Sands I went to the Riviera. Lost seven straight bets.

FRAN: Why talk about it?

JOE: From the Riviera to the Tropicana. Started betting the "Don't" side. An old lady with purple hair, three huge diamond rings, and a face like death, made five passes in a row. After each pass she looked at me and cackled.

FRAN: Must you?

JOE: On to the Dunes. Three hundred dollars left. Bet it all on one roll. Lost. The thirty-six hundred dollars, so painfully accumulated, was gone.

(*She starts from the room.*)

JOE: I'm not through.

(*She stops.*)

JOE: My cash was gone, but I was not without assets. That watch you gave me last Christmas. I sold it to a washroom attendant for ten dollars. Lost the ten dollars and—

FRAN: I don't want to hear any more.

JOE: I'm coming to the best part—about my car.

FRAN: You sold the car?

JOE: For two hundred dollars.

FRAN: It's worth three times that.

JOE: Not at four o'clock in the morning.

FRAN: What will you do without a car? And the watch—

JOE: —I'm not through.

FRAN: Do you know what I paid for that watch?

JOE: Will you let me finish?

FRAN: I thought that watch meant something to you.

JOE: It does.

FRAN: Then how could you throw it away?

JOE: I didn't throw it away! (*He pulls the watch from his pocket; holds it up.*) Voilà!

FRAN: You said you sold it for ten bucks.

JOE: And bought it back for twenty-five.

FRAN: I don't understand.

JOE: Sit down.

FRAN: Where did you get—?
JOE: *Sit down.*
   (She sits.)
JOE: You ready?
FRAN: For what?
JOE: I won.
   (She just looks at him.)
JOE: I'm a winner. A big winner.
FRAN: What do you mean?
JOE: I mean I took the two hundred I got for the car—went to the Sahara
   and started on the hottest hand you ever saw.
FRAN: You won?
JOE: I murdered them.
FRAN: How much?
JOE: A fortune.
FRAN: Where is it?
JOE: *(He takes money from a jacket pocket, puts it on the table.)* Here. *(Takes
   money from another pocket.)* And here. *(From another pocket.)* And here.
   (From another pocket.) And here!
   (She looks from him to the money, and back again, incredulously.)
JOE: Ever see a more beautiful sight?
FRAN: How much?
JOE: Twenty-two grand—give or take a hundred.
FRAN: I don't believe it.
JOE: Count it.
FRAN: I mean I don't believe any of this.
JOE: *(Indicates the money.)* Touch it and see.
   (She makes no move.)
JOE: It won't bite. Go on. *(He scoops up a fistful of currency, drops it in her lap.)*
   Believe it now?
FRAN: No.
JOE: Just between us—neither do I.
   (They regard the money in reverence and awe.)
JOE: Pass after pass. Fours, tens, hard ways. Everything I bet came up. The
   crowd was five deep and all betting *with* me. Every time I made a pass
   there was a roar that shook the casino. They kept changing stickmen,
   kept trying to slow the action. The crowd booed. I bet the eleven—fifty
   for me and ten for the boys. Hit it twice in a row. They changed the box-
   man. I made the same bet. Hit it again. It was like a dream. I kept ex-

pecting you to shake me and say get up. Pass after pass after pass. And then something funny happened: I started to get bored—uncomfortable. My legs began to hurt. My arms felt tired. I wanted to quit, but the crowd wouldn't let me. One old guy had tears in his eyes—said if I quit I was signing his death warrant. I wonder what that was all about. I kept shooting. Started making crazy bets: the field—anything. The wilder I bet, the more I won. The more I won, the more uneasy I became. Finally I couldn't stand it any more—cashed in. They handed me twenty-two thousand dollars—and I never felt worse in my life. Ask me why.

FRAN: Why?

JOE: Why do you think?

FRAN: I have no idea.

JOE: I'll give you a clue: I started to walk home. The closer I got—the worse I felt. A block from here I became dizzy: felt so faint I had to stop—sat on the curb. Care to take a stab at it?

FRAN: Blood pressure?

JOE: Guess again.

FRAN: I'm stumped.

JOE: Next clue—Where *was* I?

FRAN: Sitting on the curb.

JOE: There was a little stream of water flowing in the gutter from a lawn sprinkler up the block. It flowed right under my legs. I reached for my handkerchief, to mop my forehead, and pulled out a hundred dollar bill along with it. I folded the hundred dollar bill into a little boat, like when we were kids, put it in the stream and watched it float down the street until it came to a sewer and disappeared.

FRAN: I've got it now: You're crazy.

JOE: I thought of all the hungry kids in the world and tried to feel guilty— but I couldn't. The fact was that sailing that hundred dollar bill down the drain had cheered me enormously. A thought occurred: If throwing a *hundred* dollars away made me feel *that* good—how would I feel if I threw the whole twenty-two thousand away? And, believe it or not, for one instant I was seriously tempted to do it. *Ask me why.*
(She remains silent.)

JOE: Ask me why.

FRAN: Why?

JOE: Because I knew that if I didn't get rid of that money I had to leave you, and the prospect of that made me very sad…Shall I go on?
(She just looks at him.)

JOE: So there I was at forty thousand feet on the horns of a painful dilemma: The lady or the dough—take your choice. The lady: attractive, loyal, generous, sexy, and a good cook. The dough: twenty-two thousand dollars in twenties, fifties, and hundreds. What to do? My head was close to bursting. The sun was coming up. Something had to give. And then *presto*—an inspiration: Why the lady *or* the money? Why couldn't I have both? All it required was the courage to march in here and say I love you.
(He looks for a reaction.)
(She offers none.)

JOE: I said I love you.
(She just looks at him.)

JOE: Sorry, folks, but there seems to be a breakdown in the audio portion of our program.

FRAN: Go to bed—we'll talk in the morning.

JOE: It is the morning.

FRAN: You've been drinking.

JOE: *(Walking a "white line.")* Voilà!

FRAN: You're all keyed up now. Later you won't remember what you said.

JOE: Give me a piece of paper, I'll put it in writing.

FRAN: Don't.

JOE: Look, I'm making jokes because I'm scared, but I've never been more serious in my life…Well, what do you say?

FRAN: I don't want to talk about it.

JOE: Why not?

FRAN: I just don't.

JOE: This isn't going the way it's supposed to. When I say "I love you" that's your cue to leap in my arms, smother me with kisses, declare eternal devotion.

FRAN: I'm sorry—I didn't know.

JOE: Now you know—let's take it from the top: I love you.
(She just looks at him.)

JOE: *I love you.*
(No reaction.)

JOE: Look sister—do you want this part or don't you?

FRAN: I'm not sure.

JOE: What?

FRAN: I'm terribly confused. Please, can't we go to bed now—talk later?

JOE: Look, I know it's a lot to spring on you.

FRAN: Then why do it?

JOE: Because I love you.

FRAN: *Will you please stop saying that?*

JOE: I can't help myself—it's habit-forming. *(He tries various inflections.)* I *love* you…*I* love you…I love *you.* We have it in all styles—what's your pleasure?

FRAN: My pleasure is that this conversation or whatever it is should stop.

JOE: Maybe you prefer one of our foreign models: Je t'aime. Yo te amo. Ich liebe dich.

(She starts from the room. He blocks her way.)

JOE: Say it.

FRAN: Say what?

JOE: I love you.

FRAN: *I will not.*

JOE: Say it or I'll open the window and tell everyone you're my smoogie-oogie-boo.

(He reaches for her familiarly. She pulls back.)

FRAN: Keep away!

JOE: Now what kind of talk is that for a smoogie-oogie-boo?

(He stalks her. She retreats behind a chair.)

FRAN: Did it ever occur to you that this great love you suddenly feel might not be mutual?

JOE: The great love I feel is *not* sudden. I have *long* felt it, but never had the courage to acknowledge it before. And if it isn't mutual then you're the greatest actress in the world. You look beautiful this morning.

(He resumes his stalking. She retreats.)

FRAN: What about our agreement—no strings, no obligations?

JOE: It expired long ago.

FRAN: Not as far as I'm concerned.

JOE: The next thing you'll be telling me is that you're still waiting for Mr. Thomas Lockwood to come riding up on his white Cadillac.

FRAN: Maybe I am.

JOE: Get off it.

FRAN: You think I'd settle for a piano player if I could get someone like *him?*

JOE: I do.

FRAN: Give me the chance and we'll see.

JOE: You *had* the chance.

FRAN: What do you mean?

JOE: Two years ago he asked for your hand and you turned him down in favor of yours truly.

FRAN: *(Incredulous.)* How did you know that?

JOE: I didn't, until just now—but I've always suspected it.

FRAN: That is the cruelest, lousiest, filthiest thing that anyone's ever done to me.

JOE: Get dressed.

FRAN: Dressed?

JOE: Dressed.

FRAN: Why? What for?

JOE: Because you can't get married the way you are—even in Las Vegas.

FRAN: Married?

JOE: Married.

FRAN: You're bluffing.

JOE: Test me.

FRAN: Not like this—the spur of the moment.

JOE: Name the time.

FRAN: And not in Vegas.

JOE: Name the place—I'm waiting.

FRAN: I'll have to think about it.

JOE: For how long?

FRAN: *Stop pushing.*

JOE: Stop stalling.

FRAN: *Come in here and throw all this at me—who the hell do you think you are?*

JOE: If you think you can get off the hook by starting a fight—forget it. I'm in too good a mood.

FRAN: Some life—a piano player's wife.

JOE: A glorious mood.

FRAN: You know what's going to happen to you in New York?

JOE: A transcendent mood.

FRAN: You're not going to make it any better than you did here.

JOE: A mood of inexhaustible goodwill and patience.

FRAN: You stink!

JOE: Enough love-making—get dressed.

FRAN: Why can't we go on the way we have been? Why do we have to get married?

JOE: I didn't want to say it but you force me: I think I'm pregnant.

FRAN: That's *your* problem.

JOE: Have a little pity—you might find yourself in a similar predicament some day.

FRAN: I asked you a straight question—I'd like a straight answer: Why not go on as we are? Why get married?

JOE: That is a good question—worthy of an honest, courageous, and considered reply that I doubt I'm capable of—but I'll try. That rhymes. "Get on with it," she said impatiently. "Very well," he said, hurling himself from the building. I think we should get married because we feel more, do more, care more for each other than any two people I know: because it's too damn costly in time, money, and energy to maintain the delusion, underline delusion, that there are no strings, no commitments between us; because to fully appreciate the joy at hand one must have the guts to acknowledge it; because it will save embarrassment when we register at hotels or stay overnight with friends who have inquisitive children: finally because granted that marriage is a most faulty, pitiful, and wheezing institution, right now it's the only game in town and *we're* going to play it.

FRAN: That was beautiful.

JOE: *I* thought so.

FRAN: Like a pitchman selling a cure-all.

JOE: No such claim was intended.

FRAN: Getting married would change nothing.

JOE: You're sure?

FRAN: Positive.

JOE: Then why are you afraid of it?

FRAN: *I am not.*

JOE: You're scared to death.

FRAN: I am not.

JOE: Your lips tell me no no—but there's panic in your eyes.

FRAN: Stop!

JOE: You're terrified.

FRAN: *Stop!*

JOE: *What are you afraid of?*

FRAN: *(On the ropes.)* I don't know.

JOE: Say it.

FRAN: I don't know.

JOE: *(Shaking her.) Say it!*

FRAN: *If I marry you you'll leave me!*

JOE: Scudda-ho scudda-hey.

FRAN: Please let me go to bed now.

JOE: Why would I be more apt to leave you if we were married?

FRAN: If I don't go to bed, I'm going to be ill.

JOE: The witness will answer the question: Why would I be more apt to leave you if we were married?

FRAN: There'd be nothing to stay *for.*

JOE: In other words, I only stay *now* because I don't have you completely?

FRAN: *Can you guarantee you'll never leave me?*

JOE: No more than *you* can guarantee you'll never leave me.

FRAN: Then why get married?

JOE: So that while we're together we'll really be together.

FRAN: So that when we break up it will hurt that much more.

JOE: Not *"when"—if.* And *yes*—that is the risk we have to take.

FRAN: Well, I'm not taking it.

(He releases her. She sits on the sofa.)

JOE: For two years, I've slinked through these corridors as the villain in Apartment 2C. "He's the one who lives with that sweet little dancer— refuses to make an honest woman of her." Do you have any idea how many times our mutual friends have taken me aside to suggest that I was doing you wrong? And how well you played your part. Without ever saying a word, you conveyed the impression that you were my victim; hopelessly gone on me; standing by bravely just waiting for me to pop the question. Do you know how guilty I've felt for two years? And now here we are—the moment of truth. And what do we find? Me on bended knee, and you with your hands over your ears.

(She sits there, helpless, remote, frightened, cut off.)

JOE: You know what the tip-off on you should have been? The movie stars you worship—Bogart, Gable, Leslie Howard—all dead, unavailable.

(He looks for a response. She offers none, stares straight ahead as though he didn't exist.)

JOE: With Lockwood you had me to hide behind. What's your alibi this time?

(No response.)

JOE: You're going to blow the whole thing for both of us.

(No response.)

JOE: You're beginning to worry me. You really are.

(No response.)

JOE: My grandmother was born with a double caul which endowed her with great psychic power. That ability runs in the family. I'm now going to predict what your future will be if you *don't* marry me.

(No response.)

JOE: As I gaze into my crystal ball, I see a lonely old woman whose only consolation is the fact that she never gave her heart completely: no husband ever deceived or deserted her; no child ever caused her pain. As she nears the end of her life, she ponders a question: Which is worse—the heart abused or the heart unused?…Am I getting to you?

(No response.)

JOE: Wait a minute—is it possible this is all for the best—that you're really doing me the biggest favor of my life? Let's examine that. I've got twenty-two thousand dollars. I'm free as a bird. I know three girls I can call in New York just for openers. Wouldn't I be a fool to trade all that for a prospect that is dubious at best? The answer is yes. Talk about your close calls— *(He starts to gather up the money, shoots a glance at her in the process; sees something that gains his complete attention.)* Do I perceive the hint of a smile—the trace of a tear?

(She averts her head, he tries to get a face-to-face view of her. Her efforts not to break down are increasingly frantic and futile. Firmly but gently he compels her to look at him.)

JOE: Say it.

FRAN: I can't.

JOE: Say it.

FRAN: I can't.

JOE: If *I* can, *you* can. Come on.

FRAN: *(All but inaudible.)* I love you.

JOE: Louder.

FRAN: I love you.

JOE: Once for the West Coast.

FRAN: *(The dam giving way.)* I love you—God damn it.

JOE: *(Embracing her.)* That's my smoogie-oogie-boo. How do you feel?

FRAN: Scared.

JOE: "Be not afeared; the isle is full of noises." *(He takes her two hands in his.)* When I count three—close your eyes.

FRAN: What for?

JOE: We're going to memorize the details of this moment so that when we're old and inclined to rail against the world, we'll remember that we had our innings…Ready?

FRAN: Yes.

JOE: One…two…three.

(They close their eyes.)

THE END

LAST LICKS

ORIGINAL PRODUCTION

Last Licks opened at the Longacre Theatre in New York City on November 20, 1979. The play was produced by the Shubert Organization, Eugene V. Wolsk, Emanuel Azenberg, and Dasha Epstein. It was directed by Tom Conti. Settings were by William Rittman; costumes by Pearl Sommer, and Lighting by Tharon Musser. The cast was as follows:

Matt Quinlan . . . . Ed Flanders
Dennis Quinlan. . . . . J. T. Walsh
Fiona Raymond . . . . Susan Kellerman

INTRODUCTION

My mother had been dead some time. My father mouldering in that Bronx apartment.

Like most sons and daughters with a widowed parent, I encouraged him to resume his life to no avail.

One day I went to visit him unannounced. No answer to my ring, I used the key I retained. Let myself in. Something heating on the stove suggested he'd stepped out for a minute.

Browsing about this place where I'd grown up, I happened upon an alien item: A notebook bearing a woman's name. Opening it I found lesson plans. The owner a school teacher.

My father had entertained a woman here.

My reaction not joy and relief at this hint of resurrection but anger, outrage, and betrayal as if he'd violated a sacred shrine.

Years later I realized my reaction wasn't unique.

In their heart of hearts many (most?) good sons and daughters don't want a widowed parent to find a new life.

Thus *Last Licks* was born.

We opened at the Longacre in 1979. Eleven years since *Only Game,* during which I'd written and directed five films beginning with *Desperate Characters* starring Shirley MacLaine. As for theater, I kept my hand in via five one-acts in the annual Ensemble Studio Theatre Marathon.

Variety's box score says it all: "*Last Licks* opened November 20 to unanimous pans." Only Brendan Gill (*The New Yorker*) liked it, and he reviewed it too late to be included. Ironically the first (only?) favorable mention *The New Yorker* ever gave me.

Samuel French (Abbott Van Nostrand) wanted to publish it, but I knew the script needed work and declined.

Two years later *Last Licks* was produced on the West End in London. Same director as New York (Tom Conti): title changed to *The Housekeeper,* because *Last Licks* had no currency in England, and starring the most ideal actor I could conceive of for the leading role—Leo McKern, Rumpole of the Bailey.

I rewrote but apparently not enough.

They loved us somewhat in Brighton and Richmond. London proved the guillotine.

Reviews so scathing I've vowed never to return till the Queen apologizes.

That Leo McKern, splendid in the part, couldn't pull it off made me turn against the play with a vengeance.

And thus things stood for almost twenty years.

Then Kim Cruse, a director who had championed the play since its New York premiere, found a small theater group in New Jersey who wanted to do it.

My inclination was to let the dead rest in peace, but Kim pressured me.

Reluctantly, I read the play for the first time in two decades and saw solutions to problems I'd been blind to previously.

I gave the play a thorough overhauling, which worked.

This is the version included here.

I'll leave *Last Licks* as the title for now. But if and when it's done again I'll call it *A Thump in the Lug,* which is what my father would have given me if I'd confronted him about that notebook.

ACT I

Time: Early September, 1979, afternoon. Setting: A brownstone residence in Brooklyn. Cross section of the parlor floor: Living room and dining room. Upstage in the living room is the entrance foyer: A door opening on the street; stairs leading to the second floor offstage; a closet and a coat rack from which a man's wet umbrella dangles. Upstage in the dining room is a door to the kitchen offstage. A bay window, fronting the street, in the stage left wall of the living room would be appropriate but isn't vital. The furnishings, solid and weathered speak to long tenancy. There is a television set with rabbit ears in the living room.

At rise: It's a gray overcast day. Sounds of thunder at discreet intervals early on. We find Matt Quinlan, mid-sixties, trousers, shirt, seated immobile on a sofa in the living room. There is a cane within reach. Silence—and then:

MR. QUINLAN: *(Calling toward the stairs.)* Raining you say?

DENNIS' VOICE: *(From upstairs.)* Cats and dogs.

MR. QUINLAN: …What are you doing up there?…*What are you doing?*

DENNIS' VOICE: Trying to find you a necktie.

MR. QUINLAN: I heard drawers open. You're rummaging.
(No response.)

MR. QUINLAN: *I won't have you rummaging!*
(No response. Matt gets up. Cocks an ear by the stairs to ascertain Dennis' whereabouts; moves to the dining area where two bags of groceries, vegetables visible, stand on the table. Peering into one of the bags he extracts an apple. Rubs the apple on his sleeve and returning to his seat on the living room sofa, takes a bite.)

DENNIS' VOICE: Did you see what I brought?

MR. QUINLAN: No.

DENNIS' VOICE: Take a look.

MR. QUINLAN: I don't care.

DENNIS' VOICE: Apples.

MR. QUINLAN: *(Even as he bites.)* I'm not interested.

DENNIS' VOICE: MacIntosh. Your favorite.

MR. QUINLAN: I don't want any.
(Hearing his son descend the stairs, Matt hides the apple under the sofa cushion. Dennis Quinlan, late thirties, business suit, vest, and tie, enters bearing several neckties.)

DENNIS: Knots, stains, creases. Here's the best of the lot. Take your pick.

MR. QUINLAN: I don't care.

DENNIS: The blue goes better but the red one's clean.

MR. QUINLAN: It doesn't matter.

DENNIS: She'll be here any minute.

MR. QUINLAN: And gone the next like the rest of them.

DENNIS: Not if you behave as you promised. *(Proffering the ties.)* Your pleasure?

MR. QUINLAN: I don't care.

DENNIS: Monsieur shows excellent taste. *(Drops the red tie on his lap.)* Proceed.

MR. QUINLAN: What?

DENNIS: Put it on.

MR. QUINLAN: I can't.

DENNIS: Try.

MR. QUINLAN: I forget how.

DENNIS: Your fingers will remember.

MR. QUINLAN: *(After a lame effort.)* It's no use.

DENNIS: Allow me.
    (As Dennis knots the tie.)

MR. QUINLAN: A lot of fuss for nothing.

DENNIS: Hold still.

MR. QUINLAN: What's her name?

DENNIS: Raymond.

MR. QUINLAN: What kind of a name is that?

DENNIS: It's her last name.

MR. QUINLAN: I mean what nationality?

DENNIS: No idea—hold still.

MR. QUINLAN: She could be anything.

DENNIS: Does it matter?

MR. QUINLAN: Not to you.

DENNIS: And to you?

MR. QUINLAN: My lips are sealed.

DENNIS: Keep up the good work.

MR. QUINLAN: I know which side my bread is buttered on. *You're choking me.*

DENNIS: I remember when you could do a bow tie with your eyes closed.
    (Finishes tying the tie.) Voilà.

MR. QUINLAN: This time next week you'll be in California.

DENNIS: Right.

MR. QUINLAN: The back of the plane is safest in a crash.

DENNIS: Thanks.

MR. QUINLAN: A month or two?

DENNIS: If things go smoothly. If not it could be longer.

MR. QUINLAN: Your wife and kids will love California—won't want to come back.

DENNIS: You want it in writing?

MR. QUINLAN: You have a boy and a girl.

DENNIS: And a dog and a cat.

MR. QUINLAN: How have they been?

DENNIS: The dog's fine. The cat's…They were here last week.

MR. QUINLAN: I know that.

DENNIS: You make it sound like you haven't seen them for ages.

MR. QUINLAN: Mark and Laurie.

DENNIS: Go to the head of the class.

MR. QUINLAN: You think I don't remember my grandchildren?

DENNIS: *(Glancing at his watch.)* She said three-thirty.

MR. QUINLAN: There's nothing wrong with me.

DENNIS: And so say all of us.

MR. QUINLAN: We were married thirty-nine years.

DENNIS: Something's missing.

MR. QUINLAN: Thirty-nine wonderful years.

DENNIS: That's better.

MR. QUINLAN: Who wouldn't mourn the end of such a union?

DENNIS: Not you.

MR. QUINLAN: Bereavement used to be respected, understood. Now if you're not dancing before the grave is covered you're eccentric.

DENNIS: She died in January. It's September.

MR. QUINLAN: He's no longer the life of the party? Show the doctors in.

DENNIS: Eight months and you haven't set foot outside. You don't eat unless reminded. Don't bathe unless forced. And I'll be three thousand miles away.

MR. QUINLAN: I always knew it would come to this.

DENNIS: It could have been avoided.

MR. QUINLAN: They weren't qualified.

DENNIS: As quickly as you drove them off—who could tell?

MR. QUINLAN: I'd rather go to a nursing home than be tended by harpies.

DENNIS: "Did my son tell you I piss in my pants occasionally?" Jesus.

MR. QUINLAN: *There's no need to blaspheme.*

DENNIS: This woman is your last chance.

MR. QUINLAN: You've made that clear.

DENNIS: She sounded fine on the phone. Younger than the others.

MR. QUINLAN: I won't have a jitterbug.

DENNIS: Mature but not elderly.

MR. QUINLAN: No loud music. No friends visiting of either sex. No drinking. No smoking. No unnecessary conversation.

DENNIS: Why?

MR. QUINLAN: I don't want it.

DENNIS: Why?

MR. QUINLAN: I will not have these premises violated.

DENNIS: The shrine of Saint Margaret.

MR. QUINLAN: *You mock your mother's memory?*

DENNIS: I mock hypocrisy.

MR. QUINLAN: I feel faint all of a sudden—light-headed.

DENNIS: I don't wonder.

MR. QUINLAN: The thread eludes. You were saying?

DENNIS: *(Regarding his watch.)* A quarter of.

MR. QUINLAN: When I was fourteen I got in a fight with the leader of the Italian gang. We had it out in the yard of the deaf and dumb asylum. As we flailed away you could hear the grunts and croaks of the cheering mutes. I was getting the best of the wop when his paisans leaped in. I'd have been done for if the Tollivers, two brothers black as the ace of spades, didn't come to my rescue.

DENNIS: So what?

MR. QUINLAN: If she's a negro I won't object. Providing she meets my other requirements.

DENNIS: It could be the rain.

MR. QUINLAN: What?

DENNIS: She could be held up by the rain.

MR. QUINLAN: It doesn't matter.

DENNIS: Resigned are you?

MR. QUINLAN: What will be will be.

DENNIS: That's the old fight.

MR. QUINLAN: Remember going to see my father on Welfare Island?

DENNIS: Welfare Island was charity. This place is fifty a day plus medication. There's no comparison.

MR. QUINLAN: You don't think it cost me something to get him in there? Plus slipping the orderlies a bit every visit. Plus something for the old man to play sport—lord it over the others with. And still he was never satisfied. Always pressed me for more at the last minute so we parted in anger. *(Overcome.)* Oh Jesus.

DENNIS: You did everything you could for him and more than he deserved.

MR. QUINLAN: How do you know what he deserved?

DENNIS: I know what you told me.

MR. QUINLAN: To know a man you have to see him working—in his prime.

DENNIS: Like you in South America.

MR. QUINLAN: He was a house detective in a fine hotel on Broadway when I was a boy. That's how I remember him.

DENNIS: I remember soft stubble whiskers. That gray wrinkled handkerchief. A steady drool.

MR. QUINLAN: Who's that?

DENNIS: Your father. Our monthly visit.

MR. QUINLAN: Once a week. I went times you weren't there.

DENNIS: I wasn't accusing you of neglect. *(He sorts mail.)*

MR. QUINLAN: What are you doing?

DENNIS: Rummaging. Some bills here you forgot to mention.

MR. QUINLAN: You'll see about forwarding my mail to the home?

DENNIS: You're not there yet.

MR. QUINLAN: The eternal optimist.

DENNIS: That's me.

MR. QUINLAN: The mortgage is paid?

DENNIS: Yes.

MR. QUINLAN: It's wasteful to let the place sit empty.

DENNIS: To rent it for a month or two isn't worth the bother.

MR. QUINLAN: You gave Riley something to keep an eye on things.

DENNIS: Yes.

MR. QUINLAN: That's it then. You might as well go.

DENNIS: Give her a few minutes more.

MR. QUINLAN: I'm sure you have more important things to do.

DENNIS: Trying to get rid of me?

MR. QUINLAN: That'll be the day.

DENNIS: Do you think about South America very much?

MR. QUINLAN: Why should I?

DENNIS: Pleasant memories.

MR. QUINLAN: They were business trips.

DENNIS: In those old photographs, a young man who closely resembles you seems to be having a hell of a time.

MR. QUINLAN: Would you mind fetching the urinal. My right leg's asleep and I have to go.

DENNIS: You in that white suit. Painted senoritas pressing on every side.

MR. QUINLAN: That was a gag.

DENNIS: The girl to your immediate right had a mammoth bosom.

MR. QUINLAN: Are you going to get me the urinal?

DENNIS: Just between us—was she as good as advertised?

MR. QUINLAN: Have you lost your mind?

DENNIS: "If you're hot and bothered come to Josie's. We guarantee to cool you off."

MR. QUINLAN: Baldy stuck that card in my suitcase where mother would be sure to find it. So help me I never went there.

DENNIS: What if you did? What's so bad?

MR. QUINLAN: That'll be enough of that.

DENNIS: A vigorous man, far from home—it was only natural.

MR. QUINLAN: Snooping through other peoples' possessions it serves you right any false impressions you got.

DENNIS: You can't even admit a trip to a whore house twenty-five years ago?

MR. QUINLAN: Why are you so determined to pin that on me? What's your game?

DENNIS: I think you punish yourself for things no one else, including me, holds against you.

MR. QUINLAN: "Bless me father for I have sinned."

DENNIS: If you want to crucify yourself, go on—but I'll have no part in it.

MR. QUINLAN: *(Sings.)* "California here I come."

DENNIS: *If you go to that home it will be your fault not mine.*

MR. QUINLAN: How hard it is for kids to accept a parent's decline.

DENNIS: Ann says I give you too much attention—thinks you'd do fine on your own.

MR. QUINLAN: Saving you fifty bucks a day in the bargain.

DENNIS: More including medication.

MR. QUINLAN: When I buried my father who buried his father, I made a vow I would be the first in my line to pay for his own funeral. I would have made it except for your mother's illness.

DENNIS: The money I'm laying out is more than covered by your equity in the house.

MR. QUINLAN: Got it all figured out have you?

DENNIS: To the penny.

MR. QUINLAN: Suppose I linger.

DENNIS: You wouldn't dare.

(They both laugh.)

DENNIS: I've cheated on Ann.

MR. QUINLAN: What?

DENNIS: I've been less than a faithful husband.

MR. QUINLAN: We only hear confessions on Saturday.

DENNIS: I can't blame you for doing what I did.

MR. QUINLAN: What I did or didn't do is *my* business. That's the manly way.

DENNIS: And so he kept it bottled inside: The visits to Josie's; the Spanish dancer encountered on the *SS Wilmont;* the casuals picked up on Saturday afternoons with Mr. Sheffield at the Hotel Taft; the widow Ferguson.

MR. QUINLAN: What wouldn't I give to deal you a thump in the lug.

DENNIS: Whatever it is I double it. Go on.

MR. QUINLAN: How brave knowing I can barely lift my hand.

DENNIS: How shrewd knowing if you did, the cat would be out of the bag.

MR. QUINLAN: If it wasn't a sin I'd put my head in the oven.

DENNIS: This is where I came in.

MR. QUINLAN: You're giving up on her then?

DENNIS: That isn't what I meant.

MR. QUINLAN: If she can't be on time applying for the job what the hell will she be like if she gets it?

DENNIS: That from a man who arrived home late for dinner two nights out of three—and sometimes not at all.

MR. QUINLAN: To do business I had to socialize.

DENNIS: I think I better leave.

MR. QUINLAN: I think so.

DENNIS: Anything I can do before I go—the urinal?

MR. QUINLAN: The urge is gone.

(*Dennis starts for the entrance.*)

MR. QUINLAN: A semi-private room?

DENNIS: Yes.

MR. QUINLAN: A man, I trust.

DENNIS: Of course.

MR. QUINLAN: Some colleges now they mix them up—boys and girls all together.

DENNIS: The same floor but different rooms.

MR. QUINLAN: The same room. I saw it on TV.

DENNIS: I thought you didn't watch TV.

MR. QUINLAN: Once in a great while—almost never.

DENNIS: How did you like the fight the other night?

MR. QUINLAN: Didn't see it.

DENNIS: *You* miss a title bout?

MR. QUINLAN: *I don't watch TV.*

DENNIS: Mrs. Freedman said you play it to all hours and loud—asked me to speak to you about it.

MR. QUINLAN: *She's a lying bitch.*

DENNIS: Such language and this a holy place.

MR. QUINLAN: I *don't watch TV.*

DENNIS: I was hoping just once we might level with each other. See you Wednesday.

MR. QUINLAN: I have to go again—the urinal.

DENNIS: Get it yourself.

MR. QUINLAN: My leg's asleep.

DENNIS: Do it in your pants.

(Mr. Quinlan rises, his legs give way. He falls.)

DENNIS: Safe at first.

MR. QUINLAN: I refuse your assistance.

DENNIS: I didn't offer any.

MR. QUINLAN: I hope I broke something—that I lay here and die.

DENNIS: I have an appointment.

MR. QUINLAN: Don't be late on my account.

DENNIS: Fun's over—rise and shine.

MR. QUINLAN: Don't touch me…What are you doing?

DENNIS: *(At the phone, dialing.)* Calling Doctor Goldberg.

MR. QUINLAN: I forbid it.

DENNIS: I can't leave you lying there.

MR. QUINLAN: It's coming back—the circulation.

DENNIS: Miraculous.

MR. QUINLAN: Give us a hand.

(Dennis helps him up.)

MR. QUINLAN: You're a good son. Better than I deserve.

DENNIS: Ain't it the truth.

MR. QUINLAN: *You said you wanted straight talk—I'm trying.*

DENNIS: I'm sorry. Go on…Well?…Well?

MR. QUINLAN: Okay I admit it.

DENNIS: What?

MR. QUINLAN: I saw the fight on TV.

DENNIS: *What?*

MR. QUINLAN: Only till the tenth round. I got tired.

DENNIS: That's *it?*

MR. QUINLAN: I watch the news. Sometimes a movie when I can't sleep.

DENNIS: See you Wednesday. *(Starts to leave.)*

MR. QUINLAN: *I might have visited Josie's once or twice. It's too long ago to re-member.*

DENNIS: Go on.

MR. QUINLAN: A stranger in a foreign land I drank more than usual—might have done certain things while under the influence.

DENNIS: Go on.

MR. QUINLAN: *I humped every dame in the joint—is that what you want to hear?*

DENNIS: If that's what you did.

MR. QUINLAN: Fine opinion you must have of me.

DENNIS: Better than you think and nothing you tell me will change it.

MR. QUINLAN: Want to bet?

DENNIS: Try me.

MR. QUINLAN: So you can go to California loathing me—leave me for good with a clear conscience?

DENNIS: Fine opinion *you* must have of *me.*

MR. QUINLAN: You're the best.

DENNIS: Thank you.

MR. QUINLAN: I mean that.

DENNIS: I know.

MR. QUINLAN: It's me that ruined things.

DENNIS: You give yourself too much credit.

MR. QUINLAN: She was a wonderful person.

DENNIS: Yes.

MR. QUINLAN: Angelic.

DENNIS: I wouldn't go that far.

MR. QUINLAN: So many flowers, so many people, you'd have thought they were burying a celebrity.

DENNIS: It's true everybody loved her…

MR. QUINLAN: *But?*

DENNIS: She wasn't perfect.

MR. QUINLAN: You must know something I don't.

DENNIS: Exaggerating her virtues and magnifying your flaws fuels the mea culpa farce that's been running here.

MR. QUINLAN: Not having been to college you have the advantage of me.

DENNIS: If you want to go slinking to your grave, do it. But don't blame me!

MR. QUINLAN: Oh Jesus don't.

DENNIS: I have to go to California—can't leave you here alone.

MR. QUINLAN: I understand.

DENNIS: *I don't want you to understand. I want you to resist.*

MR. QUINLAN: The brochure said exercise programs, occupational therapy, social activities. The change might do me good.

DENNIS: I'd rather see you at the Starlight Bar and Grill.

MR. QUINLAN: Among those janitors and whores?

DENNIS: I never said "whores."

MR. QUINLAN: All that wasted time I could have spent with your mother.

DENNIS: Anything else you care to throw in my face?

MR. QUINLAN: You were right: Drinking there signaled my demise.

DENNIS: I said "decline."

MR. QUINLAN: You were always wiser than your years.

DENNIS: To keep you two together I had to be.

MR. QUINLAN: That isn't what I meant.

DENNIS: "The boy hasn't eaten in three days—says he won't till we make up."

MR. QUINLAN: We stayed together because we loved each other.

DENNIS: Years later when she asked, "What's wrong Matt?"...

MR. QUINLAN: My biggest account had just declared bankruptcy—my health was beginning to fail.

DENNIS: ..."You, you son-of-a-bitch," you said to her. "You're all that's ever been wrong with me."...

MR. QUINLAN: So much for thirty-nine years.

DENNIS: ...When she threw you out and you begged to come back, I said it might be best to make the separation permanent. And you said to me?

MR. QUINLAN: *I don't remember.*

DENNIS: You said to me, "Now you tell me that. Now that it's too late you set me free." Words that will haunt me to my dying day.

MR. QUINLAN: Anything else you want to pin on me?...Now's the time...Bottom of the ninth inning...Last licks!

DENNIS: Always the injured party!

MR. QUINLAN: *What the hell do you want from me?*

DENNIS: You know what I want? I'll tell you what I want. The pleasure of your company at the Starlight Bar and Grill.

MR. QUINLAN: That low den?

DENNIS: The same.

MR. QUINLAN: I couldn't make it.

DENNIS: It's across the street. I'll carry you.

MR. QUINLAN: I'll never set foot in that place again.

DENNIS: A vow taken in mother's name?

MR. QUINLAN: *We had thirty-nine wonderful years.*

DENNIS: Murderers get off with less.

MR. QUINLAN: *I loved her!*

DENNIS: *Then stop piling debts on her grave!*
    (The doorbell sounds.)

DENNIS: She's here!

MR. QUINLAN: Don't answer.

DENNIS: What?

MR. QUINLAN: It's a waste of time.

DENNIS: Not if you make a good impression like you promised.

MR. QUINLAN: That was before you took the heart out of me.
    (Dennis starts for the door.)

MR. QUINLAN: *Don't answer.*

DENNIS: Have it your way. *(He sits.)*

MR. QUINLAN: If I go to that home it's the end.

DENNIS: I wouldn't be surprised.

MR. QUINLAN: How well you take it.
    (Dennis offers no response. Doorbell again.)

MR. QUINLAN: You win.

DENNIS: What?

MR. QUINLAN: Let her in.

DENNIS: You're sure that's what you want?

MR. QUINLAN: Let her in.

DENNIS: Wait upstairs.

MR. QUINLAN: While you warn her that I have two heads?

DENNIS: Run a comb through both of them and put your jacket on. Go on.

MR. QUINLAN: *(Starting to the stairs.)* Remember what I said about no smoking and the rest.
    (The bell again.)

DENNIS: *Be right with you.* (To his father.) A bit of the charm that wowed them at Josie's wouldn't hurt. And no asking for the urinal.

MR. QUINLAN: Deception?

DENNIS: Anything to keep you out of that home.

MR. QUINLAN: I appreciate your concern.

DENNIS: Thanks.

MR. QUINLAN: I really do.

DENNIS: The old college try?

MR. QUINLAN: You have my word. *(Mr. Quinlan disappears up the stairs.)*
    (Dennis goes to the door as the bell sounds again. Admits Miss Raymond; an ample, handsome woman, early forties. She wears a plain suit, sensible shoes.

Hair straight back, glasses, no makeup, the overall impression advertises humorless efficiency.)

MISS RAYMOND: Mr. Dennis Quinlan?

DENNIS: Miss Raymond.

(She folds her wet umbrella which he hangs on the rack.)

MISS RAYMOND: *(Openly surveying the house as she enters the living room.)* Sorry I'm late—the rain.

DENNIS: That's all right

MISS RAYMOND: I don't like to be kept waiting. I don't like to keep other people waiting. The entire house is yours?

DENNIS: My father's—yes.

MISS RAYMOND: Where is he?

DENNIS: Upstairs. I thought it best we talk first.

MISS RAYMOND: *(Noting the other room.)* The dining room?

DENNIS: Yes.

MISS RAYMOND: He's ambulatory, your father—able to get around?

DENNIS: Yes.

MISS RAYMOND: I'm not a nurse.

DENNIS: He's ambulatory.

MISS RAYMOND: To what extent?

DENNIS: He goes dancing every night…That was a joke.

MISS RAYMOND: *(Spotting the cane.)* He uses a cane.

DENNIS: Occasionally.

MISS RAYMOND: When?

DENNIS: Stairs mostly.

MISS RAYMOND: Encouraging.

(Dennis regards her.)

MISS RAYMOND: That he can climb stairs.

DENNIS: Score one for the home team.

MISS RAYMOND: That door?

DENNIS: To the kitchen.

(She checks.)

DENNIS: May I ask what you're looking for?

MISS RAYMOND: A hospital bed on the parlor floor.

DENNIS: He sleeps upstairs.

MISS RAYMOND: Hospital beds mean the job is not for me.

DENNIS: He sleeps in his own bed.

MISS RAYMOND: Age?

DENNIS: Early sixties…sixty-four.

MISS RAYMOND: Retired?

DENNIS: Only because his business failed.

MISS RAYMOND: Which was?

DENNIS: Freight forwarding. The importing and exporting of heavy equipment like locomotives. Anything else?

MISS RAYMOND: How would you summarize his condition?

DENNIS: A sharp decline in the will to live since my mother died last January.

MISS RAYMOND: They were very close.

DENNIS: For thirty-nine years.

MISS RAYMOND: Prescribed medications?

DENNIS: Zero.

MISS RAYMOND: You've consulted a doctor?

DENNIS: Doctors.

MISS RAYMOND: Their diagnosis?

DENNIS: With all due respect, I advertised for a housekeeper not a physician.

MISS RAYMOND: Where the person I'm to keep house for is not fully functional I require a complete medical history.

DENNIS: Of course—forgive me. I've been under a bit of a strain. My firm is sending me on temporary assignment to Los Angeles—

MISS RAYMOND: —And your father can't manage on his own.

DENNIS: I don't want to risk it. On the other hand, I hate the thought of a nursing home, even though it would be temporary.

MISS RAYMOND: You live here with him?

DENNIS: No—Long Island. I'm married. I visit him twice a week—call every day.

MISS RAYMOND: "A sharp decline in the will to live."

DENNIS: He's stopped seeing friends. Refuses to go out.

MISS RAYMOND: Not unusual following the death of a loved one except for the length of time.

DENNIS: They were very close.

MISS RAYMOND: So you said.

DENNIS: I tried having him live with us but I have two young children.

MISS RAYMOND: They bothered him.

DENNIS: He didn't improve and it was causing friction.

MISS RAYMOND: So you brought him back here.

DENNIS: He wasn't easy to live with when he was a hundred percent...

MISS RAYMOND: Go on.

DENNIS: I think I've said too much.

MISS RAYMOND: I prefer candor to assurances that the person to be cared for is a saint.

DENNIS: He's not a saint. You have my word.

MISS RAYMOND: Where would I sleep?

DENNIS: Third floor. Your own sitting room and bath.

MISS RAYMOND: Your ad said one hundred and seventy-five a week plus room and board.

DENNIS: Right.

MISS RAYMOND: I require two twenty-five.

DENNIS: The going rate is two hundred tops.

MISS RAYMOND: Your ad appeared three weeks ago and the position isn't filled.

DENNIS: You think I'm over a barrel, will agree to anything.

MISS RAYMOND: Yes.

DENNIS: You're not the only one partial to candor. *(Shooting out his hand.)* Miss Raymond it's a deal.

MISS RAYMOND: *(Ignoring his hand.)* You didn't tell me what the doctors said.

DENNIS: "Aging." "Inevitable decline hastened by traumatic loss." The usual mumbo-jumbo. Deal?

MISS RAYMOND: I never accept a position before meeting the individual concerned.

DENNIS: No sooner said than done. *(Moving to the foot of the stairs—calling.)* Pop?

MR. QUINLAN'S VOICE: Yes.

DENNIS: You're on.

MR. QUINLAN'S VOICE: How am I doing?

DENNIS: So far so good.

MR. QUINLAN'S VOICE: She knows about the wooden leg—that I sing off-key?

DENNIS: Everything.

(Mr. Quinlan, resplendent in a white suit not worn in twenty years, white shoes, bow tie, Panama hat in hand, appears.)

MR. QUINLAN: I was on my way out—can spare but a minute.

DENNIS: Miss Raymond, my father—Mr. Quinlan.

MISS RAYMOND: How do you do?

(Mr. Quinlan freezes.)

DENNIS: Pop.

MR. QUINLAN: Yes?

DENNIS: Miss Raymond just greeted you.

MR. QUINLAN: Fine thanks.

DENNIS: What's the matter?

MR. QUINLAN: I feel a bit light headed.

DENNIS: *(To Miss Raymond.)* Nerves. Worried about impressing you. *(Helping him to a chair.)* Sit.

MISS RAYMOND: Are you subject to fainting, Mr. Quinlan?

DENNIS: Never.　　　　　　　　MR. QUINLAN: Occasionally.

DENNIS: When?

MR. QUINLAN: You weren't here.

DENNIS: You never mentioned it.

MR. QUINLAN: I don't like to worry you.

DENNIS: *(To Miss Raymond.)* That's a new one.

MISS RAYMOND: Don't be concerned.

DENNIS: You're still interested in the job.

MISS RAYMOND: If your father approves of me.

DENNIS: Of course he approves.

MISS RAYMOND: *(To Mr. Quinlan.)* Do you, Mr. Quinlan?
　　　(He offers no reaction.)

DENNIS: *Well go on—tell her.*

MR. QUINLAN: What?

DENNIS: Tell Miss Raymond that you'd be delighted to have her keep house
　　　for you.

MR. QUINLAN: The room's going around.

DENNIS: Pop!

MR. QUINLAN: Yes?

DENNIS: Miss Raymond will take the job if you want her to.

MR. QUINLAN: Describe her to me.

DENNIS: *(To Miss Raymond.)* He's never worn glasses in his life.

MISS RAYMOND: *(To Mr. Quinlan.)* Mr. Quinlan?

MR. QUINLAN: *(Sotto voce to Dennis.)* She sounds tiny. If I faint I want some-
　　　one who can lift me.

MISS RAYMOND: Care to feel my muscle?

MR. QUINLAN: *(To Dennis.)* What did she say?

DENNIS: *(To Miss Raymond.)* Would you excuse us a minute—wait in the
　　　kitchen?

MISS RAYMOND: All right.

MR. QUINLAN: Before she goes, I wonder if she'd mind fetching the urinal.

MISS RAYMOND: Where is it?

DENNIS: *I'll take care of it.*

MR. QUINLAN: I forgot—wasn't supposed to mention that.

MISS RAYMOND: Shall I close the door?

DENNIS: Thank you.
　　　(She enters the kitchen—closes the door.)

DENNIS: *You son-of-a-bitch.*

MR. QUINLAN: Call me mister.

DENNIS: Why?

MR. QUINLAN: I don't like her.

DENNIS: She's the only thing that stands between you and that home.

MR. QUINLAN: She looks like a keeper in a concentration camp.

DENNIS: *I thought you couldn't see her. And that crap about fainting.*

MR. QUINLAN: I was trying to reject her gracefully.

DENNIS: *Of the women who answered the ad, she's the best by far. And unlike any of them she wants the job.*

MR. QUINLAN: How much?

DENNIS: Two twenty-five.

MR. QUINLAN: Larceny.

DENNIS: Still cheaper than the home.

MR. QUINLAN: What's her background, experience, references?...Well?

DENNIS: We didn't get into that.

MR. QUINLAN: *That eager to salve his conscience and save a few bucks he'd palm me off on anyone.*

DENNIS: I'll ask for references.

MR. QUINLAN: She has a loony look.

DENNIS: *I'll ask for references.*

MR. QUINLAN: "Man Dismembered—Housekeeper Sought."

DENNIS: *I'll get references!*

MR. QUINLAN: Which won't be worth the paper they're written on.

DENNIS: What do you want me to do?

MR. QUINLAN: Get rid of her.

DENNIS: You're serious?

MR. QUINLAN: Yes.

DENNIS: Even though it means the home for sure?

MR. QUINLAN: Yes.

DENNIS: Suppose I told you the California job might turn out to be permanent?

MR. QUINLAN: You think that's news.

DENNIS: *It's not just yourself you're punishing—it's me.*

MR. QUINLAN: You've done everything a son could be expected to.

DENNIS: So why do I feel so bad?

MR. QUINLAN: The next woman I'll take sight unseen. I swear.

DENNIS: She's the final applicant.

MR. QUINLAN: *I won't have her!*

DENNIS: Congratulations.

MR. QUINLAN: She gives me the shivers.

DENNIS: You've just won yourself an indefinite stay at the nursing home.

MR. QUINLAN: *(Heading for the stairs.)* Let me know when she's gone.

DENNIS: Stuck with the dirty work as usual.

MR. QUINLAN: Go to hell.

DENNIS: You mean this isn't it?

(Mr. Quinlan exits upstairs. Dennis opens the kitchen door.)

DENNIS: All clear.

(Miss Raymond emerges from the kitchen.)

DENNIS: Ready for a switch?

MISS RAYMOND: He doesn't want me.

DENNIS: I apologize for wasting your time.

MISS RAYMOND: Did he say why?

DENNIS: Nothing personal.

MISS RAYMOND: Having invested an afternoon I deserve an explanation.

DENNIS: He feels he treated my mother badly—is determined to atone.

MISS RAYMOND: You said they were close.

DENNIS: As only life-long combatants can be.

MISS RAYMOND: What happens now?

DENNIS: On Wednesday I take him to the nursing home.

MISS RAYMOND: Which you'd give anything to avoid.

DENNIS: Yes.

MISS RAYMOND: Leave us for an hour.

DENNIS: What?

MISS RAYMOND: Leave your father and me alone for an hour.

DENNIS: He wouldn't stand for it.

MISS RAYMOND: Don't tell him—just go.

DENNIS: He'd scream bloody murder.

MISS RAYMOND: It's four-thirty now. Come back at half past five.

DENNIS: You mean it?

MISS RAYMOND: Yes.

DENNIS: Why?

MISS RAYMOND: Why am I doing it?

DENNIS: Yes.

MISS RAYMOND: The challenge appeals.

DENNIS: You really expect to win him over?

MISS RAYMOND: I've had success with similar cases…Well?

DENNIS: I don't know.

MISS RAYMOND: Just a suggestion. I'll be going now.

DENNIS: Wait a minute. What have I got to lose?

MISS RAYMOND: Exactly.

DENNIS: An hour?

MISS RAYMOND: At least. These things take time...Well?

DENNIS: He's got a terrible temper.

MISS RAYMOND: It'll be fine.

DENNIS: *(Offering his hand.)* I'll see you at five thirty. If you're not here when I get back—thanks for the effort.

MISS RAYMOND: I'll be here.

(He exits the house. She stands as is. A beat and then.)

MR. QUINLAN'S VOICE: Is that witch finally gone?...Well?...Ready or not here I come. *(Mr. Quinlan descends the stairs—enters the living room.)*

MR. QUINLAN: Why so long getting rid of her? Sonny? *(The sight of her stops him cold.)*

MISS RAYMOND: He's gone for a walk.

MR. QUINLAN: Oh dear God!

MISS RAYMOND: He won't be back for an hour. Hello Matt.

MR. QUINLAN: Mr. Quinlan to you.

MISS RAYMOND: Alone at last.

MR. QUINLAN: *Sonny!!*

MISS RAYMOND: I often wondered what it looked like—tried to picture you here.

MR. QUINLAN: Miss Raymond?

MISS RAYMOND: My mother's name.

MR. QUINLAN: Because you knew I wouldn't let you in.

MISS RAYMOND: "All's fair," as the saying goes. Nice furnishings but worn. I'll make curtains to start—recover the sofa.

MR. QUINLAN: You're not staying.

MISS RAYMOND: Two weeks and you won't recognize the place.

MR. QUINLAN: *Get out!*

(He lunges but she avoids him, moving into the dining room where he pursues—collapses into a chair at the dining table. As he sits, Dennis [out of their sight line] enters the house to get his umbrella; is reaching for it when he hears.)

MISS RAYMOND: Not as quick as you used to be but still surprising for a man en route to a nursing home.

(Dennis freezes.)

MR. QUINLAN: I'll be exhausted for a week. My heart is pounding.

MISS RAYMOND: Let me feel.

MR. QUINLAN: Keep your filthy hands off me!

(Dennis returns the umbrella to the rack; ducks into the closet leaving the door ajar.)

MISS RAYMOND: There's a switch.

MR. QUINLAN: How did you get rid of my son?

MISS RAYMOND: I told him you and I had been lovers before his mother died.

MR. QUINLAN: You wouldn't dare.

MISS RAYMOND: I will if you don't explain why you've been avoiding me.

MR. QUINLAN: Have you no regard for mourning—a decent interval of grief?

MISS RAYMOND: That's what I told myself the first three months. Give him time. He'll come around.

MR. QUINLAN: It took a great deal out of me—her illness. The fact is I'm not well.

MISS RAYMOND: You could have answered my calls.

MR. QUINLAN: I wanted you to remember me the way I was.

MISS RAYMOND: Crap.

MR. QUINLAN: *I'm sick God damn it—on my way to a nursing home.*

MISS RAYMOND: I've missed you.

MR. QUINLAN: My hearing's failed along with everything else.

MISS RAYMOND: *All those nights at the Hotel Marquette.*

MR. QUINLAN: Keep your voice down!

MISS RAYMOND: You said your hearing had failed. Remember the Hotel Marquette?

MR. QUINLAN: My memory's shot. Especially names.

MISS RAYMOND: Room four-seventeen? The king-size bed? The big mirror that if you tilted it we could see—

MR. QUINLAN: —*Enough.*

MISS RAYMOND: You remember?

MR. QUINLAN: To my everlasting shame. What do you want from me?

MISS RAYMOND: Looking for employment, I came upon your ad for a housekeeper.

MR. QUINLAN: False advertising. I'm too far gone.

MISS RAYMOND: A man in a white suit, bow tie and Panama hat on his way to the grave?

MR. QUINLAN: A pose for my son's benefit which I can't maintain.

MISS RAYMOND: Try.

MR. QUINLAN: He'll want to know your background—demand references.

MISS RAYMOND: I was a nun, easily verifiable, for eighteen years. On leave to care for my dying father, death certificate on request, I encountered the man of my dreams.

MR. QUINLAN: It's the ecumenical influence—the God damn modernization.

MISS RAYMOND: Proud, fierce, determined. It was love at first sight.

MR. QUINLAN: Priests speaking English. Sisters out of uniform. What do you expect?

MISS RAYMOND: I followed him to the Starlight Bar and Grill where he held forth like a king.

MR. QUINLAN: Business failing, I drank among janitors to shore my confidence.

MISS RAYMOND: I forced myself to drink.

MR. QUINLAN: The wanton slut to a turn.

MISS RAYMOND: The next thing I knew I was in room four-seventeen.

MR. QUINLAN: You all but dragged me there.

MISS RAYMOND: I tried to hide my virginity.

MR. QUINLAN: A shock. But nothing compared to what was in the wings.

MISS RAYMOND: I began to cry. Was still crying when you saddled up for the second round.

MR. QUINLAN: In for a penny, in for a pound.

MISS RAYMOND: "I'm a nun," I shouted.

MR. QUINLAN: *"I'm the Pope," I cheered.*
(Caught up in the memory they laugh. He catches himself—ceases abruptly. Her laughter trails.)

MISS RAYMOND: We began to see each other regularly.

MR. QUINLAN: Quit it.

MISS RAYMOND: Twice a week at least till your wife got sick.

MR. QUINLAN: Stop!

MISS RAYMOND: Want the fair Fiona to kiss it away?

MR. QUINLAN: You whore.

MISS RAYMOND: Can I help it if you bring out the best in me?

MR. QUINLAN: I'm not the man I was.

MISS RAYMOND: Half a loaf will do.

MR. QUINLAN: I had happiness in the palm of my hand for thirty-nine years—didn't realize it till she passed away.

MISS RAYMOND: Take two Hail Marys and call me in the morning.

MR. QUINLAN: *I loved her.*

MISS RAYMOND: *I'm* convinced. What about *you?*

MR. QUINLAN: I never told her. Do you suppose she knew?

MISS RAYMOND: Frankly I don't give a fuck.

MR. QUINLAN: *I will not have such language in this house.*

MISS RAYMOND: You used to *make* me talk that way.

MR. QUINLAN: The room's beginning to spin again.

MISS RAYMOND: "Say 'cunt' or daddy will spank."

MR. QUINLAN: When I'm upset I don't hear anything.

MISS RAYMOND: *Testing: Prick. Balls. Do you read me now?*

MR. QUINLAN: If I had the strength I'd strangle you!

MISS RAYMOND: If you had the strength I'd suggest other things.

MR. QUINLAN: How could a nun turn slut so completely?

MISS RAYMOND: I had a skillful teacher.

MR. QUINLAN: *Who had a more than eager pupil.*

MISS RAYMOND: Fifty-fifty's fine with me.

MR. QUINLAN: In a life of debauchery I regret you most. I, who was known in the finest watering places—had slept with the most elegant women, reduced to drinking in a dump like the Starlight and humping the likes of you!

MISS RAYMOND: … I'll be going now.

MR. QUINLAN: My son will want to know what happened.

MISS RAYMOND: Say I regretfully concluded the job is not for me.

MR. QUINLAN: Do I perceive a tear?

MISS RAYMOND: I was thinking of you in that nursing home.

MR. QUINLAN: It's a deluxe establishment—the best in the state.

MISS RAYMOND: Did you ever hear of one that wasn't?

MR. QUINLAN: It's only for a month or two.

MISS RAYMOND: Or three, or four, or—

MR. QUINLAN: —Wouldn't my son rent this house if he thought I wasn't coming back?

MISS RAYMOND: A common and well-intended ploy.

MR. QUINLAN: Not as common as your attempt to frighten me in the hope I'll reconsider—ask you to stay.

MISS RAYMOND: Caring for my father gave me my fill of hopeless invalids. But thank you anyway.

MR. QUINLAN: I know what you're after.

MISS RAYMOND: When you're settled in, have one of the nurses drop me a line.

MR. QUINLAN: *(Sings.)* "Oh ring-dang-do oh what is that, so soft and warm like a pussy cat?"

MISS RAYMOND: Shall I fetch the urinal before I go?

MR. QUINLAN: Fair Fiona's got the hots. Wants daddy to make them go away.

MISS RAYMOND: If that's an offer, I accept.

MR. QUINLAN: I curse the day we met.

MISS RAYMOND: I'm immune to flattery.

MR. QUINLAN: What did I ever see in you?

MISS RAYMOND: My eyes for one thing. *(Removes her glasses.)* You said they were irresistible.

MR. QUINLAN: Whiskey talk.

(She removes the pins that hold her hair allowing it to spill over her shoulders.)

MR. QUINLAN: What are you doing?

MISS RAYMOND: You were also partial to my hair. *(She whips him with it.)*

MR. QUINLAN: Stop that.

MISS RAYMOND: Twenty lashes for old times' sake?

MR. QUINLAN: I'm a very sick man.

MISS RAYMOND: Ten lashes then. *(She starts to flog away.)*

MR. QUINLAN: You'll pay for this.

MISS RAYMOND: Hopefully.

(He pulls her into a passionate embrace reaching fever stage when she breaks off; stands; offers her hand.)

MR. QUINLAN: *(Taking her hand.)* Now what?

MISS RAYMOND: Come. *(She leads him to the stairs.)*

MR. QUINLAN: Not up there!

MISS RAYMOND: Because it's where you and she slept?

MR. QUINLAN: Yes.

MISS RAYMOND: I think I'd find it arousing. What the kids call a turn on.

MR. QUINLAN: Perverted bitch.

MISS RAYMOND: Love's old sweet song.

MR. QUINLAN: Degenerate cunt!

MISS RAYMOND: Sing on—sing on!

(She leading the way, hand in hand, they ascend the stairs—disappear. Silence. Dennis emerges from the closet. Stares up the stairs. A burst of laughter from above activates him. He exits the house.)

END OF ACT I

ACT II

Time: An hour later, early evening. Place: The same. At rise: Mr. Quinlan and Miss Raymond, hair up, glasses on, all as before, are playing checkers. She moves.

MR. QUINLAN: *(Regarding his pocket watch.)* It's almost six.

MISS RAYMOND: Move.

MR. QUINLAN: He said he'd be back at five-thirty?

MISS RAYMOND: Yes. It's your move.

MR. QUINLAN: He's always punctual.

MISS RAYMOND: Maybe he went to a movie—lost track.

MR. QUINLAN: The Starlight Bar and Grill. Suppose he went there. Found out about us—who you are?

MISS RAYMOND: Move.

MR. QUINLAN: I don't feel like playing.

MISS RAYMOND: He'll wonder what we've been doing. Go on.
(Mr. Quinlan moves.)

MISS RAYMOND: How many games have we played?

MR. QUINLAN: Why can't we just be sitting here?

MISS RAYMOND: We've played eight games. *(Holds up a tally sheet.)* Four checks under "Mr. Quinlan." Four under "Miss Raymond." This is the deciding game.

MR. QUINLAN: *I'm sick of lies.*

MISS RAYMOND: Then tell the truth: We had a jolly romp in the hay.

MR. QUINLAN: *Keep your voice down.*

MISS RAYMOND: When he left you were dead set against my staying here. He'll want to know what changed your mind…Well?

MR. QUINLAN: I outlined my rules—no smoking, no visitors, et cetera and you agreed.

MISS RAYMOND: What else?

MR. QUINLAN: A mutual interest in checkers, religion, and sports.

MISS RAYMOND: Especially boxing—my father was an amateur fighter.

MR. QUINLAN: Too thick.

MISS RAYMOND: It's true…You sound irritated. Are you sure you want me to stay?

MR. QUINLAN: Yes.

MISS RAYMOND: Say it.

MR. QUINLAN: I want you to stay—damn it.

MISS RAYMOND: Why?

MR. QUINLAN: Don't.

MISS RAYMOND: To avoid going to the home?

MR. QUINLAN: *Please.*

MISS RAYMOND: Repeat after me: "Fair Fiona I love you with all my heart."

MR. QUINLAN: Stop.

MISS RAYMOND: "Fair Fiona I love you a little bit?"

MR. QUINLAN: What do you want from me?

MISS RAYMOND: Ultimately everything. But for openers "Fair Fiona" will suffice. Say it.

MR. QUINLAN: Fair Fiona.

MISS RAYMOND: You do have a way with words. Move.

MR. QUINLAN: The neighborhood's not what it used to be. I hope he didn't go wandering.

MISS RAYMOND: What are you really worried about?

MR. QUINLAN: My son.

MISS RAYMOND: That he won't come back or that he will?

MR. QUINLAN: What an awful thing to say.

MISS RAYMOND: He'll never know we made love in mommy's bed unless you tell him.

MR. QUINLAN: Stop!

MISS RAYMOND: Is that what you're going to do? Confess out of some misbegotten sense of guilt?

MR. QUINLAN: You don't know him. If she and I had a row, he'd come home and no matter what sort of face we tried to put on, he'd sniff it out.

MISS RAYMOND: There's nothing wrong here.

MR. QUINLAN: From the time he was knee high forcing us to say we loved each other.

MISS RAYMOND: *There is nothing wrong! (Taking his hand in both of hers.)* We are two people, late in the day, seeking a bit of joy.

MR. QUINLAN: Not too joyful or he'll catch wise.

MISS RAYMOND: And if he does?

MR. QUINLAN: Don't even mention it.

MISS RAYMOND: Would you like a signed statement I took advantage—assume all the blame? *(Indicating the checker board.)* It's still your move.

MR. QUINLAN: The shade!

MISS RAYMOND: What?

MR. QUINLAN: The window shade in the bedroom. He'll wonder why it's drawn.

MISS RAYMOND: I opened it.

MR. QUINLAN: You're sure?

MISS RAYMOND: Right before I wiped the room for fingerprints. Jump or you lose a checker.

(The doorbell sounds.)

MR. QUINLAN: Bless us and save us.

MISS RAYMOND: Ready?

MR. QUINLAN: As I'll ever be.

MISS RAYMOND: Where are we going this Sunday?

MR. QUINLAN: To church.

(The bell again.)

MR. QUINLAN: Why the bell? He has a key.

MISS RAYMOND: I prefer early mass. You prefer late. We compromised on ten o'clock.

MR. QUINLAN: Let him in before he gets suspicious.

MISS RAYMOND: He'll only be suspicious if you give him reason.

MR. QUINLAN: I don't think my nerves are up to this.

MISS RAYMOND: It's my sweet nothings or the croaking chorus at the nursing home.

MR. QUINLAN: Let him in.

(She goes to the entrance—admits Dennis.)

DENNIS: I seem to have lost my key. Everything all right?

MISS RAYMOND: Couldn't be better.

DENNIS: You mean it?

MISS RAYMOND: Come see. *(Returning to Mr. Quinlan with Dennis following.)*

MISS RAYMOND: As I was saying: Max Baer, Braddock, Joe Louis, Walcott, Marciano.

MR. QUINLAN: *(To Dennis.)* Be with you in a second. *(To Miss Raymond.)* Go on.

MISS RAYMOND: Where was I?

MR. QUINLAN: Rocky Marciano.

MISS RAYMOND: Floyd Patterson, Ingmar Johansson, Patterson again and finally Sonny Liston.

MR. QUINLAN: By George she's done it. *(To Dennis.)* She claimed to be a dyed-in-the-wool boxing fan. So I challenged her to name the heavyweight champs that preceded Mohammed Ali. *(To Miss Raymond.)* Madam, I bow.

DENNIS: Ditto for me.

MR. QUINLAN: We're going to mass on Sunday. She's Catholic.

DENNIS: And a checker player to boot. Who's winning?

MR. QUINLAN: *(Displaying the tally sheet.)* Four games each. This one tells the tale.

DENNIS: Don't let me interrupt.

MISS RAYMOND: *(To Mr. Quinlan.)* Draw?

MR. QUINLAN: Accepted.

DENNIS: I take it you want Miss Raymond to keep house for you.

MR. QUINLAN: Yes.

DENNIS: *(To Miss Raymond.)* And you've agreed? I pronounce you housekeeper and housekeeperee.

(They react.)

DENNIS: What's wrong?

MR. QUINLAN: I don't find your poor taste amusing. I'm sure Miss Raymond agrees.

MISS RAYMOND: It's all right.

DENNIS: Forgive me. I'm just so relieved it's turned out like this.

MISS RAYMOND: I understand.

DENNIS: On to practicalities: Two hundred and twenty-five a week?

MISS RAYMOND: Yes.

DENNIS: Starting?

MISS RAYMOND: Tomorrow if you like.

DENNIS: Eager to begin. I like that. No salt. No sweets. Doctor's orders. …You're surprised?

MISS RAYMOND: Mildly.

DENNIS: You're now a member of the family so to speak, privy to all. Does it put you off?

MR. QUINLAN: I'll eat and drink any God damn thing I like.

DENNIS: *(To Miss Raymond.)* See what you're in for.

MISS RAYMOND: The diet will be adhered to.

DENNIS: I'm sure it will. *(To Mr. Quinlan.)* I think you've met your match.

MISS RAYMOND: Anything else?

DENNIS: Exercise: He hasn't been out of the house since my mother died.

MISS RAYMOND: Barring inclement weather, we'll take walks twice a day.

DENNIS: *(To his father.)* You agree?

MR. QUINLAN: Yes.

DENNIS: *(To Miss Raymond.)* You must be a magician.

MISS RAYMOND: Shall we say tomorrow then—three o'clock?

DENNIS: With bells on.

MISS RAYMOND: I'll want doctors' names. Phone numbers of friends and relatives. And any other data that might be useful.

DENNIS: *(To his father.)* Offhand I'd say we've hit the jackpot. *(To Miss Raymond as he extracts checkbook and pen from his pocket.)* A month's wages in advance?

MISS RAYMOND: Two weeks will do.

DENNIS: Did you hear that? *(To Miss Raymond preparing to write the check.)* How shall I make it out?

MISS RAYMOND: There's no need until tomorrow. *(Offering her hand.)* Good day.

DENNIS: *(Ignoring her hand.)* You wouldn't be putting us on?

MISS RAYMOND: What?

DENNIS: I have a feeling it's too good to be true—that you won't come back.

MR. QUINLAN: She said she'll be here. What more do you want?

DENNIS: If you have any reservations about the job, no matter how slight, tell me.

MR. QUINLAN: Stop putting ideas in her head.

MISS RAYMOND: *(To Mr. Quinlan.)* It's all right. *(To Dennis.)* I assure you nothing will stop me from taking this job.

DENNIS: Thank you. *(To his father.)* Thank her.

MR. QUINLAN: Two hundred and twenty-five a week isn't charity.

DENNIS: Thank her anyway.

MR. QUINLAN: Thanks.

MISS RAYMOND: *(Again offering her hand to Dennis.)* Three o'clock tomorrow.

DENNIS: *(Pumping her hand enthusiastically.)* If I knew you better I'd kiss you.

MISS RAYMOND: *(Offering her hand to Mr. Quinlan.)* Good day, Mr. Quinlan.

MR. QUINLAN: *(Taking her hand briefly.)* Miss Raymond.

DENNIS: Mr. Quinlan? Miss Raymond? *(To her.)* What's your first name?

MISS RAYMOND: Fiona.

DENNIS: Fiona meet Matt. Matt—Fiona.

MR. QUINLAN: I prefer Mister and Miss.

MISS RAYMOND: So do I.

DENNIS: Forgive me. It's just that I feel so good, so great! *(To his father.)* Break out the bottle.

MR. QUINLAN: What bottle?

DENNIS: The Scotch I'm not supposed to know about.

MR. QUINLAN: You found that bottle the visit before last. Poured the contents down the drain.

DENNIS: You're right. *(To Miss Raymond.)* He's right.

MISS RAYMOND: It's just as well. I have to go.

DENNIS: The occasion demands a toast! *(Thrusting a twenty dollar bill at her.)* Get us a fifth of Johnny Walker Red.

MR. QUINLAN: Didn't you hear her say she has to go?

DENNIS: You passing up the chance of a drink? *(To Miss Raymond.)* There's a liquor store halfway down the block to your right on the opposite side of the street.

MR. QUINLAN: You want it so bad, go yourself.

DENNIS: *(To Miss Raymond.)* It will give me a chance to discuss some matters of a private nature with my father.

MISS RAYMOND: *(Taking the money.)* I understand.

MR. QUINLAN: What matters of a private nature?

MISS RAYMOND: *(To Mr. Quinlan.)* He wants to make sure I haven't cast a spell over you.

DENNIS: I cannot tell a lie. Halfway down the block on the opposite side of the street.

MISS RAYMOND: I know where it is—I'm from the neighborhood.

DENNIS: What gave me the impression you'd come a distance?

MISS RAYMOND: A fifth of Red Label?

MR. QUINLAN: Long as you're going, get a quart.

DENNIS: That's more like it. *(Accompanying her to the door.)* You're sure you don't mind?

MISS RAYMOND: Positive.

(She exits, he returns to the living room.)

DENNIS: Hallelujah!

MR. QUINLAN: You sent her off like an errand boy.

DENNIS: We have been saved.

MR. QUINLAN: Serve you right if she doesn't come back.

DENNIS: *(Shifting gears.)* Is that what you want?

MR. QUINLAN: What?

DENNIS: Despite your mutual interest in religion and checkers, and the cozy mood I interrupted, is it possible you hope she never returns?

MR. QUINLAN: Why would I hope that?

DENNIS: An hour ago you said get rid of her. Now she's fine. It bothers me.

MR. QUINLAN: You make too much of it.

DENNIS: I want to know what you really think of her.

MR. QUINLAN: She seems all right.

DENNIS: "All right"?

MR. QUINLAN: I'm willing to give it a try.

DENNIS: I'll be three thousand miles away. I can't leave you with someone who just seems all right.

MR. QUINLAN: I thought you were so impressed by her.

DENNIS: I am, but you're the one who'll be living with her.

MR. QUINLAN: We'll get along.

DENNIS: Cooped up here with someone you disliked could be worse than the nursing home.

MR. QUINLAN: I'll take my chances.

DENNIS: You really like her then?

MR. QUINLAN: *I've only met the woman.*

DENNIS: But what you've seen you like?

MR. QUINLAN: Yes.

DENNIS: You're not just saying that to relieve me?

MR. QUINLAN: No.

DENNIS: What did she tell you about herself?

MR. QUINLAN: Nothing.

DENNIS: I was gone an hour.

MR. QUINLAN: We played checkers—discussed sports.

DENNIS: I would have thought you'd ask questions—learn all you could.

MR. QUINLAN: She prefers early mass, I prefer late. We settled for ten.

DENNIS: Wouldn't mother be pleased.

(Mr. Quinlan eyes him.)

DENNIS: That you're resuming your life.

MR. QUINLAN: I agreed to go to church. Don't make a big deal.

DENNIS: How did she persuade you?

MR. QUINLAN: She asked me to go—I said yes.

DENNIS: You're blushing.

MR. QUINLAN: *I am not.*

DENNIS: My God there's life in the old boy yet.

MR. QUINLAN: *I will not have such talk in this house joking or otherwise.*

DENNIS: All I said was—

MR. QUINLAN: *—Say it again and you can chuck the whole thing—ship me off to the home as scheduled.*

DENNIS: Aren't we touchy?

MR. QUINLAN: An hour ago you were begging me to accept her. I accept her. What more do you want?

DENNIS: To be sure you're not doing it for my sake.

MR. QUINLAN: I'm not doing it for your sake.

DENNIS: While I was out, I realized it's selfish making you live with a total stranger so I can leave without a care.

MR. QUINLAN: *I'm not doing it for your sake.*

DENNIS: There's a waiting list at the good homes. If this woman doesn't work out there might not be another opening for quite a while.

MR. QUINLAN: It'll work out.

DENNIS: I'm going to ask her for references.

MR. QUINLAN: You've already told her she has the job.

DENNIS: I'm not leaving you in the hands of a person I know nothing about.

MR. QUINLAN: References don't mean shit.

DENNIS: You're right.

MR. QUINLAN: So where are we?

DENNIS: ...The Starlight Bar and Grill.

MR. QUINLAN: What?

DENNIS: She said she's from the neighborhood. I'll ask at the Starlight if they ever heard of Fiona Raymond.

MR. QUINLAN: Parade my business before that lot?

DENNIS: I'll do it discreetly.

MR. QUINLAN: I forbid it.

DENNIS: Why?

MR. QUINLAN: What would a woman like her have to do with the scum in that place?

DENNIS: Most likely nothing.

MR. QUINLAN: Exactly.

DENNIS: But if by some chance they know her it could save us a lot of grief. *(Starting for the door.)* If she gets back before me, say I had to see one of the neighbors about something.

MR. QUINLAN: Wait!

(Arrested by his father's voice, Dennis turns, sees him, eyes closed, clutching his forehead.)

DENNIS: What is it?...What's wrong?

MR. QUINLAN: A wave of dizziness.

DENNIS: Like before?

MR. QUINLAN: Worse. And pains.

DENNIS: Where?

MR. QUINLAN: All over.

DENNIS: I'll call the doctor.

MR. QUINLAN: No.

DENNIS: The pain.

MR. QUINLAN: It's subsiding.

DENNIS: The dizziness?

MR. QUINLAN: That too.

DENNIS: How often do you get these things?

MR. QUINLAN: The first time was the night of the funeral.

DENNIS: It could be psychosomatic.

MR. QUINLAN: Exactly what I thought, which is why I never told you. But lately they've been more frequent.

DENNIS: I'm calling the doctor.

MR. QUINLAN: No!

DENNIS: It could be serious.

MR. QUINLAN: Whatever it is can wait till I get to the nursing home.

DENNIS: The nursing home?

MR. QUINLAN: The jig's up my lad. Much as it pains me to say so, I'm throwing in the sponge.

DENNIS: What about Miss Raymond?

MR. QUINLAN: Thank her for everything but it wouldn't work.

DENNIS: You seemed so happy with the arrangement.

MR. QUINLAN: An act as you suspected. But my body betrays. I'll lie down for a while. *(Cane in hand, he starts for the stairs.)*

DENNIS: Shouldn't you tell her yourself—say good-bye?

MR. QUINLAN: I'm not up to it. You can explain.

DENNIS: She's going to think it's *my* fault—that for some reason I changed your mind.

MR. QUINLAN: Why would you do that when it's your dearest wish to keep me from going to that place.

DENNIS: *It is my dearest wish!*

MR. QUINLAN: I know and I appreciate it. *(He pauses.)* I think she would have got on my nerves. But there's no need to mention it.

DENNIS: You're sure it's what you want—to get rid of her?…Well?

MR. QUINLAN: Yes. *(He exits up the stairs.)*

DENNIS: You're the boss.

MR. QUINLAN'S VOICE: What?

DENNIS: I'll do it.

MR. QUINLAN'S VOICE: There's a good lad.

(Dennis looks after his father with conflicted emotions; braces himself as the doorbell rings; admits Miss Raymond carrying a paper bag, who sweeps by him into the dining room.)

MISS RAYMOND: They were out of Red Label so I took Black. It was that or a five-block walk. Your change. *(She deposits the bottle and change on the table.)* Private matters settled?

DENNIS: Yes.

MISS RAYMOND: Where is he?

DENNIS: Lying down upstairs. He had another one of those dizzy spells after you left.

MISS RAYMOND: It's from staying in—no exercise. I'll remedy that. *(Extracting the liquor bottle from the bag.)* Shall I open it.

DENNIS: No.

(She regards him.)

DENNIS: I'm afraid there's been a change in plans.

MISS RAYMOND: A change?

DENNIS: I don't know quite how to put it.

MISS RAYMOND: The plainer the better.

DENNIS: He insists on going to the nursing home.

MISS RAYMOND: Why?

DENNIS: The last attack really scared him.

MISS RAYMOND: There's nothing seriously wrong with him.

DENNIS: I'll let the doctors be the judge of that.

MISS RAYMOND: You were so desperate not to commit him.

DENNIS: It's *his* decision.

MISS RAYMOND: Which you didn't influence at all.

DENNIS: You think I want him in a nursing home?

MISS RAYMOND: Is it some reservation about me?

DENNIS: No.

MISS RAYMOND: It *was* a whirlwind interview.

DENNIS: Personally, I find you ideal. But it's his choice.

MISS RAYMOND: If it's the salary, I may have been high.

DENNIS: Exorbitant. But in my opinion, worth every cent.

MISS RAYMOND: I'd take less—considerably.

DENNIS: Why?

MISS RAYMOND: I think…I know I would be comfortable here.

DENNIS: With only a sick old man for company?

MISS RAYMOND: I've just come through a trying time. The isolation appeals.

DENNIS: A made-in-heaven arrangement if there ever was one, but I'm not in charge. *(Offering his hand.)* Good-bye, Miss Raymond.

MISS RAYMOND: *(Ignoring his hand.)* I'd like to speak to him.

DENNIS: I'm sorry—but no.

MISS RAYMOND: Another one of *his* decisions?

DENNIS: Yes.

MISS RAYMOND: I don't believe you.

DENNIS: I asked him to tell you. He said he wasn't up to it. Said I should thank you for everything.

MISS RAYMOND: I'm touched.

DENNIS: I apologize for wasting your time. Am willing to pay for it.

MISS RAYMOND: Generous to a flaw.

DENNIS: How much?

MISS RAYMOND: I insist on seeing him.

DENNIS: It's settled. Good-bye.

MISS RAYMOND: Until *he* tells me he prefers going to that home, I'm not budging.

DENNIS: I'm trying to make it easy on you.

MISS RAYMOND: You think I didn't sniff through all your praise and gratitude?

DENNIS: He said you got on his nerves.

MISS RAYMOND: Is that what he said?

DENNIS: Yes.

MISS RAYMOND: *(Shouting upstairs.) Is that what you said, Mr. Quinlan? I got on your nerves?*

DENNIS: Get out!

MISS RAYMOND: *Shall I have my say, Mr. Quinlan? Speak my piece?*
(As he moves to eject her, they are arrested by Mr. Quinlan's banging cane and:)

MR. QUINLAN'S VOICE: *What the hell's going on? (Footsteps and then Mr. Quinlan, in pajamas and robe, appears.)*

MR. QUINLAN: What's all the racket?

DENNIS: Miss Raymond was saying good-bye.

MR. QUINLAN: *(To Dennis.)* Miss Raymond?

DENNIS: The housekeeper you were going to hire until you changed your mind.

MISS RAYMOND: We talked sports, played checkers. If that doesn't jog your memory there are other things.

MR. QUINLAN: *I remember.*

DENNIS: I told Miss Raymond you insisted on going to the home. She doesn't believe me.

MR. QUINLAN: *(To Miss Raymond.)* It's true.

MISS RAYMOND: You were fine when I left. Everything was agreed on.

MR. QUINLAN: I had a dizzy spell. Realize I've been kidding myself. *(To Dennis.)* What's her name?

MISS RAYMOND: Fiona Raymond.

MR. QUINLAN: I thank you, Fiona Raymond, but it wasn't meant to be. I'm sorry. I have to rest now. *(He starts toward the stairs.)*

MISS RAYMOND: *(To Dennis.)* If you let him go to that home, you might as well shoot him.

MR. QUINLAN: It's *my* decision!

MISS RAYMOND: Born of false guilt and phony bereavement.

MR. QUINLAN: *(To Dennis.)* What did I tell you when she first came in? A loony. A nut.

DENNIS: I'll handle it—go to bed.

MR. QUINLAN: God knows what she might say next.

MISS RAYMOND: Take a guess!

MR. QUINLAN: *(Clutching his bosom.)* Oh—dear God.

DENNIS: What is it?

MR. QUINLAN: My heart—a real stabbing pain.

DENNIS: *(Helping him to a chair.)* I'll call the doctor.

MISS RAYMOND: How about a priest? Three, four, seven, six, zero, four, one. Ask for Father Mancini who has a soft spot for "sins of the flesh."

MR. QUINLAN: Get her out of here!

MISS RAYMOND: "Bless me father for I have sinned as recently as an hour ago." *(Dennis and Mr. Quinlan regard her incredulously.)*

MISS RAYMOND: Yes.

MR. QUINLAN: She made sexual advances. I wasn't going to say anything but there it is.

DENNIS: I beg you, Miss Raymond, please leave.

MISS RAYMOND: Didn't you hear what he said?

DENNIS: He's not himself. *(To his father.)* Apologize to Miss Raymond.

MISS RAYMOND: There's no need. It's true.

DENNIS: What?

MISS RAYMOND: I made sexual advances.

MR. QUINLAN: Not just crazy, but a slut.

DENNIS: You made a pass at him?

MISS RAYMOND: Which was more than reciprocated.

MR. QUINLAN: That's a lie!

MISS RAYMOND: We had sex.

(Dennis explodes with laughter.)

MR. QUINLAN: What is it?

DENNIS: She says you and she made love.

MR. QUINLAN: What's funny about that?

DENNIS: In your condition? *(Laughing again.)*

MR. QUINLAN: *(Laughing with him.)* Like I said—a loony of the first order.

DENNIS: My apologies for doubting you.

MR. QUINLAN: Accepted.

MISS RAYMOND: In the bedroom there are pink floral drapes, an oak chiffonier, and a branching crack in the ceiling that resembles the letter Y.

MR. QUINLAN: *I had to go to the bathroom. She took advantage of my absence to snoop.*

DENNIS: There's no need to explain.

MISS RAYMOND: Sniff the pillows—examine the sheets.

MR. QUINLAN: *(Jumping to his feet.)* Another word and I'll strangle you!

MISS RAYMOND: Note the agility with which he sprang from that chair?

DENNIS: Get out or I'll throw you out!

MISS RAYMOND: Can't you see he's faking? Punishing himself for a miserable marriage.

MR. QUINLAN: I blabbed a bit—but nothing derogatory.

DENNIS: I understand.

MR. QUINLAN: *A son in a million.*

MISS RAYMOND: Your father's penis is long and narrow.

DENNIS: I wouldn't know.

MISS RAYMOND: You *are* a son in a million.

MR. QUINLAN: Call Bellevue—it's the only way.

MISS RAYMOND: *(To Dennis.)* Is it possible you believe me but pretend not to so you can put him away?

MR. QUINLAN: He'd give his arm to keep me out of that home!

MISS RAYMOND: *(To Dennis—ignoring his father.)* Well?

DENNIS: The question's too ridiculous to dignify.

MISS RAYMOND: A familiar refrain that usually means bull's-eye.

DENNIS: You really think I want him to go to that home?

MISS RAYMOND: No. And that's the saddest part of all.

MR. QUINLAN: They say it's best to humor them.

MISS RAYMOND: *(To Mr. Quinlan.)* If you let your son deprive you of the little pleasure that remains, you burden the rest of his days.

MR. QUINLAN: *I would die for my son!*

MISS RAYMOND: That's the easy way out.

(Turning abruptly, she exits. father and son transfixed for a moment. And then.)

MR. QUINLAN: What was that all about?

DENNIS: Your guess is as good as mine.

MR. QUINLAN: I don't mind saying she scared the hell out of me.

DENNIS: Why?

MR. QUINLAN: There's been several murders in the neighborhood. And all that wild talk. I was afraid you might take her seriously.

DENNIS: A demented slut?

(Mr. Quinlan reacts.)

DENNIS: Isn't that what you called her?

MR. QUINLAN: *(Noting the liquor bottle.)* She got the booze I see.

DENNIS: What sort of an opinion do you think I have of you?

MR. QUINLAN: In light of our recent ordeal, a little taste is in order. All in favor?

DENNIS: What sort of an opinion do you think I have of you?

MR. QUINLAN: Better than I deserve. I'll get the glasses. *(He starts toward the dining area.)*

DENNIS: You're feeling better then?

MR. QUINLAN: A shade. On the rocks?

DENNIS: Neat will do.

MR. QUINLAN: Neat it is.

(Overwhelmed, he at the dining room table weeps silently. In the living room Dennis, equally distressed, struggles to maintain composure.)

DENNIS: How you doing?

MR. QUINLAN: Fine…I'll open the bottle.

DENNIS: Right.

MR. QUINLAN: …Neat you said.

DENNIS: Right.

MR. QUINLAN: …The glasses are dusty—need wiping.

DENNIS: Take your time.

MR. QUINLAN: …She must have peeked.

DENNIS: What?

MR. QUINLAN: When I went to the bathroom, she must have sneaked a look to describe my privates so accurately.

DENNIS: Elementary, Watson.

MR. QUINLAN: What?

DENNIS: There's no need to explain.

MR. QUINLAN: The idea of cavorting with the likes of her turns my stomach.

DENNIS: Forget about it.

MR. QUINLAN: It's a lucky thing you caught wise to her.

DENNIS: It wasn't *me* who caught wise, it was *you.*

MR. QUINLAN: Are you sure?

DENNIS: You said you changed your mind. Told me to get rid of her.

MR. QUINLAN: I can't hold a thought from one minute to the next and she accuses me of rape.

DENNIS: She didn't say rape.

MR. QUINLAN: Whatever she said—it's ridiculous.

DENNIS: Agreed.

MR. QUINLAN: A man in my condition.

DENNIS: What about that drink?

MR. QUINLAN: Come and get it.

   (Dennis joins his father at the table.)

DENNIS: Shall I do the honors?

MR. QUINLAN: Please.

DENNIS: *(Pouring.)* Your doctor would have a fit if he saw this.

MR. QUINLAN: Not if he'd been through what we've been through. Don't spare the horses.

DENNIS: What'll we drink to?

MR. QUINLAN: The two nicest fellows in the house.

DENNIS: You took the words out of my mouth.

   (They touch glasses and down the hatch.)

MR. QUINLAN: Every time you open the door these days, you take your life in your hands.

DENNIS: That's one good thing about the nursing home.

MR. QUINLAN: What's that?

DENNIS: Security.

MR. QUINLAN: She accused you of wanting to put me away.

DENNIS: Refill?

MR. QUINLAN: If I hadn't known she was crazy before, I'd have known it then.

DENNIS: Care for another? Don't mind if I do. *(He refills his glass.)*

MR. QUINLAN: If what she'd said about me going to bed with her was true, you'd have been glad.

DENNIS: Glad?

MR. QUINLAN: To learn I was equal to the task. Wouldn't you?

DENNIS: *(Raising his glass.)* Skoal.

MR. QUINLAN: Wouldn't you?

DENNIS: I've had my fill of fantasy.

MR. QUINLAN: Suppose it wasn't fantasy?

DENNIS: Suppose I could fly.

MR. QUINLAN: For the sake of argument, does a man capable of a roll in the hay belong in a nursing home?

DENNIS: What man is that?

   (Mr. Quinlan pours a shot—downs it; quickly refills his glass and downs it.)

MR. QUINLAN: You were right about me and the senoritas in South America. I cut quite a swath. Ditto the dancer on the *SS Wilmont;* the ladies at the Taft; the Widow Ferguson; and others too numerous to name.

   (Dennis reacts.)

MR. QUINLAN: Isn't that what you wanted to hear?

DENNIS: Some other time. I have to get back to the office. *(He rises.)*

MR. QUINLAN: *Now.*

(Dennis hesitates; resumes his seat.)

MR. QUINLAN: You asked what occupies my mind sitting here all day. It's them. *The women.* All shapes. All sorts. All inviting. Especially those never sampled. One in particular: A school teacher, ample and creamy, who summoned me to discuss your conduct when you were in second grade.

DENNIS: Miss Orenstein?

MR. QUINLAN: Gave me her home phone—never used for fear of complication. Foundation 8-0129.

DENNIS: Be funny if you dialed it now and she answered.

MR. QUINLAN: Funny?

DENNIS: After so many years. She, like you, probably a grandparent.

MR. QUINLAN: How about if she remembered me? Not only remembered but renewed the invitation. Still funny?

DENNIS: Funny yes. Credible no.

MR. QUINLAN: You think sex has an age limit?

DENNIS: The point eludes.

MR. QUINLAN: What Miss Raymond said was not without substance.

DENNIS: She said so much—refresh me…Well?

MR. QUINLAN: It happened.

DENNIS: It?

MR. QUINLAN: I made love to her.

DENNIS: Nice try but no cigar.

MR. QUINLAN: I swear.

DENNIS: Is there anything you wouldn't say to avoid going to that home?

MR. QUINLAN: Playing checkers and the rest was an act for your benefit.

DENNIS: Of course.

(Mr. Quinlan starts toward the stairs.)

DENNIS: Where are you going?

MR. QUINLAN: To fetch the bed sheets—show you the stains!

DENNIS: *(Studying him.)*…You really mean it.

MR. QUINLAN: Yes.

DENNIS: Well I'll be damned.

MR. QUINLAN: You're convinced.

DENNIS: Amazed.

MR. QUINLAN: That's all you have to say?

DENNIS: It's hard to know what's appropriate.

MR. QUINLAN: I thought you'd be pleased.

DENNIS: I am. A man capable of fucking is no candidate for a nursing home. We owe Miss what's-her-name an enormous debt.

MR. QUINLAN: I know where to reach her.

DENNIS: What for?

MR. QUINLAN: To say we've reconsidered—she can have the job.

DENNIS: Speak for yourself.

MR. QUINLAN: You're opposed?

DENNIS: Doesn't it strike you odd, her whisking you off to bed?

MR. QUINLAN: That was my doing.

DENNIS: Overwhelmed her did you? Or was it love at first sight—violins?

MR. QUINLAN: You begged me to quit mourning!

DENNIS: A quick jump is one thing. A live-in whore is another.

MR. QUINLAN: You're a better judge of character than that.

DENNIS: What about those thirty-nine wonderful years?

MR. QUINLAN: Is it the house? Fear she might coax me to change my will?

DENNIS: That hadn't occurred but it's worth a thought.

MR. QUINLAN: I'll sign everything over to you.

DENNIS: I've got a better idea: You're coming with us to California.

MR. QUINLAN: Your wife and I would be at each others throats in a week.

DENNIS: *I'm not leaving you with someone neither of us knew before she walked in the door.*

MR. QUINLAN: Your final word?

DENNIS: Unless you have something to add…Well?

MR. QUINLAN: Jesus, Mary and Joseph guide me.

DENNIS: I thought this was a private conversation.

MR. QUINLAN: We're not strangers.

DENNIS: What?

MR. QUINLAN: We, Miss Raymond and I, knew each other previously.

DENNIS: Of course.

MR. QUINLAN: *It's true.*

DENNIS: Rave on.

MR. QUINLAN: Wait here while I dress.

DENNIS: And then?

MR. QUINLAN: I'm taking you to the Starlight where they'll tell you she and I were lovers before your mother died.

DENNIS: I wouldn't if I were you.

MR. QUINLAN: Why?

DENNIS: If you convince me, you'll never see me again.

MR. QUINLAN: That's putting it plain.

DENNIS: I hope so.

MR. QUINLAN: …Give me your hand.

DENNIS: What for?

MR. QUINLAN: We've come to the parting of the ways.

DENNIS: You're bluffing.

MR. QUINLAN: Give me your hand and see.

> *(Dennis extends his hand. Mr. Quinlan clasps it and clings forcefully.)*

MR. QUINLAN: How about that grip for a man you'd put in a nursing home?

DENNIS: Impressive but can you sustain it?

MR. QUINLAN: Five bucks you cry uncle as always.

DENNIS: The nursing home if you fail?

MR. QUINLAN: It's a deal.

> *(All-out struggle underwrites the ensuing dialogue.)*

MR. QUINLAN: You'd rather see me in that home than here with her.

DENNIS: Affirmative.

MR. QUINLAN: You really want to punish me.

DENNIS: Same reply.

MR. QUINLAN: Why?

DENNIS: Full particulars or summary?

MR. QUINLAN: The short form will do.

DENNIS: Every son competes with his father for his mother.

MR. QUINLAN: So where's the novelty?

DENNIS: I won.

MR. QUINLAN: And *my* offense?

DENNIS: Letting me win so easily.

MR. QUINLAN: You righteous mutt.

DENNIS: Words that never fail to inspire. *(Applying increased pressure to his father's hand.)* Encore.

MR. QUINLAN: *Mutt.*

DENNIS: *(More pressure still.)* Fortissimo!

MR. QUINLAN: *(In growing pain.)* Mutt!

DENNIS: *(With an all-out surge.)* Louder still!

MR. QUINLAN: *MUTT!* *(Vanquished, he breaks off the contest, pulls away.)* Congratulations.

DENNIS: Are you all right?

MR. QUINLAN: Didn't think you had it in you.

DENNIS: I was about to say the same to you.

MR. QUINLAN: I lost.

DENNIS: By a whisker.

MR. QUINLAN: A first. Proves how poorly I am—that I belong in the home.

DENNIS: A man who can diddle?

MR. QUINLAN: Don't tell me you fell for that stuff?

DENNIS: Completely.

MR. QUINLAN: Pure make-believe.

DENNIS: It had the ring of truth.

MR. QUINLAN: It was a lie! *(He starts for the stairs.)*

DENNIS: Where are you going?

MR. QUINLAN: To pack my things. I want to go to the home immediately.

DENNIS: What's the rush?

MR. QUINLAN: I'm too ill to be alone.

DENNIS: Afraid Miss Raymond might come back and you'll weaken again.

MR. QUINLAN: *I tell you it never happened.*

DENNIS: "Fair Fiona's got the hots. Wants daddy to make them go away."

MR. QUINLAN: What?

DENNIS: I came back for my umbrella. Heard everything.

MR. QUINLAN: If there's a spark of mercy, strike me dead!

DENNIS: The easy way out. Like Miss Raymond said.

MR. QUINLAN: *Don't utter that slut's name in this house.*

DENNIS: You sang a different song at the Hotel Marquette—room four-seventeen.

MR. QUINLAN: Is there no limit to your cruelty?

DENNIS: Look at me.

MR. QUINLAN: I can't.

DENNIS: *Look at me!*

>   *(Mr. Quinlan regards him.)*

DENNIS: Put on your white suit. Go to the Starlight where you'll doubtless find Miss Raymond and ask her to live with you.

MR. QUINLAN: So you can go away relieved.

DENNIS: Yes.

MR. QUINLAN: Spare me the tears.

DENNIS: There are no tears.

MR. QUINLAN: *I can see them God damn it. The same crybaby you always were. One minute dividing us—the next begging us to stay together.*

DENNIS: *You used me as a football—a battlefield!*

MR. QUINLAN: *You volunteered!* …What are you waiting for?

DENNIS: The next line is yours.

MR. QUINLAN: "Get out of my house?"

DENNIS: That should do it.

MR. QUINLAN: *Get out of my house!*
  (Dennis just stands there.)

MR. QUINLAN: Now what?

DENNIS: I want to go but my feet won't obey.

MR. QUINLAN: Get out before I throw you out!

DENNIS: If you'd be so kind.

MR. QUINLAN: Get out!
  (He gives Dennis a shove that drives him toward the door.)

MR. QUINLAN: *Get out!*
  (Another push takes him to the door which Mr. Quinlan opens.)

MR. QUINLAN: GET OUT!
  (A final shove propels Dennis from the place. Mr. Quinlan closes the door, and, spent, leans against it catching his breath when the significance of what's happened hits him. Hoping to find Dennis there, he opens the door. Not finding him he dashes into the street. Returns, after a quick and unavailing look.)

MR. QUINLAN: Good riddance! *(Still breathing hard, he moves to the sofa. Flings the cane away. Sits. Something alien registers. Reaching under the cushion he extracts the apple. Raising his arm to hurl it, he spots the whiskey bottle on the dining table. Goes to it.)* Don't mind if I do. *(Pours a shot.)* To the two nicest fellows in the house.
  (Downs the shot. Pours another. Downs it. Realizes booze won't ease his pain and just sits until the doorbell rings. Thinking it's Dennis, he jumps to his feet. Goes to the door as the bell rings again.)

MR. QUINLAN: *I meant what I said—go away!*

MISS RAYMOND'S VOICE: It's me.
  (He admits her.)

MR. QUINLAN: I thought it was my son. I threw him out.

MISS RAYMOND: Why?

MR. QUINLAN: None of your business…Well?

MISS RAYMOND: Well?

MR. QUINLAN: What do you want?

MISS RAYMOND: What do *you* want?

MR. QUINLAN: You're the one who came calling.

MISS RAYMOND: Your son came to the Starlight—said you wanted to see me.

MR. QUINLAN: That's a lie! …What are you waiting for?

MISS RAYMOND: I can't find my earrings—think I left them in the bedroom.

MR. QUINLAN: Get them and go.

(While she disappears upstairs, he moves to the liquor bottle—is pouring himself a shot as she reappears donning her earrings.)

MR. QUINLAN: You found them I see.

MISS RAYMOND: On the night stand beside the bed, which I shall always remember fondly.

MR. QUINLAN: And I will recall as the place where we earned eternal damnation.

MISS RAYMOND: I thought we did that at the Hotel Marquette—room four-seventeen.

MR. QUINLAN: Don't start!

MISS RAYMOND: Why do you suppose your son said you wanted to see me?

MR. QUINLAN: He really did?

MISS RAYMOND: Yes… I'll be going now.

MR. QUINLAN: Do you have time for a taste?

MISS RAYMOND: That all depends.

MR. QUINLAN: On what?

MISS RAYMOND: How you ask me.

MR. QUINLAN: If you want a drink, help yourself.

MISS RAYMOND: Not good enough.

MR. QUINLAN: Would madam care for a snort?

MISS RAYMOND: That's not what I meant.

MR. QUINLAN: If Miss Raymond would have a drink with Mr. Quinlan, he'd be much obliged.

MISS RAYMOND: Close but no cigar.

MR. QUINLAN: Fiona?

MISS RAYMOND: You're getting warm.

MR. QUINLAN: Fair Fiona, God damn it!

MISS RAYMOND: I don't mind if I do.

(Curtain.)

THE END

ANY GIVEN DAY

ORIGINAL PRODUCTION

Any Given Day, directed by Paul Benedict, scenery designed by Marjorie Bradley Kellogg, costumes by Ann Roth, lighting by Dennis Parichy was presented by Edgar Lansbury, Everett King, Dennis Grimaldi, Matt Garfield and David Young on November 16, 1993 at the Longacre Theatre, New York City. The cast in order of appearance:

Carmen Benti	Andrea Marcovicci
Willis	Justin Kirk
Gus Brower	Andrew Robinson
Nettie Cleary	Lisa Eichorn
John Cleary	Victor Slezak
Eddie Benti	Peter Frechette
Doctor Goldman	Stephen Pearlman
Mrs. Benti	Sada Thompson
Timmy Cleary	Gabriel Olds

INTRODUCTION

Sometimes you do good work and get your due. Sometimes you do bad work and get your due.

Sometimes you do bad work and get away with it, but in your heart you know.

Worst of all is knowing you did good work and were struck down unfairly. Such was the case with *Any Given Day.*

John Simon (*New York Magazine*) said: "Gilroy is a shrewd observer of both internecine abrasiveness and moments of playful lightening, and knows how to construct an effective scene and stud it with whimsical, caustic or poignant language. We feel in clean, undeceitful hands with this playwright, something we can't often say nowadays."

Clive Barnes (*New York Post*) said: "A haunting chilling portrait...Gilroy knows how to write, and he knows how to write for actors."

Dennis Cunningham (CBS-TV) said: "*Any Given Day* is better, more mature, more accomplished than *The Subject Was Roses*... First class all the way."

Michael Feingold (*The Village Voice*) said: "Unlike naturalism's dabblers and fakers, Gilroy knows how to set his characters in lively motion and trace the unhappy consequences without flinching—or omitting the humor and warmth that makes every close-knit family both a nightmare and a safe haven... Very few times in the recent flood of openings have been this enjoyable."

So what went wrong?

I don't know. But it didn't help that in the week set aside for critics we gave one distinctly inferior show (a Saturday matinee) when the *New York Times* critic was present.

I doubt seeing us at our best would have changed his opinion. But it gives me a chance to voice a thought that many (most?) theater people share:

The old way, having all critics present opening night—one roll of the dice for everything—was better for several reasons:

Number one—you can't expect actors to stay at opening night pitch for an entire week.

Two: It robs you of the chance to make changes right up to the opening, which is what previews were intended for. How can you experiment (dare to blunder) with critics in the audience?

Three: It deprives opening nights of their once electric air—that sense of heightened occasion. Critics hastening up the aisles as the final curtain fell to pound out their immediate impressions for the morning edition.

Measure this against the current situation.

With several days to write their reviews, critics can ruminate, reflect, discuss with family and friends, research, and second guess.

Possibly he or she does none of the above.

But in any case, what tends to result lacks the excitement compelled by an immediate deadline.

In its place we are often treated to a scholarly exegesis telling us more about the critic (that they did their homework) than what they experienced during the two hours they were sitting there: Did their butts signal boredom as opposed to comparison to a play of similar genre done in 1822?

As for the argument that we now get better written reviews due to the hiatus twixt experience and reaction, I offer Walter Kerr's crafted reviews, written for deadline, in rebuttal. And I do so having tasted both his praise and lash.

What about the fourteen years between *Last Licks* and *Any Given Day?*

In the interim I wrote two full length plays—*Grang* and *Ace of Spads*—both of which have had public readings.

The former exposed problems I'm working on.

The latter, read successfully at the Old Globe Theatre, prompted talk of full production, which a struggle twixt the Dramatists' Guild and League of Regional Theatres derailed.

In addition, I wrote eight more one-acts for the Ensemble Studio Theatre Marathon. (See Volume Two of this collection.)

I did screen plays for hire.

And I wrote, produced, and directed four truly independent films—"truly" signifying no pre-distribution deals or safety net of any kind. Our home at risk more than once. Enough action for any gambler.

SETTING

The entire action of the play takes place in the Benti's Bronx apartment.

CHARACTERS

MRS. BENTI: 63, widowed matriarch, German extraction, which none of her three children, stamped with their late father's Italianate features, reflect.

CARMEN BENTI: 37, unwed mother of Willis.

WILLIS: nominal age 18 but instrument damage at birth has left him physically handicapped and mentally retarded (without impairment of facial features), so he appears both younger and older.

GUS BOWER: 37, Carmen's boyfriend.

NETTIE CLEARY: 36, Carmen's sister.

JOHN CLEARY: 40, her husband.

TIMMY CLEARY: 16, their son.

EDDIE BENTI: 35, Nettie's and Carmen's brother.

DOCTOR GOLDMAN: 50, the family physician.

SYNOPSIS

ACT I

Scene I: November 1941, Sunday afternoon.

Scene II: Wednesday. Two weeks later.

ACT II

Fifteen months later, early February 1943, Saturday afternoon.

ACT I
SCENE I

Time: November 1941, Sunday afternoon. Setting: The Bronx, New York, west of the Grand Concourse. The Benti's apartment (second floor) in an aging five-story walk-up. The generous room dimensions, height especially, suggest it was a superior dwelling in its prime. The dining room and living room, divided by an invisible wall, are linked upstage and downstage. From the dining room there is an entrance, by swinging door, to the kitchen (off-stage), a door to Mrs. Benti's bedroom, and the entrance to a hallway leading to the front door, two bedrooms, and bathroom—all offstage. The living room contains curtained French doors that open on Eddie's bedroom (off-stage). Furnishings in the living room include a piano and stool; a glass-fronted bookcase filled to overflowing with eclectic works; a radio; an oriental rug the worse for wear. The dining room is dominated by a rectangular table with ten chairs—not all matching. There is a sideboard which, like the furniture is sturdy, dark-hued, and weathered.

A foot-treadle sewing machine in a corner contributes to the feeling that this apartment has been much lived in for a long time. There is something melancholy and comfortable about this place—the former quality muted by ample light from the large avenue that the living room fronts and light from the side street that the dining room looks out on.

At rise: Carmen, Gus, John, Nettie, Eddie, and Doctor Goldman at the table in the dining room. Remnants of dessert. Whiskey bottle and glasses. The Doctor, three-piece suit, black bag by his chair. Gus and John in shirts, ties and vests. Eddie in shirt and tie. Carmen dressed with a tendency to flamboyance heightened by Nettie's conservative apparel. Willis, shirt and trousers, no tie, alone in the living room, seated in a wheelchair (which he never propels). As always it's impossible to gauge what he grasps of what's going on so that people often converse and conduct themselves as though he weren't there.

EDDIE: Another drink, Doctor?

DOCTOR GOLDMAN: No.

EDDIE: If you don't have one, I'll be forced to down your share, which is against your explicit orders.

WILLIS: *(Spelling is his proudest achievement.)* E-X-P-L-I-C-I-T.

DOCTOR GOLDMAN: I have calls to make.

CARMEN: *(Indicating John—the hint of a dig.)* Cleary will give you one of his breath mints.

DOCTOR GOLDMAN: One more drink would do me in as usual.

GUS: Professional standards first: I respect you, Doctor.

EDDIE: Not even a weak one?

NETTIE: *(To Eddie—indicating the Doctor.)* Keep it up and he'll never drop in again.

DOCTOR GOLDMAN: Nothing would prevent me from doing that, I assure you.

EDDIE: *(Offering his empty glass to John, nearest the whiskey bottle.)* I thought you'd never ask.

CARMEN: Should you?

EDDIE: *(To John—first hint of the constant and thinly veiled enmity between them.)* There's a wee drop left. Or are you planning on drinking it all yourself?

JOHN: There's plenty left.

NETTIE: *(To John.)* Make it a small one.
(John pours.)

EDDIE: *(Critical of the amount.)* She said small not infinitesimal.

WILLIS: I-N-F-I-N-I-T-E-S-I-M-A-L.

EDDIE: Cheers. *(He downs it.)*

DOCTOR GOLDMAN: I hate to miss your mother, but duty calls.

NETTIE: She'll be here any minute.

EDDIE: Unless the sponsor detains her.

GUS: "The sponsor"?

CARMEN: Miss Julian. The daughter of the man our father worked for.

EDDIE: An old maid worth far more than her weight in gold.

NETTIE: *(To Gus.)* She gives us money from time to time.

JOHN: Time to time? When Miss Julian doesn't cough up, Mrs. Benti stays away to punish her.

NETTIE: *(Protesting.)* That's not the only reason Mama goes to see her. They're friends.

EDDIE: Some say Miss Julian gives out of the goodness of her heart. The truth is she had a secret crush on our late father. The wages of guilt.

CARMEN: If only they'd slept together.
(Eddie and Doctor Goldman laugh; John is annoyed; Gus and Nettie are embarrassed.)

NETTIE: Carmen, really.

EDDIE: It's a one hour trolley car ride each way. Which our mother makes round trip on a single fare.

CARMEN: By browbeating the conductor until he accepts a worthless transfer to avoid a scene. That's when you know she's German.

EDDIE: Until I was thirteen she palmed me off as under six so I rode for free.

NETTIE: *(Laughing with the others in spite of herself. To Gus)* They exaggerate.

GUS: I understand. *(To the group.)* Your mother German but all of you so Italian. How do you account for it?

EDDIE: Chalk one up for the good guys.

GUS: The good guys?

CARMEN: Our father's influence.

GUS: I see *(Rising.)* Excuse me.

CARMEN: For what?

GUS: To get my jacket before your mother arrives.

CARMEN: Always the gentleman.

GUS: I try.

NETTIE: It's appreciated.

GUS: Thank you. *(Rises and exits to the living room where he retrieves his jacket from the back of a chair.)*
(Eddie has a coughing fit.)

CARMEN: You shouldn't have had that drink.

NETTIE: The smoking's worse. *(To Doctor Goldman.)* Can't you do something?

DOCTOR GOLDMAN: He's a grown man—won't listen. *(To Eddie.)* At least come in for a checkup. It's been over a year.
(Gus is donning his jacket when he becomes aware of Willis regarding him.)

GUS: And how are you today?

WILLIS: *Ex*-cellent. E-X-C-E-L-L-E-N-T.

GUS: You're a fine speller.

WILLIS: *(In the secret language he resorts to frequently.)* Koopie-say.

GUS: *(Uneasily.)* I never know quite how to converse with you. Am never sure how much you comprehend…But somehow today, I feel compelled to say what I have to say whether you grasp it or not. Just so there are no misunderstandings…
(In the dining room Eddie has a new coughing fit.)

EDDIE: Pardon me. *(He exits into the living room, en route to his bedroom behind the French doors.)*

WILLIS: *(Hailing him.)* How are you Eddie dear?

EDDIE: *(Detouring to tweak Willis' nose reassuringly, he pronounces a word from the secret vocabulary they share.)* Poop-shla.

WILLIS: *(Brightening at his touch.)* "Sometimes we're happy."

EDDIE: "And sometimes the bottle's empty."

GUS: *(To Eddie indicating Willis.)* I'm never sure how much he understands.

EDDIE: Nothing significant escapes him.

WILLIS: S-I-G-N-I-F-I-C-A-N-T.

EDDIE: Bravo.

WILLIS: Bravissimo.

(A renewed fit of coughing sends Eddie to his room from which we hear muf-fled coughs that soon cease.)

GUS: *(To Willis.)* Let me start again…Your mother and I are going to an-nounce our engagement when your grandmother returns…I have been direct and honest with her where you're concerned…I've said…I've told her that while I most definitely will not raise another man's child, I will agree to have you live with us for a month every year…I'm a business-man and I put it to her as a business proposition…We each bring assets to the partnership. And like any partnership it will succeed only in so far as the foundation is firm. Which means truth without equivocation from the start. And please understand there is nothing personal in my refusal to have you live with us permanently. I mean I would feel the same regardless of your condition…

(Willis has been writing in the air, a frequent activity, while Gus speaks.)

GUS: If you grasp any of this, *please* let me know.

WILLIS: "Hi ya, captain, how's your ship? Pardon me, captain, my finger slipped." *(He goes from a salute to a nose-thumb while reciting the above.)*

GUS: Is that aimed at me or nonsense?

WILLIS: N-O-N-S-E-N-S-E.

GUS: I don't think you like me which is understandable…Well I've tried. *(He returns to the dining room.)*

DOCTOR GOLDMAN: I really must go.

NETTIE: Mama will be so sorry she missed you.

DOCTOR GOLDMAN: Likewise.

JOHN: Did I ever tell you about the first time I met my wife's family?

DOCTOR GOLDMAN: *(Something always guarded between them.)* I don't believe so.

NETTIE: *(To John—embarrassed.)* Not that again.

JOHN: I was talking to the doctor.

DOCTOR GOLDMAN: *(In deference to Nettie's feelings.)* I'm late now.

JOHN: *(Overriding the Doctor's protest.)* "I'd like you to meet my family," she said. So I came to their home for dinner. We're about to sit down when I hear all kinds of whistles in the street. "What's that?," I asked. "That's the rest of my family. They're engineers," she says.

(In the living room, Eddie emerges from his bedroom, is patting Willis' cheek.)

NETTIE: Doctor Goldman doesn't know what you're talking about.

JOHN: *(He won't be silenced.)* I went to the window and the street was full of peanut vendors.

DOCTOR GOLDMAN: *(Blankly.)* Peanut vendors?

JOHN: With their carts. Blowing their steam whistles.

DOCTOR GOLDMAN: What about them?

NETTIE: It's a dumb thing.

CARMEN: Italians.

DOCTOR GOLDMAN: Italians?

CARMEN: It's Cleary's way of suggesting he married beneath him.

JOHN: *It's a joke.*

EDDIE: *(Entering the dining room—to John, caustically.)* You want a real laugh try organ grinders and monkeys.

JOHN: Another county heard from.

DOCTOR GOLDMAN: *(To Nettie.)* Tell your mother—

(The doorbell sounds: three short brisk rings.)

EDDIE: Speak of the devil.

NETTIE: Forgot her keys again. *(She disappears down the hallway.)*

EDDIE: Judging by the ring, I'd say the sponsor coughed up a hundred, minimum. Any wagers?

JOHN: *(Pointedly.)* How would you pay if you lost?

EDDIE: *(Stung, but lightly to hide it.)* He's got me there.

(Mrs. Benti, energized, an unwavering gaze reinforced by ramrod posture, precedes Nettie into the dining room.)

MRS. BENTI: *(To Doctor Goldman.)* How nice.

DOCTOR GOLDMAN: It's been a while and I have a patient in the neighborhood.

EDDIE: *(To his mother.)* Where's the loot?

MRS. BENTI: You've been drinking.

EDDIE: If it's more than a hundred blink three times.

MRS. BENTI: *(Taking her place at the head of the table. To Nettie.)* Get me a cup of coffee and one for the doctor.

NETTIE: We're drinking tea.

MRS. BENTI: Tea then.

GUS: *(Tapping a knife against a glass to get their attention.)* I'm afraid tea doesn't suit the occasion. *(To Carmen.)* Shall I?

CARMEN: *(Matter-of-fact.)* Gus and I are getting married.

GUS: *(In a rush.)* We decided last night, which is why there's no ring. But we are officially engaged. *(To Eddie.)* There's a bottle of champagne in the ice box.

EDDIE: Coming right up. *(He exits to fetch it.)*

CARMEN: …A deathly silence gripped the room.

NETTIE: It's such a surprise. Congratulations. *(Hugging her sincerely.)*

DOCTOR GOLDMAN: Congratulations.

NETTIE: I'm so pleased for you. *(To Gus.)* And for you.

JOHN: *(To Gus—ambiguously.)* Welcome to the club.

CARMEN: That the best you can do?

JOHN: *(Exaggeratedly.)* Heartfelt wishes to you both. Okay?

GUS: *(The subtext eluding him.)* Thank you. Thank you very much. *(To Mrs. Benti.)* And you, Mrs. Benti? I should call you mother, but I don't feel comfortable enough. Perhaps in time. What do you say?

MRS. BENTI: You'll take the boy one month a year and contribute financially?

GUS: Everything as stipulated. You have my word.

NETTIE: *(To Carmen.)* Have you set the date?

CARMEN: As soon as we find an apartment.

GUS: I already have several leads.

   (Eddie returns from the kitchen with an open champagne bottle and glasses. Gus pours.)

DOCTOR GOLDMAN: *(As Gus proffers a glass.)* Not for me, thanks.

GUS: Just a sip.

NETTIE: You must, Doctor. Everyone must or it's bad luck.

GUS: *(To Mrs. Benti.)* I tried explaining to your grandson but doubt he got it.

DOCTOR GOLDMAN: *(Taking a glass.)* I shouldn't be doing this.

EDDIE: *(Bringing a glass to Willis.)* Care to drink to the bride and groom?

WILLIS: Ka-vilda ka-vilda.

EDDIE: My sentiments exactly.

   (He wheels Willis to the dining room table. Stays Willis' hand as he lifts the glass.)

EDDIE: Wait for the toast.

WILLIS: Whatever you say, Eddie darling.

GUS: Who'll give the toast? Eddie?

EDDIE: Unaccustomed as I am to public speaking.

NETTIE: *(Amiably.)* Just do it.

EDDIE: *(Solemnly.)* …They say a man is not complete until he takes a wife…And then he's finished.

GUS: *(The only laugher.)* That's a good one. *(To Carmen.)* Don't you get it?

CARMEN: I should. I've heard it often enough.

GUS: It's a new one on me.

JOHN: What was the show where someone asks "Who gave the bride away?" and Jimmy Durante says "Nobody said a word"?

NETTIE: *(Hastily to cover her husband's gaffe.)* Will somebody say something sensible before the champagne is flat?

GUS: Perhaps Doctor Goldman will honor us.

EDDIE: Second the motion.

DOCTOR GOLDMAN: It should be a family member.

MRS. BENTI: Which is how we consider you.

EDDIE: Hear-hear.

NETTIE: Please, Doctor.

DOCTOR GOLDMAN: *(Looking about.)* No objections?...All right—if you insist. *(He gets to his feet—glass in hand.)* It's fitting your mother includes me in this family because that's how I feel after so many years as physician and, hopefully, friend to each and every one of you with the exception of the groom to be.

GUS: Be assured if my doctor retires—

CARMEN: *(To Gus.)* —Let him speak.

GUS: Sorry.

DOCTOR GOLDMAN: I knew you first in the East Bronx on West Farms Road when, fresh from medical school, I sat in my office—all the money I could borrow and beg invested in equipment and furnishings—waiting for my first patient. Had been waiting for three days and was losing confidence when this dear lady...*(Indicating Mrs. Benti.)* entered with you...*(Indicating Eddie.)* A handkerchief wrapped around the finger you'd sliced with a knife. The blood leaking so, I remember thinking, "Please don't let it get on my new rug." "Can you save the finger?" she asked. I knew it would be difficult and my first impulse was to send him to a hospital. But the way she eyed me, playing safe wouldn't do. My first patient and I was facing a test that I knew would determine my career. "I'm willing to try," I said. She studied me so, I felt I was being x-rayed to the depths of my soul, and said...

MRS. BENTI AND DOCTOR GOLDMAN: *(Together.)*..."Go ahead."

EDDIE: *(Displaying the finger.)* Eighteen stitches.

DOCTOR GOLDMAN: Word spread. My practice flourished. And little by little I got to know all of you. I shared your burdens which have been many. And I shared your joys, such as I hope today's occasion will prove to be...To the happy couple.

THE OTHERS: *(With the exception of Willis.)* To the happy couple.

WILLIS: *(Delayed action.)* To the happy couple.

(Everyone except John Cleary and Mrs. Benti laughs.)

CARMEN: *(Noting the Doctor's glass.)* You barely tasted yours.

DOCTOR GOLDMAN: It's the thought that counts.

MRS. BENTI: Drink up, Doctor.

DOCTOR GOLDMAN: I have calls to make.

MRS. BENTI: Unfinished toasts are bad luck. *(She wheels Willis back to the living room.)*

DOCTOR GOLDMAN: Why do I think she just made that up? But as usual I'm helpless in her hands. L'Chaim.

EDDIE: *(As the Doctor drains his glass.)* So drink chug-a-lug.

DOCTOR GOLDMAN: If I behave like a fool, you've only yourselves to blame.

NETTIE: *(To Carmen.)* Where are you looking for an apartment?

CARMEN: Any place for the right price.

GUS: We saw one I felt was ideal in Manhattan but she didn't like it.

(Mrs. Benti returns to the dining room as John taps a knife against a glass.)

JOHN: *We* also have an announcement. *(To Nettie.)* Tell them.

NETTIE: Tell them what?

JOHN: *(To the others.)* I've had an offer to go to Brazil and run operations for one of the biggest coffee importers in America.

GUS: Congratulations.

NETTIE: *(Minimizing it.)* He's had offers before.

JOHN: This one is too good to turn down.

NETTIE: We're just talking about it.

JOHN: You said—

NETTIE: —There's been no decision.

DOCTOR GOLDMAN: It might be the sort of change he needs.

(They regard him.)

DOCTOR GOLDMAN: Your son Timmy.

NETTIE: *(Belittling the idea.)* Tropical diseases and God knows what?

DOCTOR GOLDMAN: *(His tongue loosening.)* There are balancing considerations.

JOHN: That's what I told her.

WILLIS: *(Affected by the champagne—sings.)* "Without a song, the day would never end."

EDDIE: One drink one drunk.

DOCTOR GOLDMAN: Make that two. My head spins. I warned you.

EDDIE: *(Refilling the Doctor's glass.)* You can't walk on one leg.

DOCTOR GOLDMAN: Why do I let this happen? What is this spell you people cast over me?

(Taking the replenished glass while Eddie refills the others.)

DOCTOR GOLDMAN: But if I make a fool of myself among friends, so what?

MRS. BENTI: *(Raising her glass to Nettie with hidden emphasis.)* Here's to your new life in South America

NETTIE: *(Emphatically.)* I told you we're just talking.

MRS. BENTI: Good luck.

(She drinks, as do the others with the exception of Nettie.)

DOCTOR GOLDMAN: Where is Timmy?

NETTIE: Home.

JOHN: *(Sarcastically.)* Too sick to go to mass.

NETTIE: *(To Doctor Goldman.)* Nothing serious or I would have called.

DOCTOR GOLDMAN: Fever?

NETTIE: No. Just the usual: pain over his right eye—stomach upset.

DOCTOR GOLDMAN: South America might be just the thing.

MRS. BENTI: *(Wanting him gone.)* We mustn't keep you any longer, Doctor.

DOCTOR GOLDMAN: I don't have any other calls to make. I merely said I did as an excuse not to drink. But now that I've had a drink the deed is done. In for a penny as they say. *(He downs what's in his glass.)*

EDDIE: *(Poised to refill the Doctor's glass.)* Hung for a sheep?

DOCTOR GOLDMAN: Why not? I need a break—relaxation. And it's only here I can let my hair down with impunity.

WILLIS: I-M-P-U-N-I-T-Y!

DOCTOR GOLDMAN: *(Referring to Willis' spelling.)* Is he ever wrong?

EDDIE: Not that I remember.

DOCTOR GOLDMAN: Amazing.

JOHN: Why do you think South America might be good for Timmy?

NETTIE: *(To John—not wanting to resume that topic.)* It's the doctor's day off.

DOCTOR GOLDMAN: *(Increasingly expansive.)* A change of venue might be beneficial for all concerned. And you know I'm sincere when I say that since this dear woman…*(He touches Nettie's face with great affection.)* will be missed by everyone—myself high on the list…*(To John pointedly.)* She's a darling—this girl. An angel. You're a fortunate man.

NETTIE: *(Embarrassed but pleased.)* No more champagne for the Doctor.

DOCTOR GOLDMAN: You're right. Why am I so affected by the tiniest bit of alcohol? Beyond that why are so many Jews similarly afflicted? Not affliction because it's really a saving grace supported by Darwin's theory of evolution.

JOHN: *(Derisively.)* The guy who said we're descended from apes?

EDDIE: *(Eager for battle.)* Which we are.

JOHN: Speak for yourself.

DOCTOR GOLDMAN: *(On his own wavelength.)* I think Jews with a low tolerance in ancient times, who therefore abstained, were more apt to survive than Jews who imbibed making them less sensitive to impending danger—pogroms. Natural selection.

JOHN: *(Regarding Eddie.)* One week he's spouting communism. The next it's creatures from outer space.

EDDIE: At least I read.

JOHN: What else do you have to do? .

EDDIE: Besides taking care of Willis?

JOHN: I mean a real job!

MRS. BENTI: *(To John and Eddie.)* How do you think that sounds to Willis? Or do you think he has no feelings?

GUS: *(To John and Eddie.)* Mrs. Benti, I almost said mother that time, is right. This is an occasion for rejoicing. A time of new beginnings to bury the hatchet. What must the doctor think?

DOCTOR GOLDMAN: I am like the hub of a wheel and all of you the spokes. I know you to the tips of your toes and depths of your souls. And I love you all. *(Eyes Gus.)* Of course I've only met you, but you impress me as a good and decent man.

GUS: Thank you, Doctor.

DOCTOR GOLDMAN: A man who will always deliver what he promises…

GUS: *(Flustered.)*…Merci beaucoup.

DOCTOR GOLDMAN: But unfortunately… *(He catches himself—stops.)*

GUS: Go on.

CARMEN: *(To Gus.)* Quit while you're ahead.

GUS: I'd like his complete opinion. *(To the Doctor.)* As you were saying?

EDDIE: *(Devilishly.)* In vino veritas. You're on, Doctor.

DOCTOR GOLDMAN: The trend…I mean the thread eludes.

GUS: I impressed you as a good and decent man who would always honor his promises.

DOCTOR GOLDMAN: Exactly.

GUS: Then you said "unfortunately" and stopped.

DOCTOR GOLDMAN: One look as I come through the door, my wife will say, "You've been to the Benti's again."

GUS: What is there about me that's unfortunate?

JOHN: Talk about leading with your chin.

CARMEN: *(To Gus.)* Drop it for God's sake.

GUS: *(To Carmen.)* What's needed is a wart or two to highlight my virtues. *(To Doctor Goldman.)* I will always deliver what I promise but unfortunately what?

DOCTOR GOLDMAN: …I'm afraid you will never promise very much.

CARMEN: *(To Gus.)* Satisfied?

DOCTOR GOLDMAN: No offense intended.

GUS: No offense taken. A man who doesn't overpromise will never disappoint you. Isn't that what you were saying?

DOCTOR GOLDMAN: Close enough.

GUS: I put it to Mrs. Benti: Is a man whose word is gold a good marital prospect—all other things being equal?

JOHN: *(A Groucho Marx insinuation.)* Depends what you mean by "all other things."

MRS. BENTI: My late husband was such a man. Reliable in every way.

GUS: You see?

MRS. BENTI: It's a quality least appreciated by those who should value it most.

CARMEN: Is that a dig at me or drawn from personal experience?

JOHN: If the shoe fits. *(Feigning a wince.)* Ouch—my wife just kicked me.

NETTIE: *(She'd never do such a thing.)* I did not.

CARMEN: *(To Doctor Goldman.)* Did you know my mother was married before she met my father?

DOCTOR GOLDMAN: *(Surprised.)* No.

MRS. BENTI: This hardly seems—

CARMEN: *(Refusing to be silenced.)* —She was put out to work as a young girl in the home of a wealthy family with a playboy son who took a shine to her.

DOCTOR GOLDMAN: *(To Mrs. Benti.)* A romantic secret. You've been holding out on me.

MRS. BENTI: There was nothing romantic about it.

CARMEN: You married him.

MRS. BENTI: *(To Doctor Goldman.)* He was a drunkard. His family, thinking I might be a good influence, pushed the marriage. My family, impressed by their money, pushed as well.

CARMEN: I found a picture of him she kept hidden. *(To Eddie and Nettie.)* Remember?

NETTIE: Don't.

CARMEN: *(Ignoring Nettie—to the Doctor.)* He was extremely handsome.

MRS. BENTI: The picture wasn't hidden.

CARMEN: "To my dearest dearest darling."

MRS. BENTI: I never loved him!

CARMEN: Catching us, she tore up the picture on the spot.

MRS. BENTI: I hate snooping.

CARMEN: That from a woman who opens every letter that comes to this house; eavesdrops on every call.

MRS. BENTI: That's a lie.

CARMEN: *(In a bantering manner calculated to infuriate.)* I think he was the love of your life.

MRS. BENTI: *(To Doctor Goldman—adamantly.)* Three months till I realized he'd never stop drinking and left him. A year later his family notified me he was dying and wanted to see me. I refused. *(To Carmen.)* Does that sound like I loved him?

GUS: How long till you married again?

MRS. BENTI: Several years.

DOCTOR GOLDMAN: *(To Gus.)* Mr. Benti was a gentleman in every sense of the word. Blessed with a dignity that never faltered, even at the end when his pain was extreme.

JOHN: *(Derisive.)* The meek shall inherit the earth.

NETTIE: *(To John.) He had a wealth that money can't measure.*

CARMEN: *(To Gus.)* He loved opera, concerts, ballet.

JOHN: And horses.

GUS: Horses?

JOHN: He played the ponies.

CARMEN: *(To John—pointedly.)* I can think of worse things.

WILLIS: *(Breaking into song.)* "Celeste Aida...forma divina."

DOCTOR GOLDMAN: He has a nice voice.

JOHN: He *should.*

(Carmen, Nettie, and Eddie regard John reprovingly.)

JOHN: What did I say?

(Before they can respond, Mrs. Benti addresses Gus.)

MRS. BENTI: Not a penny.

GUS: What?

MRS. BENTI: I didn't inherit anything from my first husband.

(Gus reacts.)

MRS. BENTI: Isn't that what you were wondering?

GUS: Yes. *(To Carmen.)* She read my mind.

CARMEN: Born with a double caul as I told you.

JOHN: Heigh-ho it's magic time.

NETTIE: Don't mock what you don't understand.

JOHN: Give her a little encouragement, she'll be reading cards again.

GUS: Cards?

JOHN: People came from all over to have her read their futures till the girls made her stop because a rumor began to circulate they were gypsies.

GUS: I'm by nature a skeptic but I try to keep an open mind in all things. *(To Doctor Goldman.)* Doctor, what is your scientific opinion?

DOCTOR GOLDMAN: I think, by virtue of my nose tingling, that I'm intoxicated.

GUS: Do you believe in psychic phenomena?

DOCTOR GOLDMAN: I hold no brief with magic, under which heading I include any and all religions... *(To John.)* No offense... *(To Gus.)* But, if you're asking whether this lady... *(Indicating Mrs. Benti.)* possesses an understanding of human nature so keen that she is capable of predictions that come true with startling frequency, then the answer, based on personal observation for more than twenty years, is yes.

GUS: Like most skeptics I long to believe there's more to life than meets the eye. But where's the proof—alas?

JOHN: *(To Carmen—sarcastically.)* Tell him about the lady everyone thought was dying of cancer who came to your mother as a last resort.

GUS: *(To John.)* What about her?

JOHN: Mrs. Benti read the cards and predicted what the doctor took for a tumor was an unsuspected pregnancy.

MRS. BENTI: *(With compelling authority.)* I'd abandoned the cards by then. Read tea leaves as a special favor because the woman traveled so far and was desperate.

JOHN: Six months later the lady gave birth to twins.

CARMEN: It's true.

JOHN: You should have sent it to Ripley.

MRS. BENTI: *(To Gus—indicating John.)* He makes fun because it scares him.

JOHN: *(To Gus.)* Sure you want to marry into this family now that you've had a preview?

MRS. BENTI: *(To John—challenging.)* Would you like me to read *your* future?

JOHN: *(Routed.)* This is where I came in.

NETTIE: Where are you going?

JOHN: A breath of fresh air if that's all right with you. Where's my jacket?

EDDIE: My room.

JOHN: *(As Eddie moves to fetch it.)* I'll get it.

(As he passes through the living room en route to Eddie's room, Willis hails him.)

WILLIS: How's tricks?

JOHN: You talking to me?

WILLIS: But of course.

JOHN: *(Never sure how to deal with Willis—torn between sympathy and loathing.)* Fine. How's tricks with *you?*

WILLIS: C-O-P-A-C-E-T-I-C.

JOHN: Come again?

WILLIS: Copacetic.

JOHN: Right. *(He exits into Eddie's room.)*

GUS: *(To Nettie.)* Carmen tells me your husband supported his entire family, five sisters, and a crippled father, from the time he was twelve.

NETTIE: Yes.

DOCTOR GOLDMAN: *(Expansively.)* An admirable achievement.

GUS: Indeed. But while such things build character, they take their toll.

CARMEN: What are you talking about?

GUS: *(To Nettie.)* With all due respect, your husband always seems to have a chip on his shoulder.

CARMEN: Because you only see him in this house. Out in the world he's the life of the party.

MRS. BENTI: At home anywhere but home.

CARMEN: Did Willis call me just now?

MRS. BENTI: No.

CARMEN: I think he did.

(The dining room conversation continues unheard as Carmen goes to Willis.)

CARMEN: Are you all right?

WILLIS: Yes, Mother dear.

CARMEN: I'm going to marry Gus—Mr. Brower.

WILLIS: Hepsha-pepsha.

CARMEN: It means I'll move away—won't be living here.

WILLIS: "Shake the hand that shook the hand—"

CARMEN: *(Irritated.)* —Do you understand?

WILLIS: To perfection.

CARMEN: What do you think about it?

WILLIS: Be of stout courage, my darling.

(He caresses her face reassuringly. The two of them in silent tableau while we tune in on the dining room.)

GUS: Don't you think, Mother... *There*—I said it: "Mother" spontaneously. Indicating I'm comfortable here since by nature I'm a formal person. *(Eddie has a coughing fit.)*

DOCTOR GOLDMAN: You must come to my office for a checkup.

MRS. BENTI: He'll be there this week.

DOCTOR GOLDMAN: *(To Eddie.)* For sure?

EDDIE: *(Indicating Mrs. Benti.)* You heard the warden.

GUS: *(To Mrs. Benti.)* The point I intended to make has slipped my mind.

MRS. BENTI: *(Reading him as before.)* You were going to say that my experience with my first husband, who promised to stop drinking but didn't, supports your belief that what the doctor said about you is a compliment.

GUS: *(Dumbfounded.)* She's done it again! My exact thought verbatim! Amazing!

EDDIE: You ain't seen nothing yet.

(Sometime during this last sequence, John, jacket on, emerges from Eddie's room; has been watching Carmen, her back to him, caressing Willis. Darting a look at the dining room where they are absorbed in conversation, he crosses to Carmen; slips his arms around her cupping her breasts. Startled, she turns. He embraces her fiercely. She breaks free in a way suggesting this isn't a first—that it's the timing she objects to rather than what took place.)

WILLIS: *(Like an alarm going off.)* KOOPIE SAY KAVILDA...KAVILDA... KAVILDA!

EDDIE: *(Realizing something's wrong.)* Now what?

(He goes to the living room where Carmen and John regard Willis who spouts a continuous flow of nonsense words with mounting agitation.)

EDDIE: What set him off?

CARMEN: Who knows?

WILLIS: It's these God damn sons of bitching legs!

EDDIE: *(Gripping his shoulders reassuringly.)* Have no fear Eddie's here.

GUS: Is there anything we can do?

MRS. BENTI: Eddie will take care of it.

DOCTOR GOLDMAN: *(To Gus—indicating Mrs. Benti.)* He should be in a home but she won't hear of it.

MRS. BENTI: *(To Doctor Goldman.)* You better go before your wife calls.

EDDIE: *(To Willis—calmingly.)* What do you think of the high price of putty?

WILLIS: Yes Eddie dear.

EDDIE: *(Gently insistent.)* What do you think of the high price of putty?

WILLIS: It's putty high.

EDDIE: That's my boy. *(Tweaks his nose.)* Poop shla.

WILLIS: *(Tweaking Eddie's nose in return.)* Poop shla, my darling.

JOHN: *(To Eddie—guilt expressed in anger.)* Why do you encourage that gibberish?

WILLIS: *(Pointing at John accusingly.)* Corbo…Krow-posk ah-see!

EDDIE: *(To John.)* You've heard the charge. How do you plead?

JOHN: *(Fearful what Willis might be communicating.)* What?

EDDIE: *(Does he suspect?)* Don't play the innocent.

JOHN: I'm getting out of this mad house.

CARMEN: Anyone stopping you?

JOHN: *(Pointedly.)* Congratulations on your engagement.

CARMEN: *(In similar vein.)* And to you on South America.

GUS: *(To John as he moves from the living room with the intention of leaving.)* I hope you won't go to South America before the wedding.

NETTIE: *(Before John can reply.)* We'd never do that. Besides nothing's settled.

DOCTOR GOLDMAN: Go there. If for no other reason than Timmy's health.

GUS: What exactly is wrong with him?

NETTIE: He's underweight for one thing.

GUS: Delicate, in other words.

JOHN: *(Boorishly.)* He likes girls.

GUS: I wasn't suggesting…

DOCTOR GOLDMAN: *(To Nettie.)* If you go to South America, I'll lose one of the two women who invest my dreams…*(He turns to Gus.)* And the other one I'll lose to *you*. Such different types for sisters. In my dreams they combine. It's ideal. *(He giggles.)*

GUS: You'll be invited to the wedding of course. Not a big wedding since, contrary to custom, I'll bear the cost. Which I'm glad to do. But I don't want you to expect a grand affair.

DOCTOR GOLDMAN: A word of advice if I might?

GUS: By all means.

DOCTOR GOLDMAN: It's not bad occasionally to promise more than you're sure you can deliver. It will give you something to strive for.

GUS: I'm not sure I agree but we'll discuss it another time. Perhaps when my doctor retires and I become your patient as I intend.

DOCTOR GOLDMAN: *(Preparing to leave.)* I can hear my wife now. *(He goes to the living room. To Eddie.)* You *will* come for a checkup?

MRS. BENTI: *(Before Eddie can speak.)* Yes.

EDDIE: *(To Doctor Goldman.)* You see? Guaranteed.

DOCTOR GOLDMAN: *(To Carmen.)* And again felicitations.

CARMEN: Thank you.

DOCTOR GOLDMAN: I'm disappointed you didn't sing today.

CARMEN: The next time.

DOCTOR GOLDMAN: At your wedding most likely. *(To Gus.)* What a voice she had—still has.

GUS: So I'm told.

DOCTOR GOLDMAN: You've never heard her?

GUS: No. But I have no judgment of such things.

DOCTOR GOLDMAN: *(To Willis.)* Good-bye.

(Willis ignores him—writes in the air.)

DOCTOR GOLDMAN: He doesn't like me.

CARMEN: Don't be silly.

DOCTOR GOLDMAN: *(Philosophically.)* I don't take it personally. It's my black bag. Doctors as a whole have served him poorly…What do you suppose he's writing? It seems to be in script but that's all I decipher…It might be the key to the universe—who knows?…*(Takes Carmen's hand.)* It's fortunate you and your sister are so different that I could never decide which one I preferred…I'll let myself out. *(He exits.)*

JOHN: I'm going too.

NETTIE: *(To John.)* Don't make Timmy go to your mother's if he doesn't feel up to it.

JOHN: *(Exiting—acerbically.)* Like I always do.

NETTIE: That isn't what I meant.

GUS: *(Writing in his notebook.)* "…a wife and then he's finished"…*(To Mrs. Benti.)* Ordinarily I'm not partial to them but he seems likable.

MRS. BENTI: Them?

GUS: The Doctor—Jews.

MRS. BENTI: *(Warning him not to pursue that line.)* He's helped this family through many emergencies.

EDDIE: *(To Gus—emphasizing his mother's point.)* He came every day for two months when my father was dying. And we had to beg him to send a bill.

GUS: *(Backing down.)* A good man—like I said.

(In the living room Carmen has moved to the piano. Sits, lost in thought, absently picking out single notes while Eddie sets up a checker board to play with Willis.)

EDDIE: Red or black?

WILLIS: Red, monsieur.

EDDIE: *(Setting the pieces.)* Usual stakes?

WILLIS: All the money in the world.

EDDIE: I'll take half the bet…Your move…Well, go on.

(Willis moves—the game proceeding silently from that point.)

CARMEN: *(Calls.)* Nettie?

NETTIE: *(Gathering glasses in the dining room.)* Yes?

CARMEN: Play for me.

NETTIE: Soon as I clear the table. Pick out something.

(Nettie carries a tray of glasses into the kitchen while Carmen goes through a stack of music on the piano top.)

GUS: *(To Mrs. Benti.)* At what age did you discover it?

(She regards him.)

GUS: The knack. Your psychic propensity.

MRS. BENTI: When I was ten years old the doctors said I would die if they didn't operate. The day before the operation was scheduled, I begged my mother to take me to the ocean. Thinking it might be my last wish, she took me to Coney Island where I watched the waves till the sun went down. The doctors pronounced me cured next day.

GUS: And from that day—

MRS. BENTI: —Yes.

GUS: *(Politely.)* Fascinating.

EDDIE: *(To Willis.)* I see a double jump.

WILLIS: *(Makes the jumps.)* Excellent on the hour. Sorry, Eddie dear.

GUS: *(To Mrs. Benti.)* As I said I'm skeptical but open-minded. Perhaps you'll read *my* fortune one day.

MRS. BENTI: Carmen wouldn't like that.

GUS: Just between us—our little secret.

MRS. BENTI: I threw the cards away.

GUS: You read tea leaves for the woman who had twins. *(He looks for his cup which Nettie cleared.)* She took my cup. I'll get it.

MRS. BENTI: No.

GUS: Afraid you won't be able to convince me?

MRS. BENTI: *(Accepting the challenge—indicating Carmen.)* You won't tell her?

GUS: You have my word—I almost said "mother" again.

(Gus exits into the kitchen. Nettie enters and passes through to the living room.)

NETTIE: *(To Carmen.)* What's it to be?

CARMEN: *(Handing her the music she's selected.)* Here.

NETTIE: *(Regarding it.)* You haven't done this one since…

CARMEN: Since Papa died. Can't you even say it?

NETTIE: Why this one?

CARMEN: Because it's about time.

NETTIE: I don't think I can.

CARMEN: It's been five years. New beginnings: Gus and I to marry; you to South America. Time to bury the past.

NETTIE: John and I are only talking about it.

CARMEN: You've been talking about it as long as I can remember.

NETTIE: How would Mama manage without me?

CARMEN: I think you've got it backwards.

NETTIE: What do you mean?

CARMEN: Nothing. Play.

(Nettie plays the opening chords of Non Ti Scordar Di Me. Carmen begins to sing with a voice that displays talent and training despite disuse. Mrs. Benti, unable to bear it, retreats to her room. Gus reenters from the kitchen carrying his tea cup, sits; listens.)

CARMEN: Non ti scordar di me
    La vita mia legataea te
    Io t'amo sempre piu
    Nel sogno mio rimani tu
    Non ti scordar di me
    La vita mia legataea te
    C'e sempre un nido nel
    Mio cor perte
    Non ti scordar di me!

    C'e sempre un nido nel
    Mio cor perte
    Non ti scordar di me!

(Carmen sings with such feeling that Nettie, overwhelmed by the memories and sensations evoked, is unable to continue; they clasp each other lovingly.)

NETTIE: I see Papa with that special smile. How he loved it when you sang.

CARMEN: I to become a prima donna. You my accompanist.

NETTIE: I wasn't cut out for appearing in public.

CARMEN: And I wasn't good enough. Gus doesn't want me to work after we're married. Perhaps I'll study again and who knows?

NETTIE: I hope so.

CARMEN: I know you do. You've always wished me nothing but the best. While I...

NETTIE: Don't.

CARMEN: Doctor Goldman's right. Two sisters so different. One pure, trusting. The other a devil.

NETTIE: That isn't what he said.

CARMEN: All you do for me: helping with Willis. And how do I repay you?

NETTIE: You do the best you can.

CARMEN: You really believe that?

NETTIE: Yes.

CARMEN: *(Studying her.)* Yes you do. Like Papa you're incapable of thinking anything but the best about everyone. Even those you have every reason to hate.

NETTIE: I could never hate you.

CARMEN: You should—and probably will one day.

NETTIE: *(With total certainty.)* Never.

CARMEN: *(Angrily.)* Don't say that!

NETTIE: It's true.

CARMEN: How do you know what I might do?

NETTIE: It wouldn't matter.

CARMEN: Was I always a hellion or did it start because everyone praised your angelic qualities?

NETTIE: You take after Mama. I take after Papa. There's nothing we can do about it.

CARMEN: I don't like Mama.

NETTIE: Of course you do.

CARMEN: I don't. At times I loathe her…At times I loathe you.

NETTIE: *(Unperturbed.)* What would you like to sing next?

(Carmen and Nettie search the music. Mrs. Benti emerges from her room: enters the dining room.)

EDDIE: You're about to get a king.

WILLIS: Yes.

EDDIE: Go on so I can crown you.

WILLIS: Ah-ven-deal Ah-ven-dahta.

EDDIE: *(Pointing.)* You have to move that checker.

WILLIS: But of course.

EDDIE: …Well do it.

WILLIS: But of course. *(He moves it.)* Crown me.

EDDIE: *(Tapping him on the head.)* I dub thee Sir Willis.

GUS: *(To Mrs. Benti, who has been studying the leaves in his cup—his tone indulgent, patronizing.)* Well?

MRS. BENTI: What part of your life most concerns you? Wait…*(Looking from the cup as though she'd just seen the answer.)* It's business.

GUS: *(Good humored.)* Yes. What about business?

MRS. BENTI: *(Regarding the leaves.)* Your prospects where you work are most promising.

GUS: *(Unable to stifle his skepticism.)* Would I contemplate marriage if they weren't?

MRS. BENTI: There's a chance for promotion.

GUS: As your daughter's no doubt mentioned.

MRS. BENTI: *(Looking from the cup to him abruptly.)* You won't take it.

GUS: *(Surprised.)* What?

MRS. BENTI: *(Matter-of-fact.)* If the promotion is offered you'll turn it down.

GUS: *(With dawning wonderment.)* Why would I do that?

MRS. BENTI: *(Back to the leaves.)*...I see a sign with your name...

GUS: Go on.

MRS. BENTI: *(Studying the leaves a moment more.)*...Of course.

GUS: What is it?

MRS. BENTI: *(Regarding him.)* You've decided to go in business for yourself.

GUS: *(Jolted.)* No one knows that. Not even Carmen.

MRS. BENTI: What else would you like to know?...

GUS: *Amazing.*

MRS. BENTI: ...Personal relationships? Marriage perhaps? You'll be happily married with three children.

GUS: Ah. But about going into business for myself. How will I fare?

MRS. BENTI: Hard going at first.

GUS: And then?

MRS. BENTI: You'll wind up a millionaire.

GUS: I knew it!

NETTIE: *(Selecting a piece of music.)* Here's one we can all sing. *(To Willis.)* Remember "Dreamland"?

WILLIS: *(Sings.)* "Meet me in dreamland, Sweet dreamy dreamland."

NETTIE: *(Setting the music on the piano.)* Now if I can still play it. *(She plays the introduction to "Meet Me Tonight in Dreamland"—and at a nod from her they begin.)*

CARMEN, EDDIE, AND WILLIS: "Meet me tonight in dreamland. Under the silvery moon."

(Eddie is seized by a coughing fit.)

NETTIE: Are you all right?

EDDIE: Yes. There will be a brief intermission. *(He exits into his room; closes the door.)*

CARMEN: It's the damn cigarettes.

NETTIE: He's cut way down.

CARMEN: Then why is he coughing?

NETTIE: I don't know. Don't worry. Doctor Goldman will give him something.

CARMEN: *(Touching her cheek.)* The bright side of everything. How I envy you.

GUS: *(Entering the living room.)* Incredible!

CARMEN: *(To Gus.)* What's that?

GUS: Your mother! I'm not saying I'm entirely converted, but if there are people endowed with psychic powers she is certainly one of them! *(Catches himself.)* I'm sorry—it was supposed to be a secret.

CARMEN: *(To Mrs. Benti—accusing.)* You read his fortune.

MRS. BENTI: He insisted.

GUS: She told me things no one knows. Not even you.

CARMEN: *(Facetiously.)* Did she warn you marrying me would be your downfall?

GUS: Just the opposite. She said, "You'll be happily married with three children."

CARMEN: *(To Mrs. Benti—suspiciously.)* You saw that in the leaves?

MRS. BENTI: As clear as I've ever seen anything.

CARMEN: *(In spite of herself.)* I know it's all humbug but suddenly I'm happy.

GUS: *(Seizing her.)* And me as well. *(To Nettie.)* Play something we can dance to. *(Nettie plays* The Blue Danube. *Gus and Carmen dance. Eddie emerges from his room.)*

NETTIE: Are you all right?

EDDIE: Hepsha-pepsha.

NETTIE: Really?

EDDIE: Watch. *(Inviting Mrs. Benti to dance.)* May I have the honor?

MRS. BENTI: No.

NETTIE: Go on, Mama

MRS. BENTI: I forget how.

EDDIE: *(Whisking her off.)* It'll come back to you. *(Once launched Mrs. Benti throws herself into it. Nettie raises volume and tempo—exuberance spirals as the dancers whirl. Willis infected by their gaiety, claps in rhythm.)*

GUS: *(To Carmen as they spin about.)* Did I tell you I've decided to go in business for myself?

CARMEN: No.

GUS: Well I have and your mother envisions great success!

WILLIS: *(Increasingly animated.)* See what the boys in the back room will have.

EDDIE: And tell them I died of the same.

MRS. BENTI: *(To Willis as they waltz by.)* Some day *you're* going to dance with me.

WILLIS: To be sure! *(Unnoticed by the dancers or Nettie, stimulated by the atmosphere, he struggles to his feet; attains a standing position, hands on chair arms, by a supreme effort. Then daringly lets go. Shouts.)* Look! Look at me! *(Nettie stops playing. All turn to Willis who wavers for an instant and then collapses to the floor before Eddie, who makes a lunge, can reach him. Curtain.)*

SCENE II

Time: Two weeks later, a weekday, a little past noon. At rise: Nettie, Gus, John, Willis in the living room. She in everyday clothes. Gus and John in business suits. Willis, in his chair, seemingly detached from the tension and anxiety that prevails. Two weathered suitcases, unmatched, are conspicuous.

GUS: What time is it?

JOHN: Five minutes later than the last time you asked.

NETTIE: I gave Eddie a wallet for his birthday.

(John regards her uncomprehendingly.)

NETTIE: It has his name and address in case of an accident.

GUS: What time does his train leave?

JOHN: Three forty-five...

GUS: Wouldn't you think he'd call?

JOHN: Not if you knew him.

GUS: I don't want to alarm the ladies any more than they are, but I think the police should be notified.

NETTIE: He's right.

JOHN: You know where the phone is.

GUS: I was hoping you'd do it. Being a member of the family. Please?

NETTIE: Please.

(John exits down the hallway.)

GUS: I passed through there once on my way to Canada. It's like a resort. One of those places the rich go to in Switzerland. If you didn't know different, you'd think—

CARMEN: *(Entering.) Must you.*

GUS: All I'm saying is that one *could* look at it as a holiday. Expenses paid.

WILLIS: *(To Gus.)* B-E-R-N...B-E-R-N-E.

GUS: *(To Nettie—indicating Willis.)* What's he saying?

NETTIE: You mentioned Switzerland. He's giving alternate spellings of the capital.

MRS. BENTI: *(Apron on, enters from the kitchen.)* What would you like to eat?

CARMEN: How can you think of food?

MRS. BENTI: I've cooked three meals a day, three hundred and sixty-five days a year, for as long as I can remember. I did it when Papa died. I did it when Aunt Anna died.

CARMEN: *Who said anything about dying?*

GUS: *(To Carmen.)* What your mother meant was life goes on.

CARMEN: *(To Gus—heatedly.) Our* lives aren't going on. Till Eddie gets better—no wedding bells.

MRS. BENTI: Nettie and I can't manage your son on our own.

CARMEN: In case you missed it, "your son" is to remind me of my responsibility.

GUS: Doctor Goldman said seven or eight months. A slight interruption.

CARMEN: You take it so cheerfully. Could it be what you were hoping?

NETTIE: *(To Gus.)* Don't pay attention. She's just upset.

CARMEN: *(Aimed at Mrs. Benti.)* I know it's what *she* was hoping.

MRS. BENTI: *(Ignoring Carmen.)* There's pot roast from yesterday.

CARMEN: Break out the party hats—cue the band.

MRS. BENTI: We all can't behave like opera singers!

CARMEN: That's more like it. *(To Gus.)* She hates opera because Papa loved it. *(To Mrs. Benti.)* Because it was a bond between him and me that no one else shared.

NETTIE: Really, Carmen.

CARMEN: *(Whirling on her.)* Not even *you.* His favorite in everything else. But not when it came to opera.

(Nettie weeps silently.)

MRS. BENTI: *(To Carmen.)* Satisfied?

CARMEN: *(To Nettie—remorseful.)* I'm sorry.

NETTIE: It's all right.

CARMEN: I didn't mean—

NETTIE: *(Reassuringly.)* —I know.

GUS: *(To Mrs. Benti—indicating Carmen and Nettie.)* Does anyone understand these two?

CARMEN: *We* do. We understand each other perfectly.

WILLIS: *(To Nettie.)* What is it, Auntie?

NETTIE: *(Wiping her eyes.)* Nothing, dear. I'm fine.

GUS: Everyone's upset. Which is only natural given the circumstances.

(John Cleary appears from the hall corridor with a piece of paper in his hand.)

JOHN: You have to be missing twenty-four hours before they'll do anything. I've got the number. *(To Mrs. Benti.)* He went out about four?

MRS. BENTI: Yes.

GUS: *(Regarding his watch.)* Three hours and twenty-five minutes. *(They look at him.)*

GUS: Till he qualifies. Not that I expect him to.

JOHN: *(To Mrs. Benti.)* How was he dressed?

MRS. BENTI: I told you, I was in the kitchen.

JOHN: Just said he was going out and you heard the door close.

MRS. BENTI: Yes.

CARMEN: Remarkable.

JOHN: What's that?

CARMEN: *(Indicating Mrs. Benti.)* For anyone to leave without providing her with an itinerary.

NETTIE: *(Quickly—to head off another skirmish between Carmen and Mrs. Benti.)* Shouldn't we call Doctor Goldman so he doesn't make the trip for nothing?

MRS. BENTI: *(With omniscient certainty.)* Eddie will be here.

GUS: *(To Carmen.)* Your mother's right.

CARMEN: *(Sarcastic.)* Because she predicted you'd become a millionaire.

GUS: The very next day they offered me a partnership.

JOHN: Did anyone check his closet to see what's missing?

CARMEN: *(Indicating the suitcases.)* He packed everything he was taking.

NETTIE: Except the blue suit he was going to wear. *(She goes into Eddie's room to check.)*

JOHN: If he was just going out for the paper—something in the neighborhood he wouldn't doll up.

GUS: *(Impressed.)* You should have been a detective.

CARMEN: You just made a friend for life.

GUS: Why?

CARMEN: *(Indicating John.)* He loves being taken for a cop.

NETTIE: *(Emerging from Eddie's room.)* The suit's gone. Also the shirt and tie he laid out.

JOHN: Sounds like he went downtown.

CARMEN: Probably to say good-bye to Charlie Winegarten and they tied one on.

MRS. BENTI: I called Charlie. He hasn't seen Eddie in a month.

NETTIE: He has other friends.

GUS: *(Regarding the suitcases.)* Why did he pack yesterday?

JOHN: Maybe he knew he wasn't coming home.

GUS: If so, that's encouraging.

NETTIE: Why?

GUS: If his absence was premeditated it rules out mishap—accident.

CARMEN: *(Indicating John and Gus.)* Holmes and Watson ride again.

MRS. BENTI: You need money to carouse. Eddie's broke.

CARMEN: I'm sure Rosemary, Olive, or what's her name would pick up the tab.

GUS: Who are they?

CARMEN: Anonymous ladies who phone Eddie and drive my mother crazy.

MRS. BENTI: Don't talk nonsense.

CARMEN: See what I mean.

JOHN: He shouldn't be out in public.

CARMEN: It's not the plague!

GUS: It is contagious.

CARMEN: *(To the others—indicating Gus.)* Ten to one he's researched it.

GUS: I believe in facing facts.

CARMEN: You have researched it.

GUS: How can you face facts if you don't know what they are?

WILLIS: Tuberculosis…T-U-B—

MRS. BENTI: —I forbid that word in this house!

WILLIS: Apologies.

MRS. BENTI: You want people treating us like we're lepers? Eddie is going away because he got a job in Albany.

WILLIS: To be sure, Mama dear.

MRS. BENTI: *(Rehearsing Willis.)* Where is Eddie going?

WILLIS: I know.

MRS. BENTI: *Say it.*

WILLIS: A-L-B-A-N-Y.

GUS: *(To Mrs. Benti.)* I wasn't implying any stigma. They're making remarkable strides. Some authorities predict sanitariums like Saranac will be unneeded in twenty years.

JOHN: *(To Gus.)* You can get it out of the air—breathing other peoples' germs right?

GUS: Yes.

JOHN: *(To Nettie.)* You see.

NETTIE: It's not like he got it yesterday.

JOHN: Why take more chances than we have already?

MRS. BENTI: That's enough!

(The doorbell sounds.)

CARMEN: I'll get it.

(Carmen disappears down the corridor. Returns with Doctor Goldman.)

DOCTOR GOLDMAN: I'm sure he's all right.

MRS. BENTI: *(Indicating Carmen.)* She told you about Eddie?

DOCTOR GOLDMAN: A last fling. Quite common.

GUS: I've been telling them what a beautiful place Saranac is.

DOCTOR GOLDMAN: I've never been there but several patients said they hated to leave.

JOHN: How many have you treated?

DOCTOR GOLDMAN: With TB, more than I can count.

NETTIE: And you never caught it.

DOCTOR GOLDMAN: Knock wood.

NETTIE: *(To the Doctor indicating John.)* He wouldn't let Timmy come to say good-bye.

DOCTOR GOLDMAN: If the boy's susceptible he'd have it by now.

JOHN: How do we know he doesn't?

DOCTOR GOLDMAN: We don't. Which is why I recommend a thorough checkup—the sooner the better.

JOHN: *(To Nettie.)* What did I tell you?

DOCTOR GOLDMAN: It's just a precaution. I wouldn't mention it to Eddie.

GUS: *(To the Doctor.)* Would you classify his condition as a primary infection?

CARMEN: *(To the Doctor—indicating Gus.)* He's trying to impress you he's done his homework.

DOCTOR GOLDMAN: Nothing wrong with that.

GUS: Thank you, Doctor.

DOCTOR GOLDMAN: Providing you don't get carried away. A little knowledge, as they say. He went out yesterday afternoon.

NETTIE: And no word since.

DOCTOR GOLDMAN: One more night on the town won't kill him.

GUS: What about the rest of us getting checkups?

DOCTOR GOLDMAN: If you're concerned. But I'd be surprised if they found anything.

WILLIS: Good day, Doctor.

DOCTOR GOLDMAN: Good day to you.

WILLIS: The capital of Switzerland is Bern.

DOCTOR GOLDMAN: I thank you for the information. *(Aside to Mrs. Benti.)* Does he know what's happening?

MRS. BENTI: Yes.

DOCTOR GOLDMAN: You're sure you can manage with Eddie gone?

MRS. BENTI: Positive.

DOCTOR GOLDMAN: If you change your mind—

MRS. BENTI: —We can manage.

DOCTOR GOLDMAN: *(To everyone.)* I can't say I'm in favor of what you're doing. But I admire it.

GUS: Seven or eight months isn't long.

DOCTOR GOLDMAN: That was a rough estimate.

GUS: Instead of an apartment for expediency, we have time to find one that's ideal. Plus I'm about to go into business for myself which will require undivided attention in the beginning. Status quo for a while could be a blessing.

CARMEN: *(To the Doctor.)* Suppose he misses the train?

DOCTOR GOLDMAN: There's another train tomorrow. *(To Nettie.)* South America postponed once again.

NETTIE: Yes.

DOCTOR GOLDMAN: *(To John.)* Most generous of you.

JOHN: You make it sound like I had a choice.

NETTIE: *(To John.)* You can go. If it's everything it's cracked up to be, Timmy and I can join you.

JOHN: There's a laugh. *(To Doctor Goldman—indicating Nettie.)* You know what it took to get her to spend summers at the lake? And that's only Jersey—an hour away.

NETTIE: *(A rare outburst.)* I hate the lake: No heat. No hot water. No phone.

JOHN: Put them all together they spell *mother!*

WILLIS: *(Shouts.)* Order in the court!

GUS: *(To Willis—grateful that his exclamation silenced John and Nettie.)* From the mouths of babes.

CARMEN: He's eighteen.

GUS: I was speaking figuratively. *(To Doctor Goldman.)* Rod-shaped organisms—the bacilli?

DOCTOR GOLDMAN: Correct.

GUS: Called lupus when it invades the skin.

CARMEN: *Must you?*

DOCTOR GOLDMAN: He doesn't have lupus.

GUS: I didn't mean to suggest—

WILLIS: —E-M-P-Y-E-M-A.

DOCTOR GOLDMAN: *(Regarding Willis.)* Remarkable.

JOHN: What's remarkable?

DOCTOR GOLDMAN: E-m-p-y-e-m-a, empyema relates to Eddie's condition.

JOHN: English translation?

DOCTOR GOLDMAN: The presence of pus in a bodily cavity.

JOHN: In other words he's sicker than I was led to believe. *(To Nettie, accusing.) Why wasn't I told?*

DOCTOR GOLDMAN: Probably to avoid upsetting you any more than you are already.

GUS: *(To Doctor Goldman—extracting pad and pencil.)* Would you spell it again?

DOCTOR GOLDMAN: I'm not here to give a medical lecture.

GUS: *(Laughing it off as he pockets pad and pencil.)* Of course—of course.

WILLIS: *(To Gus.)* When does it rain in the circus?

GUS: What?

WILLIS: *(Insistent.)* When does it rain in the circus?

GUS: *(Humoringly.)* I don't know: When does it rain in the circus?
(Before Willis can reply the doorbell rings.)

NETTIE: I'll go.

GUS: *(As Nettie exits up the corridor.)* I'll bet it's Eddie—forgot his keys.

CARMEN: The eternal optimist. You should have married my sister. *(In response to voices at the door.)* Sounds like Timmy.

JOHN: It better not be.
(Nettie reappears with Timmy, sixteen, thin to the point of frailty; possessed of a superior intelligence and sensitivity he isn't aware of. Fearful of his father's reaction he stands at the room entrance diffident but resolute.)

NETTIE: *(Primarily to John.)* He wants to say good-bye to Eddie.

JOHN: I thought we settled that.

NETTIE: He insists.

JOHN: Let me guess who seconded the motion.

DOCTOR GOLDMAN: *(To John.)* I assure you it will do no harm.

JOHN: That's not the point.

TIMMY: *(Displaying a small gift-wrapped box.)* I just want to give him this.

NETTIE: He'll be here soon.

TIMMY: *(To his father.)* Can I wait?

JOHN: What are you asking me for?

NETTIE: *(To John.)* Please.

TIMMY: I just want to see him.

JOHN: Suit yourself. Doctor Goldman says it's too late to lock the barn door anyway.

NETTIE: Stop it.

TIMMY: What's that mean?

JOHN: You're going to be tested.

DOCTOR GOLDMAN: *(To Timmy.)* A routine checkup—nothing to worry about.

TIMMY: *(Shrewdly.)* Is everybody being tested?

DOCTOR GOLDMAN: If they're concerned.

TIMMY: It's voluntary for them but not for me.

DOCTOR GOLDMAN: Young people are at greater risk. Merely a precaution.

TIMMY: Suppose I have it? What then?

NETTIE: *(To John.)* Satisfied?

JOHN: Who encouraged him to be here?

TIMMY: *(The buffer as always.)* She had nothing to do with it.

JOHN: "She"?...

TIMMY: *(To Doctor Goldman.)* Would I be sent where Eddie's going?

JOHN: ...Since when do you call your mother "she"?

DOCTOR GOLDMAN: *(To Timmy.)* If and when the time comes, I'll answer all questions. Right now it's premature. *(Measuredly.)* You understand?

TIMMY: Yes.   •

MRS. BENTI: *(To Timmy with certainty.)* Timmy. You have nothing to worry about.

JOHN: Mind if we get a second opinion that doesn't involve a crystal ball?

WILLIS: *(To Timmy.)* Greetings, cousin.

TIMMY: *(Moving to Willis to avoid his father.)* What do you say, Willis?

WILLIS: Pals to the finish.

TIMMY: *(He knows the routines.)* Lend me five dollars.

WILLIS: That's the finish!

DOCTOR GOLDMAN: I once had a patient who gave a party the night before major surgery. A huge party he couldn't pay for because he was sure he was going to die.

NETTIE: How did it go?

DOCTOR GOLDMAN: Memorable: orchestra, champagne, caviar—the works.

NETTIE: I meant the operation.

DOCTOR GOLDMAN: He made a hundred percent recovery.

GUS: How did he pay for the party?

DOCTOR GOLDMAN: I have no idea.

CARMEN: *(To the Doctor.)* He likes stories with a moral.

GUS: If you mean with a point, yes.

CARMEN: *(To the Doctor.)* You want to make him happy say the man worked so hard to pay for the party that it killed him.

GUS: Somebody had to pay for it. *(To John.)* What do *you* say?

JOHN: Sounds like Eddie.

CARMEN: Meaning?

JOHN: *He* lights the candle at both ends and *we* get burned.

NETTIE: *(To John in Eddie's defense.)* Except to go job hunting he hasn't been downtown in ages.

JOHN: He didn't get sick overnight. *(To Timmy.)* If he's not here in ten minutes, beat it.

TIMMY: School doesn't start till one o'clock.

JOHN: *Ten minutes.*

NETTIE: *(To Timmy.)* Want a sandwich?

JOHN: There isn't time.

NETTIE: Sure there is.

JOHN: *Can he once do as I say without you butting in?*

MRS. BENTI: *(To the Doctor.)* Does washing everything in boiling water kill the germs?

DOCTOR GOLDMAN: Yes.

MRS. BENTI: *(To John.)* Now can he have a sandwich or would you like me to get new knives, forks, dishes?

JOHN: *(She's read him accurately.)* I was just being cautious.

MRS. BENTI: *(Hurling a plate to the floor so it shatters.)* Is this what you want?

NETTIE: Mama don't!

JOHN: *(Routed.)* All I said was—

CARMEN: —Too much as always.

JOHN: *(To Timmy.)* Have a banquet!

TIMMY: *(Anything for peace.)* I had lunch before I came.

JOHN: *(To Doctor Goldman.)* I took time off from work to be here. Can you beat it?

DOCTOR GOLDMAN: Everyone's under a strain.

JOHN: In this house that's a permanent condition.

CARMEN: Especially when you're here.

JOHN: Fine. Good-bye.

NETTIE: *(To John as he starts to go.)* What do we do if he doesn't show up?

JOHN: Call missing persons. Here's the number. *(He puts the slip of paper on the table.)*

NETTIE: *(A reluctant admission.)* I'd feel better if you stayed. I think everybody would.

JOHN: Not your sister.

CARMEN: Stay—go, it's all the same.

GUS: *(To Carmen.)* You're not being fair.

CARMEN: *(To John with an exaggeration that doesn't hide she wants him there.)* Pretty please?

GUS: *(To John.)* I'm sure you're more knowledgeable dealing with the police than I would be. I mean if it comes to that, which I don't expect.

CARMEN: *(Who has turned her back on the proceedings—is looking out a window.)* At last.

NETTIE: Eddie?

CARMEN: Getting out of a cab.

WILLIS: *(Merrily as Nettie, Gus, and Timmy join Carmen at the window.)* Happy days are here again.

MRS. BENTI: *(To those at the window.)* Don't let him see you.

CARMEN: I don't think he sees much of anything.

GUS: Three sheets to the wind as they say.

(Those at the window react sharply to something they see.)

MRS. BENTI: What is it?

GUS: He almost fell—caught himself.

JOHN: I'll go down.

DOCTOR GOLDMAN: *(To John.)* He wouldn't appreciate it.

JOHN: Someone has to pay for the cab.

CARMEN: Someone is paying for it.

GUS: A very attractive someone.

CARMEN: *(Turning to Mrs. Benti.)* You always wondered what they looked like. Here's your chance.

(Mrs. Benti doesn't budge, but John can't resist a peek.)

JOHN: Typical bimbo.

CARMEN: You should know.

NETTIE: She's trying to help him.

MRS. BENTI: She's not coming in this house.

(With the exception of John, those at the window laugh.)

MRS. BENTI: Now what?

TIMMY: They're dancing.

MRS. BENTI: How nice for the neighbors.

CARMEN: Long red hair.

MRS. BENTI: Spare me the details.

CARMEN: Which one do you suppose it is? Rosemary, Gladys—

MRS. BENTI: *(To Doctor Goldman.)* —Would you please go down and see to him?

NETTIE: They're at the entrance.

MRS. BENTI: *She's not coming in this house.*

TIMMY: ... *Wow.*

JOHN: Boy, oh boy.

CARMEN: …Talk about clinches.

MRS. BENTI: *(To Doctor Goldman.)* If you don't go down, I will!

NETTIE: He's on his way up.

MRS. BENTI: With *her?*

GUS: No. She's walking away.

(They follow her progress until:)

NETTIE: She's gone.

(They turn from the window in anticipation of Eddie's arrival.)

CARMEN: How do we greet him?

DOCTOR GOLDMAN: As matter-of-factly as possible.

CARMEN: No interrogation?

DOCTOR GOLDMAN: Above all.

CARMEN: That's going to be tough on my mother.

MRS. BENTI: *That's enough from you.*

NETTIE: Will he be able to travel?

MRS. BENTI: Doctor Goldman will decide

DOCTOR GOLDMAN: Is there coffee?

MRS. BENTI: I'll make some.

GUS: *(To the Doctor as Mrs. Benti enters the kitchen.)* What do you mean by "matter-of-fact"?

DOCTOR GOLDMAN: Act normal—be yourselves.

JOHN: You can't have it both ways.

GUS: Did we see him get out of the taxi just now?

DOCTOR GOLDMAN: No.

GUS: We should be surprised when he enters.

CARMEN: *Don't be anything.*

JOHN: *(To Timmy.)* Say good-bye and scram.

DOCTOR GOLDMAN: *(To Timmy.)* No mention of the checkup…*(Turning to John.)* Or anything else that might upset him.

JOHN: How long does it take to climb two flights?

NETTIE: Maybe he needs help.

TIMMY: Want me to see?

MRS. BENTI: *(At the kitchen entrance.)* He's at the door.

CARMEN: Places everyone.

MRS. BENTI: Don't be like statues—talk.

GUS: *(To John as Mrs. Benti disappears into the kitchen.)* How do you feel about lend lease to Britain?

JOHN: What?

NETTIE: *(Hushed.)* He's coming. *Talk.*

TIMMY: *(To Willis—eager to do his part.)* "You can lead a horse to water but…"

WILLIS: Argo—argo-say-vah.

NETTIE: *(To Doctor Goldman.)* Are you going to Florida this year?

DOCTOR GOLDMAN: Ask my wife.

CARMEN: *(To Nettie.)* They're doing *Traviata* on Thursday. Want to go if I can wangle tickets?

NETTIE: Yes. *(She nudges John to participate.)*

JOHN: *(To Gus.)* I think we'll be in it sooner or later.

GUS: An opinion I share despite Roosevelt's assurances.

(Eddie appears at the hallway entrance. Considerably disheveled [hair mussed, tie loosened, mouth lipstick-smeared] and overly erect, he waits to be acknowledged while they studiously ignore his presence.)

NETTIE: *(To Carmen.)* Dinner before the opera?

CARMEN: If I get off early.

GUS: *(To Doctor Goldman.)* What's *your* opinion on the chances of our going to war?

TIMMY: *(Prodding Willis.)* "You can lead a horse to water but"—*what?*

EDDIE: "But a pencil has to be lead."

(They turn to him affecting surprise.)

EDDIE: You're probably wondering why I called you here.

DOCTOR GOLDMAN: How are you?

EDDIE: Never better. *(Looking about.)* Where's my mother? Let me guess: Missing Persons.

MRS. BENTI: *(Appears beside him.)* I'm making fresh coffee.

EDDIE: I'm back.

MRS. BENTI: I'm glad.

EDDIE: That's it?

MRS. BENTI: I'll get you something to eat. Sit.

EDDIE: I must be in the wrong apartment.

WILLIS: *95 Brandt Place—Apartment ten.*

EDDIE: You're sure?

WILLIS: *Indubitably.*

MRS. BENTI: *(To Eddie.)* What would you like?

EDDIE: A bit of third degree to make me feel at home.

DOCTOR GOLDMAN: You have time for a nap before the train.

EDDIE: And miss the festivities? What holiday is this? And if it isn't a holiday what are you all doing here?

GUS: We came to see you off.

EDDIE: I'm touched despite that "see you off" sounds like I'm boarding a cruise ship instead of going to a TB sanitarium...*(To Mrs. Benti.)* Apologies...*(To the others, confidentially.)* She hates that word.

MRS. BENTI: *(To Doctor Goldman.)* Is he fit to travel?

DOCTOR GOLDMAN: I think so.

EDDIE: Observe. *(He takes a few steps on an imaginary chalk line.)* Convinced?

JOHN: *(In an effort to speed things up.)* Timmy has something to give you before he goes back to school.

EDDIE: *(Turning to Timmy who offers his gift.)* Just what I always wanted.

TIMMY: It's a razor and blades.

EDDIE: *(Feeling the stubble on his face.)* Not a moment too soon. But you know what they say.

TIMMY: "If you can get them with a beard you can hold them with a shave."

EDDIE: Give that boy a star.

WILLIS: Right with Eversharp.

EDDIE: *(Indicating Willis.)* And another for the gentleman in the balcony.

JOHN: *(To Timmy, pointedly.)* It's five after.

EDDIE: *(To Timmy.)* You better go.

(Timmy would hug him but Eddie keeps him at arms' length; offers his hand which Timmy takes.)

TIMMY: I'll write to you.

EDDIE: I'm counting on it.

TIMMY: I'll make sure Willis writes too.

EDDIE: *(Hand to mouth in mock whisper indicating Mrs. Benti.)* Beware the censor.

TIMMY: Good-bye. *(At the verge of tears he goes off.)*

EDDIE: *(Lightly to mask his own feelings.)* One down—seven to go. Who's next?

DOCTOR GOLDMAN: I'll be monitoring your progress and have every expectation things will turn out fine if you cooperate.

EDDIE: Scout's honor.

MRS. BENTI: That means no cigarettes.

EDDIE: *(His breezy air giving way momentarily to anger.)* I know what it means.

DOCTOR GOLDMAN: *(Offering his hand.)* I'll say good-bye then.

EDDIE: *(Shaking with him.)* Good-bye and thanks for everything.

DOCTOR GOLDMAN: I wish I could have done more. *(To the others.)* Good-bye. *(To Mrs. Benti who would accompany him.)* I'll let myself out. *(To Eddie.)* Three forty-five—the train.

EDDIE: Wouldn't miss it for the world.

(Doctor Goldman exits.)

JOHN: I've got to go too. *(Offering an envelope.)* This is from Nettie and me.

EDDIE: Thanks.

NETTIE: It isn't much but we'll send something regularly.

EDDIE: No donation, regardless of size, will be refused.

JOHN: *(Sympathy momentarily tempering enmity.)* Good luck.

EDDIE: *(In similar vein.)* The same to you.

JOHN: *(To Nettie.)* I'll call you later. *(To the others.)* Bye. *(He starts to go.)*

EDDIE: *(Calling after him.)* I'm sorry about South America.

JOHN: So am I. *(He exits.)*

EDDIE: And then there were four.

CARMEN: *(To Gus.)* Don't you have appointments?

GUS: No, but I can take a hint. *(To Eddie.)* Rather than get you something useless I thought it best to wait till you're settled—know what you need.

EDDIE: Good thinking.

GUS: You'll let me know?

EDDIE: To be sure.

GUS: *(Impulsively—uncharacteristically.)* I love your sister with all my heart and nothing will ever change that.

EDDIE: *(Airily.)* Why is he telling me this?

GUS: To relieve you about the wedding postponement.

CARMEN: *(To Gus—touched by his declaration despite a semblance of irritation.)* Will you please get out of here?

GUS: *(Regarding Carmen.)* I made her blush—a first. *(To Eddie.)* But she's right. It's time to leave the floor to the immediate family. Good-bye.

WILLIS: *(To Gus.)* Go-venda koop-la-ta.

GUS: Whatever you say. *(Gus exits.)*

EDDIE: Who *was* that masked man?

CARMEN: Don't knock him.

EDDIE: What did I say?

CARMEN: He's better than I deserve.

EDDIE: I'm not sure what for but pardon me. Make that a blanket apology to everyone I've inconvenienced.

NETTIE: It's not your fault.

EDDIE: *Timmy hasn't been checked.*

NETTIE: He's going to be.

EDDIE: How will you feel if he's got it?

NETTIE: I'll feel the same.

EDDIE: *(Pained by her infinite good will.)* You really know how to hurt a guy.

NETTIE: *(Embracing him tearfully.)* Please...please...please.

EDDIE: You'll tell me the result no matter what?

NETTIE: Yes.

EDDIE: Swear it!

NETTIE: I swear.

MRS. BENTI: *(Rejoining them.)* There's nothing wrong with Timmy.

CARMEN: *(To Eddie—seconding her mother.)* I think she's right.

EDDIE: *I* think you're all too kind. *(To Nettie.)* I prefer your husband's accusing eyes.

CARMEN: *(Striking her chest mockingly.)* Mea culpa—mea maxima culpa.

WILLIS: *(Agitated.)* This darn life!

EDDIE: *(To Willis.)* Care to repeat that stranger?

MRS. BENTI: *(To Eddie.)* Don't get him started.

EDDIE: *(Reading Willis.)* He's wondering what will happen with me gone?

NETTIE: Everyone will pitch in a little harder. It's all arranged.

EDDIE: Suppose it doesn't work out?

CARMEN: *It will.*

EDDIE: *(To Mrs. Benti.)* Your word he'll be here when I get back?

MRS. BENTI: *(Sealing a compact between them.)* Yes.

EDDIE: The good Doctor favors putting him away, temporarily, of course, in my absence.

MRS. BENTI: He's not leaving this house. I promise.

NETTIE: So do I.

EDDIE: *(To Carmen.)* What do *you* say?

CARMEN: The same.

MRS. BENTI: I have a steak I've been saving.

EDDIE: The condemned man ate a hearty meal.

CARMEN: If that's your attitude—

EDDIE: *(Flaring.)* —Spare me the positive thinking!

CARMEN: I have to get back to work.

EDDIE: *(To Nettie.)* Don't you have some place to go?

NETTIE: If that's what you want.

EDDIE: I'd like a few minutes alone.

MRS. BENTI: Who'll take you to the train?

CARMEN: He's not a kid going to summer camp.

EDDIE: Thanks for noticing.

CARMEN: You'll let us know anything you need.

EDDIE: Guaranteed.

> *(She embraces him with great feeling for a moment. Then breaks off and leaves.)*

NETTIE: *(Weeping anew.)* I'm sorry, I can't help it.

EDDIE: *(Hugging her.)* It wouldn't be you if you did.

NETTIE: You'll do what they tell you?

EDDIE: So help me.

CARMEN'S VOICE: *(To Nettie from the hallway.)* Are you coming?

> *(A final squeeze and Nettie goes off. We hear the door close after her and Carmen.)*

EDDIE: *(To Mrs. Benti.)* I'll have that steak.

MRS. BENTI: How do you want it?

EDDIE: I *don't* want it. But I can't think of any other way to get rid of you while I have a word with my buddy here.

MRS. BENTI: About what?

EDDIE: Have you no respect for the attorney-client privilege?

> *(Stung, she exits into the kitchen, closing the door.)*

WILLIS: P-R-I-V-I-L-E-G-E.

EDDIE: Alone at last.

WILLIS: "When does it rain in the circus?"

EDDIE: I want to talk to you.

WILLIS: *Ex-*cellent.

EDDIE: *(Earnestly.)* It's important.

WILLIS: Ko-balla-vay.

EDDIE: *(Angered.) Stop that!*

> *(Willis, startled regards him.)*

EDDIE: I'm sorry. But you have to pay attention.

WILLIS: Yes Eddie, dear.

EDDIE: You know I'm going away.

WILLIS: Yes my darling.

EDDIE: While I'm gone it's important to help yourself as much as you can.

WILLIS: Aye-aye.

EDDIE: Try to dress yourself in the morning.

WILLIS: *(Bridling.)* I do.

EDDIE: Try even harder.

WILLIS: It's these damn legs!

EDDIE: Above all: Ask for the urinal when you need it.

WILLIS: *(Tuning out.)* Bro-go-low-me-say.

EDDIE: *(Seizing his shoulders to compel attention.) I want you to be here when I get back.*

WILLIS: *(Patting Eddie's face reassuringly.)* Everything will be delightful.

EDDIE: I have your word?

WILLIS: "Sometimes we're happy and sometime's the bottle's empty."

EDDIE: And sometimes you drink enough to sink a battleship and wind up soberer than when you started…Can you keep a secret?

WILLIS: Mum's the word.

EDDIE: I've never been away from home for more than a week and I'm scared.

WILLIS: Be of stout courage.

EDDIE: Tell me more.

WILLIS: Koopie-say-ka-vilda.

EDDIE: Brang-volda-kay.

WILLIS: Gar-anta-kap-a-sat.

EDDIE: Oh-ska-par-di-valt.

WILLIS: *(As Mrs. Benti reappears.)* Are-van-da-pane.

MRS. BENTI: *(To Eddie.)* Why do you encourage that?

EDDIE: What's the harm?

MRS. BENTI: It makes people think he's demented.

EDDIE: Wake me in an hour.

MRS. BENTI: Doctor Goldman said it wouldn't matter if you went tomorrow.

EDDIE: *(Firmly.)* I'm going today.

MRS. BENTI: *(She thrusts a wad of currency at him.)* Here.

EDDIE: *(Riffling the bills—surprised by the amount.)* I knew you loved me but not this much.

MRS. BENTI: It's from Miss Julian.

EDDIE: Hats off to the sponsor…*One* hour. *(He exits into his room—closes the door.)*

(Mrs. Benti retreats to the dining room. Face to the wall, she weeps for a moment, then catches herself, stiffens, and returns to the living room as Willis begins to write a story in the air, which he recites as he goes.)

WILLIS: *(The opening syllables and inflection suggesting "Once upon a time.")* Cope a-vay a-konda, eel-ya tri mar-si-pool. Go-veel-da go-van-da la door-may…

MRS. BENTI: Stop that.

WILLIS: *(Increasingly caught up in the tale, ignores her.)*…Or-voo do-blah-sand key-mar-dash key-vor-zend key-plarto…

MRS. BENTI: *I said stop.*

WILLIS: *(Volume and cadence increasing—a rapturous look suffusing his face.)*…Don-too-val or-deal-ya, Don-too-val fro-to-mal-say…

(Mrs. Benti goes to the sideboard; opens a drawer; extracts a cat-o'-nine-tails, a whip made of nine knotted lines attached to a handle; goes to Willis who, oblivious to her, "writes" faster and faster—speaks louder and louder.)

WILLIS: *Corto-sen-vi-dar, ven-dar-seel-yay op-toe op-tima.*

MRS. BENTI: *(Brandishing the cat.)* Will you stop?

WILLIS: *(Nearing climax—in ecstasy.)* VON-DO-LAY-TAR-MENT-OH-BLED-SO-OH-CAR-WAND-OH-CAR-VANE-OH—
(She lashes him—one savage swipe that breaks the spell. He regards her like one awakened from a dream.)

MRS. BENTI: *WHY DO YOU MAKE ME DO IT?...WHY?*

WILLIS: *(Beatifically.)* Because I love you, my darling.

END OF ACT I

ACT II

Time: Fifteen months later, early February 1943, Saturday afternoon. At rise: A wedding cake, topped by a bride and groom, on the dining-room table. Nettie standing on a chair attaching streamers...John, highball glass in hand—not his first—watching her skeptically. At the dining room table, Timmy, suit and tie emphasizing his maturation, helps Willis to read aloud from a copy of Treasure Island.

WILLIS: *(Labored.)* "Hands off, if you like John Silver," said the other. "It's a black..."

TIMMY: Go on.

WILLIS: I know it.

TIMMY: A black what?

WILLIS: Ko-valta mar-say.

TIMMY: What does C-O-N-S-C-I-E-N-C-E spell?

WILLIS: "Lucky Strike Green has gone to war."

TIMMY: *(Exasperated.)* Conscience..."Black conscience."

WILLIS: But of course.

TIMMY: *(Taking the book from him.)* Forget it.

NETTIE: What's the matter?

TIMMY: He's not in the mood.

NETTIE: Coax him.

TIMMY: I tried.

NETTIE: Try again.

JOHN: *(Disdainful.)* Waste of time.

NETTIE: *(To John—shortly.)* He read more books last year than you've read in your life.

JOHN: If he remembers one title I'll... Ah the hell with it.

(Mrs. Benti emerges from the kitchen, shakes her head in disapproval of the streamers.)

MRS. BENTI: *(To Nettie.)* Why are you doing that?

NETTIE: Eddie not here, I want to make it as nice as possible.

JOHN: Out of sight—out of mind.

(They regard him.)

JOHN: He's been up there a year and you only hear from him when he needs something.

NETTIE: He's busy with his jewelry business.

JOHN: Carmen getting married. The least he could have done was phone.

NETTIE: It's early yet.

(The doorbell rings.)

NETTIE: Them already?

MRS. BENTI: No. She has her keys. *(She goes off to see who it is.)*

NETTIE: *(As John drains his glass.)* That's your third.

JOHN: Fourth. But who's counting on this joyous occasion?

(Mrs. Benti ushers Doctor Goldman in.)

DOCTOR GOLDMAN: I understand I beat the bride and groom.

NETTIE: Yes. I'm so glad you're here.

DOCTOR GOLDMAN: Would I miss it? *(Eyeing the cake.)* Very nice… Everyone well?

NETTIE: Yes.

DOCTOR GOLDMAN: *(To Timmy.)* How's the back?

TIMMY: A lot better.

DOCTOR GOLDMAN: *(Repeating advice previously given.)* Avoid lifting heavy things.

JOHN: *(To the Doctor indicating Nettie sarcastically.)* No fear of that with her around.

NETTIE: You make it sound like a crime.

DOCTOR GOLDMAN: *(To John.)* I still recommend a brace.

JOHN: No.

DOCTOR GOLDMAN: It would only be temporary.

JOHN: No brace and that's it!

TIMMY: *(To Doctor Goldman.)* I don't feel like I need one.

NETTIE: You're just saying that.

TIMMY: No—really. I haven't had any pain in weeks.

WILLIS: S-A-C-R-O-I-L-I-A-C.

DOCTOR GOLDMAN: Sacroiliac. Correct. And how is the world's champion speller today?

WILLIS: Delighted…delirious…delectable.

JOHN: *(Regarding his watch.)* What's keeping them?

NETTIE: They say City Hall is swamped with weddings since Pearl Harbor.

JOHN: *(To Doctor Goldman.)* A taste of marriage and the war will seem like a picnic. Right?

DOCTOR GOLDMAN: *(To John—refusing to ally himself with that remark.)* I understand you're also to be congratulated: South America.

JOHN: We're not there yet.

DOCTOR GOLDMAN: I thought it was all arranged.

NETTIE: Except for Timmy.

DOCTOR GOLDMAN: I thought he was going with you.

NETTIE: That depends on the draft board. He goes for his physical in two weeks.

DOCTOR GOLDMAN: There's no chance they'll take him.

NETTIE: They say because of casualties they've lowered standards.

DOCTOR GOLDMAN: The sacroiliac condition alone would disqualify him. Plus the stomach upsets—chronic headaches.

NETTIE: You're sure?

DOCTOR GOLDMAN: Positive.

JOHN: *(To Nettie—caustically.)* Happy?

NETTIE: Yes. *(To Doctor Goldman, indicating John.)* Missing out on World War One is still the regret of his life.

JOHN: He's going to be Four-F. Why talk about it?

NETTIE: Because you secretly hope they'll take him.

JOHN: *It's no secret: I want him to be normal.*

NETTIE: What a thing to say!

JOHN: *(To Timmy—apologetic.)* You know what I mean.

TIMMY: Yes.

JOHN: It isn't that I think—

TIMMY: *(Truthfully.)* —I understand…I really do.

DOCTOR GOLDMAN: *(To Mrs. Benti—indicating Willis.)* Has everything been explained to him?

MRS. BENTI: Yes.

DOCTOR GOLDMAN: *(Voice lowered.)* They expect to have an opening in a week or so.

MRS. BENTI: There's no need to whisper.

DOCTOR GOLDMAN: You're sure he understands?

MRS. BENTI: *(To Willis by way of demonstration.)* Where are you going?

WILLIS: *(As though she'd asked a question so easy he was embarrassed to answer.)* I know that.

MRS. BENTI: Tell Doctor Goldman.

WILLIS: *(Blithely.)* I'm going to Shadybrook your excellency.

MRS. BENTI: Why are you going there?

NETTIE: *(Can't bear it.)* Mama please.

MRS. BENTI: *(To Willis—ignoring Nettie.)* Why can't you live here any more?

WILLIS: Uncle Eddie…

MRS. BENTI: *(Relentless.)* Go on.

WILLIS: I forget.

MRS. BENTI: Because Uncle Eddie has decided to stay in Saranac and without him we're not able to take care of you any longer.

WILLIS: *(As though she'd given the right answer on a quiz show.)* Correct.

MRS. BENTI: Show Doctor Goldman the tie clasp Eddie made you.

NETTIE: *(To Mrs. Benti—knowing where this will lead.)* Must you?

WILLIS: *(Indicating his tie clasp to the doctor.)* See?

DOCTOR GOLDMAN: *(Peering closer.)* And with your initials. Fine work. *(To Mrs. Benti.)* He must have a natural aptitude to pick it up so fast.

NETTIE: He always had an artistic streak.

JOHN: *(Disparaging.)* Oh boy.

NETTIE: *(Displaying a bracelet she wears.)* Handwrought silver. You don't think it took talent and skill? *(To Doctor Goldman.)* I sold over three hundred dollars worth of jewelry from the catalog Eddie sent.

MRS. BENTI: *(To Doctor Goldman with more than a hint of disapproval.)* That's how he intends to support himself up there.

DOCTOR GOLDMAN: I know.

JOHN: *(To Nettie.)* What happens when you run out of friends and relatives?

NETTIE: They bought because they liked it—not out of sympathy.

MRS. BENTI: I hope so, because I'm not sending him any more money.
(She moves from the dining room to the living room drawing the others [except Timmy and Willis] with her.)

NETTIE: You sound like you want him to fail.

MRS. BENTI: I want him to face facts.

DOCTOR GOLDMAN: Whether he fails or not it's a step in the right direction for all of you. *(To Nettie and John.)* You're going to South America at last. Your sister marrying at last. *(To Mrs. Benti.)* And you will be free for the first time in all the years I've known you.

NETTIE: *(To Doctor Goldman, indicating her mother.)* Miss Julian invited her to take a trip—all expenses paid.

DOCTOR GOLDMAN: There you see. And as for Eddie? If the jewelry business doesn't work out, he'll find something else. Nothing taxing because even though he's cured he's far from robust. Which makes Saranac the safest place to be. Plus I understand there's a girl.

NETTIE: The daughter of a local businessman.

DOCTOR GOLDMAN: So he won't starve. *(To Mrs. Benti.)* I repeat As painful as it is, it's for the best.

MRS. BENTI: For everyone but Willis.

DOCTOR GOLDMAN: Including him. Not in the short run but ultimately. Even *with* Eddie here how long do you think it could continue?…Him deteriorating, you getting older, you'd have to put him away eventually. Only by then he'd be less adaptable. And the longer you waited the more painful. Saddest of all, by the time you did it your lives would be over. *(Extracting a pamphlet from his pocket.)* Here I brought a brochure. Clean rooms. Recreational facilities.

(Mrs. Benti making no move to take the brochure he offers it to Nettie.)

DOCTOR GOLDMAN: It might ease your mind.

(Nettie turns her back fighting tears. John takes the brochure.)

JOHN: *(Regarding the photo on the cover.)* Nice grounds.

NETTIE: *(At a window.)* Gus and Carmen are getting out of a brand new car! *(Timmy runs to the window to see.)*

DOCTOR GOLDMAN: *(Surveying Nettie, Mrs. Benti, John.)* What's the sense of a wedding cake and decorations if you're all going to frown?

NETTIE: The doctor's right. It's their day. Nothing must spoil it. *(Determined to be happy.)* We've done all we could.

DOCTOR GOLDMAN: Exactly.

NETTIE: We could be at the brink of something wonderful.

DOCTOR GOLDMAN: Which you've more than earned.

(Nettie, infected by her own words, turns to John exultantly.)

NETTIE: I've always said no to South America. But suddenly I see it differently: I wish we were leaving this minute. *(She kisses him impulsively; rushes to the piano; plays the first chords of the "Wedding March" to make sure she knows it, poises to play.)*

WILLIS: *(Merrily.)* Happy days are here again.

DOCTOR GOLDMAN: That's the spirit.

NETTIE: Tell me when.

JOHN: Make sure they're married first.

DOCTOR GOLDMAN: *(Ear cocked to the hallway.)* The door's opening…*(To Nettie.)* They're coming.

(Nettie plays the "Wedding March" as Gus and Carmen, both looking their best—she wearing a corsage—enter. Doctor Goldman leads the applause. Timmy and Willis follow suit enthusiastically. John claps dutifully. Mrs. Benti just stands there.)

WILLIS: *(As he claps.)* Bravo…Bravissimo…Encore.

(Nettie stops playing, rushes to embrace Carmen who seems slightly embarrassed.)

NETTIE: I'm so happy for you.

GUS: How about *me?*

NETTIE: *(Hugging him.)* And for you

GUS: Thank you, sister.

DOCTOR GOLDMAN: *(Taking Gus's hand.)* Congratulations.

GUS: Thank you, Doctor. Thank you all.

DOCTOR GOLDMAN: May I kiss the bride?

GUS: By all means.

(While the Doctor kisses Carmen, John offers his hand to Gus.)

JOHN: Congratulations.

GUS: Thank you.

JOHN: I almost said "many happy returns" but that's for birthdays.

NETTIE: *(To John.)* Get the champagne.

JOHN: Coming right up.

CARMEN: *(To John as he heads for the kitchen.)* Aren't you going to congratulate me?

JOHN: Congratulations. *(He exits into the kitchen.)*

GUS: *(To Mrs. Benti.)* Well, Mother? Did you think this day would ever come?

MRS. BENTI: Yes.

GUS: Of course you did. You predicted it: "Happily married with three children." I must say there were times this past year when I began to lose faith. But my business is going first rate just as you forecast so I persevered. And here we are: all come true like you said. Though I do think "three" children might be overdoing it.

MRS. BENTI: I'll get the glasses.

CARMEN: *(Blocking her way.)* Not till you give us your blessing.

MRS. BENTI: Yes.

CARMEN: Yes what?

MRS. BENTI: Don't be silly.

(She would go around Carmen who grips her shoulders.)

CARMEN: Say it.

MRS. BENTI: *(Fuming.)* Let me go.

CARMEN: *(In a playful manner that doesn't hide serious intent.)* Not till you say it.

GUS: *(Sensing something deeper at issue and trying to ease the moment.)* I'm sure we have your mother's best wishes.

MRS. BENTI: *(Meaning it.)* I wish you both the best.

GUS: You see.

(They all assemble at the dining room table as John working the cork from a champagne bottle, emerges from the kitchen.)

DOCTOR GOLDMAN: *(To Gus.)* Will there be a honeymoon?

GUS: Yes. But don't ask where.

CARMEN: He hasn't even told *me*.

GUS: Suffice to say we will proceed by car, purchased for the occasion, and follow an itinerary known only to me for two weeks.

JOHN: Why all the secrecy?

GUS: So no one can get in touch with us. Not my office. Not anyone for any reason. And to doubly insure this, we've pledged to make no phone calls the entire time. *(To Carmen.)* Correct?

CARMEN: Yes.

GUS: A complete interruption in our lives. A break with the familiar to launch us properly.

JOHN: Suppose something happens—an emergency?

GUS: It will have to happen without us.

NETTIE: *(To Carmen.)* Doctor Goldman just told us the home might have an opening in a week.

GUS: At the risk of being misunderstood, I hope so…
(They react.)

GUS: Yes…Because it's my deepest fear that when the moment comes to part with him someone will get cold feet. Since Carmen is the most likely candidate, I think it's vital she be out of touch when it happens and greeted with a fait accompli on her return.

DOCTOR GOLDMAN: *(Gauging Gus anew.)* That's very wise.

GUS: You don't think it's callous—cruel?

DOCTOR GOLDMAN: Not at all.

GUS: *(To Carmen.)* You see?

CARMEN: *(To John—regarding the champagne bottle.)* Are you opening it or aging it?

JOHN: *(Displaying the cork.)* It's open.

NETTIE: I didn't hear it.

GUS: A tribute to the opener.

CARMEN: That or it's cheap.

JOHN: *(Thrusting the label at her.)* Good enough?

NETTIE: The cork popping is the best part.

GUS: Most people would agree. But in the best restaurants—

CARMEN: —Can we drink it before it evaporates?

GUS: *(To John as Mrs. Benti sets a tray bearing stemmed glasses before him.)* Proceed.

DOCTOR GOLDMAN: *(As John pours.)* Not for me.

CARMEN: You must.

DOCTOR GOLDMAN: Helpless as usual—but only a sip.

TIMMY: What about Willis and me?

CARMEN: Of course.

MRS. BENTI: No. Not for Willis.

NETTIE: Just a little to toast.

WILLIS: *(To Mrs. Benti.)* Please?

CARMEN: *(To John.)* Give him some.

(John looks to Mrs. Benti for permission.)

MRS. BENTI: *(Acquiescing and dealing Carmen a subtle jab.)* He's *her* son.

NETTIE: *(To John as he pours for Timmy and Willis.)* Light for both of them.

(Glasses are distributed. Timmy brings Willis his.)

TIMMY: Here you go.

WILLIS: For medicinal purposes only.

(He would drink but Timmy stops him.)

TIMMY: Wait for the toast.

(Carmen [champagne glass in hand] moves to the living room. The others follow. Timmy wheeling Willis so he can be part of the toast.)

CARMEN: I can't believe Eddie isn't here.

NETTIE: He said the doctors advised against it even though he's cured.

CARMEN: I know what he said. But I thought he'd call at least.

GUS: *(To Doctor Goldman.)* Would you do us the honor, Doctor?

DOCTOR GOLDMAN: I wasn't good luck the last time.

GUS: That was *before* the fact. *(Displays his wedding band.)* This time it's after…Please?

DOCTOR GOLDMAN: My best wishes to the bride and groom. And to everyone in the family near and far. I could say more but why tempt the Gods by drawing attention to this happy scene. What we Jews call conna hooris.

(He drinks. They all follow suit.)

GUS: *(Looking about.)* Anyone else care to speak?

WILLIS: *(Boisterously.)* "With liberty and justice for all."

MRS. BENTI: *(To Carmen—blaming it on the champagne.)* You see?

NETTIE: He'll be fine.

GUS: Perhaps he has something to say. *(To Willis.)* The floor is yours.

WILLIS: *(Impassioned.)* Oh-gan kay-vil-do-say dee-min-tar-vah!

GUS: Anyone care to translate?

(No response.)

GUS: …In that case I have a few words.

CARMEN: After we have the cake.

GUS: I'll be brief.

CARMEN: I'm starving.

GUS: *I insist.*

JOHN: Married an hour and already he's cracking the whip.

MRS. BENTI: *(Sensing something of more than routine interest.)* Let him speak.

GUS: Thank you, Mother.

CARMEN: What are you waiting for?

GUS: *(Having second thoughts.)* Perhaps I shouldn't...

CARMEN: Where's the cake knife?

GUS: ...But if I don't say it now I won't ever be able to. Not that I attach any real significance to it. But even a grain of sand becomes a nuisance if it isn't attended to. "Speak now or forever hold your peace" as the saying goes.

CARMEN: *(Lightly to cover a dawning apprehension.)* Are you drunk?

GUS: Quite the contrary. But it might be better if I was. A man who's imbibed too much makes a fool of himself, it's expected. *(Extending his empty glass to John.)* If you please.

JOHN: *(Pouring.)* Say when.

CARMEN: *(The glass half full.)* When.

(John stops pouring, regards her as do the others puzzled by her uncharacteristic behavior which she tries to gloss over.)

CARMEN: We have a long drive.

JOHN: I thought you didn't know where you were going.

GUS: She doesn't. The fact is we're staying in New York overnight—don't ask where—and getting an early start in the morning.

CARMEN: *(Caution to the winds.)* Never let it be said I killed a party. Bring on the reserves.

DOCTOR GOLDMAN: I'm afraid duty calls.

GUS: *(To the Doctor.)* Stay.

CARMEN: He has patients waiting.

GUS: Please. Just a minute. As someone close to this family, I want you to witness that I love this woman...*(Regarding Carmen with curious intensity.)* Love her with all that I am or ever will be...Love her now and for eternity...

CARMEN: *(Uneasily.)* Your minute's up.

GUS: ...To know she's my wife is too overpowering to contemplate...Like looking at the sun.

CARMEN: *(Seeking to stop him.)* And I love you too. *(She kisses him.)* Now can we cut the cake?

MRS. BENTI: *(Reading Gus.)* He isn't finished.

CARMEN: What more is there to say?

GUS: Nothing perhaps.

CARMEN: Why not let it go at that?

GUS: I want to—am tempted to.

DOCTOR GOLDMAN: *(Thinking he understands the situation.)* They say confession is good for the soul. But my advice to newlyweds is hold your fire. Don't bombard your mates with all your prior transgressions until you're sure how much they really want to know or can stand.

JOHN: I'll drink to that.

GUS: *(To Doctor Goldman.)* It's nothing like that.

NETTIE: What then?

GUS: It's possibly a misperception, a figment, caused by inability to accept my good fortune. If it is, please feel free to laugh.

CARMEN: *Will you spit it out before I scream?*

GUS: *(Quietly.)* The man at the entrance to City Hall when I got there.

CARMEN: What man?

GUS: The one you were talking to: tan raincoat—green fedora. My first impression was you were giving him directions.

CARMEN: What was your second impression?

GUS: That he might be someone you knew because he seemed to have his right hand in close proximity to, if not touching, your arm. Of course from fifty yards, if not further, I could easily have been mistaken. And if I wasn't, if I perceived correctly, it was at most a momentary contact which people, even perfect strangers, are apt to make in the course of gesticulating as people do if lost in a big city they are strangers to which I took this man, who had a vaguely foreign look, to be. And then he turned full face and I had the distinct impression he was someone I knew. Nobody I could name or had ever met. But his face was known to me the way we feel when we encounter a movie star in the street.

CARMEN: Why didn't you—

GUS: *(Putting his fingers to her lips.)* —Please let me say it all before you speak.

WILLIS: When does it rain in the circus, cousin?

TIMMY: *(To Willis.)* Shush.

GUS: By the time I reached you he was gone. And since you didn't mention the encounter I assumed my first impression—someone asking directions—was correct. And so I put it out of my mind and we proceeded to get married. "I pronounce you man and wife at eleven-eleven a.m." the clerk or what ever he was said pointing to a clock that read eleven minutes after eleven precisely. Then into my…*our* new car, which will enable us to visit Willis and take him for rides. And here we are. And I never thought of that man until I viewed Willis' face and suddenly I realized why he looked familiar…He resembled your son: the same nose, chin, eyes. A delusion brought on by nerves? More than likely, given how little sleep I've been getting because I was sure that at the last minute you would be snatched from my hands again. That's it—the whole kit and kaboodle which sounds even more far-fetched as I recount it. So now tell me the fellow was asking how to get to Times Square and we'll all have a fine laugh on me…Well?

CARMEN: If I say he was asking directions you'd believe me?

GUS: Of course.

CARMEN: Suppose I said he was trying to pick me up?

GUS: As beautiful as you are, who could blame him?

CARMEN: Suppose I said it was Willis' father? That we'd bumped into each other accidentally.

GUS: Those things happen.

NETTIE: *(To Carmen—anxiously.) Stop teasing. (To Gus.)* She's teasing you.

CARMEN: *(To Gus—ignoring Nettie.)* Bumped into each other accidentally. Which I should have mentioned when you arrived but I didn't realize you'd seen him and, figuring what you didn't know wouldn't hurt you, decided to keep it to myself so as not to intrude on our wedding day. If I said that's what happened would you find it acceptable?

GUS: *(Bewildered.)* I can live with anything but I must have the facts.

CARMEN: *Do you think I'd meet my ex-husband minutes before I was getting married if there was anything to hide?*

GUS: If you're saying that wasn't him, I'll never mention it again…
    (He looks for her to affirm this but she says nothing.)

GUS: Well?

NETTIE: *(To Carmen.)* Say it.

CARMEN: I can't.

GUS: Why not?

CARMEN: Because it was him.

NETTIE: Armand?

CARMEN: Yes.

GUS: *(Incredulous.)* Willis's father?

CARMEN: The same.

GUS: *(Desperately trying to put the best face on it.)* Who hasn't run into people not seen in years at the strangest times and most unlikely places? A small world as they say.

NETTIE: *(To Carmen.)* Was that it? A coincidence?

CARMEN: No.

JOHN: You knew he'd be there?

CARMEN: No.

GUS: *(Hopeful.)* Then it wasn't prearranged?

CARMEN: Not by me.

JOHN: *What the hell was he doing there?*

CARMEN: *(Indicating her mother.)* Ask her.

MRS. BENTI: *(With cold intensity.)* I wouldn't pursue this if I were you.

CARMEN: What would you do?

MRS. BENTI: Leave immediately.

CARMEN: My welfare your primary concern as usual?

GUS: *(Suddenly fearful—to Carmen.)* Your mother's right. Let's go.
    (He would take her arm but she brushes him off.)

CARMEN: *(To Mrs. Benti.)* Tell them why he was there today.

GUS: I don't want to know!

CARMEN: *Then you shouldn't have asked. (To Mrs. Benti.)* Well?

MRS. BENTI: *(Flatly.)* He phoned…

CARMEN: *(For Gus's benefit.)* Seven years since he was last seen or heard from.

MRS. BENTI: …He wanted to see Willis. I said he'd have to get your permission.

CARMEN: Me in charge—that's a hot one.

GUS: *(To Carmen.)* Why didn't he contact you at work or here?

CARMEN: *(Forwarding the question to her mother.)* Well?

MRS. BENTI: I thought it best to let him know you were getting married.

CARMEN: *Did you have to give him the time and place?*

MRS. BENTI: *(Defiant—challenging.)* I thought it was over between you.

CARMEN: *It is!*

MRS. BENTI: Then what's the harm?

GUS: *(To Carmen.)* Your mother's right.

CARMEN: My mother's lying! *(To Mrs. Benti—savagely.)* He didn't call *you.*
    You called him.

MRS. BENTI: *(Pleading guilty but not yielding an inch.)* As the father, he has
    the right to know Willis is being put away.

CARMEN: *(Incredulous.)* Did she really say that?

GUS: *(To Carmen—supporting Mrs. Benti.)* What's fair is fair.

CARMEN: *(To Gus.) Are you that simple?*

GUS: I think he's entitled by law.

CARMEN: *(To Gus as to a dull-witted child.)* Her calling him was a last ditch
    effort to come between us—stop the wedding.

GUS: Why?

CARMEN: *She can't bear the thought of putting Willis away.*

GUS: *(Understanding beyond belief.)* All the love and care she's lavished on him, can you blame her.

CARMEN: *(In a final attempt to breach his confident assessment.)* He said walking out on Willis and me was the biggest regret of his life! Begged me to take him back!

GUS: *(Unperturbed.)* Which you rejected in no uncertain terms, judging by his expression as he walked away…Correct?

CARMEN: Yes.

GUS: *(Exuberantly.)* Yes. And they lived happily ever after! Cut the cake before the Doctor, who has been glancing at his watch, departs.

DOCTOR GOLDMAN: I *do* have to go.

(Taking Carmen by the hand, Gus sweeps the others up, leads them to the dining room.)

GUS: The cake toute suite.

WILLIS: I want a big piece.

GUS: And you shall have it, my boy.

DOCTOR GOLDMAN: Small for me.

JOHN: None for me.

GUS: I think it's bad luck if everyone doesn't partake. *(To Mrs. Benti.)* Correct, Mother?

MRS. BENTI: Yes.

(Mrs. Benti passes the cake server to Carmen who, totally routed by Gus's impervious joy, cuts and fills the plates which Nettie distributes.)

GUS: *(Squeezing Carmen affectionately as she cuts.)* This time tomorrow we shall be well on our way to…Whoops. Almost gave it away.

JOHN: *(To Gus—casually.)* One thing puzzles me.

GUS: What's that?

JOHN: Why didn't you ask who he was then and there?

NETTIE: *(To John—sharply.)* It's over.

JOHN: I was just curious.

CARMEN: *(To John emphatically.)* Case closed.

JOHN: *(Butter would melt.)* If it's a sensitive subject, forgive me.

GUS: *(Good naturedly.)* Not at all. I didn't ask because something told me that to do so moments before the wedding might be interpreted as a sign I was getting cold feet—grasping at straws in an effort to derail things. If I loved this woman as I said, and as I do, then I should say nothing that might indicate otherwise. Especially something so asinine and farfetched as quizzing her about an apparent stranger.

JOHN: But he wasn't a stranger.

GUS: Which is why I'm glad I raised the matter. A man marrying a woman deserted by her first love can't help wondering if she still cares for him.

JOHN: You're satisfied on that point.

GUS: Completely. He begged her to take him back and she turned him down: the frosting on the wedding cake. If everyone's got a piece— begin.

NETTIE: First the bride and groom feed each other.

GUS: *(Taking a forkful of cake.)* Don't you wonder how such customs originate?

NETTIE: *(To Carmen.)* Go on.

(Carmen scoops a piece of cake on her fork, poises it at Gus's mouth as he does the same to her.)

NETTIE: One…Two…

MRS. BENTI: Wait.

CARMEN: Now what?

MRS. BENTI: *(Ear cocked.)* Someone's at the door.

(They all listen…We hear a key turn—the door open and close…approaching steps.)

CARMEN: *(Calls.)* Who's there?

(No reply…Eddie, new suit, tie, looking better than we've ever seen him, bearing a gift-wrapped package, appears.)

EDDIE: I come in peace.

(He moves to the living room to deposit the package. Nettie and Carmen rush to embrace him. The others, with the exception of Willis, follow him. Gus and Timmy are delighted. John and Doctor Goldman are puzzled. Mrs. Benti is impassive.)

WILLIS: *(Sings.)* "Roll out the barrel."

CARMEN: *(To Eddie.)* I should have guessed when you didn't even phone.

GUS: *(Pumping Eddie's—indicating Carmen.)* I can't tell you how upset she was when you said you couldn't be here.

EDDIE: I take it the dirty deed is done.

CARMEN: *(Displaying her wedding ring.)* As of eleven-eleven this morning, I am an honest woman.

EDDIE: *(Like a priest sanctifying their union.)* Bless you my children.

TIMMY: What do you say, unk?

EDDIE: *(Regarding Timmy.)* Can this strapping lad be my little nephew?

NETTIE: You've been gone over a year.

EDDIE: Fifteen months, twelve days and six hours.

DOCTOR GOLDMAN: *(Offering his hand.)* Time well spent judging by your appearance. *(To the others.)* Have you ever seen him look better?

JOHN: *(Sarcastically.)* Nothing to do but eat and sleep—who wouldn't?

EDDIE: *(Regarding John—in similar vein.)* And I was afraid everyone would change.

MRS. BENTI: Why didn't you let us know you were coming?

EDDIE: Spur of the moment decision. *(To Doctor Goldman—indicating his mother whose undemonstrative reception bothers him more than he wants anyone to suspect.)* Contrary to appearance, she's really glad to see me.

MRS. BENTI: Of course I am.

EDDIE: That's what I said.

WILLIS: *(By way of calling Eddie to him.)* Fee-fie-fo-fum.

EDDIE: *I smell the blood of an Englishman.*
(Eddie returns to the dining room—the others following in his wake.)

WILLIS: I can button my shirt.

EDDIE: Medals later. Right now "Shake the hand"…That what?

NETTIE: *(Prompting Willis.)* "That shook—"

EDDIE: —No coaching from the audience. *(To Willis.)* Five seconds to beat the clock…Well?…Three seconds…Two—

WILLIS: *(Clasping Eddie's hand.)* "That shook the hand of John L. Sullivan."

EDDIE: Give this man eight silver dollars.

MRS. BENTI: *(Probing.)* I thought the doctors advised against your coming.

EDDIE: Hey I'm cured.

DOCTOR GOLDMAN: *(To Mrs. Benti.)* A brief visit won't do any harm. *(To Eddie.)* The jewelry you're making is excellent.

EDDIE: We aim to please.

NETTIE: I have three more orders since I wrote you.

EDDIE: *(To Willis.)* What's this rumor I heard about you buttoning your shirt?

WILLIS: Go-wanda-say go-laga-veel.

EDDIE: *(As though he understood.)* Even the cuffs. Impressive.

CARMEN: How's Miss Gunther?

EDDIE: First rate.

NETTIE: *(To Doctor Goldman.)* She's the one in Saranac.

CARMEN: A lovely girl. I met her when I visited.

NETTIE: You should have brought her with you.

EDDIE: How do you know I didn't? *(Calls in the direction of the hallway.)* You can come in now.
(They all turn to the entrance expectantly.)

EDDIE: …Emily?

(Timmy overwhelmed by curiosity, disappears up the hallway.)

EDDIE: …She's very shy.

TIMMY: *(Reappearing.)* There's no one there.

EDDIE: She must be sleeping it off.

CARMEN: *(First to get the joke.)* You humbug.

(With the exception of Mrs. Benti, who regards him searchingly, and John, who shakes his head, they all laugh.)

EDDIE: *(To Mrs. Benti pointedly.)* Cheer up, Mom, it was only a gag.

MRS. BENTI: *(Defensively.)* She'd be more than welcome.

NETTIE: Why *didn't* she come?

EDDIE: Probably because she wasn't invited. *(To Willis.)* You were saying?

WILLIS: *(Delighted Eddie's there.)* Koopie-say ka-vilda.

MRS. BENTI: How long can you stay?

EDDIE: Trying to get rid of me already?

CARMEN: Gus and I were about to leave.

EDDIE: Don't let me detain you.

GUS: *(To Carmen.)* We're staying in New York tonight. No need to rush.

EDDIE: *(To Willis.)* What other skills have you mastered in my absence?

TIMMY: *(To Eddie, indicating Willis.)* I taught him Chinese checkers.

EDDIE: *(To Willis.)* Is that a fact?

WILLIS: Wee-wee.

EDDIE: And learned to parlez-vous. You *have* been busy.

MRS. BENTI: Are you staying overnight?

EDDIE: Yes.

DOCTOR GOLDMAN: *(To Eddie.)* The last report I received was excellent: weight up again. Lab report negative for the fourth month in a row.

EDDIE: And they said it couldn't be done.

DOCTOR GOLDMAN: Frankly I had doubts.

EDDIE: *(Mimicking a prize fighter after a victory to disguise the depth of feeling behind his words.)* It was a tough fight which I couldn't have won without you people in my corner. I thank you all.

MRS. BENTI: Have you eaten?

EDDIE: Copiously.

WILLIS: C-O-P-I-O-U-S-L-Y.

EDDIE: Is there no end to this fellow's talents?

GUS: We just cut the cake. *(To Nettie.)* Give him a piece.

JOHN: *(To Eddie with an edge as Nettie serves him.)* How does New York seem after Shangri La?

EDDIE: Dirty, smelly, noisy, *and* wonderful.

GUS: A nice place to visit et cetera.

EDDIE: Just the opposite. *(To Willis.)* Knock-knock…

GUS: *(To Carmen—puzzled.)* Opposite?

WILLIS: …Who's there?

EDDIE: Po-lice.

WILLIS: Po-lice who?

EDDIE: Po-lice don't talk about me when I'm gone. Knock-knock.

MRS. BENTI: Stop it!

EDDIE: Stop it who?

MRS. BENTI: Doctor Goldman says there may be an opening at the home next week.

EDDIE: What's that got to do with knock-knock?

MRS. BENTI: *(Indicating Willis.)* It's cruel to make him think everything's fine.

EDDIE: Everything *is* fine.

MRS. BENTI: Where *he's* going isn't a country club like Saranac.

CARMEN: *(To Eddie as kindly as possible.)* I'm glad you came but it might have been better if you didn't. He's finally used to you not being here.

MRS. BENTI: *(To Carmen—indicating Eddie.)* Tell him how long that took: "Where's Eddie?" "When's he coming back?" till we were ready to scream.

EDDIE: Riddle: Why is Saranac like a wedding cake?…Well?

GUS: I give up.

EDDIE: Because after the first few bites the sweetness sticks in your throat.

GUS: *(To Carmen.)* What's he saying?

CARMEN: *(To Gus but eyeing Eddie apprehensively.)* Shut up.

EDDIE: Don't you get it?

NETTIE: Get what?

EDDIE: *(Regarding Mrs. Benti.)* You mean to tell me even the great swami is in the dark?

MRS. BENTI: Not any more.

NETTIE: *(To Mrs. Benti.)* What is it?

EDDIE: *(To Mrs. Benti.)* Before you reveal the answer, have we ever met before?

MRS. BENTI: *(To the others.)* He's home to stay.

(Shocked they turn to Eddie for confirmation.)

EDDIE: How *does* she do it?

CARMEN: You're not going back?

EDDIE: I opt for quality of life over quantity.

DOCTOR GOLDMAN: *(Adamant.)* You're making a grave mistake.

EDDIE: No pun intended I trust.

GUS: *(Hoping he's right.)* Don't you see? He's pulling your leg like about the girl.

JOHN: *(Seconding the notion.)* If he was staying he'd have luggage.

EDDIE: *(To Timmy—gesturing down the hallway.)* My bags if you please.
(Timmy scampers off. Eddie glances around the room.)

EDDIE: You should see your faces. And I thought I was bringing good news.
(Timmy reappears with the two valises seen previously.)

EDDIE: Voilà.

NETTIE: The jewelry business. All those orders?

EDDIE: Send the money back.

NETTIE: It was going so well.

EDDIE: *(Defensive—a flash of irritation.)* Thanks to the war you can't get silver. And who do we sell to when we've exhausted friends?

JOHN: That's what I told her.

EDDIE: *(Pointedly.)* I'll bet you did.

GUS: It's quite a bombshell.

CARMEN: Why didn't you tell us?

EDDIE: I didn't make up my mind till last night.

GUS: Just like that?

EDDIE: I'd been thinking about it.

NETTIE: What about Emily?

EDDIE: She'll survive.

JOHN: Leave it to you to ruin a good thing.

EDDIE: *(To Gus—indicating John.)* In case you missed it that was a reference to when my brother-in-law and I went into business together with predictable results.

JOHN: *It was you running around every night that killed it!*

NETTIE: *(To them both.)* Stop it!

GUS: *(Suddenly apprehensive—to Carmen.)* We should have left when I said.

CARMEN: Who kept asking questions?

GUS: *(To Eddie.)* You may have noticed the DeSoto by the door. I bought it for our honeymoon.

EDDIE: What's keeping you? *Go.*

GUS: *(To Carmen.)* He's right. Come.

CARMEN: *(To Eddie—ignoring Gus.)* What are your plans?

GUS: He just got here.

CARMEN: *(To Eddie.)* Do you intend to get a job?

EDDIE: Of course.

MRS. BENTI: When?

EDDIE: *(Sarcastically.)* Would this afternoon be soon enough?

NETTIE: *(To Eddie.)* It's just that we've all made plans. Including Mama who's taking a trip with Miss Julian.

MRS. BENTI: She invited me but nothing's settled.

EDDIE: *(Hands raised.) Time out...*
(They regard him.)

EDDIE: If I thought I was lousing things up for everyone, I wouldn't be here.

CARMEN: We just want to know what's what.

EDDIE: I intend to seek gainful employment. Okay?

GUS: I let a salesman go last week. Would you be interested?

EDDIE: Once I'm settled in, which I'm sure Doctor Goldman would not only recommend but insist on.

DOCTOR GOLDMAN: For the rest of his life he must guard against over-doing. Which is why I deeply regret his leaving Saranac.

EDDIE: Strike the Doctor's statement after "over-doing"

GUS: *(With more confidence and enthusiasm than he really feels.)* All's well that ends well! My bride and I away to places unknown as scheduled... *(To John and Nettie.)* My new sister and brother off to South America where I look forward to visiting you... *(To Mrs. Benti.)* And you, Mother, to embark on the first of what I hope will be many pleasurable trips you so richly deserve.

MRS. BENTI: And Willis?

GUS: To the home as planned.

MRS. BENTI: I don't think so.

GUS: Why not?

MRS. BENTI: *(Presciently.)* Eddie has other ideas.

CARMEN: What are you talking about?

MRS. BENTI: *(To Eddie.)* Tell them.

EDDIE: *(All eyes on him—his attention on his mother.)* Once again she peers into her crystal ball...

NETTIE: Ideas about what?

EDDIE: ...Only this time she came up empty.

MRS. BENTI: *(Challenging him.)* If Doctor Goldman said there was an opening tomorrow, you'd let Willis go with no objections?

EDDIE: We do not dignify hypothetical questions.

CARMEN: *(Entreating.)* Eddie listen. It's taken more pain than you can imagine to decide about Willis.

EDDIE: And I think you've made the right decision.

NETTIE: Really?

EDDIE: Absolutely…Except now you don't have to rush.

CARMEN: What do you mean?

EDDIE: While I'm readjusting, you can shop around—make sure it's the best place for him.

CARMEN: We've done that.

EDDIE: Consider it a reprieve then. A few weeks grace.

DOCTOR GOLDMAN: *(Firmly.)* There's a waiting list. If you say no when the opportunity comes, there's no telling how long till the next opening.

EDDIE: We'll take our chances. *(To Willis.)* Right?

WILLIS: Correct, your highness!

CARMEN: *Eddie, you can't manage him alone. (To Doctor Goldman.)* Tell him!

DOCTOR GOLDMAN: *(To Eddie.)* It would be a strain your system couldn't tolerate.

EDDIE: *(To Timmy—tensing his right arm à la Popeye.)* Feel my musk-el.

JOHN: *How I'd love to smash you.*

NETTIE: *John!*

JOHN: *Don't you see what's happening?*

EDDIE: *(To Mrs. Benti.)* Why don't we leave it to the supreme authority. What do you say about postponing for a month?

MRS. BENTI: A month isn't worth it.

GUS: I couldn't agree more.

EDDIE: *(Surprised by her response.)* I see said the blind man.

TIMMY: *(Reflexively.)* As he put down his hammer and saw.
(Hastily as Nettie shoots him a look.)

TIMMY: Sorry.

GUS: *(Hopefully.)* That would appear to settle it then.

DOCTOR GOLDMAN: In everyone's best interest.

EDDIE: *(To Mrs. Benti—impulsively.)* How about *six* months?

GUS: What?

EDDIE: *(To his mother.)* You say postponing for a month isn't worth it. How many months *would* be worth it?

GUS: *(To Eddie.)* We all know what deep feelings you have for the boy but—

EDDIE: *(To Mrs. Benti—ignoring Gus.)* —How about I promise not to take a job for a year?

NETTIE: *(Distraught.) Why are you doing this?*

EDDIE: *(To Mrs. Benti.)* Say no and that's it. I'll go back to Saranac.

MRS. BENTI: You and I can't manage him.

EDDIE: We can try.

DOCTOR GOLDMAN: *The two of you with no relief? It wouldn't work.*

CARMEN: *(Rashly.)* Suppose Gus and I got an apartment nearby?

GUS: *What?*

CARMEN: *(To Gus.)* To help out now and then—in case of emergency.

GUS: *NO!*

CARMEN: He *is* my son!

GUS: *(To Carmen—fervent, resolute, pleading.)* How can we build a life together if what happens in this house is your first concern?…Whatever
they decide must be done without your assistance.

CARMEN: Are you saying I have to choose?

GUS: Yes. Yes I guess I am. And I beg you, weigh things carefully before you
answer.

CARMEN: *(To Mrs. Benti.)* If I don't promise to lend a hand he goes to the
home as scheduled?

MRS. BENTI: There's no other way.

CARMEN: *(To Gus—indicating Willis.)* Most people with his condition don't
live twenty years.

GUS: *(Unmoved.)* Most people with his condition don't get the devoted attention he receives.

CARMEN: What a cruel joke if after all these years we put him away just before the end.

DOCTOR GOLDMAN: I've seen worse cases live to fifty.

EDDIE: *(Explodes.) Why don't we draw lots? Winner shoves him out the window.*

CARMEN: *(To Gus—desperately.)* It would just be a year.

GUS: I gave you more than a year. And, if I thought that would end it, I'd
give you another year. But there is no end and never will be if you don't
declare it here and now.

CARMEN: *(Helpless.)* I don't think I can.

GUS: I mean what I say.

CARMEN: I know.

GUS: *My God are you really going to let me go?*

EDDIE: *(Genuinely dismayed.)* I didn't want anything like this.

GUS: What *did* you want?

EDDIE: The best for everyone.

GUS: I think things work better when people aren't so generous—pursue
their own interest selfishly. Like a busy intersection where traffic flows
smoothly as long as everyone pushes ahead ruthlessly. And then some
kind soul hangs back—touches the brake instead of the gas—and suddenly there's pandemonium. Which I realize has little relevance to the

situation at hand, but hope that while I've been babbling, my wife…my darling wife…might have reconsidered…

CARMEN: I can't deprive him of what might be the last year of his life.

GUS: But you *can* deprive us of a lifetime…That's it then. What more is there to say? *(Appealing to Nettie.)* Can *you* think of anything?…*(To Doctor Goldman.)* Can *you?*…*(To everyone.)* The saddest moment of my life and you know what's going through my mind? I'm wondering what to do about the hotel where I've reserved the bridal suite…Having paid in advance, shall I use it myself?

NETTIE: Go there and wait. She'll come to you.

GUS: You're an angel. But for that to happen she would have to know the name of the hotel.

NETTIE: What is it?

GUS: *(Regarding Carmen.)* That question must come from *her.*

NETTIE: *(Imploring Carmen.) Ask him what hotel it is.*

CARMEN: *(Resigned, almost peaceful, as though some monumental decision had been made.)* I had one of the earliest shows on radio. Sustaining, they called it because there weren't any advertisers so I didn't get paid. But radio was growing and my program, fifteen minutes three nights a week was popular. Everyone said if I stuck with it my future was assured…

MRS. BENTI: *(She knows what's coming.) Papa was out of work. We needed to eat.*

CARMEN: Because we needed to eat, I, at my mother's insistence took a job in vaudeville—four of us, a tenor, Armand was the baritone, a coloratura and me—performing famous arias from coast to coast. Usually after the magician and before the juggler for one hundred dollars a week…

MRS. BENTI: Great money in those days.

CARMEN: Plus I got to see the country. And, for the first and only time in my life, I was free.

MRS. BENTI: *Did I tell you to sleep with everyone? Be a tramp?*

CARMEN: *(Unperturbed.)* I was a bit wild but "tramp" is an exaggeration.

MRS. BENTI: What did I say when you phoned you were pregnant?

CARMEN: "Come home and Doctor Goldman will take care of it so nobody knows."

MRS. BENTI: But you stayed on the road hoping he'd marry you until it was too late and…

CARMEN: Go on. Say it.

NETTIE: Don't.

CARMEN: *(Exploding.) Until I wound up in the hands of a doctor in Kansas City who botched the delivery! Say it! Say it!*

GUS: No! Ancient history. What's the point?

CARMEN: *(To Gus—matter-of-fact.)* The point is I never loved anyone so much before or since.

GUS: Willis' father?

CARMEN: Yes.

NETTIE: *(Appalled.)* Why are you saying this?

CARMEN: *(Regarding Gus more tenderly than she ever has before.)* Because he's too good a man to leave here with regrets or delusions.

GUS: *(Desperate.)* Suppose I said the boy can live with us?

CARMEN: To use one of your favorite words: impractical.

GUS: *I don't care what happened with what's his name. What's past is past.*

CARMEN: How do you *know* it's past?

GUS: You said he begged you to take him back and you refused.

CARMEN: Because he's broke and a cheater and always will be.

GUS: *(Shocked.)* That's the only reason?

CARMEN: Yes.

GUS: In that case I'm well out of this.

CARMEN: I think so.

GUS: *(Stupefied—helpless.)* What more can I say?…*(To Doctor Goldman.)* I better stay with my current doctor under the circumstances.

DOCTOR GOLDMAN: I think so.

GUS: Imagine gaining and losing a family in one day?…Tomorrow I'll think of something befitting the occasion but right now good-bye is the best I can do…Good-bye. *(He starts to exit. Stops.)* There's one thing which if I don't ask I'll always wonder about…*(He goes to Willis.)* When *does* it rain in the circus?

WILLIS: When the man on the flying trapeze.

GUS: What?…Oh yes—I see. *(He exits.)*

NETTIE: The poor man.

JOHN: *(To Eddie—viciously.)* You son-of-a-bitch.

EDDIE: Call me mister. *(Snapping his fingers as something occurs to him.)* Gus loves the Taft!

CARMEN: What?

EDDIE: The Hotel Taft. That's probably where he reserved the suite if you change your mind.

(She just looks at him.)

EDDIE: Want me to check?

CARMEN: *(Bitter—accusing, as what she's done sinks in.)* You've done enough!

EDDIE: *(With false bravado.)* If that's the way everyone feels, say the word and I'm on the next train to Saranac.

JOHN: *(With scorn.) How typical.*

EDDIE: Been nice seeing you!

(He starts from the room but John blocks his way.)

JOHN: *Make a mess and leave others to clean up like always.*

EDDIE: *UP YOURS!*

(He tries to shove John aside. Exhausts himself to the point of collapse in the brief wrestle. Doctor Goldman and Carmen help Eddie to a chair in the living room where he breathes heavily.)

EDDIE: *(As Doctor Goldman takes his pulse.)* What round is it?

NETTIE: *(To John.) Happy now?*

CARMEN: *(To the Doctor as he finishes.)* Well?

DOCTOR GOLDMAN: He'll be all right but he better lie down.

(As Doctor Goldman and Nettie help Eddie to his feet.)

MRS. BENTI: *(To Eddie.)* Can I get you anything?

EDDIE: Kind words in short supply, I'll settle for a shot of rye—water on the side.

MRS. BENTI: *(To Doctor Goldman.)* Is that good for him?

DOCTOR GOLDMAN: No. But under the circumstances.

EDDIE: Drinks for the house. *(To Timmy as Nettie and Doctor Goldman help him to his room.)* Did you get my birthday card?

TIMMY: Yes.

EDDIE: And greetings from Uncle Sam?

TIMMY: I go for my draft physical two weeks from tomorrow.

EDDIE: Grand Central Palace?

TIMMY: Yes.

EDDIE: Having been through it, remind me to give you a few tips. *(To Willis.)* See you in the morning, pardner.

WILLIS: *I didn't ask to be born!*

EDDIE: So say we all.

NETTIE: *(To Timmy by way of calming Willis.)* Play checkers with him.

TIMMY: The guys are waiting for me.

NETTIE: *(Uncharacteristically harsh.) Do as I say.*

(Doctor Goldman and Nettie, with Eddie between them disappear into his bedroom closing the door.)

TIMMY: *(To Mrs. Benti.)* Where are the checkers?

MRS. BENTI: Willis' room.

(Timmy disappears down the corridor.)

JOHN: *(To Mrs. Benti.)* I'll have one too.

(She regards him.)

JOHN: A drink when you pour his.

MRS. BENTI: *(To Carmen.)* How about you?

CARMEN: Yes.

(Mrs. Benti exits into the kitchen.)

JOHN: *(Mimicking her words to Gus.)* "I never loved anyone so much before or since."

CARMEN: *(Measuredly.)* I meant it.

(John embraces Carmen who breaks away furiously.)

CARMEN: *Are you crazy?*

JOHN: Kissing the bride is all. I knew you wouldn't go through with it.

CARMEN: Then you knew more than I did.

JOHN: *(Vehemence a measure of his uncertainty.) You said it to get rid of him.*

CARMEN: *(Mocking.)* I wish I had your capacity for self-delusion.

JOHN: If I thought you still loved Armand, I'd get tickets for South America tomorrow.

CARMEN: Bon voyage.

(Before John can react, Doctor Goldman and Nettie emerge from Eddie's room; Timmy, appears with the Chinese checker board at the hallway entrance; Mrs. Benti emerges from the kitchen with a whiskey bottle and six filled shot glasses on a tray.)

DOCTOR GOLDMAN: *(To Mrs. Benti—referring to Eddie.)* You can forget his drink.

NETTIE: Fell asleep as soon as his head touched the pillow.

TIMMY: *(As Mrs. Benti passes shots to Carmen and John.)* I'll take Eddie's.

NETTIE: You will not. *(To Mrs. Benti.)* Skip me.

DOCTOR GOLDMAN: And me.

JOHN: *(To Nettie—indicating Timmy.)* Old enough to fight for his country but not to drink. That's a hot one.

NETTIE: He's not in yet. And if all goes well—

JOHN: *(To Mrs. Benti.)* —Give him a drink.

TIMMY: *(In No Man's Land again.)* It doesn't matter. Skip it.

JOHN: *Take it!*

(Timmy, figuring there will be less fireworks if he takes the drink than if he refuses, reaches for a shot glass.)

DOCTOR GOLDMAN: *(Eager to be gone—to Mrs. Benti.)* Let me know how he is tomorrow. *(To Carmen.)* I hope you reconsider.

JOHN: *(To the Doctor indicating Nettie and himself defiantly.)* We're not changing our plans! I'm booking us on the first ship to Rio in the morning!

(However opposed Nettie may be, she knows this isn't the time to fight that battle.)

DOCTOR GOLDMAN: I see...Well—good. *(To Mrs. Benti.)* Till tomorrow then. *(Doctor Goldman exits.)*

NETTIE: Something I wanted to ask him I forgot. *(She follows the Doctor off.)*

JOHN: *(Raising his glass sardonically.)* What'll we drink to?

CARMEN: *(Regarding her mother—bitter, derisive.)* How about to the world's greatest fortune teller who assured Gus he'd be happily married and have three children.

MRS. BENTI: *(With cold certainty.)* He will. But not with you.

(Carmen hurls the contents of her glass into her mother's face. Everyone freezes except Willis who begins to babble agitatedly.)

WILLIS: Go-vanda say...Go-vilda-say...Go-bane-ya...Go-vanda-say. *Go-vilda say. Go-bane-ya! GO-VANDA SAY. GO-VILDA-SAY. GO-BANE-YA!*

(Carmen goes to Willis; sits beside him stroking his hand reassuringly.)

CARMEN: It's all right...It's all right.

WILLIS: *(Still agitated but less so.)* Garva-garva-tankay.

CARMEN: You're staying here. We're all staying here. Do you understand?

WILLIS: Yes mother dear.

(Carmen breaks down; weeps silently. Willis, interpreting her concern as exclusively for him, pats her cheek.)

WILLIS: Don't cry my darling—I'm fine.

(Mrs. Benti exits to her room. John pours himself a drink.)

TIMMY: *(Eager to be anywhere else.)* I'll see how Eddie's doing.

(As he approaches Eddie's door, it opens. Eddie appears.)

EDDIE: I heard Willis.

TIMMY: It's nothing.

EDDIE: You strip to your shorts and single file.

TIMMY: What?

EDDIE: Your physical next week. It's like an assembly line. Doctors poking and probing, till you come to a desk where they say you're in or out. The rejected brag about the great times they're going to have while the others are getting their asses shot off. But in their hearts most 4-Fs, including me, leave that building with their tails between their legs.

TIMMY: I had no idea you were so patriotic.

(Unnoticed by Eddie and Timmy, Mrs. Benti emerges from her room—is listening.)

EDDIE: *(Adamant.)* Don't tell them about your back.

TIMMY: *(Sarcastic.)* You think the army will make a man of me?

EDDIE: *(Fervently.) I think it's the only way for you not to be sucked in here like the rest of us.*
(He exits to his bedroom. Mrs. Benti sits on the sofa as Nettie returns to the living room after seeing Doctor Goldman out.)

NETTIE: *(To Mrs. Benti.)* The Doctor is going to write a letter for Timmy to take. He said when they read his medical history they'll reject him. I'm sure he's right but I still feel uneasy. If I make tea will you read the leaves?

MRS. BENTI: *(Roused from private thoughts.)* What?

NETTIE: *(As John enters the living room.)* I want you to read the leaves and tell me if Doctor Goldman is right—that Timmy will be turned down when he goes for his physical.

MRS. BENTI: I'm through with that.

NETTIE: *I have to know...* Please.

MRS. BENTI: All right.

NETTIE: I'll put the kettle on.

MRS. BENTI: It isn't necessary.

NETTIE: You know?

MRS. BENTI: Yes

NETTIE: Tell me.

MRS. BENTI: He's going to war.
(Nettie gasps. John reacts in spite of himself.)

JOHN: And then what?

MRS. BENTI: It's all nonsense. What do you care?

JOHN: *And then what?*

MRS. BENTI: He'll come home.

NETTIE: The way he was? Uninjured?

MRS. BENTI: Uninjured but not the way he was.

JOHN: How about the winner of the Kentucky Derby while you're at it?

MRS. BENTI: I can't do that. But I can tell you why you won't go to South America.

JOHN: *(Indicating Nettie.)* Because she's going to insist on staying here to help out with Willis. Big deal.

MRS. BENTI: I mean your reason. *(She eyes him challengingly.)* Would you like to hear?

JOHN: *(Afraid she might know about him and Carmen.)* No thanks. I've heard enough bull for one day

NETTIE: Uninjured?

MRS. BENTI: Uninjured.

NETTIE: *(Hugging Mrs. Benti who accepts it stoically.) I can't tell you how relieved I feel.*

JOHN: *(In private reverie.)* When I was seventeen I was sent to Brazil on an expense account. Everyone liked me. Everyone wanted to do business with me.

CARMEN: *(To Willis.)* I saw your father today.

WILLIS: Hep-sha. Pep-sha.

CARMEN: I told him you had a nice voice. He said he might come to hear you one day.

WILLIS: *(Begins to sing.)* "In your dear eyes of blue. Meet me tonight in dreamland, sweet dreamy dreamland." *(Carmen joining in.)* "There let my dreams come true."

(Nettie, moved by their voices, goes to the piano and as they conclude, she plays the opening chords leading into "Dreamland," which she sings as well. Carmen and Willis, hearing Nettie sing join in. Drawn by the music, Eddie emerges from his bedroom, adds his voice to the song. Now Timmy joins in.)

Meet me tonight in dreamland

Under the silvery moon

Meet me tonight in dreamland

Where love's sweet roses bloom.

Come with the love light gleaming

In your dear eyes of blue

Meet me in dreamland

Sweet dreamy dreamland

There let my dreams come true.

(They conclude on a note of impressive harmony.)

EDDIE: We do have our moments.

MRS. BENTI: *(Detached—on her own wavelength.)* I was ten when my mother took me to Coney Island. A cold winter day. We had the beach to ourselves. I sat looking at the water for hours until I understood everything. Then I said, "We can go home now."

(They freeze in tableau from which Timmy detaches himself and exits. The curtain falls.)

THE END

PRODUCTION NOTE

We were blessed with Andrea Marcovicci. her extraordinary voice made the song "Non Ti Scordar di Me" ideal. Subsequent productions, espeically amateur, might not be so fortunate. I recommend simpler songs, popular or classical, that the actress playing Carmen is comfortable with which will show her voice to best advantage.

CONTACT WITH THE ENEMY

ORIGINAL PRODUCTION

Contact with the Enemy was presented by the Ensemble Studio Theatre (Curt Dempster, Artistic Director; M. Edgar Rosenblum, Executive Director; Jamie Richards Executive Producer) in November 1999. Set design by Kert Lundell, Lighting design by Michael Lincoln, sound design by Beatrice Terry, costume design by Julie Doyle, production stage manager Jim Ring, casting by Nina Pratt. The play was directed by Chris Smith with the following cast:

Hank Naylor . . . . Nesbitt Blaisdell
Bill Duffy . . . . Christopher Murney
Mrs. Grayson . . . . Cynthia Hayden
The Guide . . . . Kathryn Gayner
Bartender . . . . Paul Bartholomew

INTRODUCTION

In April, 1945 Patton's Third Army overran the first Concentration Camp the Allies discovered: A satelite camp called Ohrdrf-Nord, where Jews were worked, starved, beaten, and shot to death in lieu of gas chambers and ovens. Eisenhower, Bradley, and Patton went to see for themselves.

Patton puked. Eisenhower ordered every GI in the area who could be spared to witness it so we'd know what we were fighting for.

Seeing Ohrdruf (thirty-two hundred matchstick corpses piled like cordwood) proved the most influential day of my life, though it took years for the full impact to register.

Longing to bear witness in a way that might resonate, I wrote reams about Ohrdruf without success.

A visit to the Holocaust Museum in Washington, D.C., several years ago, resurrected the horrors but provided no inspiration.

And then, in that spontaneous combustion way in which plays come to life, another parallel experience entered the equation and *Contact with the Enemy* was conceived.

It was hailed by several producers who called within twenty-four hours of receipt to register their enthusiasm. This, invariably, followed by a subsequent call saying that upon reflection it didn't seem commercial enough, which I sensed was a euphemism for what really bothered them: The Holocaust—such an emotional topic that any treatment of it in less than the most doctrinaire way would occasion alarm. Remember the furor over Hannah Arendt's "banality of evil"?

A week from today (October 11, 1999) we begin rehearsals for a showcase production at the Ensemble Studio Theatre. Did someone say "break a leg"?

SCENE I

Time: Morning. 1993. Place: Outside the entrance to the Holocaust Museum, Washington, D.C. At rise: Hank Naylor, late sixties, is taking a photo of the museum sign. Enter Bill Duffy—mid-sixties.

NAYLOR: Wonder if you'd do me a favor?

DUFFY: What is it?

NAYLOR: *(Indicating his camera.)* Would you take my picture with the sign in the background?

DUFFY: Sure.

NAYLOR: *(Handing him the camera.)* Automatic focus—just press that button.

DUFFY: Right.

(Naylor positions himself.)

NAYLOR: Be sure you get the sign in.

DUFFY: *(Camera to his eye.)* Ready?

NAYLOR: Yes.

(Duffy snaps; returns the camera to Naylor.)

NAYLOR: Thanks a lot.

DUFFY: You're welcome. What time's it open?

NAYLOR: Ten o'clock.

DUFFY: What time you got?

NAYLOR: A quarter of. *(Indicating the museum.)* They say it's really something.

DUFFY: So I hear.

NAYLOR: Friend of mine and his wife got to where you pick a card out of a basket with one of the victim's names and pictures, she almost passed out...I'm traveling with a group. Tried to get some of them to come but they said they were sick of the Holocaust. My own wife wouldn't come. "You've seen it once," she said. "Why do you want to see it again?"

DUFFY: You've been here before?

NAYLOR: No.

DUFFY: I don't understand.

NAYLOR: When my wife said "You've seen it once," she meant the real thing.

DUFFY: Real thing?

NAYLOR: The first concentration camp they came across. I saw it.

DUFFY: When was that?

NAYLOR: Right after they found it.

DUFFY: What was it called?

NAYLOR: It was a small one nobody ever heard of.

DUFFY: Ohrdruf-Nord?

NAYLOR: Ohrdruf-Nord. Right.

DUFFY: I saw it too.

NAYLOR: No.

DUFFY: Yes.

NAYLOR: Well how about *that*.

DUFFY: Courtesy of General Eisenhower who ordered everyone in the area to see it—

NAYLOR AND DUFFY: —So we'd know what we were fighting for.

DUFFY: Right.

NAYLOR: What outfit you with?

DUFFY: Eighty-ninth division.

NAYLOR: Talk about a small world.

DUFFY: You in the 89th?

NAYLOR: Yes.

DUFFY: What unit?

NAYLOR: Cavalry Reconnaissance.

(Duffy reacts sharply.)

NAYLOR: What's the matter?

DUFFY: The world just got a lot smaller.

NAYLOR: You don't mean—

DUFFY: —Yes.

NAYLOR: *You* were in the 89th Recon Troop?

DUFFY: Right.

NAYLOR: Well I'll be damned. *(Offering his hand.)* Put it there. Hank Naylor.

DUFFY: From Cranberry Falls—South Dakota.

NAYLOR: *North* Dakota. Who are *you?*

DUFFY: *(Mimicking someone as a clue.)* "Listen boy. I order you to do something and you refuse, we settle it man-to-man. You whip me, I'll turn in my stripes and recommend you get them."

NAYLOR: *(Remembering.)* Sergeant Black's welcome when you joined the first platoon.

DUFFY: Right.

NAYLOR: *(Incredulous.)* We were in the same platoon?

DUFFY: Yes.

NAYLOR: The first?

DUFFY: The first.

NAYLOR: Why don't I recognize you?

DUFFY: It's been a long time.

NAYLOR: *You* recognized *me.*

DUFFY: Not till you said your name.

NAYLOR: *(Taking a stab at it.)* Bowen?

DUFFY: Bowen was a corporal. I was a PFC.

NAYLOR: *(Determined to get it.)* Don't tell me…Which section?

DUFFY: Third.

NAYLOR: Armored car?

DUFFY: Mortar jeep.

NAYLOR: Not Hamsun.

DUFFY: No.

NAYLOR: *(Sure he's got it.)* Collins—you're Collins!

DUFFY: Strike three.

NAYLOR: I give up.

DUFFY: Duffy.

NAYLOR: No.

DUFFY: Yes.

NAYLOR: From Brooklyn.

DUFFY: The Bronx.

NAYLOR: Well I'll be. *(Studies Duffy's face.)* Bill Duffy—Right?

DUFFY: Right.

NAYLOR: Loved to gamble—bet on anything.

DUFFY: Bull's-eye.

NAYLOR: You rode with that psycho.

DUFFY: Ezekiel Potter.

NAYLOR: Were buddies with that Italian kid.

DUFFY: Torelli.

NAYLOR: Torelli—right.

DUFFY: *He* was from Brooklyn.

NAYLOR: How old were you then?

DUFFY: Nineteen. You were older.

NAYLOR: Still am.

  (They laugh.)

DUFFY: You were married to a woman named Alice.

NAYLOR: Still am. How the hell you remember that?

DUFFY: *(Recalling a story Naylor told.)* You were at a dance with Alice and this big tough guy made an insulting remark. You called him on it and he invited you to step outside. You were about to chicken out when Alice whispered—

NAYLOR: —"You can take him Hank," she said. And I did. Beat the bejesus out of him then and there.

DUFFY: I heard you tell that story I made up my mind I wanted a woman like Alice.

NAYLOR: Won't she get a kick out of that. I'm meeting her later. How about joining us?

DUFFY: Love to.

NAYLOR: *(Still can't get over it—regarding him anew.)* The Duffy I remember was this crap shooting kid—thin as a rail. And what happened to the New York accent?

DUFFY: *(Laughing.)* Believe it or not, you're talking to an Ivy League graduate.

NAYLOR: Go on.

DUFFY: Dartmouth College.

NAYLOR: How'd you manage that?

DUFFY: The GI Bill, deception and luck.

NAYLOR: Sounds like quite a story.

DUFFY: It is.

NAYLOR: Save it till we meet Alice. She'll love it. I'm Vice President of a farm equipment company: H. C. Blair—second biggest west of the Mississippi. What do *you* do?

DUFFY: I'm a writer.

NAYLOR: What do you write?

DUFFY: Books—short stories.

NAYLOR: Anything I might know?

DUFFY: I had a novel called *The Bridge Jumper* did pretty well.

NAYLOR: *(Searching his memory.)* Can't place it.

DUFFY: They made a movie out of it.

NAYLOR: Tell you the truth I'm not up on that stuff. But I bet Alice will know. *(Something off gains his attention.)* Looks like they're getting ready to open the doors.
(Duffy turns to the entrance. Both facing off, there's a shift in mood as what they're about to see sinks in.)

NAYLOR: I feel nervous all of a sudden.

DUFFY: Like going back to a bad dream.

NAYLOR: Wasn't for you I don't think I'd go through with it…You know there are people who say the Holocaust never happened?

DUFFY: Yes.

NAYLOR: I used to talk about Ohrdruf but no one ever heard of it, so I quit.

DUFFY: First time I came across it was in a book called *The Last Hundred Days* by John Toland.

NAYLOR: He mentions Ohrdruf?

DUFFY: Yes. I was beginning to think I made it up and there it was: "Ohrdruf Nord."

NAYLOR: What did he say about it.

DUFFY: That it was the first concentration camp discovered; how when Eisenhower, Bradley and Patton saw it, Patton puked.

NAYLOR: Anything about all those bodies?

DUFFY: Yes.

NAYLOR: I often wondered how many there were.

DUFFY: Thirty-two hundred.

NAYLOR: The book says that?

DUFFY: Yes.

NAYLOR: Thirty-two hundred?

DUFFY: Thirty-two hundred.

NAYLOR: So why isn't Ohrdruf better known?

DUFFY: It was a satellite camp where they worked people to death instead of gassing them. Compared to Auschwitz, Buchenwald and the others it was small potatoes.

NAYLOR: They're going in.

DUFFY: Ready?

NAYLOR: Let's do it.

(*They move off.*)

SCENE II

Time: Several minutes later. Place: Inside the museum. Duffy alone staring at a basket on a table. Several beats then Naylor, fussing with the zipper on his fly, appears.

NAYLOR: When you gotta go you gotta go. (*He realizes Duffy, preoccupied, didn't hear him.*) Hello.
(*Duffy turns.*)

DUFFY: This is where your friend's wife almost lost it.

NAYLOR: What?

DUFFY: The basket with the pictures and history of Holocaust victims. *(Pointing.)* That's it. Take one.

NAYLOR: After you.

DUFFY: I already did. *(Displays a card—reads aloud from it.)* "Evelyn Golub. Born April 7, 1930. Killed at Dachau with her mother and two sisters March 1942. A promising violinist, she—"

NAYLOR: —That's enough.

DUFFY: *(Indicating the basket.)* Your turn.

(Naylor takes a card reluctantly.)

DUFFY: What's it say?

NAYLOR: *(Reading.)* "Leonard B. Klickstein."

DUFFY: …Go on.

NAYLOR: "Born August 23, 1925."

DUFFY: Same year I was born.

NAYLOR: "Killed at Bergen-Belsen 1943."

DUFFY: Let's see.

(Naylor hands him the card. Duffy holds the two cards side by side.)

DUFFY: They would have made a nice couple.

NAYLOR: That's not funny.

DUFFY: It wasn't meant to be.

NAYLOR: Which way do we go?

DUFFY: *(Gesturing off.)* The elevator.

(Naylor starts away; realizes Duffy, regarding the cards, hasn't moved.)

NAYLOR: You coming?

(Duffy pockets the cards—follows Naylor off.)

SCENE III

Time: Moments later. Place: Fourth floor of the museum. At rise: Naylor and Duffy emerge from the elevator.

NAYLOR: How long you think the tour will take?

DUFFY: No idea.

NAYLOR: I'm meeting Alice two o'clock at the—

DUFFY: —*Holy Christ.*

NAYLOR: What is it?

DUFFY: The photo covering that wall.

NAYLOR: *(Following Duffy's gaze, he reacts.)* Pow right in the kisser.

(They move downstage; regard the fourth wall as though it contained a massive photograph. Naylor dons glasses; reads an inscription in the lower left hand corner of the photo.)

NAYLOR: "Shortly after liberating Ohrdruf concentration camp in central Germany, American troops encounter the charred remains of prisoners April, 1945." *(To Duffy indicating the inscription.)* There it is: Ohrdruf.

DUFFY: They could be us.

NAYLOR: What?

DUFFY: The guys looking at those bodies. That might have been the day we were there.

NAYLOR: I never saw bodies like that.

DUFFY: Like what?

NAYLOR: They're all burned.

DUFFY: It's a pyre. Like they use for cremation in India.

NAYLOR: I know what a pyre is.

DUFFY: They were trying to destroy the evidence.

NAYLOR: I know that too. *(Peering at the photo.)* They're lumps of ash—faceless.

DUFFY: Right.

NAYLOR: The ones I saw had faces.

DUFFY: There were bodies everywhere: Ditches, sheds, on the ground. Some were burned like those.

NAYLOR: You remember seeing what's in that picture?

DUFFY: Yes.

NAYLOR: Maybe it's another camp—they got the name wrong.

(A guide—a girl, twentyish, a pinkish sport jacket by way of uniform goes by.)

DUFFY: Pardon me.

THE GUIDE: Yes?

DUFFY: You work here?

THE GUIDE: Yes.

DUFFY: *(Indicating the photo.)* Would you mind identifying that picture for my friend?

THE GUIDE: That's Ohrdruf-Nord, the first concentration camp the allies overran.

NAYLOR: The one Eisenhower, Patton, and Bradley visited?

THE GUIDE: Yes. Would you like to see a picture of them there?

NAYLOR: Yes.

THE GUIDE: It's over here.

(The Guide leads them to another photo on the fourth wall; points left to right.)

THE GUIDE: That's General Patton with his famous pearl-handled revolver...
There's Eisenhower... And that's General Bradley.

NAYLOR: At Ohrdruf?

THE GUIDE: At Ohrdruf.

DUFFY: *(To Naylor.)* Satisfied?

NAYLOR: *(Troubled.)* Why don't I remember those burned bodies?

DUFFY: It was over forty years ago.

THE GUIDE: Excuse me.

DUFFY: Yes?

THE GUIDE: Were you at Ohrdruf?

DUFFY AND NAYLOR: Yes.

THE GUIDE: Both of you?

NAYLOR: Yes.

THE GUIDE: You saw Ohrdruf-Nord personally?

NAYLOR: Yes.

THE GUIDE: When?

DUFFY: A day or two after that picture was taken.

THE GUIDE: The museum is always looking for eyewitnesses. Would you be
willing to be interviewed?

NAYLOR: Okay by me. *(To Duffy.)* You?

DUFFY: No.

NAYLOR: Why?

DUFFY: I'd rather not.

THE GUIDE: *(To Naylor.)* I'll make arrangements. See if you can convince
him. *(She exits.)*

NAYLOR: You'd be in good company.

DUFFY: What?

NAYLOR: *(Glasses on—reading inscription.)* "I made the visit deliberately in
order to be in a position to give *first hand* evidence of these things if ever
in the future there develops a tendency to charge these allegations merely
to propaganda." General Dwight D. Eisenhower. *(To Duffy.)* You'd be
doing what Ike did. What do you say?

DUFFY: No.

NAYLOR: Have it your way. *(He regards the stage right photograph.)* What's
"REVIER" mean?

DUFFY: Revier?

NAYLOR: *(Pointing to the photo.)* The sign on that barracks or whatever it is:
"R-E-V-I-E-R."

DUFFY: I don't know.

NAYLOR: *(Shifting focus on the photo.)* Phew!

DUFFY: What?

NAYLOR: *(Pointing.)* That guy's mouth—like he was killed in the middle of a scream. You think that's when Patton threw up?

DUFFY: Could be.

NAYLOR: Ike and Bradley don't look too chipper.

DUFFY: It wasn't the day they'd planned.

NAYLOR: Planned?

DUFFY: They toured a mine shaft in the morning where the Nazis kept a lot of the gold and stuff they looted. The war almost over. They were having lunch—feeling good—when someone told them about Ohrdruf and they went to see for themselves.

NAYLOR: You really know this stuff.

DUFFY: I've read a lot about it.

NAYLOR: Ever write about it?

DUFFY: I tried lots of times.

NAYLOR: And?

DUFFY: No cigar.

NAYLOR: That figures.

DUFFY: Why?

NAYLOR: What can you say that hasn't been said before?

DUFFY: Thanks for the encouragement.

NAYLOR: I didn't mean—

DUFFY: —I know.

NAYLOR: *(Making a connection.)* You still hope to write about it.

DUFFY: Yes.

NAYLOR: That's why you don't want to be interviewed. Afraid you'll give something away you might be able to use.

DUFFY: Yes.

NAYLOR: I hope you succeed.

DUFFY: Thanks.

NAYLOR: But if you don't it would be a shame to miss a chance like this.

DUFFY: You don't give up do you?

NAYLOR: More and more nuts saying the Holocaust never happened—it's your duty.

DUFFY: *(Capitulating.)* All right already.

NAYLOR: You'll do it.

DUFFY: Yes.

NAYLOR: *(Slapping him on the back.)* Our words and Ike's preserved forever.

DUFFY: *(Good naturedly.)* I said I'd do it—stop selling. You remember a smell when we reached Ohrdruf?

NAYLOR: No.

DUFFY: Neither do I. Bradley wrote about a God-awful stench.

NAYLOR: *(Eyeing the photo.)* I don't see anyone holding their noses.
(The guide returns.)

THE GUIDE: *(To Naylor.)* Well?

NAYLOR: He'll do it.

THE GUIDE: Thank you. *(To Duffy.)* Thank you. After I show you around, I'll take you to Mrs. Grayson's office for the interview.

NAYLOR: *(To Duffy.)* You hear that—a private tour.

THE GUIDE: Two men who witnessed the same thing the same day is unusual. We don't want to lose you.

DUFFY: *(Indicating the photo.)* What does "r-e-v-i-e-r" mean?

THE GUIDE: It's German for "quarter" or "district."

NAYLOR: I don't remember seeing that sign, do you?

DUFFY: No. *(Duffy takes out a notebook and pen—jots it down.)*

NAYLOR: *(To the Guide—indicating Duffy.)* He's a writer.

DUFFY: Okay to take notes?

THE GUIDE: Yes. *(Noting Naylor's camera.)* But no pictures of exhibitions. Now if you'll follow me.
(The Guide goes off. They follow.)

SCENE IV

Time: an hour and a half later. Place: Mrs. Grayson's office. She, fiftyish, intelligent, simply but expensively dressed, businesslike, at her desk perusing papers. A knock at the door.

MRS. GRAYSON: Come in.
(The Guide ushers Duffy and Naylor in.)

THE GUIDE: These are the two gentlemen who witnessed Ohrdruf: Mr. Naylor and Mr. Duffy. *(To them.)* This is Mrs. Grayson.
(Mrs. Grayson rises. There is a polite exchange of greetings.)

THE GUIDE: They were in the same outfit—haven't seen each other since the war. Met today by chance.

MRS. GRAYSON: *(Dismissing the Guide.)* Thank you.

THE GUIDE: *(Taking her cue—to Duffy and Naylor.)* Nice meeting you.

NAYLOR: Same here.

DUFFY: Thanks for the tour.

THE GUIDE: You're welcome.

NAYLOR: You're ever in North Dakota look me up like I said.

THE GUIDE: I will. *(The Guide exits.)*

NAYLOR: *(To Mrs. Grayson re: the Guide.)* She does a good job for you.

MRS. GRAYSON: Thank you. You're Mr. Naylor.

NAYLOR: Right.

MRS. GRAYSON: *(Back at her desk—pen poised.)* Your full name?

NAYLOR: Henry Z. Naylor.

DUFFY: Z?

NAYLOR: Zebediah. *(To Mrs. Grayson.)* Everyone calls me Hank.

MRS. GRAYSON: *(To Duffy.)* And you?

DUFFY: William J. Duffy.

MRS. GRAYSON: *(Writing as she goes.)* The military unit in which you served?

NAYLOR: 89th Reconnaissance Troop attached to the 89th Infantry Division.

DUFFY: Ditto.

MRS. GRAYSON: Commanding officer's name?

NAYLOR: Of the division or the Troop?

MRS. GRAYSON: Preferably both.

NAYLOR: The troop CO was Captain Engel. I forget division.

DUFFY: Major General Thomas Finley.

NAYLOR: Finley—right.

MRS. GRAYSON: Your rank?

NAYLOR: I was a T-five. That's—

MRS. GRAYSON: —I know what a T-five is. *(She turns to Duffy.)*

DUFFY: PFC.

(She notes this then rises.)

MRS. GRAYSON: I'll be back in a minute. *(She exits.)*

NAYLOR: *(Looking after her.)* Not the warmest reception I ever got.

DUFFY: You worked here—how friendly you think you'd be?

NAYLOR: I wouldn't work here for anything. You know what hit me hardest? The boxcar: Walking through it knowing people had been packed in there shitting, puking, dying before they even reached the camps. *(He shivers at the memory.)* What got to you?

DUFFY: The shoes.

NAYLOR: I saw you making notes about it. What did you write, if it's not too personal?

DUFFY: I copied the first line of the poem.

NAYLOR: Poem?

DUFFY: There was a poem about the shoes.

NAYLOR: I missed it. What did it say?

(Duffy takes out his notebook; finds the page.)

DUFFY: *(Reads.)* "We are the shoes. We are the last witnesses." Moses Schulstein 1911 to 1981.

NAYLOR: One of the lucky ones.

DUFFY: Lucky?

NAYLOR: 1981 means he survived.

DUFFY: Some survivors felt anything but lucky. Felt guilty in fact.

NAYLOR: I know.

(Duffy regards him with mild surprise.)

NAYLOR: I've done some reading about it too. "We are the shoes" then what?

DUFFY: "We are the last witnesses."

NAYLOR: They should make anyone who says the Holocaust never happened go through this place.

DUFFY: In some cases it wouldn't help.

NAYLOR: A Nazi is a Nazi is a Nazi.

DUFFY: I was thinking of my mother.

NAYLOR: Your mother?

DUFFY: When I showed her the pictures I took at Ohrdruf, she asked where I got them. I told her I took them myself. "No you didn't," she insisted, "who gave them to you?"

NAYLOR: Your mother didn't believe the Holocaust?

DUFFY: To her dying day.

NAYLOR: Why?

DUFFY: She couldn't accept a world in which such a thing was possible.

(Mrs. Grayson returns—resumes her place at the desk.)

MRS. GRAYSON: *(To Naylor.)* You didn't mention your Bronze Star.

NAYLOR: How do you know about it?

MRS. GRAYSON: We have the history of every division. Including rosters of the men who served with their rank and decorations if any.

NAYLOR: *(Good naturedly.)* You were checking on us. *(To Duffy.)* She was checking on us.

MRS. GRAYSON: It's standard procedure. Shall we begin?

DUFFY: You're going to interview us together?

MRS. GRAYSON: You were there the same day.

DUFFY: We might remember things differently.

MRS. GRAYSON: After so many years it would be unnatural if you didn't. Plus in tandem you might recall things that wouldn't surface otherwise.

NAYLOR: That makes sense.

DUFFY: Together it is.

MRS. GRAYSON: *(Making notes from here on.)* Let's start with the date.

NAYLOR: When we saw Ohrdruf?

MRS. GRAYSON: Yes.

NAYLOR: 1945—April. A few weeks before VE Day.

MRS. GRAYSON: Could you be more exact?

DUFFY: Probably April thirteenth or fourteenth because Eisenhower was there on the twelfth.

NAYLOR: That's when Patton puked and Ike ordered every GI in the area to see Ohrdruf so we'd know what we were fighting for.

MRS. GRAYSON: What we're interested in is what you personally experienced. Not what you read or learned subsequently.

NAYLOR: No second hand information.

MRS. GRAYSON: Exactly.

NAYLOR: Got ya.

MRS. GRAYSON: How did it begin?

NAYLOR: We entered this stockade and there were all these bodies.

MRS. GRAYSON: I mean how did that day begin? The weather, et cetera.

NAYLOR: It was a perfect spring day.

MRS. GRAYSON: *(To Duffy.)* Is that how you remember it?

DUFFY: Yes.

MRS. GRAYSON: Where were you situated?

NAYLOR: Situated?

MRS. GRAYSON: When you woke up. Where were you?

DUFFY: Just south of a city called Gotha we'd taken the day before. Wait a minute: it might have been Eisenach.

MRS. GRAYSON: E-I-S-E-N-A-C-H?

DUFFY: Close enough.

MRS. GRAYSON: *(To Naylor.)* Was it Gotha or Eisenach?

NAYLOR: Beats me. All I remember is we were on the side of a hill. Vehicles spread out. Laundry drying.

MRS. GRAYSON: Laundry?

NAYLOR: We'd been on the move for weeks. There was a stream nearby. We made the most of it.

(Mrs. Grayson turns to Duffy for confirmation.)

DUFFY: I recall the hill and the stream—not the laundry.

NAYLOR: *(To Mrs. Grayson.)* He was probably shooting craps or playing poker.

DUFFY: I don't think Mrs. Grayson is interested in that.

MRS. GRAYSON: Quite the contrary: Details reinforce credibility. *Were* you shooting craps?

DUFFY: As a matter of fact I was sunbathing.

MRS. GRAYSON: Sounds like a holiday.

NAYLOR: It was, until the lieutenant came back from headquarters and said, "Be ready to roll in ten minutes."

DUFFY: We figured it was a mission.

NAYLOR: Another chance to be ducks in a shooting gallery.

MRS. GRAYSON: "Ducks in a shooting gallery?"

NAYLOR: *(To Duffy.)* You're the writer—explain.

DUFFY: The primary duty of a Reconnaissance Troop is to maintain contact with the enemy. The Germans in full retreat made that extremely dangerous.

NAYLOR: Down the road we'd go.

DUFFY: Highway.

NAYLOR: Road—highway, whatever. Nine vehicles—thirty men. Sometimes we'd go five miles. Sometimes fifteen or twenty till they fired at us.

MRS. GRAYSON: Like ducks in a shooting gallery.

NAYLOR: Right.

MRS. GRAYSON: And then?

DUFFY: Contact with the enemy established we'd hightail it home.

NAYLOR: Laughing and shouting like maniacs.

DUFFY: Providing no one got hit.

MRS. GRAYSON: When the Lieutenant said 'get ready to roll' that day, you thought that's what you were in for?

DUFFY: Right.   NAYLOR: Yes.

MRS. GRAYSON: But it wasn't.

DUFFY: No. Just before we took off, he said we were going to visit a concentration camp.

NAYLOR: Which was the first time I ever heard those words.

MRS. GRAYSON: *(Not surprised—just verifying.)* You'd never heard of concentration camps?

NAYLOR: No.

MRS. GRAYSON: *(To Duffy.)* Did you?

DUFFY: No.

NAYLOR: I don't think anybody did because when the Lieutenant said it, we cheered.

MRS. GRAYSON: Cheered?

NAYLOR: Because we wouldn't have to risk our necks—were one day closer to the end.

MRS. GRAYSON: *(To Duffy.)* Did *you* cheer?

DUFFY: I remember feeling like a kid when school was called off.

MRS. GRAYSON: The Lieutenant didn't explain what a concentration camp was?

DUFFY: He might have said it was a prison or something but I don't think he had any real idea.

NAYLOR: *(To Mrs. Grayson.)* In one of the exhibits it says our government knew about the camps and the killing years before they discovered Ohrdruf.

MRS. GRAYSON: True.

NAYLOR: So why didn't *we* know?

MRS. GRAYSON: A good question that's never been answered satisfactorily. *(To Duffy.)* The Lieutenant said you were going to visit a concentration camp. Then what?

NAYLOR: We drove there.

MRS. GRAYSON: How long a ride?

NAYLOR: Beats me.

MRS. GRAYSON: *(To Duffy.)* You?

DUFFY: An hour—maybe more, maybe less.

NAYLOR: We weren't in any hurry.

MRS. GRAYSON: What do you recall about the ride?

NAYLOR: Meadows. Farmland. The war seemed a million miles away.

MRS. GRAYSON: *(To Duffy.)* You?

DUFFY: The same until we were stopped by some infantry guys who'd picked up a German soldier trying to escape in civilian clothes.

NAYLOR: The German—right. I forgot about that.

DUFFY: Since they were on foot and we had vehicles, they asked us to take him, which we did.

NAYLOR: Mounted him on the hood of a jeep—hands on his head like so. *(He demonstrates.)*

MRS. GRAYSON: And then?

NAYLOR: We kept going.

DUFFY: Till we reached a fork and turned left up a dirt road-

NAYLOR: —Which is when the German gave himself away.

MRS. GRAYSON: What do you mean?

NAYLOR: He started babbling like he knew where we were going which meant he had something to do with it. *(To Duffy.)* Right?

DUFFY: Right.

MRS. GRAYSON: Go on.

DUFFY: We topped a rise and there it was.

MRS. GRAYSON: Ohrdruf-Nord.

DUFFY: Ohrdruf-Nord.

NAYLOR: Nord means north in German?

MRS. GRAYSON: Yes.

NAYLOR: North of what?

MRS. GRAYSON: The town of Ohrdruf.

NAYLOR: I didn't know there *was* a town. *(To Duffy.)* You?

DUFFY: Yes. After they viewed the camp, the mayor and his wife committed suicide.

NAYLOR: *No shit. (To Mrs. Grayson hastily.)* Pardon my French.

MRS. GRAYSON: What did it look like from the outside?

NAYLOR: A stockade with a high wire fence.

DUFFY: The gates open—we drove in.

NAYLOR: I don't remember driving in.

DUFFY: We drove in and parked our vehicles.

NAYLOR: I don't remember that.

MRS. GRAYSON: In any case you entered. And then?

NAYLOR: The bodies. *(To Duffy.)* Right?

DUFFY: Yes.

NAYLOR: *(To Mrs. Grayson.)* Naked bodies piled five high like cordwood stretching I don't know how far.

DUFFY: I remember uniforms with vertical stripes.

NAYLOR: *(To Duffy.)* They were naked. *(To Mrs. Grayson.)* Heads shaved and so wasted you couldn't tell if they were men or women.

DUFFY: They were all men.

NAYLOR: I know they were men but you had to look close because their privates were so shriveled. *(To Mrs. Grayson.)* Sorry about that.

MRS. GRAYSON: No need to be. *(To Duffy.)* You disagree?

DUFFY: Let's just say there were bodies everywhere in every conceivable condition.

NAYLOR: They were naked.

DUFFY: Including naked.

MRS. GRAYSON: *(To Naylor.)* What was your immediate reaction?

NAYLOR: Like I was watching a movie.

MRS. GRAYSON: It didn't seem real.

NAYLOR: It still doesn't. That's why I came here today: To convince myself I saw what I saw.

MRS. GRAYSON: *(To Duffy.)* Do you remember *your* reaction?

DUFFY: Yes.

MRS. GRAYSON: What was it?

DUFFY: Nothing.

MRS. GRAYSON: You didn't feel anything?

DUFFY: I knew I should, and I wanted to but I couldn't. It took years for the whole thing to register.

NAYLOR: There were no gas chambers at Ohrdruf—right?

DUFFY: Right.

NAYLOR: So how were they killed?

DUFFY: Starvation, beatings, a bullet in the back of the head.

NAYLOR: *(To Mrs. Grayson—for confirmation.)* Is that right?

MRS. GRAYSON: Yes. You saw the bodies—then what?

DUFFY: We must have separated because the next thing I remember are the bodies burned on railroad ties.

NAYLOR: Which I don't remember at all.

MRS. GRAYSON: *(To Naylor.)* What's your next memory?

NAYLOR: A long ditch filled with arms and legs sticking out where they didn't finish burying them.

MRS. GRAYSON: Was there someone showing you around—explaining things?

DUFFY: No.

NAYLOR: Yes.

NAYLOR: *(To Duffy.)* There *must* have been someone.

DUFFY: Why?

NAYLOR: *(To Mrs. Grayson.)* There was this butcher's block where they smashed peoples' skulls to get the gold out of their teeth.

DUFFY: What about it?

NAYLOR: How would we know what it was for if someone didn't explain? *(To Mrs. Grayson.)* Same with the rack where they strung people up to torture them.

MRS. GRAYSON: *(To Duffy.)* Did *you* see the rack?

DUFFY: There was a platform outdoors with rope loops.

NAYLOR: To hold their arms while they beat them.

DUFFY: I wouldn't call it a rack.

NAYLOR: Call it whatever you like. The point is someone showed it to us and explained. How do you think we got to the building with survivors?

MRS. GRAYSON: You met survivors?

NAYLOR: We glimpsed them.

MRS. GRAYSON: Describe it.

DUFFY: We stuck our heads in this filthy shack...

NAYLOR: ...For as long as we could hold our breath...

DUFFY: ...Floor to ceiling wood platforms...

NAYLOR: ...Crawling with lice...

DUFFY: ...At the far end of the room were these living skeletons.

MRS. GRAYSON: The survivors.

DUFFY: Yes.

MRS. GRAYSON: How many?

naylor and DUFFY: Three.

MRS. GRAYSON: How did they react?

DUFFY: React?

MRS. GRAYSON: When they saw you.

NAYLOR: There's a laugh.

MRS. GRAYSON: What do you mean?

DUFFY: They were like animals caught in headlights.

NAYLOR: Like zombies.

MRS. GRAYSON: You didn't speak to them?

NAYLOR: They were more dead than alive.

MRS. GRAYSON: There was no communication?

NAYLOR: Zero.

MRS. GRAYSON: *(To Duffy.)* Is that what you remember?

DUFFY: Yes.

MRS. GRAYSON: Anything else?

DUFFY: Yes...

MRS. GRAYSON: What is it?...Well?

DUFFY: I hated them.

MRS. GRAYSON: Them?

DUFFY: The survivors.

MRS. GRAYSON: You hated the survivors?

DUFFY: Yes.

MRS. GRAYSON: Why?

DUFFY: I didn't want to know that people could be reduced to that.

MRS. GRAYSON: *(To Naylor.)* Anything you care to add?

NAYLOR: When we got outside I couldn't believe the sun was still shining.

MRS. GRAYSON: What happened next?

NAYLOR: I don't remember anything after that. *(To Duffy.)* You?

DUFFY: No. That was the final stop.

MRS. GRAYSON: That's it then. *(Rising—notebook in hand.)* I'll have this typed at once and you can sign it.

DUFFY: You want us to wait?

MRS. GRAYSON: If you can.

DUFFY: Fine with me. *(To Naylor.)* You?

NAYLOR: Sure.

MRS. GRAYSON: It won't take long. *(She starts to exit.)*

NAYLOR: *(Remembering something.)* The German.

MRS. GRAYSON: What?

NAYLOR: The German we picked up on the way to Ohrdruf.

MRS. GRAYSON: What about him?

NAYLOR: He toured the camp with us. *(To Duffy.)* Remember?

DUFFY: Yes.

NAYLOR: *(To Mrs. Grayson.)* Nobody in the platoon spoke German. But one of our guys spoke Yiddish which was close enough for him to understand.

NAYLOR: *(To Duffy.)* What was his name—the Jewish guy—corporal?

DUFFY: Borowsky.

NAYLOR: Borowsky—right. *(To Mrs. Grayson.)* The Lieutenant told Borowsky to tell the German he's gonna tour the camp with us. Any doubts the guy was a guard there ended when he started blubbering. Sweat rolling off him in sheets. "Tell him to shut up," the Lieutenant says. Borowsky told him but the guy wouldn't quit. *(To Duffy.)* Remember what happened next?

DUFFY: The cigarette case.

NAYLOR: *(Relishing the story.)* Right. *(To Mrs. Grayson.)* To shut the guy up, the lieutenant takes a gold cigarette case from his pocket; jams it in the German's mouth and tells Borowsky to tell him if he drops it, he'll shoot him on the spot.

MRS. GRAYSON: Why are you telling me this?

NAYLOR: You said you wanted to know everything that happened—details.

MRS. GRAYSON: …Go on.

NAYLOR: Even with the cigarette case in his mouth the guy kept pleading. But he never dropped it.

MRS. GRAYSON: What became of him?

DUFFY: We turned him over to a tank outfit headed for the rear.

MRS. GRAYSON: *(To them both.)* Anything else?

NAYLOR: That's it.

MRS. GRAYSON: If you prefer to go to lunch while I have this typed.

DUFFY: This place doesn't leave you with much of an appetite.

MRS. GRAYSON: I understand. *(She exits.)*

NAYLOR: Whew.

DUFFY: Really brings it back huh?

NAYLOR: What was the name of that city we took right before Ohrdruf?

DUFFY: Gotha or Eisenach.

NAYLOR: You remember *every* place we were?

DUFFY: Most of them.

NAYLOR: I think I'm losing it.

DUFFY: Why?

NAYLOR: I didn't even remember that German until you mentioned it. *(Snaps his fingers as he recalls something.)* There were teeth marks!

DUFFY: What?

NAYLOR: When the Lieutenant got his cigarette case back there were teeth marks where the German bit it.

DUFFY: I don't remember that.

NAYLOR: I saw them…What did we do the rest of that day?

DUFFY: After Ohrdruf?

NAYLOR: Yes.

DUFFY: No idea.

NAYLOR: Me either. It's like a car accident I had: Everything leading up to it is clear. What happened after I don't have the foggiest…Why you suppose she does it?

DUFFY: Mrs. Grayson?

NAYLOR: Yeah. You see those pearls—that ring?

DUFFY: What about them?

NAYLOR: She's a lady of means. Why's she working here?

DUFFY: Probably a volunteer.

NAYLOR: …I know what you mean about hating the survivors: If it happened to them, it could happen to you. Right?

DUFFY: Something like that.

NAYLOR: Before I ended up that way I'd kill myself.

DUFFY: A lot of people did: Ran into the electrified fences; stopped eating.

NAYLOR: I don't see how anyone could bear it.

DUFFY: Years ago I was taking a cab to the airport. The driver had his arm resting on the divider. I saw numbers tattooed on his wrist.

NAYLOR: He'd been a prisoner?

DUFFY: Auschwitz—four years. When I told him about Ohrdruf, he pulled the cab to the shoulder of the road and invited me to get in front with him which I did. I asked him how come he'd survived when so many others gave up. "Nobody ever asked me that before," he said. For the next few miles we drove in silence while he thought about it. Then suddenly he turned to me, a big smile on his face, and said, "I wanted to know how it would end."

NAYLOR: You think about Ohrdruf a lot.

DUFFY: It was the most influential day of my life.

NAYLOR: How do you mean?

DUFFY: It ended any belief I had in religion.

NAYLOR: You don't believe in God?

DUFFY: Not in any formal way.

NAYLOR: I do.

DUFFY: I'm glad.

NAYLOR: Is that a crack?

DUFFY: No.

NAYLOR: …You don't believe in anything?

DUFFY: I believe there's something unknowable and I bow to the mystery. As for other peoples' beliefs, I subscribe to what the Irish playwright, Brendan Behan, said: "I'm in favor of anything that gets you up in the morning, through the day, and keeps the old folks warm."…Ohrdruf have any effect on your life?

NAYLOR: Somebody makes an anti-Semitic remark, I let them know I don't like it. I helped open the country club to Jews.

DUFFY: Good for you.

NAYLOR: You in touch with anyone from the troop?

DUFFY: No.

NAYLOR: I used to see Junior Henry when I visited Chicago. After a few visits we ran out of things to say. What about Torelli?

DUFFY: What about him?

NAYLOR: You and he so tight and both from New York, I figured you'd be friends forever.

DUFFY: He died.

NAYLOR: Sorry to hear it. How old?

DUFFY: Early forties. I was living in Los Angeles. His brother wrote me.

NAYLOR: What did he die of?

DUFFY: His brother was vague. My guess is suicide.

NAYLOR: *Suicide?*

DUFFY: Yes.

NAYLOR: He was such a happy-go-lucky guy.

DUFFY: Not really.

NAYLOR: Why do you think he did it?

DUFFY: At his wedding, a few months after we were discharged, he told me he was high on the list to become a fireman. I went to college and we lost touch until one day I'm on a subway and see this conductor go by. Just a glimpse but he looked like Torelli so I followed till I caught up to him.

NAYLOR: Torelli?

DUFFY: Torelli. He'd flunked out as a fireman because he couldn't climb ladders. Can you believe that after all the stuff we'd been through. Became a subway conductor which he was so embarrassed about he tried to duck me.

NAYLOR: He committed suicide because he didn't become a fireman?

DUFFY: Partly.

NAYLOR: Partly?

DUFFY: He insisted I come to his house for dinner. After dinner, while his wife put their son to bed, we got talking about the war. I asked if he ever thought about that day.

NAYLOR: What day?

DUFFY: I meant Ohrdruf but he thought I meant the day we were ambushed when Bevan and Hatcher were killed. The next thing I know he's crying because Hatcher was riding where he usually rode and—

NAYLOR: *(Shortly.)* —I remember.

DUFFY: I got the feeling he blamed himself for Hatcher's death.

NAYLOR: *(Regards his watch impatiently.)* She said it wouldn't take long.

DUFFY: It's only been a few minutes…I tried to convince Torelli he wasn't responsible. But he was inconsolable.

(Naylor reacts.)

DUFFY: What's the matter?

NAYLOR: You mind we change the subject?

DUFFY: You asked about him.

NAYLOR: It isn't Torelli.

DUFFY: What then?

NAYLOR: Forget it. You ever find her?

DUFFY: Her?

NAYLOR: You said you wanted a girl like Alice. Did you succeed?

DUFFY: As a matter of fact I did.

NAYLOR: Kids?

DUFFY: Three sons. You?

NAYLOR: A son and two daughters. Six grandchildren. *(Regards his watch.)* What's keeping her?

DUFFY: What's the rush?

NAYLOR: Rush?

DUFFY: You seem pressed for time all of a sudden.

NAYLOR: This place gives me the willies.

(Awkward silence—Naylor preoccupied. Duffy looking for something to say.)

DUFFY: …Want a little known fact about Ohrdruf I picked up recently?

NAYLOR: *(Disinterested.)* What's that?

DUFFY: There's a street named after Johann Sebastian Bach, who lived in Ohrdruf. Composed some of his music there. Bach and Ohrdruf—some sweet duet huh?

(Naylor offers no reaction… Silence…Duffy tries again.)

DUFFY: …You saw Junior Henry?

NAYLOR: Years ago.

DUFFY: What was he doing?

NAYLOR: Salesman.

DUFFY: There's a guy who should believe in miracles: Bevan and Hatcher killed and Junior in the back seat never got a scratch.

NAYLOR: *(Irritated.)* Back to that again.

DUFFY: What do you mean?

(Before Naylor can reply, Mrs. Grayson returns holding two typewritten pages.)

DUFFY: That was quick.

MRS. GRAYSON: I combined what you said into one report. *(She hands a page to each of them.)*

MRS. GRAYSON: When you sign, include your address.

NAYLOR: *(With an edge.)* What for?

MRS. GRAYSON: So we can send you a copy.

NAYLOR: *(Sarcastic.)* Along with a request for donations.

MRS. GRAYSON: *(Taking it as a joke.)* No.

DUFFY: Name and address?

MRS. GRAYSON: Yes.

(Duffy takes out his pen—is about to sign.)

MRS. GRAYSON: After you read it.

DUFFY: I'm sure it's okay.

NAYLOR: *(To Duffy—with a puzzling edge.)* Anyone signs anything without reading it is a damn fool.

MRS. GRAYSON: As a matter of fact we insist you read it before signing.

(As Naylor takes out his reading glasses, Duffy and Mrs. Grayson exchange looks.)

DUFFY: *(After a swift read.)* Looks fine.

(He signs. Naylor, still reading, comes to the bottom of the page; turns it over as though expecting more.)

NAYLOR: *(Finding the other side blank.)* That's it?

MRS. GRAYSON: Yes… Something wrong?

NAYLOR: There's nothing about the German those infantry guys turned over to us.

MRS. GRAYSON: It seemed extraneous.

NAYLOR: He was there.

MRS. GRAYSON: If you like I'll add a footnote.

NAYLOR: Saying what?

MRS. GRAYSON: That you picked up this German on the way to Ohrdruf.

NAYLOR: *(Pointedly.)* Don't forget the cigarette case.

MRS. GRAYSON: Is that really necessary?

NAYLOR: You said you wanted details.

MRS. GRAYSON: The cigarette case will be included. Anything else?

DUFFY: *(Eager to end it.)* No.

NAYLOR: *Yes.*

MRS. GRAYSON: What is it?

NAYLOR: When the Lieutenant got his cigarette case back there were teeth marks where the German bit it.

MRS. GRAYSON: I don't recall you saying that.

NAYLOR: I remembered after you left the room.

(Mrs. Grayson looks to Duffy for confirmation.)

DUFFY: I don't remember teeth marks.

NAYLOR: *There were teeth marks, God damn it!*

(His inexplicable anger floods the room with tension.)

MRS. GRAYSON: *(To Naylor—evenly.)* You feel the cigarette case and teeth marks are relevant?

NAYLOR: Yes. And I'll give you another detail: I don't think the tank guys we turned him over to had any intention of delivering him to a POW camp.

MRS. GRAYSON: What do you mean?

NAYLOR: Dollars to doughnuts they killed him.

DUFFY: What are you talking about? *(To Mrs. Grayson.)* I don't know what he's talking about.

NAYLOR: *(To Duffy.)* You didn't see that tanker wink when he said, "We'll take care of him"?

DUFFY: No.

NAYLOR: Well I did and I want it in there.

MRS. GRAYSON: Mr. Naylor.

(He turns to her.)

MRS. GRAYSON: Do you think the cigarette case in the German's mouth and the possibility he was killed compare with the horrors you witnessed at Ohrdruf?

NAYLOR: Of course not.

MRS. GRAYSON: Then why demand their inclusion which will be seized on by people who excuse the Germans by saying everyone is capable of doing what they did?…Well?

NAYLOR: *(Quietly—with deep seated conviction.)* I think everyone *is* capable of it.

MRS. GRAYSON: In other words you object to the Holocaust in black and white—would like to add a bit of gray.

NAYLOR: *(Averting his gaze.)* Nothing's pure.

MRS. GRAYSON: Mr. Naylor, look at me.

(He does so.)

MRS. GRAYSON: If you put a gun to my head and said you'd kill me if I didn't spit in Mr. Duffy's face, I wouldn't do it. Do you believe me?

NAYLOR: *(Evasive.)* I'm not signing that paper the way it is.

MRS. GRAYSON: *Do you believe me?*

NAYLOR: Yes.

MRS. GRAYSON: So everyone wouldn't do it.

NAYLOR: I didn't say everyone would do it. I said we all have the potential.

MRS. GRAYSON: *(To Duffy.)* Do you share his opinion?

DUFFY: No.

NAYLOR: *(Whirling on Duffy.)* How can you say that after…

DUFFY: After what?

NAYLOR: Forget it.

MRS. GRAYSON: *(To Naylor.)* Mr. Naylor, my father was twelve, at school in England when the Nazis invaded Poland where he was born and raised. Unable to go home, he remained in England for the duration of the war. During which his parents, two brothers and three sisters were killed in concentration camps despite their grandfather having converted from Judaism to Christianity. My father grieved about this every day of his life. When I was eleven, I came home from school and found him dead, the gun still in his hand. I tell you this to explain why I don't share your outrage because someone shoved a cigarette case in a German's mouth and the rest of it. *(Taking the paper from his hands.)* As for this. It will be amended to include everything you said: the cigarette case, bite marks, everything.

NAYLOR: I don't care any more.

MRS. GRAYSON: I do! I don't want you going around saying you were censored.

NAYLOR: Let's get something straight: I'm no Nazi.

MRS. GRAYSON: Give me your address and I'll send the revised statement for your inspection.

NAYLOR: *I hate the Nazis and what they did as much as anyone!*

MRS. GRAYSON: *(Meaning it.)* I believe you.

NAYLOR: Really?

MRS. GRAYSON: Really.

NAYLOR: So what's this all about?

MRS. GRAYSON: A good question you should ask yourself. Your address?

NAYLOR: *(Dazed—befuddled.)* Here's my card. *(He drops it on the desk and exits.)*

DUFFY: *(To Mrs. Grayson—exonerating himself.)* I bumped into him on line— haven't seen him in over forty years.

MRS. GRAYSON: If I were you I'd go after him.

(Duffy hesitates—then exits.)

SCENE V

Time: Fifteen minutes later. Place: A bar. Naylor and Duffy, an empty chair between them, sit silently. A Bartender, bearing drinks, appears.

BARTENDER: Gin and tonic?

DUFFY: Here.

(The Bartender sets it down.)

BARTENDER: And bourbon neat. *(He places it in front of Naylor.)* Anything else I can do for you gentlemen?

DUFFY: No.

(The Bartender goes off.)

DUFFY: What'll we drink to?

(When Naylor doesn't respond, he raises his glass.)

DUFFY: To Bevan, Hatcher, Rodowski, Spooner and the guy in the third platoon. What was his name?

NAYLOR: Olmstead.

DUFFY: Bevan, Hatcher, Rodowski, Spooner and Olmstead.

(He sips his drink. Naylor downs his in a gulp.)

NAYLOR: *(Calling off.)* I'll have another.

BARTENDER'S VOICE: *(To Duffy.)* How about you?

DUFFY: Not yet.

NAYLOR: *(Calling off.)* Make it a double.

DUFFY: Every time I get a new ache or pain I think of them.

NAYLOR: *(Deeply preoccupied.)* What?

DUFFY: It's one thing they've been spared.

NAYLOR: What are you talking about?

DUFFY: The guys who were killed.

NAYLOR: What about them?

DUFFY: They avoided the penalties of aging.

NAYLOR: Enough gloom for one day—okay?

DUFFY: Okay.

> *(The Bartender arrives. Deposits the double bourbon in front of Naylor and exits. Naylor downs it without preamble.)*

DUFFY: …You want to talk about it?

NAYLOR: It?

DUFFY: What's bothering you.

NAYLOR: *Nothing's bothering me.*

DUFFY: Something happened back there between you and Mrs. Grayson.

NAYLOR: I don't want to talk about it.

DUFFY: Meaning something *did* happen.

> *(Naylor shoots him a look.)*

DUFFY: Sorry. *(Silence. Then Duffy chuckles.)*

NAYLOR: What's funny?

DUFFY: I just remembered how when anyone asked you where someone was, you'd always say, "He's lying down over in the corner drunker than hell but better than he was."

NAYLOR: Look, I know you're trying to cheer me up but you want to do me a favor, let me collect myself.

DUFFY: You got it.

NAYLOR: …I didn't mean to jump you.

DUFFY: Forget it…I'm looking forward to meeting her.

> *(Naylor regards him questioningly.)*

DUFFY: Alice…You invited me to join you.

NAYLOR: I don't think that's a good idea.

DUFFY: You don't want me to meet her?

NAYLOR: Not today.

DUFFY: Why?

NAYLOR: I've been on the wagon for twenty years. There'll be a scene.

DUFFY: Have a cup of coffee—take a walk. She'll never know.

NAYLOR: She'll know. *(He takes a twenty dollar bill from his wallet—lays it on the bar.)*

DUFFY: It's on me.

NAYLOR: I insist. *(Offers his hand.)* It was nice meeting you.

DUFFY: *(Ignoring his hand.)* You're leaving?

NAYLOR: Yes.

DUFFY: Just like that?

NAYLOR: Alice is waiting.

DUFFY: You said you were meeting her at two o'clock. It's not even one.

NAYLOR: I'm going to try and walk it off like you said.

DUFFY: I'll walk with you.

NAYLOR: *(Emphatically.)* No.

DUFFY: Suit yourself. *(Stung by the rejection he turns away.)*

NAYLOR: Nothing personal.

    (Duffy offers no reaction.)

NAYLOR: I need time to collect myself.

    (No reaction. Naylor gives up—starts away.)

DUFFY: *(Without turning.)* One thing before you go?

NAYLOR: What is it?

DUFFY: What happened back in that office that upset you? *(Turning to Naylor.)* I'd really like to know…Well?

NAYLOR: *(Facetiously.)* I'm a Nazi sympathizer like she said.

DUFFY: She didn't say that. And I don't believe it.

NAYLOR: Thanks.

DUFFY: You know the odds against two guys meeting like we did after all these years?

NAYLOR: What about it?

DUFFY: The powers that be go to all that trouble and it ends like this?

NAYLOR: Would you feel better if I kissed you?

DUFFY: I'd feel better if you leveled.

NAYLOR: Cut the bullshit!

DUFFY: Bullshit?

NAYLOR: *You* know what happened.

DUFFY: No.

NAYLOR: Get off it.

DUFFY: *(Solemnly.)* I have no idea what you're talking about.

    (Naylor regards him, trying to gauge if he's telling the truth.)

DUFFY: So help me.

NAYLOR: I'm talking about that day.

DUFFY: Ohrdruf?

NAYLOR: *Fuck Ohrdruf!*

DUFFY: Fuck Ohrdruf?

NAYLOR: *Ohrdruf wasn't the worst thing that happened.*

DUFFY: It was to me.

NAYLOR: Count your blessings.

DUFFY: Hank listen—I'm trying very hard to follow you.

NAYLOR: *You really want to know?*

DUFFY: Yes.

NAYLOR: *(Calling off as he resumes his seat at the bar.)* Bring us another round.

BARTENDER'S VOICE: You got it.

DUFFY: What about Alice—the booze?

NAYLOR: "Hung for a sheep" as they say.

   (The Bartender sets drinks before them; exits. Naylor raises his glass.)

NAYLOR: To Boris Becker.

DUFFY: The tennis player?

NAYLOR: Bullseye.

   (Naylor downs his double shot. Duffy sips.)

NAYLOR: It wasn't her set me off—it was you.

DUFFY: Me?

NAYLOR: You.

DUFFY: What did I do?

NAYLOR: How you asked Torelli about that day meaning Ohrdruf and he thought you meant the day we were ambushed.

DUFFY: So what?

NAYLOR: You have no idea where this is going?

DUFFY: I swear.

NAYLOR: *(Calling off.)* Another bourbon.

DUFFY: Don't you think you've had enough?

NAYLOR: Do you want to hear it or don't you?

   (The Bartender appears with the bottle; refills Naylor's glass; goes off. Naylor downs it.)

NAYLOR: What do you remember about it?

DUFFY: It?

NAYLOR: The ambush.

DUFFY: Routine patrol. Lieutenant's armored car the point. The road starts to curve. Disappears into a forest…Germans hidden in foxholes on both sides. They let the first few vehicles pass. Then one of them fires that thing that looks like a bazooka.

NAYLOR: —A panzerfaust—

DUFFY: Panzerfaust—right. I see this bright orange ball an instant before the explosion... *(The memory too vivid to continue.)*

NAYLOR: *(Prodding gently.)* And?

DUFFY: Bevan killed instantly. Hatcher, right leg hanging by a thread, bleeding to death.

NAYLOR: What happened next?

DUFFY: You were there.

NAYLOR: I'd like your version.

DUFFY: My version?

NAYLOR: What you saw and did. Please.

DUFFY: While they pump morphine into Hatcher I'm telling him stupid things like he's going to be home soon and reminding him I owe him two hundred bucks from a card game.

NAYLOR: *(Impatient.)* Bevan and Hatcher die. Then what?

DUFFY: I wasn't through.

NAYLOR: Go on.

DUFFY: Hatcher kept saying he had to take a leak and was afraid of doing it in his pants. Before we could move him he was dead. "I have to take a leak." How's that for last words?

NAYLOR: What was happening while you were taking care of Hatcher?

DUFFY: Happening?

NAYLOR: Around you.

DUFFY: Pandemonium.

NAYLOR: Describe it.

DUFFY: You were there.

NAYLOR: People running all over the place? Cursing? Screaming? Crying?

DUFFY: Right.

NAYLOR: Shooting?

DUFFY: Yes.

NAYLOR: What about the Germans?

DUFFY: What about them?

NAYLOR: What were they doing?

DUFFY: They were dead.

NAYLOR: Killed?

DUFFY: Yes.

NAYLOR: Because they ambushed us.

DUFFY: Yes. *(Warily.)* Where you going with this?

NAYLOR: Except for that panzerfaust, did any of them fire a shot?

DUFFY: Who knows?

NAYLOR: I know and *you* know! You want me to level—you do the same: Did any of them fire a shot after the panzerfaust?... *Well?*

DUFFY: No.

NAYLOR: Then they weren't killed—they were murdered.

DUFFY: *(Passionately.)* The war was almost over! They should have surrendered *before* they killed Bevan and Hatcher not *after!*

NAYLOR: The defense will get its chance. Right now it's the prosecution's turn: They tried to surrender?

DUFFY: Maybe.

NAYLOR: Maybe?

DUFFY: I don't speak German.

NAYLOR: Did *you* shoot any of them?

DUFFY: No.

NAYLOR: Who did?

DUFFY: What's the difference?

NAYLOR: How about Ezekiel Potter?

DUFFY: Yes.

NAYLOR: You saw him kill someone?

DUFFY: Yes.

NAYLOR: More than one?

DUFFY: Yes.

NAYLOR: Did you try to stop him?

DUFFY: *(Defensive.)* No one did! Bevan and Hatcher lying there—we were out of our minds!

NAYLOR: You plead insanity?

DUFFY: *I don't plead shit! (He drains his glass; rises to leave.)* Give Alice my regards.

NAYLOR: One last question?...Please?

DUFFY: Go ahead.

NAYLOR: Did he look like Boris Becker?

DUFFY: Who are you talking about?

NAYLOR: The kid who fired the panzerfaust and then came out of his foxhole smiling like he hoped we'd excuse him.

DUFFY: You think he looked like Boris Becker?

NAYLOR: The spitting image.

DUFFY: All I remember is he was young.

NAYLOR: You *did* see him.

DUFFY: Yes.

NAYLOR: Saw him get out of the foxhole?

DUFFY: Yes.

NAYLOR: And then?

DUFFY: What's this all about?

NAYLOR: *And then?*

DUFFY: He started toward us—hands raised. Was half-way when someone gunned him down.

NAYLOR: Someone?

DUFFY: I didn't see who—figured it was Potter.

NAYLOR: It was me.

DUFFY: You?

NAYLOR: Surprised?

DUFFY: Yes.

NAYLOR: I don't seem the type.

DUFFY: No.

NAYLOR: Potter was about to shoot but I beat him to it.

DUFFY: Why?

NAYLOR: I don't know.

DUFFY: That's why you got upset.

NAYLOR: Yes.

DUFFY: Because I mentioned the ambush.

NAYLOR: Yes.

DUFFY: It still bothers you.

NAYLOR: Give that man five silver dollars.

DUFFY: Ever hear of the statute of limitations?

NAYLOR: It doesn't apply in murder cases.

DUFFY: It was combat.

NAYLOR: *(With quiet but total certainty.)* It was murder.

DUFFY: Did you ever think about getting help?

NAYLOR: Psychiatry?

DUFFY: Yes.

NAYLOR: Been there—done that.

DUFFY: And?

NAYLOR: It got me over the worst of it so I quit drinking.

DUFFY: Until today.

NAYLOR: Alice didn't want me to visit the museum—had a hunch it might set me off.

DUFFY: There was a war on. Two of your best friends had just been killed. We were kids.

NAYLOR: There's nothing you can say I haven't told myself a thousand times. But thanks anyway.

DUFFY: Punishing yourself won't change anything.

NAYLOR: Easy for you to say.

DUFFY: No it isn't.

NAYLOR: You were a bystander—a spectator.

DUFFY: No.

NAYLOR: No?

DUFFY: No.

NAYLOR: What do you mean?…Well?

(Duffy takes a long swig of his drink.)

NAYLOR: …Well?

DUFFY: *(Matter-of-fact.)* I took part.

NAYLOR: Took part?

DUFFY: In the craziness. After Bevan and Hatcher were killed.

NAYLOR: Took part how?

DUFFY: Like you did.

NAYLOR: You said you didn't shoot anyone.

DUFFY: I didn't.

NAYLOR: What then?

DUFFY: Remember the guy who came out of the woods when we thought they were all dead?

NAYLOR: The lieutenant said "Get rid of him." Evans shot him.

DUFFY: Goofy looking guy. Eye glasses. Wore an armband with a cross.

NAYLOR: So what?

DUFFY: Before the lieutenant said "Get rid of him," he debated because the guy was a medic. Then someone reminded him the guy had seen everything that happened. That did it.

NAYLOR: So what?

DUFFY: That "someone" was me.

NAYLOR: You think you signed his death warrant?

DUFFY: I know I did.

NAYLOR: Welcome to the club.

DUFFY: Thanks.

NAYLOR: You don't seem bothered about it.

DUFFY: That's why I told you.

NAYLOR: You never lost any sleep over it?

DUFFY: In the beginning.

NAYLOR: And now?

DUFFY: I'm sorry I did it but that's it.

NAYLOR: No bad dreams?

DUFFY: Not about that.

NAYLOR: What's the secret?

DUFFY: Secret?

NAYLOR: Of your miraculous adjustment.

DUFFY: There's nothing miraculous about it.

NAYLOR: Care to share it?

DUFFY: Ohrdruf.

NAYLOR: Ohrdruf?

DUFFY: Eisenhower wanted us to see it so we'd hate the Germans.

NAYLOR: So what?

DUFFY: He succeeded.

NAYLOR: What's that got to do with the ambush?

DUFFY: Ohrdruf primed us to do what we did.

NAYLOR: If we hadn't seen Ohrdruf we wouldn't have killed those guys?

DUFFY: Yes.

NAYLOR: You really believe that?

DUFFY: Completely.

NAYLOR: Dream on.

DUFFY: The day Patton, Bradley, and Eisenhower saw Ohrdruf, Patton jumped on the hood of his jeep and screamed, *"See what those sons-of-bitches did. I don't want you to take any prisoners."*

NAYLOR: *(Mocking a la the Nazis.)* Achtung! The next thing you're going to say is, "We were only following orders."

DUFFY: You don't think Ohrdruf had anything to do with you shooting that kid?

NAYLOR: *(With certainty.)* I know it didn't. *(Rising.)* I've gotta go.

DUFFY: You think I'm kidding myself.

NAYLOR: If it works for you, I'm glad. *(Offers his hand.)* Good luck.

DUFFY: *(Ignoring his hand.)* He said smugly.

NAYLOR: Smugly?

DUFFY: You think punishing yourself makes you superior to me?

NAYLOR: No.

DUFFY: Sure you do. I can see it.

NAYLOR: Have it your way.

DUFFY: *(Angrily.)* I love it. I try to help you—tell you something I never told anybody—you end up looking down your nose at me.

NAYLOR: I appreciate what you tried to do.

DUFFY: *You're doing it again you son-of-a-bitch!*

NAYLOR: *(Stung.)* I wouldn't say any more if I were you.

DUFFY: What are you gonna do—hit me?

NAYLOR: Worse.

DUFFY: Worse?

NAYLOR: I wish you all the best. I mean that.

> *(Naylor starts to leave. Duffy grabs his shoulder.)*

DUFFY: What do you mean "worse"?

NAYLOR: Alice is waiting.

> *(He tries to free himself but Duffy tightens his grip.)*

DUFFY: *What do you mean "worse"?*

NAYLOR: You tried to do me a favor—I'm trying to return it.

DUFFY: *Fuck favors!*

NAYLOR: *(Losing control.) Ohrdruf had nothing to do with the day we were ambushed!*

DUFFY: That's your opinion.

NAYLOR: It's fact!

DUFFY: Seeing all those bodies had no effect on what happened after Bevan and Hatcher were killed?

NAYLOR: It couldn't have.

DUFFY: Why?

> *(Naylor makes a final effort to leave but Duffy restrains him.)*

DUFFY: *Why?*

NAYLOR: The ambush happened *before* we saw Ohrdruf.

DUFFY: *Bullshit!*

NAYLOR: *(With total certainty.)* We saw Ohrdruf on April thirteenth or fourteenth. We were ambushed on April the second.

DUFFY: *(Doubts leaking in.)* How do you know?

NAYLOR: After the ambush we took over a house where we found a wine cellar; tried to drink ourselves into oblivion.

DUFFY: What's that got to do with—

NAYLOR: —As we drank, someone remembered it was my birthday; opened a can of Spam—

DUFFY: *(Remembering.)* —And put a candle on it.

NAYLOR: Right.

DUFFY: That was April second?

NAYLOR: Yes.

DUFFY: You're sure?

NAYLOR: It's my birthday.

DUFFY: I would have bet my life Ohrdruf came first.

NAYLOR: You would have lost.

DUFFY: (As the full import registers.) Wow!

NAYLOR: I shouldn't have told you.

DUFFY: My fault for pressing.

NAYLOR: I'm really sorry.

DUFFY: That makes two of us.

NAYLOR: I should have listened to Alice—never gone to the museum.

DUFFY: April second?

NAYLOR: April second.

DUFFY: Can I see your driver's license? Just kidding.

NAYLOR: I can't tell you how bad I feel.

DUFFY: April second?

    (Naylor nods.)

DUFFY: It's like I got kicked in the stomach.

NAYLOR: One last round before I go back on the wagon?

DUFFY: Yeah.

NAYLOR: (Calling off.) Two more.

DUFFY: (Calling.) Both doubles.

    (They sit reflectively.)

DUFFY: He *must* have seen everything.

NAYLOR: What are you talking about?

DUFFY: The German.

NAYLOR: The one you told the lieutenant to kill.

DUFFY: *I didn't say "kill him." I said... (He catches himself.)* How about that? I'm making excuses already.

NAYLOR: (He's been there.) Goes with the territory.

    (Silence. Then Duffy laughs ironically.)

NAYLOR: I miss something?

DUFFY: It doesn't matter which came first—Ohrdruf or the ambush. Either way it's murder.

NAYLOR: Congratulations.

DUFFY: For what?

NAYLOR: It took me three years on the couch to admit that.

DUFFY: On the other hand you can't compare what we did to what the Nazis did—the camps and all.

NAYLOR: True.

DUFFY: I couldn't shove people in gas chambers—no matter what. Could you?

NAYLOR: Wrong question.

DUFFY: Why?

NAYLOR: It's too easy.

DUFFY: Easy?

NAYLOR: You ask anyone out of the blue if they'd shove people in gas chambers they'll say no and they'll mean it. Want a tougher question?

DUFFY: Go on.

NAYLOR: You're at a meeting with business associates. They start making cracks about one man because he's Jewish. Do you speak up? *(To Duffy directly.)* Well do you?

DUFFY: Yes.

NAYLOR: The guy is fired because he's Jewish. Do you protest?

DUFFY: Yes.

NAYLOR: Do you continue to socialize with him?

DUFFY: Yes.

NAYLOR: Even after he's forced to wear a star marking him a Jew?

DUFFY: What?

NAYLOR: *(Overriding Duffy's confusion, gaining momentum.)* Do you patronize his store after they break his windows? Do you offer him a ride when Jews are forbidden to drive cars? Do you offer him shelter when he's kicked out of his home? Do you ask what happened when he and his family vanish one night?

DUFFY: What's your point?

NAYLOR: It doesn't begin with gas chambers and ovens.

(The Bartender sets their drinks down—departs. Several beats. Then.)

NAYLOR: Maybe you'll get a story out of it.

DUFFY: Your mouth—God's ear.

NAYLOR: You don't believe in God.

DUFFY: I might if she delivers.

NAYLOR: *(Raises his glass.)* Cheers.

DUFFY: *(Lifting his glass.)* Cheers.

(Lights down as they touch glasses.)

SCENE VI

Time: moments later. Place: lights up on Mrs. Grayson answering her ringing phone:

MRS. GRAYSON: Hello?

DUFFY'S VOICE: Mrs. Grayson?

MRS. GRAYSON: Speaking.

(Lights up on Duffy at the same bar—phone in hand.)

DUFFY: Bill Duffy. I was in your office this morning with another guy about Ohrdruf.

MRS. GRAYSON: Mr. Naylor.

DUFFY: Right.

MRS. GRAYSON: Did you catch up with him?

DUFFY: Yes.

MRS. GRAYSON: How is he?

DUFFY: He's okay.

MRS. GRAYSON: I was concerned about him.

DUFFY: He's fine.

MRS. GRAYSON: I appreciate your letting me know.

DUFFY: That's not why I called...

MRS. GRAYSON: Go on.

DUFFY: I want to set the record straight.

MRS. GRAYSON: Record?

DUFFY: What Naylor and I told you.

MRS. GRAYSON: What about it?

DUFFY: When he said he thought everyone had the potential to do what the Nazis did, you asked if I shared his opinion.

MRS. GRAYSON: You said "no."

DUFFY: I want to amend that.

MRS. GRAYSON: You think everyone *does* have the potential?

DUFFY: I don't know about everyone. Just me.

MRS. GRAYSON: What made you change your mind?

DUFFY: I don't want to talk about it.

MRS. GRAYSON: I see. That it?

DUFFY: Yes.

MRS. GRAYSON: Are you all right Mr. Duffy?

DUFFY: Yes.

MRS. GRAYSON: Really?

DUFFY: No.

MRS. GRAYSON: Anything I can do?

DUFFY: No. But thanks for asking.

(Lights down on Mrs. Grayson. As Duffy hangs up he reaches for his drink— is raising it to his lips—when something stops him. Returning the glass to the bar, he extracts the two Holocaust victim cards from his pocket; regards them as lights dim to black.)

THE END

AFTERWORD

It's several days since *Contact with the Enemy* concluded its premiere four-week showcase run at the Ensemble Studio Theatre.

The production (all hands) delivered the play beyond my fondest hopes.

Of the nine reviews I'm aware of, *The New York Times* was respectful to good. *The Village Voice* offered nice quotes but misread my intention. The other seven leave a glow I can't resist sharing:

The Daily News: "*Contact with the Enemy* tackles the Holocaust without a trace of sentimentality—and packs a wallop that implicates all of us."

Back Stage (Victor Gluck): "One of the most disturbing plays you will see this or any year."

New York Calling (William Wolf): "Gripping new drama. This is definately a work that needs a continued showing."

Aisle Say—Internet Magazine (David Spencer): "The most compelling accolade is that you can spend the rest of the evening in passionate debate about it."

Show Business (Dan Callahan): "The consummate intelligence of the play should not conceal its passion, nor should we be anything but grateful for a drama which deals with the Holocaust in such a way as to incriminate all of us."

The Irish Echo (Joseph Hurley): "Gripping and unforgettable. Plays as compellingly and breathlessly as the mystery thriller it comes to resemble."

I wish you'd been there.

STOP THE PRESSES!

Contact with the Enemy just nominated by the Drama Desk for best new play of 1999–2000.

Frank D. Gilroy is a playwright, novelist, television writer, screen writer, director, and independent filmmaker. His awards include a Pulitzer Prize, a Tony Award and a New York Drama Critics Award for *The Subject Was Roses*. His play *Who'll Save the Plowboy?* won the Obie for Best American Play of the Year. *Desperate Characters,* which he wrote and directed, won two Silver Bears at the Berlin Film Festival. Born and raised in the Bronx, he graduated from Dartmouth (courtesy of the GI Bill) after service in World War II. He is a past president of the Dramatists Guild.